Ingenious Citizenship

INGENIOUS CITIZENSHIP

Recrafting Democracy for Social Change

Charles T. Lee

Duke University Press   Durham and London   2016

Printed in the United States of America on acid-free paper ∞
Designed by Natalie F. Smith
Typeset in Quadraat Pro by Copperline

Library of Congress Cataloging-in-Publication Data
Lee, Charles T., [date] author.
Ingenious citizenship : recrafting democracy for social
change / Charles T. Lee.
pages cm
Includes bibliographical references and index.

ISBN 978-0-8223-6021-6 (hardcover : alk. paper)
ISBN 978-0-8223-6037-7 (pbk. : alk. paper)
ISBN 978-0-8223-7483-1 (e-book)

1. Democracy—United States—Citizen
participation. 2. Marginality, Social—Political
aspects—United States. 3. Social change—United
States. 4. Political participation—United States.
5. Political culture—United States. I. Title.
JK1764.L427 2016
323'.0420973—dc23
2015030380

Cover Art: Do Ho Suh, *Floor* (detail), 1997–2000. PVC figures,
glass plates, phenolic sheets, polyurethane resin. Forty parts
each 100 × 100 × 8 cm. © Do Ho Suh, courtesy of the artist
and Lehmann Maupin Gallery, New York and Hong Kong.

For Celia, Tristan, and Kamina

Contents

Acknowledgments

This book originated as a dissertation and went through innumerable iterations as my thinking about politics and justice evolved and transformed over the years. To recount the kindness of people who have been a part of this journey with me—whether by sharing their critiques and insights, offering encouragement and prodding, providing institutional assistance and support, or giving emotional and physical care—makes my undertaking of this project a humbling endeavor. While all flaws and shortcomings remain mine alone, I wish to acknowledge the many people who not only helped me complete what I once thought was an impossible journey but also enriched it with their generosity.

At the University of Southern California, my dissertation committee first helped me give life to this project. Marita Sturken taught me about cultural studies and opened up a new intellectual horizon for me. I learned from her the importance of doing original work while maintaining one's political sensibility and responsibility. She has been the backbone of my intellectual adventure, and I could not possibly have done the kind of work that I do today without her steadfast mentoring, guidance, support, and savvy. Alison Dundes Renteln has provided pivotal comments and mentoring on my writing, teaching, and professional development and always answered my calls for help with unflinching support and encouragement. I especially thank her for planting the seed in my thinking about human rights from a relativistic and contextual vantage point, enabling me to expand on the direction of my narrative in this book in important ways. Nora Hamilton offered enduring support from beginning to end and is a remarkable treasure of wisdom and insights. I cherished and learned greatly from all of my conversations with her on immigrant workers. For years I have marveled at Sarah Banet-Weiser's critical and creative scholarship. She is an intellectual role model for me in many ways, and I thank her for her exceedingly perceptive insights on my methodology, writing, and conceptual arguments.

At Arizona State University, I have been surrounded by colleagues at the School of Social Transformation (SST) who provide sustaining support to my interdisciplinary work. Karen Leong and Ann Hibner Koblitz read the entire manuscript and gave constructive feedback and painstaking critiques at the most critical time, raising questions about my ideas and picking out issues with my prose line by line when I most needed them. I thank Karen for her amazing strength and mentoring, and I thank Ann for her magic sense with words, including suggesting the book's title. Mary Margaret Fonow read the draft chapters with crucial suggestions and guidance in spite of her exceedingly busy schedule as the director of the SST. I am grateful for her sage advice and unwavering support. Beth Swadener is a godsend and a tremendous mentor: I thank her for her pivotal advice, support, and comments on the project at the most urgent time. For their wise counsel, expert advice, and help and support in many ways, I thank Mary Romero, Pat Lauderdale, Marjorie Zatz, Karen Kuo, Vanna Gonzales, Vera Lopez, H. L. T. Quan, Gray Cavender, Nancy Jurik, Bryan Brayboy, and Daniel Schugurensky. I also thank Vanna Gonzales and Vera Lopez for their friendship, which helped ease my transition to Arizona. And I thank the colleagues in my home unit, Justice and Social Inquiry, for their collegiality and commitment to justice, with routinely democratic spirit and good sense of humor.

Portions of ideas in the book were conceived and developed during my participation in the transnational feminist research cluster "Local to Global Feminisms and the Politics of Knowledge," funded by the Jenny Norton Grant in the Institute for Humanities Research at Arizona State University. I thank the cluster participants—especially Karen Leong, Ann Hibner Koblitz, Karen Kuo, Heather Switzer, and Roberta Chevrette—for the many critical readings and discussions that stimulated my thinking on the book project. And thanks to Sally Kitch, the director of the Institute for Humanities Research, and to Reverend Jenny Norton for providing the funding that made this engaging and supportive space possible.

I am most fortunate to have found a superlative editor in Courtney Berger at Duke University Press. Her keen understanding of the book, perceptive insights for my revisions of the manuscript, and belief in this project have been indispensable. I am so grateful for her responsiveness, efficiency, and savvy in guiding me through the editorial process. I also thank Courtney for securing two superb anonymous reviewers. My deepest thanks to Barbara Cruikshank and another anonymous reader, whose many excellent and incisive suggestions pushed me to hone my argument, deepening and refining it so that it has more force and theoretical usefulness. Their brilliant and dynamic engagement with the manuscript inspired confidence and infused energy into my revision more than I could imagine. I cannot thank them enough for their intellectual rigor and generosity. Finally, I also thank Erin Hanas for her important and timely editorial assistance.

Numerous teachers and scholars have had an important impact on my intellectual trajectory and thinking on this project at different stages. For their exceptional teaching and training in political theory, I thank Alyson Cole, Judith Grant, Mark Kann, and Raymond Rocco. Alyson first kindled my passion for theory during my undergraduate years, and I am thankful to have had the opportunity to continue that passion in exploring different theoretical approaches and inquiries with Judith, Mark, and Ray in graduate school. I thank Dana Polan for making my arguments more nuanced and reminding me of the role of history in his critical comments on the draft chapters in early forms. I am in awe of Chandan Reddy's brilliant mind and thank him for his immense kindness in reading the manuscript on short notice and offering his insightful comments at a critical stage. I have benefited from his wealth of interdisciplinary knowledge. I was also fortunate to have met Rita Dhamoon and learned very much from her inspiring critical work. I thank her for her friendship, generosity, and sharp insights on the project, especially chapter 2.

The critical scholarship by Engin F. Isin and Peter Nyers in citizenship studies has been pivotal to my thinking on citizenship. I thank Peter for his generous comments and continuing support of my work over the years, and I thank Engin for his critical feedback and guidance on a book chapter based on materials included in this manuscript. I have also benefited greatly from input from and conversations with Minoo Moallem, Renya Ramirez, Richard Jackson, Jinee Lokaneeta, Vicki Squire, Larin McLaughlin, and Ara Wilson. I thank Jinee Lokaneeta and Sangay Mishra for their friendship, including the many memorable food excursions and conversations back in the days of graduate school. Early draft chapters were presented at numerous conference meetings at the American Political Science Association, Western Political Science Association, American Studies Association, Cultural Studies Association, Critical Ethnic Studies Association, National Women's Studies Association, and International Studies Association. I thank the co-panelists and audience for their questions and comments, which helped me reshape this project from different angles.

Other individuals have also provided assistance in varying forms. I acknowledge the graduate students Natalie Lopez, Sangmi Lee, a de la maza pérez tamayo, and Lucía Stavig for their first-rate research assistance. The doctoral scholarship of Nancy Perez on domestic workers has informed my own work and is helpful for my analysis in chapter 2. Conversations with Lucía Stavig inspired insights and energy for the project, and I value our chats on a range of subjects, from social justice to ethnic food and mind-body practices. Editing assistance by Kristie Reilly and Deanna Wilson improved the organization, clarity, and simplicity of the manuscript. Portions of ideas in the book were fleshed out in my two graduate seminars, "Democracy, Citizenship, and Globalization" in Fall 2011 and "Theoretical Perspectives on Justice" in Fall 2014, and I thank the students in the seminars for the dynamic and engaging discussions that enriched my thinking.

Sections of ideas in chapter 2 have appeared in other forms in the following publications: "Tactical Citizenship: Domestic Workers, the Remainders of Home, and Undocumented Citizen Participation in the Third Space of Mimicry," Theory and Event 9, no. 3 (2006), published by the Johns Hopkins University Press; "Undocumented Workers' Subversive Citizenship Acts," Peace Review: A Journal of Social Justice 20, no. 3 (2008): 330–38, published by Taylor and Francis; and "Bare Life, Interstices, and the Third Space of Citizenship," Women's Studies Quarterly 38, no 2 (2010): 57–81, published by the Feminist Press. An early development of the ideas in chapter 5 originally appeared as "Suicide Bombing as Acts of Deathly Citizenship? A Critical Double-Layered Inquiry," Critical Studies on Terrorism 2, no. 2 (2009): 147–63, published by Taylor and Francis. Parts of the introduction, chapter 1, and chapter 3 appeared in "Decolonizing Global Citizenship," in Routledge Handbook of Global Citizenship Studies, ed. Engin F. Isin and Peter Nyers (London: Routledge, 2014), 75–85.

Although they have not played a direct intellectual role in this project, my family and friends outside academia have been an inseparable part of this journey for the emotional and physical care and support they have given me. I thank my parents, Ronny and Vera Lee, and my sister, Melody, for their enduring love, encouragement, and support. I also thank the extended Lee family, in Taiwan and in diaspora. Special acknowledgment to my aunt Linda Lee and cousin Peggie for their sage counsel and encouragement. To the Ho family: I thank Hsin-Chi and Judy Ho, as well as Daisy, Joe, Terry, Kitty, Jo-anne, Chloe, Ethan, Jayden, and Kaitlyn, for sharing another world of family life with me. My friends Jason Chen and Steve Su have been with me through thick and thin, and I thank them for simply, and always, being there. For their treasured friendship and support, I thank Irona Wang, Tina Chen, and Lawrence Tsai.

Since college, Celia Ho has been my closest companion and a loving (and subversive) presence in my life. She pushes me harder than anyone to pursue what I want to do while always finding a way to deviate from my suggestions for what she should do. I thank her for her extraordinary strength, her un-countable sacrifices, and, above all, for bringing love and ingenuity into our everyday life. Our two children, Tristan and Kamina, were born while I was revising the book. Their playful and unruly presence constantly "disrupts" my work schedule while also creating a needed, healthy distraction in stress-ful times. Not only have they changed my work habits; they have also trans-formed my life's horizons. My life would not have been complete without the three of them, and I thank them for entering into the heart of my life. It is to them that I dedicate this book.

On a last note, for the past decade or so Zen Buddhism has informed some of my perspectives in life and enabled me to regain calm and composure in times of flux and struggle. As I wrote this book, I found that its influence has also subtly and indirectly found its way into the narrative. Although I have not made direct reference to Zen thought or literature in the pages that follow, I wish to acknowledge its (nonlinear) insight and spirit, which has formed an unobserved but indispensable element of this book.

Introduction. Ingenious Agency
Democratic Agency and Its Disavowal

Two Tales of Democracy: Rethinking Democratic Agency

Ten days after the terrorist attack on the United States on September 11, 2001, the American Ad Council, a nonprofit organization known for producing public service announcements (PSAs) to deliver civic messages to the American public on national television, launched a new advertising campaign. Called "I Am an American," the campaign sought to unite U.S. citizens in the wake of national trauma.[1]

As the reincarnation of the former War Advertising Council created during World War II to mobilize public support for the war effort, the Ad Council has collaborated closely with the federal government in promoting positive, forward-looking, and democratic civil behavior among U.S. citizens (see, e.g., its litter prevention, drunk driving prevention, domestic violence prevention, and AIDS prevention ads of the past several decades). In this particular post–9/11 campaign, made in tribute to the tragedy, the ad features citizens of varying ages, races, national origins, occupations, religions, and genders, each one firmly declaring, "I am an American." Via delicate emotive and aesthetic effects—a banner carrying the U.S. motto "E Pluribus Unum" (Out of Many, One) appears at one moment on the screen, and the ad concludes with a girl waving an American flag—the PSA highlights diversity as a unique strength of the U.S. national body, which is capable of regenerating hope, recovery, and democratic life following the terrorist-inflicted deaths and casualties.

Professor Cynthia Weber of Sussex University recently produced a multimedia project, "I Am an American": Video Portraits of Unsafe U.S. Citizens, that compiles narratives and images that challenge the harmonious tale of diversity in the name of patriotic nationalism presented by the Ad Council (Weber 2011).[2] At the heart of Weber's critique is the Ad Council's vacuous vision of democracy, which subsumes racial, class, gender, and sexual differences into a unified citizenry in a time of national crisis. This celebratory vision is devoid of, and in fact represses, critical social discussion of structural oppression, injustice, and inequality, which could pose a danger to the cohesiveness of the U.S. nation-state in a post–9/11 climate (Weber 2010, 81).

Using the Ad Council's declaration, "I am an American," as a reference point and site of contestation, Weber staged a series of on-camera interviews with a number of individuals whose identities are not easily melded into the concept of "ordinary American," who remain othered as, in her terms, "unsafe U.S. citizens." These dissonant and dissenting subjects are imbued with unsettling differences: a Chinese American Muslim chaplain wrongly accused as a terrorist spy and imprisoned as an enemy combatant; African American Hurricane Katrina evacuees treated as "refugees" and divested of U.S. citizenship; the U.S.-born son of an undocumented Mexican immigrant on the verge of deportation; an Iraq War conscientious objector forced to seek political asylum in Canada. By looking into the video camera and stating emphatically, "I am an American," they contest their nonbelonging as U.S. (second-class) citizens and voice a desire for equality and inclusion. Weber's critical art thus exposes the unequal access to and realization of U.S. citizenship for these unassimilatory subjects and the unseen systematic marginalization of nonnormative citizens in everyday liberal democratic life. In doing so, her political intervention interrupts the Ad Council's professed "tolerance of difference" and illusive celebration of "diversity patriotism," the hallmark of contemporary U.S. national identity (Weber 2010).[3]

These two opposing media productions lay out seemingly contrasting juxtapositions of democracy as conceived in Western political thought. The Ad Council presents a mainstream ideal of liberal democracy that appeals to public "common sense," embracing national loyalty and melting-pot harmony as its constitutive inclusive logic ("One Nation under God, indivisible, with liberty and justice for all," as the Pledge of Allegiance has it). As Russ

Castronovo and Dana Nelson argue, however, this dominant articulation of constitutional liberalism presents democracy as "a sacred and reified thing" that must be guarded with "conservation and protection" and represses any antagonistic struggle staged by dissenting subjects regarding the naturalness of its own self-formation (2002a, 1–2). By assembling a diverse pool of ethnic subjects uttering resolutely in consensus, "I am an American," the Ad Council's advertising campaign mythically attunes citizens to a "fantasy scene of private, protected, and sanctified 'American' life" (Berlant 1997, 220), and "takes form as an antipolitical gesture that closes down disagreement, contestation, and meaningful conflict" (Castronovo and Nelson 2002a, 1).

In contrast, Weber's multimedia project points toward a vision of radical democracy that, as the political theorists Ernesto Laclau and Chantal Mouffe (1985) deploy the term, is constitutive of perpetual struggles for racial, class, gender, and sexual justice in political institutions and civil society. Focusing on difference, disagreement, and contestation from subordinate positions, radical democratic politics formulates itself as a critique of the dominant liberal emphasis on social harmony and consensus.[4] It rattles the illusive naturalness of the liberal patriotic discourse of diversity and belonging and contests hypocritical closure to marginal struggles for social membership and inclusion. In calling attention to the precarious material conditions of social life on the margins, Weber's work is meant to shock the pacified mainstream citizenry absorbed in a life of static privilege out of its complacency by confronting it with vivid narratives and imageries of violent exclusion and displacement. By rupturing the sterilized order of the Ad Council's normative democracy, the unsafe citizens' rendition of "I am an American" constitutes an agonistic disruption of the status quo and a contestation for democratic equality.

Weber's critical project, in my view, provides an indispensable opposition to, and an important corrective of, the Ad Council's hegemonic representation of liberal America. Yet the political campaigns' contrasting ideologies notwithstanding, these two visions of democracy actually converge with and mirror each other. Specifically, both campaigns imagine and enact a similar kind of citizen subjectivity that fits within the familiar, conventional mode of "democratic agency"—that is, a capacity to act politically in ways that are public and collective, with generally forward-looking and romantic connotations. Crucially, this linear and one-dimensional construction of political agency throughout the genealogy of Western political thought has long been interpreted as, and comes to stand in for, the only (proper) way to enact oneself as a citizen.

Hence, the Ad Council's PSA, aligned ideologically with constitutional liberalism via the motto "E Pluribus Unum" flashing across the screen, connotes the proper forms of citizen activity, which include mainstream acts of voting, representing, deliberating, or campaigning. These ordinary forms of political participation are imbued with democratic agency and laden with public and collective qualities that are central to the making of democratic citizens.

Weber's multimedia project also manifests these same qualities, albeit in a dissenting and radicalizing fashion. For instance, the unsafe citizens are seen openly resisting the Iraq War, speaking out against unjust treatment of Guantánamo detainees, taking church sanctuary to fight a deportation order, and issuing public complaints about mistreatment of Hurricane Katrina evacuees. All of these political acts—in being vocal and openly contestatory—resonate with the civic ethos of democratic practices such as protests, demonstrations, and sit-ins. Although the general public tends to look at these contentious acts less favorably than, say, voting, they do converge with mainstream liberal forms of political participation in formulating the range of activities commonly understood as practices of democratic citizenship in Western political thought. Weber's progressive critique of the Ad Council's campaign thus expands the spectrum of the political, yet remains based in democratic agency. By laying bare the limits of the original "I am an American" ad as insufficiently democratic, Weber's "unsafe citizens" project supplants it with what she sees as a *more* genuine and substantive vision of radical democratic agency. In spite of the ideological differences between these two visions of democracy, their conceptions of citizen subjectivity and political agency actually constitute two sides of the same coin.

I begin this book with these two tales of democracy because, in their respective ideological inclinations, they roughly capture the predominant spectrum of modes of political participation among citizens in an actually existing democracy: from mainstream liberal (the Ad Council's PSA: voting, representing, deliberating) to radical democratic (Weber's multimedia project: protesting, demonstrating, sitting in). This suggests that the massive terrain of political participation and social activism in actually existing democracy is prevailingly contained within the preconceived vocabulary and trajectory of democratic agency in liberal and progressive thought.

But why does it matter if these citizens act out their political agency and citizenship in a democratic way? Is that not how we, as citizens, should participate in a political community? In fact, not only should the historical strug-gles for suffrage staged by African Americans and women not be taken for granted, but both mainstream liberal forms of participation *and* the radical practices of dissent and protest have been employed by subordinate groups. Racial minorities, manual laborers, women, sexual minorities, and the dis-abled have embraced both positions as indispensable tools in advancing their interests and voices in society, empowering them to fight for the inclusion, rights, and equality that historically and continually have been denied to them as citizens. This democratic agency—especially the radical democratic invigoration Weber gestures toward—has continued to animate and revive our vision and aspiration for justice and equality, however fragile and precar-ious these ideals may in fact be in capitalist democracies.

I wish to suggest, however, that when this democratic mode of enactment takes hold as the only (proper) way to imagine oneself as a political subject or participating citizen, it implicitly valorizes democratic agency as some-thing sacred and heroic, while insidiously defining *other* forms of political agency as less proper and honorable. This romance of democratic agency, in envisioning "acting democratically" as the central mode of political action, crystallizes an invisible form of ideological judgment and normative exclu-sion that systematically remainders *other* forms of political agency. Even more important, its linear delineation of political agency forecloses a serious and open-ended investigation of how marginalized subjects lacking access and resources may contest and resist in surprising and even unthinkable ways to improvise and expand spaces of inclusion and belonging, thus obtaining "citizenship" via nonlinear routes.

This book explores agency from abject positions in lived conditions as well as the larger social and political lessons that such agency offers for re-thinking critical intellectual intervention and social movement activism from a nonlinear perspective. To the extent that democratic agency constitutes the dominant frame for thinking about and articulating political life and social change, critical blind spots also punctuate its constructed vision, prevent-ing it from fulfilling its potential strength. The preeminence of democratic agency is attributable to its articulation in Western political thought in its lib-eral, civic republican, communitarian, deliberative, and radical democratic variants.[5] This has framed the mainstream and progressive understanding of democratic citizenship in both discursive and material forms and cohered as the common perception of "proper" political subjectivity.

Saba Mahmood has previously examined how the normative liberal assumption that "all human beings have an innate desire for freedom" has become "integral to our humanist intellectual traditions" (2005, 5), including feminism. Mahmood writes, "Freedom is normative to feminism, as it is to liberalism" (10), such that human agency is conceived in forms of "acts that challenge social norms" rather than those who inhabit norms (5), and "critical scrutiny is applied to those who want to limit women's freedom rather than those who want to extend it" (10). Indeed, what happens when political agency is exercised via a deliberate subjection of oneself in order to realize freedom—or other desired values or ends—in other ways? As I argue, democratic agency in Western liberal and progressive thought has exerted disseminating effects and become the way in which many commentators, scholars, and activists apprehend and conceive the "political." I suggest that we reexamine this normative assumption, particularly the ways in which it can preempt an engagement with forms of agency that are not necessarily democratic, but nonetheless engender fluid configurations of change.

To further clarify this point, I pinpoint two critical blind spots that existing conceptions of democratic agency persistently disavow via normative repetition: (1) the subtle and roundabout improvisation of resistance every day by subordinate people; and (2) the nonlinear and circuitous social change that is *always occurring* in liberal social life. These two blind spots will be made progressively clear throughout this introduction and the book's chapters, but I provide a brief explication here.

First, the preeminence of democratic agency prevents many political theorists and activists from seriously tracing and uncovering the minute yet myriad ways in which episodes of social resistance might be subtly staged by marginalized populations in everyday liberal social life. The textures and qualities of these mercurial forms of quotidian resistance may not necessarily follow conventional democratic trajectories. The protean multitude of such resistant acts and practices, however limited they might be, can be understood as creating momentary fissures and ruptures in the seemingly rigid and immobile terrain of hegemonic liberal life.

Second, the recognition that political contestation is constantly staged further suggests that change and movement are instigated in ambiguous and indirect ways in everyday social life governed by liberal sovereignty. Here, Asef Bayat's insights on sociopolitical transformation can help provide a glimpse into how such nonlinear change might take place. Bayat points out that "the vehicles through which ordinary people change their societies are not simply audible mass protests or revolutions," but often involve what he calls *social nonmovements*—the collective endeavors and common practices carried out in everyday life "by millions of noncollective actors" who remain dispersed and fragmented (2010, ix, 20). In contrast to social movements that advance "organized, sustained, self-conscious challenge to existing authorities" (Tilly 1984, 304) through "the unity of actors" (Bayat, 20), Bayat argues, "The power of nonmovements rests on the *power of big numbers*"—that is, "the (intended and unintended) consequences of the similar practices that a 'big number' of subjects simultaneously perform" (20–21; emphasis in original). Although they lack a common ideological front and the extraordinary staging of mobilization and protestation, the effects of these multitudes are not to be underestimated. As Bayat asserts, first, "a large number of people acting in common has the effect of normalizing and legitimizing those acts that are otherwise deemed illegitimate. The practices of big numbers are likely to capture and appropriate spaces of power in society within which the subaltern can cultivate, consolidate, and reproduce their counterpower" (20). Second, "even though these subjects act individually and separately, the effects of their actions do not of necessity fade away in seclusion. They can join up, generating a more powerful dynamic than their individual sum total. Whereas each act, like single drops of rain, singularly makes only *individual* impact, such acts produce larger spaces of alternative practices and norms when they transpire in big numbers—just as the individual wetting effects of billions of raindrops join up to generate creeks, rivers, and even floods and waves" (20–21; emphasis in original).

These nonmovements of big numbers, which describe "the silent, protracted, but pervasive advancement of the ordinary people on the propertied, powerful, or the public, in order to survive and improve their lives" (56), constitute what Bayat calls the "quiet encroachment of the ordinary," which effects change in microscopic and manifold ways. Here, Bayat's observation moves away from the conventional linear concept of democratic social movements by indicating that the cumulative encroachment of nondemocratic acts and practices, "without clear leadership, ideology, or structured organization" (56), can nonetheless lead to change and movement in society. As James Scott has similarly observed, "the accumulation of thousands or even millions of . . . petty acts can have massive effects on warfare, land rights, taxes, and property relations" (2012, xx). Bayat's nonlinear delineation of social change, though grounded in the Middle Eastern context, bears important implications that subordinate people's subversion in other contexts may similarly generate cumulative and encroaching effects, albeit through differential trajectories and varying compositions.[6]

In sum, the subtle and roundabout improvisation of resistance, with its nonlinear and circuitous production of social change disavowed by democratic agency, suggests a needed shift of angle in viewing the horizon and potential of social justice activism. In the predominant progressive social justice paradigms, democratic agency has long functioned as motor and modus operandi. Driven by the democratic motor, social justice is often articulated as being *critical of* and *oppositional to*—in a linear fashion—the structural conditions of injustice, especially in racialized, classed, gendered, and sexualized forms. To create change means that we must seek out the structural roots of social problems and overturn any undemocratic structures of social relations—to imagine a *purer* world, so to speak. To a large extent, democratic agency precludes social justice movements from the kind of impure ethos that would reproduce unjust logics and unequal conditions. Such incomplete social transformation cannot be considered bona fide.

Yet in this way there is a general tendency to render the social world in starkly binary, black-and-white terms—justice versus injustice, equality versus inequality, democratic versus antidemocratic, and good versus evil—that impossibly ignores innate complexity and variability. Indeed, in its most romantic (and problematic) form, the conventional social justice paradigm can progress into an implicit belief that its vision and operation are (or should be) quintessentially sacred and untainted. Thus, the illusion that democratic ideals and progressive activism can transcend, without being implicated in, the instrumental exchange of liberal economy is created. This overlooks how—living in a liberal social world, with our bodies immersed and embedded in its structural material economy—we as human subjects cannot be immune to that world's instrumental effects. We may, in fact, actually need to negotiate with instrumentality (thus inextricably replicating conditions of injustice and inequality) in order to generate configurations of social change.[7] This impossibility of transcendence, and the messy entanglement and complicity of *all* political actors in the liberal economy, may in effect constitute the *given basis* for us, as critical scholars and activists, to recover and generate a complex and contingent process of transformation.

This is not a refusal of the exhortation of democratic agency (which we sorely need), but a sobering acknowledgment. The impossibility of detaching social justice from the necessity of instrumental calculation and democratic progressivism from the reinscription of a liberal hegemonic order cannot be ignored. As Joshua Gamson argues in another context, social change may inevitably involve "walking the tight rope" between purifying and contaminating elements and moving through "the turbulence of these attached conflicts" (1998, 220)—if only because, as he puts it on a nonlinear note, sometimes "the more diverse and democratic" the transformative process, "the more the dilemma," and thus contamination, may also come alive (224).

My comments in this introductory section are thus offered in the spirit of continuing the generation of democratic social change, calling forth a reinvestigation of what we can learn from nondemocratic manifestations of agency in everyday liberal social life in order to pluralize and expand the spheres and potency of such change. Such inquiry, however, is preempted and disavowed if we continue to be trapped within the discursive assumptions of liberal and progressive thought by upholding democratic agency as the "truest" enactment of political subjectivity.

Ingenious Agency:
The Immanent Coexistence of Purity and Contamination

To open this inquiry, I wish to identify and conceptualize an unpredictable and flexible way of acting politically that I term *ingenious agency*. The word "ingenious" suggests being clever, original, inventive, and resourceful. I use the term "ingenious agency" to refer to the capacity of creatively devising and contriving different ways of enacting oneself politically with limited tools and resources to generate change in one's immediate surroundings and even the larger social sphere. I provide a more detailed articulation of this agency through a four-pronged frame (i.e., oppositional, negotiated, interstitial, and subcultural) in chapter 1. Here, the above characterization provides a preliminary understanding of the term.

My conception of ingenious agency owes intellectual debt to several scholars who have artfully delineated the ever present emergence of creative resistance staged by subordinate people under repressive conditions (Hebdige 1979; de Certeau 1984; Scott 1985, 1990, 1998, 2009; Kelley 1994). Of crucial importance is the political anthropologist Scott, whose inventive concepts, from "weapons of the weak," "hidden transcripts," and "infrapolitics," to "mētis" and "ungovernability," have provided exceedingly helpful vocabularies and directions by which to analyze the varied and multitudinous dimensions of subversive contestation. While some suggest his idea of everyday resistance is more about defensive coping strategies that preserve "an already achieved gain" than an aggressive "making [of] fresh demands" that advances its own claims (Bayat, 54–56), I think subversive contestation more often than not demonstrates a fluid motion between these two characteristics and blurs the lines between aggressive "encroachment" and defensive "survival strategies" (56). For instance, unauthorized migration can be seen as a defensive survival strategy for undocumented migrants as well as aggressive encroachment on their destination countries. In addition, as Scott's work illustrates, weapons of the weak—in the forms of theft; pilfering; foot dragging; arson; and sabotage of crops, livestock, and machinery directed at slave owners, landlords, and employers (Scott 1985, 288)—are not merely defensive but can be aggressively deployed vis-à-vis "the state, the rich, and the powerful" (Bayat, 56). As Scott argues, "Infrapolitics is . . . always pressing, testing, probing the boundaries of the permissible" (1990, 200). An especially valuable contribution of Scott's formulation of creative resistance is thus its organic and polymorphous character, which takes on both defensive and aggressive qualities.

However, despite this versatile notion of subversive contestation, I argue that Scott's overall conceptual frame leaves the binary of purity and contamination intact as *exogenous* opposites. As such, in spite of his astute awareness of subordinate people's pragmatic disposition and practical knowledge, there is a strong interpretive tendency in his work to retrieve the "purity" of subaltern resistance (and even their entire way of life, as shown in his *The Art of Not Being Governed*) away from the "contamination" of state control rather than seeing the two elements as intricately intertwined. By "purity," I refer to the inviolable ideals and vision for justice, equality, and freedom; by "contamination," I mean the immersion and enactment of one's thoughts and behavior—in varying ways and degrees—in alignment with the dominant logics of existing power structures. In my view, the tendency of Scott's work to interpret subaltern struggles as a retreat from the contaminating influences of all-seeing sovereign states and their embodied high-modernist regimes (Scott 1985, 1990, 1998, 2009, 2012) misrecognizes the intimate connection between purity and contamination, as well as between creative resistance and social movements.

Hence, as Tom Brass points out, Scott consistently aspires for the resistant purity of "state-evading" agency and regards "state-making" projects such as "development, progress and modernization as three historical evils" (Brass 2012, 127). But it is not clear that subordinate people's state-evading acts necessarily preclude their involvement in, and support for, certain state-making projects. Brass thus remarks in his critique of Scott:

> Broadly speaking, grassroots agency labelled by Scott as a process of "resistance" against the state frequently entails attempts to get the state involved and, thus, does not correspond to a wish to "avoid" this institution. Much rather the opposite, in that agency by slum-dwellers and poor farmers on occasion is designed to make the state proactive on their behalf and put into practice its own policies or legislation enforcing minimum wage levels and land reform programs. Accordingly, his unambiguously all-embracing concept of anti-state agency overlooks the presence of contrary instances. (126)

In fact, Scott himself acknowledges the poor's enthusiastic support for land reform in his early work on Southeast Asian peasants (1985, 326), suggesting that the weapons of the weak are intricately connected with, rather than radically detached from, the operations of the modern state and global capitalism.

Nonetheless, Scott's conceptual avoidance of contamination and attempt to set it apart from the resistant purity and humanity of subaltern subjects carries forward throughout his empirical analysis, which preempts a critical linkage between these subjects' creative contestation and a potential reformulation of collective movements. In fact, his disposition toward purity leads him to position infrapolitics as being fundamentally at odds with formal organizations and institutional politics (which he regards as being part of the contaminating apparatus). He writes,

> The strategic imperatives of infrapolitics make it not simply different in degree from the open politics of modern democracies; they impose a fundamentally different logic of political action. . . . The elementary organizational units of infrapolitics have an alternative, *innocent* existence. . . . If formal political organization is the realm of elites, . . . of written records, . . . and of public action, infrapolitics is . . . the realm of informal leadership and nonelites, of conversation and oral discourse, and of surreptitious resistance. The logic of infrapolitics is to leave few traces in the wake of its passage. (1990, 200; emphasis added)

This binary construct thus precludes an investigative inquiry into the transference between these two types of political activities.

To sum up, what is missing at the heart of Scott's empirical analysis is a conceptual redisposition that sees the ineradicable, *endogenous* coexistence of purity and contamination in the eruption of subordinate contestation. This redisposition would enable a rereading of how subaltern subjects' improvisational complicity with the existing system—or, to put it another way, their active reuse of contamination—may actually offer valuable lessons for a useful reformulation of democratic organizations and movements. Therefore, while my concept of ingenious agency is indebted to Scott's conception of creative resistance, I nonetheless depart from his formulation by repositioning purity and contamination as organically and interactively constituted in the formation of such agency. Contra Scott, I suggest that the notion of ingenious agency offers a theoretical illumination, via its inevitable immersion in the dominant logics of existing power structures, that we need to inventively engage rather than negatively repel. Ingenuity, in my frame, embodies the notion that contamination is intrinsic to struggles for change and purity.

This dilemma compels us to confront the ineradicable coexistence of purity and contamination in any struggle for social change within the vicissitudes of liberal democratic life. There is always contamination in purity, just as there is always purity in contamination. That is the paradox, but also the opportunity: *purity and contamination may never fully annihilate each other, but actually require each other to survive and thrive.* Indeed, if contamination is an endogenous part of purity, the forces of contamination may circuitously lead to the material realization of purity in unpredictable and nonlinear ways. And if that is the case, perhaps the way to achieve and realize greater purity in the direction of social justice is not to futilely run away from or eliminate contamination, but rather to more positively, and even *ingeniously*, engage, reuse, and reorient it in order to improvise and generate social change in potent and surprising ways. It is by recentering this notion of ingenious agency at the core of political theorizing—both *with* and *against* the normative current of democratic agency—that this book hopes to offer a renewed lesson on contentious politics and social change.

This lesson runs contrary to much of what we have been taught by the existing critical scholarship on social transformation, which assumes that to realize transformative change, we must move toward the visions and values of purity (i.e., equality, justice, freedom) at the center of our struggles and away from any contaminated association with the governing normative logics of the dominant power structure. This normative desire for "decontamination" and "purification" is a prevalent ethos embedded throughout varying critical theoretical traditions (from Marxist, post-Marxist, and radical democratic to critical racial, feminist, and queer theories) as well as progressive ethnographies. We must unlearn our participation in structural oppression, so the thinking goes, in order to purify our consciousness and engage in democratic struggles for social justice.

In fact, in some of the most astute recent scholarship, critical scholars have fiercely exposed the ways in which even progressive movements may perpetuate and reproduce the enactment of injustice and inequality such that they enable freedom for certain subjects while furthering the marginalization of others. For instance, Jasbir Puar's *Terrorist Assemblages* provides a powerful account of the complicit operations of U.S. sexual exceptionalism, white ascendancy, and homonationalism, which enfold gay-rights advocates and mainstream queer subjects into the privileged liberal U.S. war on terror while ostracizing *other* "monstrous," racialized queer bodies (Puar 2007). Similarly, Lisa Marie Cacho's *Social Death* points forcefully to the replication of dominant cultural and political grammars and logics in social justice and rights-based politics and pushes for a radical, purified vision of inalienable personhood and humanity (Cacho 2012).

While this aspiration and hope for purity vis-à-vis global capitalism, whiteness, and racialized sexualization is crucial, such critical analysis can nonetheless misrecognize or underestimate the degrees to which and ways in which the relational forces of social change may actually hinge on complicity in the given system. What if the way to reach a vision of purity is actually to traffic through an inevitable journey of contamination? Just when critical scholars and progressive activists are seeking purity through the refusal of contamination, I suggest that recognizing the immanent presence of contamination as inseparably linked to purity is not defeating to the progressive cause, but can actually be used in a creative and resourceful way toward such a cause—if interpreted properly through what I call the method of "critical contextualization," discussed below.

While existing critical intellectual literatures have made an immense contribution in pointing sharply to the massive prevalence of injustice in every aspect of liberal democratic life, I wish instead to foreground the endogenous relationship between purity and contamination as a given in order to open up a space for a different theory of social change to emerge. This alternative theory and politics calls on us not to position purity and contamination as distinctive opposites (and to forsake the latter in order to save the former), but to reconsider them as endogenous entities that organically coproduce each other. In fact, if purity may only arise from and through a deeply contaminated matrix, then instead of foregrounding purity as the standpoint of critical intellectual and activist inquiry, I suggest that it might be more helpful to foreground contamination as the very context and condition we need to work with in order to bring its immanent purity from its dim and obscure background in actually existing democracies into light.

Linking Abject Subjects, Ingenious Agency, and Social Change

I further argue that it is those whom I call abject subjects who can most productively illuminate the improvisations of ingenious agency and the lessons such agency holds for the regeneration of social transformation. I use the term "abject subjects" to refer to people who are located in lowly, marginalized, and impoverished material conditions defined and produced by liberal societies. As such, they often have to act in ingenious ways to survive within a liberal social order that systematically exploits or remainders them. Their abjection is especially acute when seen in light of their unequal relations to the normative Western liberal subject (i.e., white, male, middle class, educated, professional, able-bodied, and heterosexual). In a sense, abject subjects are thus not entirely different from persons who are designated as marginal or subordinate subjects. However, I argue that *abject/abjection* contains three levels of meaning, which are particularly useful for the current investigation in thinking about ingenious agency and social change.

First, at the basic, conceptual level, "abject" carries meanings that are commonly defined in the English dictionary: lowly, cast-off, and discarded. In this respect, "abject" shares many connotations with marginalized, subordinate, or excluded. Yet "abject" also specifically conjures up affective qualities of being contemptible and degraded. What is it, then, about the abject that evokes such emotive feelings? This will become clear when we get to its final level of meaning. What is important to note at the first level is that, for my purpose, "abject" as a term offers more nuance and intricacy in describing the experience and dynamic of exclusion. One critical caveat I will provide here is that, like "marginalized," "subordinate," or "excluded," "abject" as a referential designation does not suggest the subjects' natural condition. Rather, it underlines a material and political force that determines, marks, and "throws" the subjects into such a condition. As Peter Nyers argues, " 'being abject' is, in fact, always a matter of 'becoming abject' " (2003, 1074). Nikolas Rose elaborates:

Abjection is an act of force. This force may not be violence, but it entails the recurrent operation of energies that initiate this casting off or a casting down, this demotion from a mode of existence, this "becoming abject." Abjection is a matter of the energies, the practices, the works of division that act upon persons and collectivities such that some ways of being, some forms of existence are cast into a zone of shame, disgrace or debasement, rendered beyond the limits of the liveable, denied the warrant of tolerability, accorded purely a negative value. (1999, 253)

The conceptual description of "abject" thus cannot be understood outside the historical-political context of liberal socialization—its continuing material production of inequality, displacement, and abjection.

Second, as critical social theorists who examine abjection have argued, not only is the abject always defined in relation to the normal, but the normal also requires the existence of the abject as its own precondition. Julia Kristeva writes that the abject "is something rejected from which one does not part, from which one does not protect oneself as from an object" (1982, 4). In other words, the normal subject defines itself by always being in relation with what it rejects: the abject. Judith Butler puts it more explicitly: "The forming of a subject requires . . . a repudiation which produces a domain of abjection, a repudiation without which the subject cannot emerge" (1993, 3). She writes, "The abject designates here precisely those 'unlivable' and 'uninhabitable' zones of social life which are nevertheless densely populated by those who do not enjoy the status of the subject, but whose living under the sign of the 'unlivable' is required to circumscribe the domain of the subject. . . . In this sense, then, the subject is constituted through the force of exclusion and abjection, one which produces a constitutive outside to the subject, an abjected outside, which is, after all, 'inside' the subject as its own founding repudiation" (3).

The abject is thus an inherent constitution within the normal/subject, or, in Kristeva's words, "a precondition of narcissism" (1982, 3). Indeed, if we take citizenship to be a narcissistic embodiment through which democratic citizens can realize themselves as legitimate and authoritative insiders, then those populations that we call abject subjects located in lowly and impoverished conditions are not merely rejected by citizenship but are also necessary to its constitution. As Engin Isin argues, citizenship is made possible only by its alterity/otherness (e.g., strangers, outsiders, aliens): "It requires the constitution of these others to become possible" (2002, 4). The abject and its converse—the *pure*, the *normal*, the *subject*, and the *citizen*—are thus mutually constitutive.

Finally, extending this crucial observation regarding the mutually constitutive relations of normality/abjection, I argue that we might further understand such relations not as remaining in a fixed and static state, but as continually challenged and disrupted by the abject themselves, such that these relations are always shifting in liberal social life. That is, on this third level of meaning, what is salient about the abject is that they are subjects imbued with agency who use and improvise the elements in their surroundings in response to their abjection. In fact, because they resort to whatever tools and resources are available to ameliorate their abjection and to survive, such agency does not manifest in any predictable or predetermined way but flows in diverse directions. Abject subjects thus are perceived as wretched and contemptible not only because of their marginality and exclusion, but also because of the general public's fear of their unpredictable agency, which threatens and disrupts the existing social order, as well as moral assumptions and power relations. Kristeva gestures toward such agency when she writes, "It is thus not lack of cleanliness or health that causes abjection but what disturbs identity, system, order. What does not respect borders, positions, rules. The in-between, the ambiguous, the composite" (4). She continues, "The abject is perverse because it neither gives up nor assumes a prohibition, a rule, or a law; but turns them aside, misleads, corrupts; uses them, takes advantage of them, the better to deny them" (15). The properties of the abject, in short, in Isin's words, "are experienced as strange, hidden, frightful, or menacing" (2002, 3).

Without prejudging ethical character or presuming the emotive effects such agency might evoke (since these often depend on the eyes of the beholder, varying according to political-ideological position), I use a more neutral term, "ingenious," to describe such unpredictable agency of the abject. This term recognizes how, in their limited and oppressive conditions, abject subjects come up with original and resourceful ways to enact themselves politically. Regardless of whether we agree or disagree with such acts and practices, it is important to recognize, without prejudgments or presumptions, the political *ingenuity* of these acts and practices. This acknowledgement is crucial for us to see how abject subjects contest and resist in inventive and nonlinear ways when democratic agency is not possible or effective. One may thus say that the abject are feared and rejected precisely because of their ingenious acts, which politically disturb the given liberal order while generating more inhabitable spaces.

This ingenious agency signals fluidity in the abjects' status and quality, since they might, through the constant deployment of such agency, *normalize* themselves by appropriating spaces of inclusion, belonging, and citizenship, thus unsettling the existing relations. In fact, even abjection itself may be strategically embraced and redeployed as a weapon through which to obtain normality/citizenship. While abject subjects will remain abject vis-à-vis liberal citizenship, the limited degree and extent of normality they obtain also helps alleviate their abject conditions and place them in relatively more "advantageous" positions.

So what, then, if abject subjects do not act democratically but instead improvise their actions? Given that the general public would rarely consider such acts or practices politically worthy, what larger political lessons can we draw from ingenious agency? As I argued earlier, the preeminence of democratic agency emanating from Western political thought disavows the subtle and roundabout improvisation of resistance in everyday marginal spaces by the abject. It is even less likely to conceive such hidden contestation as being linked to meaningful social change. Yet even though such ingenious acts and practices are enacted in nondemocratic ways, they create hope—both for the subjects and those affected by them—for more humane spaces in liberal life.

Each instance of such agency is certainly fraught with limitations and contradictions. In chapter 1, I describe how the domestic worker Lita's refusal of dehumanizing exploitation is enabled not through an emancipatory realization of her human rights but through a self-demeaning act that fools and manipulates her employer. In chapter 5, I consider how Ayat Akhras's enactment of suicide bombing in an effort to revive the political cause of a sovereign Palestinian state must eventually traffic in the liberal discursive language of "life, liberty, and property," given the reality of the international system of states governed by the liberal world order. Neither subject is capable of transcending the liberal structure that governs, disciplines, and regulates her life; in fact, both subjects are implicated in it even as they seek to create change. Despite these limits, they nonetheless resort to creative and unordinary means, with the tools they have, to generate spaces of greater inclusion, dignity, and belonging. In fact, one may say that these limits actually provide the tools and channels the abject creatively reassemble and redeploy in expanding livable spaces. All of this suggests that ingenious agency indeed induces change and movement, not according to any linear or predetermined trajectory, but through ambiguous and indirect means. And to think: these two examples are merely a minuscule sample of the protean multitude (or the encroaching "big number") of ingenious acts and practices staged in hetero-geneous ways every day by the abject in liberal social life.

The observation that the process of social change creates transformation even as it replicates the normative liberal order can be further illustrated by examining the tangled linkages between abject subjects. Specifically, their agency may normalize and redeem them in ways that simultaneously ab-jectify others. For instance, while Lita is marginalized in her position as an impoverished migrant, her occupation as a dignified and rightful domestic worker may stigmatize other female migrants who make a living as "way-ward" prostitutes. At the same time, the orientation of the migrant sex work-ers discussed in chapter 3, who participate in the sex trade to acquire a better living standard, raise their children, and even marry their prospective (white) clients and form a heterosexual family may also provide a semblance of "nor-mal life" that offers them certain degrees of opportunity and belonging in capitalist democracies. Such opportunities are denied to Akhras, the female Palestinian suicide bomber who is condemned and vilified for violently and lethally breaking with this liberal pursuit of life, liberty, and happiness. Yet, conversely, Akhras's awful act of sacrificial violence also enables her commu-nity to recast her as a noble martyr whose heroic deed contributes immea-surably to the potential founding of Palestinian (liberal) statehood, by which standard the acts of other abject subjects might pale in comparison.

These linkages among abject subjects, which are seemingly invisible in their disparate social positions, demonstrate the impossibility of transcen-dence but also the spectrum of opportunities for disruption and appropria-tion vis-à-vis liberal citizenship. No one is completely oppressed or abject in relation to the other; everyone is relatively normalized in certain ways and abjectified in others, depending on contingent contexts and circumstances. The abjects' agency may never fully recover them as normative subjects. How-ever, their ingenious improvisations may ameliorate their abjection, even if in such amelioration they also reify the standard order that sets others in relative places of abjection. These fluid and unpredictable relations to ab-jection vis-à-vis liberal social life suggest that the hegemonic terrain is not wholly fixed. Rather, it leaves room for malleable reshaping by political sub-jects to assuage their abjection and create change (albeit with complicities and within limits). Such abjection may never be surpassed or transcended within the liberal lifecycle, but it can nonetheless be mitigated, sublimated, and transformed.

What these flashes of ingenious agency signal is that the process of creating change may not be able to escape complicity in reproducing the hegemonic liberal order, which forever circumscribes any radical potential of social justice movements to exceed its transactional terrain. Social justice movements are always already lodged inside the liberal economy, and their hope for change may similarly hinge on their submitting to a complex process of instrumental negotiation with this economy, a transformative process that is tainted by complicity and never completely achieved. All of us, critical theorists and social activists alike, do not stand outside or above this contaminated cycle, but are ourselves implicated in tangled relations of normality and abjection. But even though there is no "outside" to the liberal economy where one may stage transformative change, the episodes in this book point to the possibility that we, like the abject, may devise more clever and unordinary methods to remold and recraft the given "democratic terrain" in manifold ways and thus generate more livable spaces for all citizen-subjects. It gestures toward an ingenious futurity that entails creative reconfiguration of the system at a collective level (with whatever means are available), and inventively reshapes the terrain of the battlefield, without transcending the battlefield.

Returning to the example that opened this introduction, even for Weber's radical democratic project, the appeal to "I am an American" contains a certain layer of meaning that evokes the same narcissistic desire for "America the Beautiful" that is embedded in the Ad Council's campaign (Ling 2010, 99). Those citizens marked as unsafe courageously indict the U.S. government even as they reinscribe the liberal myth of American exceptionalism. As L. H. M. Ling notes, these statements, "ranging from the geographical (for example, I live/work in this space) to the legal (for example, I have/want the papers) to the psycho-cultural (for example, I am entitled to certain rights)" (100), appeal to American audiences through the high principles of "democracy, freedom, and justice for all." Bonnie Honig has argued that dramatizing consent validates the "universal charms of American democracy" by showing the continuous streams of immigrants voluntarily consenting to the constitutional liberal regime (2001, 92). In Weber's project, American democracy is persistently critiqued but also continually shored up by the unsafe citizens who consent explicitly, and who would "suffer exile, indignities, and loss to be a real American" (Ling, 100). What does this critical, socially conscious project thus tell us about complicity, contamination, and social change?

Perhaps Weber's project not only exemplifies democratic agency, after all, but also contains an *ingenious* element. Specifically, the complicity of the project in reifying "America the Beautiful" may be read as partially strategic. That is, for Weber to achieve her desired political effect—winning support for the cause of her project—she may actually need to traffic in this kind of nationalist-cum-American-exceptionalist language to establish identification with the public viewing audience, showing how these unsafe citizens are just like "us." They strongly identify with being Americans, they love "our" democracy, and they are even more democratically conscious and engaged than most citizens are. How could "our" government deny them fundamental rights and liberties when every bit of their character deserves to be American?

Thus, Weber's project may be reread not as merely producing a linear replica of democratic agency, but as circuitously and cleverly *using* the representation of democratic agency and consent to the liberal constitutional regime as a critical instrument to achieve her larger goal of obtaining rights and inclusion for unsafe citizens. In addition, for her radical democratic project to generate her envisioned social change, it has to work with limits and operate *inside* the given hegemonic liberal construct that circumscribes its radicalizing vision. In the end, like Lita and Akhras, Weber's critical art can in this instance be read as an ingenious political act, one that uses whatever tools and resources are available (including limits and complicities) to generate transformative change.

Toward a Political Theory of Social Change

In asking how we may look at abject subjects' quotidian acts and practices as creative resistance and how such resistance may offer lessons for us to recraft ways to generate transformation, the foregoing sections lay out the central themes of this book. What *Ingenious Citizenship* seeks to advance, then, is a *political theory of social change* that turns to and draws on the everyday lived experiences of the abject as contextual resources and inspirations for its critical theorization. I suggest that the customary spaces of the abject that generally have been assumed to be apolitical, insignificant, or even deviant in Western political thought (bound by its constrictive vision of democratic agency) may actually offer valuable insights and lessons regarding alternative modes of political intervention and social justice. Although much contemporary scholarship in political theory from critical and progressive angles is also essentially about normative theorization of social transformation, I wish to accentuate *social change* as a descriptive qualifier of this work, because I think the way we conceive the term needs to be creatively and fluidly rethought. To do so requires a departure from, and a recrafting of, the predominant methodology of political theory.

While racial, anticolonial, feminist, queer, and comparative political theories have made important advances in recent decades, the predominant works of political theory still look to Western (male) philosophers and theorists for their intellectual resources on agency, democracy, and transformation. Without taking away the important contributions these works have made to the reconceptualization of democratic politics, there is nonetheless a way in which such disciplinary practice and methodological imagination can both confine and skew our perception of resistance, citizenship, and social change toward certain cultural mores and political contours. Specifically, I argue that restricted intellectual sources can inhibit our notions about the possible and desirable forms of agency, politics, and social change *within* a prevailingly Western democratic landscape and value system, which have a tendency to prescribe democratic agency (whether in liberal, communitarian, postmodern, or radical terms) as the universally preferred form of political subjectivity to confront any unjust conditions without attention to contexts.

Take, for example, Romand Coles's radical democratic scholarship, *Beyond Gated Politics*. In it, Coles shrewdly moves beyond "democracy" as it is commonly understood by arguing that democracy is always about *democratization*—that is, the continuous effort to "embark beyond democracy's dominant forms to invent greater equality, freedom, and receptive generosity toward others" (2005, xi). Significantly, this intent of perpetual democratization leads him to move beyond traditional practice in political theory by pointing to the insufficiencies of prevailing Anglo-American and European democratic theories for their disengaged, inward-looking, and hermetic character. Instead, he advocates for a more radical mode of democratic theory and action that orients toward "'strangeness, risks, and world-making'" and "multidimensional modes of public engagement" (xix).

However, even with this admirable challenge to the core terrain of political theory, Coles's aspiration for perpetual democratization (beyond prior political theorists) as the foreground of his interpretive lens remains shaped by, and confined within, the universalizing democratic ethos of Western political thought and ignores the critical question of contexts.[8] What if, for instance, the generation of greater equality and freedom sometimes, and in certain contexts, actually requires that we take other routes besides democratic politics? Like that of many critical scholars before him, Coles's interpretive schema creates an exogenous binary between "democratic" and "antidemocratic" without accounting for the intricate ways in which antidemocratic powers—such as global capitalism and corporate technology—may already constitute an essential, endogenous part of the matrix and infrastructure of democracy (including radical democracy).

As Inderpal Grewal observes, "The forms of civil society that enable democratic citizenship are the new technologies and new media that are controlled by multinational corporations" (2005, 26). In the new information age, democratizing existing forms of citizenship, civil society, and social consciousness often entails using, and relying on, global capitalist-consumerist circuits of media and information technologies to deliver and disseminate a message, which enable its critical disruption but also perpetually delimit the contours of its rupture. When one attends to material contexts, it reveals that what Coles takes to be the two contrasting spheres of "democratic citizenship" (rights, equality, justice) and "corporate culture" (neoliberal, neocolonial, antidemocratic) have become so deeply interwoven in their liberalized global dissemination that the former cannot be untangled from the latter simply by way of democratic consciousness-raising or counterhegemonic politics.

All this is not to refute the value of democratic politics, but it does point to the problem of the prevailing ethos of democratic agency derived from the existing intellectual resources and methodological practice of political theory, which constrict its interpretive framework toward a universalizing conception of (democratic) political agency and (democratic) social change without attention to contextual intricacies. As such, we need a different kind of interpretive methodology to read abject subjects' nondemocratic agency properly and to help us conceive a more fluid horizon of making political change.

Critical Contextualization as Interpretive Strategy

To move us toward this goal, I propose an alternative strategy, what I call *critical contextualization*, to shift our interpretive lens from the "high" vision of Western political theorists to the "low" angle of the lived experiences of the abject to reopen a once foreclosed horizon in understanding abject subjects' everyday practices as original and creative ways to act politically. This method of critical contextualization, I argue, consists of three steps.

First, it makes a methodological shift to decenter political philosophers and theorists and recenter an eclectic assemblage of abject subjects—from migrant domestic workers and global sex workers to trans people and suicide bombers—as resources for a critical reinterpretation of political agency, citizenship practices, and social transformation. The political theorists Shannon Bell and Paul Apostolidis have reread subordinate subjects such as prostitutes and immigrant workers, respectively, as political philosophers, thus destabilizing the epistemological assumptions and trajectory of Western political thought (Bell 1994; Apostolidis 2010). This move is significant, for it opens up a way for "the subaltern to speak" (and to be heard) in political theory and not simply be irrelevant, discarded, or invisibilized objects in intellectual "high theory" conversations. Yet both of them still operate within the democratic theory tradition and present their subjects primarily through a counterhegemonic, radical democratic lens.

To move past this confinement, I wish to look for something even more fluid and polymorphous in the retrieval of the agency of the abject. Specifically, instead of setting up the subjects as speaking explicitly and directly like democratic theorists, I look into and reinterpret their everyday acts (which are not visible to us as political at all) as *already* politically significant—that is, as often subversive improvisations of citizenship in everyday liberal social life that do not conform to the linear democratic trajectory. In other words, I do not require the subjects to be in the position of being like "political theorists" for them to provide lessons about democratic change. I simply take them where they are and look for meanings that might offer us a different way to approach agency and change. Also, while I recognize that what I characterize as abject subjects are not all abject to the same degree or in the same way, I deliberately use the term "abject" in conceptualizing their shared lowly and marginalized locations vis-à-vis Western political philosophers and theorists to accentuate the distinctive lessons these subjects could bring us as compared with the dominant standard formulation.

Second, in addition to placing abject subjects' everyday acts at the center of political theorizing instead of canonical texts, critical contextualization further calls for a decentering of our unitary subjectivity (e.g., as theorists, intellectuals, professionals, the educated) to relate to the abject and see things from their social positions in more fluid and organic ways. This does not entail our identification with all of the acts and deeds committed by the abject, but it does call on us to imagine and embody a contextual shift of our locations between us–them, normal–abject, spectator–gazed, and subject–object positionings to blur these boundaries and enable the possibility of an alternative interpretation of their acts and deeds. As James Ferguson argues from an anthropological perspective, "What we see . . . depends on where we are looking from" (2006, 29). When we practice looking at the everyday acts and practices of the abject through their "low" vantage point rather than from our unbendable "high" positions, it could bring "into visibility things that might otherwise be overlooked and [force] us to think harder about issues that might otherwise be passed over or left unresolved" (29).

One way to approach this decentering of self-subjectivity might be by going through the simple exercise of asking oneself: What if any of my friends, loved ones, or children—or even myself—is in the position of being an abject subject? What kinds of limitations, dangers, violence, or precarity would they or I be facing? How would their or my needs, desires, and dreams shift? How would that make me think differently about the occurrence or eruption of their or my abject acts and practices? And if I become one of the abject (say, a domestic worker), what happens to my worldview and life outlook when I shift again to the position of another abject figure (say, sex worker)? Contextually shifting our imagined or embodied locations helps challenge and destabilize our existing assumptions and open up new possibilities of interpretation.

Kobena Mercer's critical essay, "Just Looking for Trouble: Robert Mapplethorpe and Fantasies of Race," illustrates how our interpretive lens could be expanded through such a decentering shift of our locations and contexts. In it, Mercer discusses his initial shock and disgust on seeing the grotesque photos of nude black men in the white gay photographer Robert Mapplethorpe's homoerotic artwork, with images such as a black man whose face is out of the frame "holding his semitumescent penis through the Y-fronts of his underpants" (Mercer 1997, 242). Mercer's initial emotive interpretation of the images is constructed via his ideological perception of Mapplethorpe's racial fetishism and colonial fantasy, which, in his eyes, reduces "these individual black men to purely abstract visual 'things'" (243). However, this ideological framework is destabilized and transformed when Mercer comes to acknowledge a shifting context of his own embodied subjectivity: as a gay black man, he is also "a desiring [gay consumer] subject . . . [with] an identical object-choice" in his "own fantasies and wishes" (247). From this changed location, he begins to recognize "another axis of identification—between white gay-male author and black gay-male reader—that cut across the identification with the black men in the pictures" (247). In fact, here the reader may even expand on Mercer's example to enact another kind of shift and conceive oneself *as* the desired object (the nude black man) in the photos, which can further destabilize the boundaries in other ways and open up other kinds of cross-identifications.

Significantly, the shifting location from being strictly critical of Mapplethorpe's racism to being identified with his homoeroticism enables Mercer to expand his interpretive horizon in seeing Mapplethorpe's deliberate subversion in the larger material context of "the exclusion of the black subject from one of the most valued canonical genres of Western art—the nude" (248). Mercer writes, "One can see in Mapplethorpe's use of homoeroticism a subversive strategy of perversion in which the liberal-humanist values inscribed in the idealized fine-art nude are led away from the higher aims of 'civilization' and brought face-to-face with that part of itself repressed and devalued as 'other' in the form of the banal, commonplace stereotype in everyday culture" (249).

As Mercer concludes, the textual ambivalence of Mapplethorpe's artwork "foreground[s] the uncertainty of any one, singular meaning" (248); it is precisely meant to deny "a stable or centered subject-position" and arouse "an emotional disturbance that troubles the viewer's sense of secure identity" (247). The decentering of subject position that Mapplethorpe opens up enables readers, from their fragmentary subjectivities and pluralized contexts, to bring conflicting and open-ended interpretations to the image that are foreclosed by certain ideological predispositions with their dichotomous "good and bad, positive and negative" frame (247).

Taking insights from Mercer, our embodied locations always already shape and formulate our interpretations. As Dagmar Lorenz-Meyer writes, "The knower is part of the matrix of what is known, and . . . the location from which we speak is one from which other voices . . . [or even] those within ourselves, may be sanctioned" (2004, 795). And if a contextual shift of location can open up a once sanctioned or foreclosed interpretation, then the method of critical contextualization helps facilitate this goal by requesting that we embody ourselves through the located subjectivity of others—or, in Kuan-Hsing Chen's words, "to actively interiorize elements of others into the subjectivity of the self" (1998, 25).

Indeed, as an analogy, I suggest that the reader take this book like Mapplethorpe's artwork, in its "subversive strategy of perversion," in the material context of the prevailing exclusion of abject subjects from being protagonists and architects in political theory, and consider abject subjects as being in a position similar to that of the nude black man in the racialized homoerotic photo. Together for me as the author and you as the reader, it is by following Mercer's example, undergoing "a thorough investigation of . . . [his] own subject position and identifications and disidentifications, his desires and investments, and his use of a single interpretive category . . . versus the adoption of a dialogical mode of interpretation for specific knowledge claims" (Lorenz-Meyer, 796), that we may shift from the dominant interpretive lens of democratic agency in political theory to retrieve, reread, and recover abjects' nondemocratic agency—in their given contexts—as possibly dynamic, organic, and ingenious political enactments.

Finally, as the last step of critical contextualization, I argue that this interpretive method cannot be complete without resorting to its own intellectual resources to actually conduct its alternative interpretation of agency and change through the lived experiences of the abject. Moving beyond the terrain of Western political thought, I find works in other interdisciplinary fields—namely, cultural theory and cultural anthropology—to be especially helpful in enabling me to craft a different political theory of social change: one that does not take democratic agency as its automatic starting point. Specifically, Ingenious Citizenship bridges and interweaves cultural theory with existing ethnographies; qualitative interviews; news reports; films and documentaries; and autobiographical statements, writings, and documents through a critical layering of textual rereading, reinterpretation, and reconstruction in advancing an ingenious story of citizenship that is grounded in, and informed by, the lived experiences of the abject. This methodology is necessarily interdisciplinary, working at the interface of cultural theory and ethnographically informed analysis. While I have not carried out ethnographic research on my own given the diverse range of populations in the current study, I have been consciously attentive to the human narratives in existing ethnographic and autobiographic accounts to ensure that the theoretical story I weave is built on and illustrated through their concrete experiences in everyday life—specifically, in the ways these subjects negotiate their daily struggles within the hegemonic liberal order.

This combination of cultural theory and ethnography enables me to conceptualize "citizenship" differently. While common understanding of citizenship focuses on institutional rights, political participation, or street activism (formal channels that embody the enactment of democratic agency), I understand it as a cultural script inscribed and utilized by liberal sovereignty to govern and regulate how citizen-subjects should conduct themselves in different realms of social life (the political realm, economic realm, gender realm, etc.).

As I explicate in chapter 1, this liberal citizenship script produces normality (proper citizens) and abjection (abject subjects) as mutually constitutive relations. At the same time, this notion of script also serves as a critical template for us to trace and investigate how abject subjects may be read as disrupting and appropriating the script in informal and nondemocratic ways to improvise more humane and inhabitable spaces for themselves.

The term "ingenious citizenship" specifically describes how the abject, who are remaindered by the script and lack status, power, and resources to access "full" juridical rights and social acknowledgement as normative citizens, come up with original and creative ways to reinsert themselves into the script. Because such improvisations do not go through formal channels, the forms of citizenship generated are not (yet) officially recognized. I call the kind of citizenship thus appropriated and acquired "nonexistent citizenship"— that is, inclusion, belonging, equality, or rights that are not formally guaranteed and codified.[9] By delineating how abject subjects appropriate and reuse the script to assuage their abjection and make themselves "count," ingenious citizenship enables a viewing horizon of the liminal change and movement that are effected in the hegemonic liberal terrain.

Note that this is certainly not to say that such change is sufficient or that abject subjects' politics should remain at this informal, precarious level. There is no doubt that such subversive contestations are limited—in fact, even formal citizenship itself is a limiting political concept that is never instituted to effect social emancipation. But, placing such creative resistance in context, I wish to ask: What is the value of these limits? What if this limited change and movement actually offer unexpected lessons for us to tap creatively and fluidly into the unending, shifting field of abjection and strategically create more livable spaces for human subjects to inhabit, in their discrepant and differential contexts?

In all, the three steps of critical contextualization—(1) recentering abject subjects as critical resources for political theory; (2) decentering our unitary subjectivity by imagining ourselves or our immediate affiliates through shifting contexts; and (3) the intellectual borrowing from cultural theory and cultural anthropology to chronicle abject subjects' simultaneous disruption and appropriation of the citizenship script—formulate the interpretive method that constructs the ensuing story of ingenious citizenship. This new interpretative method brings into view a new horizon of creative agency.

As I wish to further suggest, this renewed interpretation of creative resistance at the individual level offers important lessons for collective movements and intervention strategies. Employing critical contextualization to elicit a political theory of social change leads to a more flexible and variable notion of politics than is often conceived in democratic political theory, especially concerning democratic political theory's emphasis on "rights" and "rights-based movements" in social justice struggles. Specifically, I argue, whether critical scholars and activists ought to resort to rights-based politics at all should depend on contexts rather than presuming its values and effects (or lack thereof) in advance.

The issue of rights has been subject to intense debate by progressive and left scholars. On the one hand, in addition to the early critique by theorists such as Wendy Brown (1995), recent works in the fields of critical ethnic studies and queer of color critique have tenaciously indicted the limitations of rights and the complicity of rights-based politics in perpetuating normative violence (Reddy 2011; Spade 2011; Cacho 2012). On the other hand, those working within political theory have sought to engender new rationales through the constellation of radical democratic theory to advocate for the continuing importance of rights, rights discourse, and making rights claims as an agonistic and performative democratic practice that perpetually thwarts and disrupts normative liberal foundations (Chambers 2004; Zivi 2011).

From my view, both sides contain their own insufficiencies. I agree with radical democrats that an excessive focus on the limits of rights may obscure the fundamentally unpredictable character of democratic politics and social change. As Karen Zivi asserts, "No language or practice of resistance can bring about the end to political debate and struggle, no matter how liberated from an ancient theory of sovereignty" (2011, 81). However, as I have indicated throughout this introduction, to foreground democratic politics as the immanent basis of social change (as radical democrats suggest) can also become an inflexible and predictable politics. As the method of critical contextualization shall remind us: there exist contexts and moments in which rights may constitute the contingent bedrock for the expansion and furtherance of social change, just as there exist contexts and moments in which it may be impractical or ineffective to resort to rights-based politics as tools of advocacy—for instance, when abject subjects live in certain authoritarian regimes, socialist republics, or non-Western cultural contexts that are not readily prone to persuasion by rights discourse.

Taking cues from abject subjects' ingenious citizenship, critical contextualization would suggest that social movements adopt a more variable use of political strategies, creatively negotiating with complicitous logics and antidemocratic powers to recraft spaces of social change in varied locations and contexts. In particular, this would imply that social movements may need to deemphasize their rights claims, or even drop their focus on rights in specific circumstances, in order to achieve a de facto actualization of humane life for the abject in concrete situations.

Such nondemocratic political processes, I argue, can appropriate and generate "nonexistent rights" for the abject—that is, de facto realization of inclusion, belonging, and rights that are not officially guaranteed or codified. Insisting that we must either renounce or embrace rights, then, prevents us from invoking and deploying the diverse tools and repertoires we need to crack open the manifold, interstitial spaces of transformation in different locations. Hence, while scholars such as Monisha Das Gupta have articulated a flexible and moveable "transnational complex of rights" that traverses local, state, national, and international contexts (Das Gupta 2006), I suggest that we need to cultivate an even more fluid and elastic relation with rights, including making political claims and doing social advocacy through non–rights-based and nondemocratic discourses and channels.

Here is also the central lesson of ingenious citizenship for organized movements: social movements need to be reconceived in an ever more fluid and creative fashion in order to maximize their effectiveness in helping the abject in global capitalism. My discussion in this book by no means rules out the critical role of rights-based movements in struggles for social justice; it does, however, decenter taken-for-granted assumptions about social movements and suggest that they take on a more flexible and amorphous orientation beyond a predetermined "pure" and "democratic" character. As abject subjects' creative acts will show, while contestation is often inspired by a vision for purity, change is often mobilized and advanced by contamination and complicity—and the more ingenious the uses of contamination, the more transformative the results we might expect to see.

This book should thus be understood as angling for an alternative kind of left politics, advancing a different conception, and political theorization, of ways to produce social transformation in much more fluid and open-ended terms than are commonly assumed in progressive and radical thought. It suggests that once we reexamine the process of social change and recognize it as always embodying the endogenous elements of purity and contamination, it opens up a nonlinear view that what are usually thought of as nondemocratic approaches (sometimes working in conjunction with democratic politics) might circuitously and deviously lead to social change in minute, polymorphous ways. What is more, we might *seize that change to create further change* in concrete circumstances and situations. Conversely, when we insist that only a method of purity can lead to "genuine" change—that is to say, when our thoughts and actions are already confined to, and constricted by, a preconceived democratic schema—we commit the mistake of overlooking both how complexity can beset and thwart the most inviolable vision and plan and how we are always entangled in the intricacies of contamination, even without our conscious recognition.

Other scholars have similarly signaled this direction in their work. Ferguson, for instance, has argued that the popular practice of left critique often repeats the same unsurprising conclusion of "the politics of the 'anti'" (i.e., anti-neoliberalism, anti-globalization, anti-imperialism) that leads to "a rather sterile form of political engagement" (2011, 62). He asks: "But what if politics is really not about expressing indignation or denouncing the powerful? What if it is, instead, about getting what you want?" (2009, 167). Ferguson suggests another kind of left politics beyond denunciatory analyses: a "left art of government" that would "*take advantage of* (rather than simply fighting against)" neoliberal rationality and "identify new possibilities and openings in the current transnational regime" (2011, 64; emphasis in original).

Such reconception of agency and change beyond the normative democratic contour and interpretation in political theory and social justice literatures, I argue, is crucially needed in these neoliberal times of ours. As Bayat asserts, "In a world of un-equals, the weak will certainly lose if it follows the same rules of the game as those of the powerful. To win an unequal battle, the underdog has no choice but to creatively play different, more flexible and constantly changing games" (23–24). And, I would add, the pivotal lesson on ways for social movements to win the perpetual battles of neoliberal times might come from the most unlikely places: the abject themselves.

The Book's Chapters

This book is divided into three parts: part I: "Beginning" (chapter 1); part II: "Episodes" (chapters 2–5); and part III: "(Un)Ending" (conclusion). Part I provides my central theoretical frame of ingenious citizenship. As indicated earlier, I look at liberal citizenship as a *cultural script*, a standardized way of life brought into being by European capitalist modernity that governs ideologically and materially how human subjects ought to live and participate as "proper" citizens. I then suggest a four-pronged frame to theorize how abject subjects may disrupt and appropriate this hegemonic citizenship script into the constellation of ingenious citizenship.

Chapters 2–5 weave together part II as each of these chapters presents a momentary example of ingenious citizenship performed by different abject subjects. Specifically, I investigate how migrant domestic workers stage hidden tactics to appropriate political citizenship (chapter 2), global sex workers use calculated abjection to appropriate economic citizenship (chapter 3), trans people adopt morphing technologies to appropriate gendered citizenship (chapter 4), and suicide bombers exert sacrificial violence to appropriate life itself (chapter 5).

By interpreting how these subjects can be understood as disrupting and appropriating scripts of citizenship, I do not suggest that their ingenious agency defines their essence as humans. Rather, I focus on one aspect of their complex lives to illustrate and illuminate recurring and persistent episodes of ingenious agency and the unexamined lessons about social change inherent in the improvisations of these acts. Thus, rather than dwelling on the personal qualities of the subjects, what I am focusing on (and what I want the reader to take away from these episodes) is how the momentary and recurring eruptions of ingenious acts and practices generated through these myriad subjects enable more livable spaces for themselves and others, without assuming any totalizing understanding of these subjects. This is addressed by looking specifically at how different abject subjects appropriate the scripts in their own distinctive and challenging ways given their respective conditions, so as to accord them crucial specificity in their humanity.

It is also important to contextualize my use of the word "episodes" here, since the implicated approach of "viewing" abject subjects seemingly borders on a voyeuristic "spectator–gazed" relationship that reinscribes the power hierarchy between the "normal" and the "abject" (Mulvey 1975). The concept of episodes is closely connected to the property of ingenious agency.

Given its inventive quality, ingenious agency is not a stable state of being as the subject undergoes the flow of life, but is necessarily fleeting and ephemeral. I thus present in this book a collage of flashing scenes (drawing from myriad sources) in which ingenious agency takes momentary hold before it evaporates and vanishes, even as it also continuously reemerges. Since the materials I draw from are existing sources available for public viewing, I cannot control how other audiences may read, interpret, or view the subjects in these documents. Rather, I wish to refocus the reader's attention on the very moments in which these subjects can be understood as acting politically in ingenious ways. Abject subjects are as complex as any other human beings, and the following portraits are not meant to describe their subjectivity in any reductive or totalizing sense (as if that is what they are in *essence*, whether in a celebratory or an indicting tone). Rather, each episode simply signifies and magnifies *one* of the manifold and heterogeneous aspects of each subject—an aspect that I argue offers significant lessons for all of us in reconsidering political agency and recognizing ways to improvise social transformation. I also hope that this exercise can help unsettle and disrupt the problematic binary between the "normal" and the "abject" by causing readers to see the abject within themselves and understand these subjects' nondemocratic agency and enactment as having always already been part of the liberal democratic norm.

Each episode of ingenious citizenship also offers unconventional insights and lessons for generating fluid social justice strategies. As I illustrate in chapters 2–4, while the current rights-based movements for migrant domestic workers, global sex workers, and trans people have displayed notable signs of ingenious agency, the foregrounding of democratic agency in their formal modus operandi prevents them from adopting a more extensive incorporation of ingenuity into their organizing strategies. In each case, I point to some tentative directions in which rights-based movements may incorporate the lessons of the ingenious politics of hidden tactics, calculated abjection, and morphing technologies, respectively, into their repertoire of intervention and activism strategies when advocating for the abject. In chapter 5, I take a different approach, using the recent neoliberal reforms spearheaded by the Palestinian Authority to illustrate how its deployment of the sacrificial violence of neoliberalism (appropriating the sacrificial logic of suicide bombing) to mobilize and enhance its claim for sovereign statehood provides a nondemocratic lesson on social change for critical scholars and activists concerned about the Palestinian rights of return and self-determination.

Finally, I construe the concluding part of the book as "(Un)Ending" not only because it constitutes the end of the book, but also because it gestures to the continuous formation of ingenious citizenship in liberal social life that lives on unendingly, flash after flash. What these unending episodes of ingenious citizenship improvised by the abject teach us, I suspect, is a futurity in which we make fluid use of political intervention and movement strategies in recrafting the lived spaces of social change. Here I turn to an unlikely figure, the Chinese diasporic martial artist Bruce Lee, as a resource to characterize the guiding position that I call "politics without politics" in this nonlinear transformation. This refers to an art of combat without combat, engaging in political contestation without it appearing so, and eclectically drawing on the use of different tools for different situations without any preconceived method or approach. My hope is that this positioning will inform critical scholars and activist groups regarding ways to incorporate the lessons of abject subjects' ingenious citizenship into political intervention and organizing strategies. It is to these lessons that I turn in the chapters that follow.

Part I

Beginning

1. Improvising Citizenship
Appropriating the Liberal Citizenship Script

In *Consumers and Citizens*, Néstor García Canclini urges a rethinking of the social practice of commodity consumption as a key site in reinvigorating citizenship. Deconstructing the conventional binary frame that juxtaposes the rational and deliberative citizen against the passive and irrational consumer, he writes, "The exercise of citizenship has always been associated with the capacity to appropriate commodities and with ways of using them" (García Canclini 2001, 15).

Here, García Canclini significantly updates prior political thought by indicating that the exercise of citizenship, including the ways in which we organize our social belonging and network, are steeped in practices of consumption and their accompanying logics of negotiation and appropriation (20). Yet his critical rendering of consumption as constitutive of citizenship nonetheless leaves citizenship as something external and immune to consumption and appropriation. Specifically, García Canclini's reading of citizenship as a capacity to appropriate commodities overlooks that citizenship may also be seen as a *cultural commodity* in itself—an object that is constantly appropriated and negotiated by citizen-subjects and "citizens in waiting."[1]

In this chapter, I extend García Canclini's revision of political thought to propose a reconception of liberal citizenship as an appropriable, globalized cultural script—a mundane material and cultural artifact that is continually revised and reused by "abject consumers" in devising informal spaces of rights, inclusion, and belonging. While existing scholarship has conceptualized and investigated citizenship in different ways,[2] I understand liberal citizenship as a *materially scripted way of life*—that is, as a standardizing and domineering cultural script of citizenship brought into being by European capitalist modernity to govern how human subjects ought to live and participate as "proper" citizens in different realms, such as the political, the economic, the gender binary, and life itself.

To speak of this script as being ripe for appropriation is not to understate its power in mapping a broad cultural-material terrain of human social life that it facilitates in making and reproducing. Embedded in the modern liberal world order, this full-blown cultural script of citizenship interpellates the "proper" ways for humans to be citizens in different social spheres to reproduce domesticated subjects who will be kept in place. It works to minimize and soften the presence and potency of deviant transgressions in ensuring the mundane reproduction of social life. Citizenship, *the script*, might be seen by many as necessary rules and social norms. But it is also ideological and biopolitical—a particular way to perform citizenship that has been crafted, articulated, and disseminated as "common sense" and materialized and reproduced into a way of life in contemporary liberal democracy. The script does not merely define or impose a life of citizenship externally on citizens; it is itself the *life to be lived*, through and through and cycle after cycle, by citizen-subjects. It is this human cycle of citizenship that sustains liberal democracy, but in acting the same script over and over, it performs a life that is banal and cannot grow outside itself.

Understanding liberal citizenship as a cultural script serves two critical objectives. First, to the extent that the script instructs human subjects on the "normal" way to conduct themselves as citizens in different social spheres and institutions, this conception illustrates how the ideological and material force of normality takes hold through the script and becomes crystallized as common sense in liberal life. The citizenship script is utilized by liberal democracy as an essential tool of surveillance and control to ensure the continuation of its lifecycle. In its production of liberal citizenship, the script produces normality (proper citizens) and abjection (abject subjects) as mutually constitutive formations. As indicated in the introduction, the normality of proper citizens presupposes the existence of the abject—those who could not "measure up" or conform to the script—for its own constitution. Thus remaindered but also serving as its constitutive outside, the abject exists precariously in the interstices of liberal citizenship.

Second, conceiving citizenship as script not only underlines its seemingly invincible production of normality and abjection, but it can also serve as a template to trace how abject subjects inventively and resourcefully disrupt and appropriate the script to generate more inhabitable spaces for themselves. The mutually constitutive formation between the proper and the abject is never stable, in essential part because the abject are imbued with agency, and their everyday acts and practices can be read as constantly improvising ways to resist their state vis-à-vis the liberal citizenship script. In this way, seeing citizenship as script can enable a horizon in viewing and theorizing abject subjects' ingenious agency and illustrating the limited change generated through such agency in hegemonic liberal life. In sum, it activates a rethinking about abject subjects' quotidian practices as *ingenious citizenship*.

Linking citizenship to the liberal script thus provides the structural and political context for my theorization of ingenious agency and change in relation to the abject. In this book, I direct my analysis to four major sites at which the liberal citizenship script is disrupted and appropriated: migrant domestic workers' workplace tactics staged against employers, global sex workers' purposeful abjection of their bodies, trans people's remodeling of gender identification and sexual practices, and acts of suicide bombing. Ingenious agency shines through prominently in the capacity of these abject subjects, who fall through the cracks of conventional citizenship, acting inventively and resourcefully to survive and reclaim limited spaces of dignity, inclusion, and belonging. In all of these instances, ingenious agency does not simply register a direct deviation from the norm. Rather, it imparts a subtle and subversive quality that involves appropriating the liberal citizenship script—thus, both fissuring and inhabiting the norm—to circuitously reanimate a remaindered and dispossessed citizenship.

As I articulate below, while my focus in this book is on the liberal script, I do not see it as the only existing script: whether in the Unites States or elsewhere, there are always competing scripts in different local contexts. I wish to emphasize, however, that the liberal citizenship script does manifest its hegemonic aspirations to the extent that local scripts in non-Western regions often have to compete or negotiate with its disseminating effects, resulting in discrepant formations of liberal subjects. I understand the liberal citizenship script as containing elements of ideology (à la Marx), hegemony (à la Gramsci), and discourse (à la Foucault) that exist in a constantly shifting continuum. This moving continuum molds different types of liberal citizen-subjects in varied sites, rendering the script both *durable* (hegemonic) and *elastic* (heterogeneous) in its distribution across geographic borders. It may be helpful to understand the globalized liberal script in terms of what Inderpal Grewal and Caren Kaplan have conceived as "scattered hegemonies," which, in traveling across national boundaries, produce syncretic, irregular, and discrepant effects (1994, 7).

In fact, the notion of scattered hegemonies allows us to understand the hegemonic aspirations of the liberal script even when it does not neatly encompass the entire globe. As James Ferguson reminds us from the vantage point of Africa, while neoliberal networks in the forms of transnational capital and nongovernmental organizations (NGOs) "do indeed 'span the globe,' . . . they do not cover it. Instead, they *hop over* (rather than flowing through) the territories inhabited by the vast majority of the African population" (2006, 14; emphasis added). This hopping effect of neoliberalism, which connects enclaved points "in a selective, discontinuous, and point-to-point fashion," results in "highly elective and spatially encapsulated forms of global connection combined with widespread disconnection and exclusion," leaving "most Africans with only a tenuous and indirect connection to 'the global economy'" (14).

Yet even such exclusion and disconnection from globalization do not take place *outside* neoliberal forces. As Ferguson notes, there exist among African populations strong "aspirations to 'development,' 'modernity'" (2006, 16), or "yearnings for cultural convergence with an imagined global standard" (20). He writes, "The same processes that produce exclusion, marginalization, and abjection are also producing new forms of non-national economic spaces, . . . new forms of government by NGO and transnational networks, . . . and new kinds of more or less desperate claims to membership and recognition at a supranational level" (14).

The "global" in Africa consists of "capital flows and markets [that] are at once lightning fast and patchy and incomplete; where the globally networked enclave sits right beside the ungovernable humanitarian disaster zone" (Ferguson 2006, 49). As Aihwa Ong has argued in another context, neoliberal rationality involves calculations regarding which populations or sites are included for investment and mobilization in relation to capital accumulation and which populations or sites are excluded from such enterprise, thus resulting in "varied effects on the constitution of citizen-subjects and the spaces that they inhabit" (2005, 257). I suggest that these splintering effects can be attributed to the moving continuum and scattered hegemonies of the traveling liberal script.

I also wish to note that the abject subjects in my reading intervene in the global power dynamics of liberal citizenship from varying positions in, relations to, and distances from U.S. citizenship: some as formal citizens, some as aliens who participate within the arrangement of formal citizenship, and others as nationals of other sovereign states and localities. Extending on Engin Isin's conception that citizenship is irreducible to matters of membership but instead is dynamically constituted through political subjectivity (Isin 2002, 2008, 2009), I argue that what is central about the abject subjects in the present study is precisely how their everyday acts, practices, and discourses can be read as politically interrupting and appropriating the widely disseminated script of liberal citizenship across national geographic boundaries, irrespective of their formal membership status. This reading expands the scope of understanding the abject as contributing to the rewriting of the liberal citizenship script in original and resourceful ways, thus contriving and extending new lineations of social change. In addition, since the liberal script interacts with competing scripts in different local and regional contexts, attention will be given to local complexity in accordance with the objective of critical contextualization. Given that this project is not meant as an ethnographic study, my objective is not to provide detailed information on the local background of every case. However, I will provide an appropriate amount of analysis of contextual differences among subjects in their local conditions to add nuance to my observation.

One question may be raised here. As recent critical scholarship from various disciplines has charged, citizenship is a limiting political category, a bourgeois concept and institution that is riven by and incapable of transcending Western, imperial, racial, class, gender, and sexual exclusion and subordination. So can a political project inspired by the conception of ingenious citizenship provide any substantive vision of social transformation? In response, I suggest that while we ought to recognize the limits of citizenship, the analysis should not stop there. Instead, we can extend the analysis by asking: *Can there be value even in these limits, especially if one considers the subjects' contexts?*

That is to say, whether there is political value in a social phenomenon depends on the locations from which one observes: what might appear to be a limiting political concept from one angle might be redeployed and used for innovative empowerment in another context. Ferguson's research on Africa provides a useful illustration of this phenomenon. As he notes, while critics of neoliberalism often hold in contempt the "homogenizing" goods and forms of global culture, they ignore that these things are unavailable to most Africans (Ferguson 2006, 20). The hardships of Africa thus "have very little to do with being overrun with Western factories and consumer goods" when countries there "are begging in vain for foreign investment of any kind and unable to provide a significant market for the consumer goods stereotypically associated with globalization" (26). In this scenario, African desires for "'likeness' with real and imagined Western standards" should not simply be interpreted as "mental colonization or capitulation to cultural imperialism." Rather, they should be seen as "an aspiration to overcome categorical subordination" (20). Ferguson writes, "Claims of likeness, in this context, constitute not a copying, but a shadowing, even a haunting—a declaration of comparability, an aspiration to membership and inclusion in the world, and sometimes also an assertion of a responsibility" (17; emphasis added).

Similarly, when we place abject subjects in the critical context of their "uninhabitable" abjection from the citizenship script that immanently defines them, their aspirations for inclusion should not simply be dismissed—or defined—as capitulation to an unequal structural order. Rather, these limited and complicit aspirations for normative citizenship might be reinterpreted as "a powerful claim to a chance for transformed conditions of life—a place-in-the-world, a standard of living, a 'direction we would like to move in'" (Ferguson 2006, 19). Following Ferguson, claiming a place in the world can disruptively compel the "normal" to acknowledge their "relationships and responsibilities in a larger system" (22).

Taking this a step further, and more specifically for my purpose, I suggest that it is precisely the limiting category of citizenship that provides an entry point for us to understand how abject subjects, situated in their contexts, are obtaining what I term *nonexistent citizenship*, or the informal and nonguaranteed spaces of inclusion, equity, and rights that are gained through inventive disruption and appropriation of the liberal script. It is also through these improvisations of nonexistent citizenship that we see how the abject resort to creative and unordinary means, with the limited tools and resources they have, to obtain the essentials they need to survive.

Ultimately, recognizing the value of limits in given contexts also turns the tables on critics who adopt an emancipatory political positioning that refuses any limits without consideration of context. By looking at how the abject appropriate citizenship to generate livable spaces for themselves, the current investigation points incisively to the ways in which abject people—and, by implication, all of us, who are abject in one way or another—are inevitably implicated in hypostatizing liberal hegemony even in resistant improvisation and subversive appropriation. One critical (and sobering) lesson I seek to elucidate in this book is thus the inevitable complicity and contamination of any performance of resistance—even the most radical kinds—in the material cycle of liberal social life. Yet I also wish to emphasize that the messy webs of complicity and contamination do not spell doom or futility; rather, they formulate the instrumental conduits to create circuitous and nonlinear processes of social change. This book thus sheds light on the perpetual tension between the immanent potentiality of social change and the inescapable circumscription of such change in liberal hegemony. It also further suggests that critical scholars and social activists may want to seize such tension as the foundation for expanding social transformation.

A Shifting Continuum: Citizenship as Cultural Script

I conceive the cultural script of liberal citizenship as an array of shifting subscripts, according to which human subjects need to perform as "proper citizens" in different social fields of liberal life. Several major examples are *politics, economics, gender,* and *life itself.* The *political script* divides human subjects into citizens of different national territories (at birth as *ius sanguinis* or *ius soli,* or through naturalization) and denotes democratic participation in a political community within predetermined bureaucratic parameters: voting, lobbying, and campaigning through the representative matrix; serving on a jury; deliberating in a town hall meeting; or protesting at a restricted street assembly without causing public disturbance. The *economic script* embodies the ideal citizen-worker in the unending rituals of working, consuming, saving, investing, and—increasingly in the neoliberal economy—enterprising, and as such contributing lawfully to the productive cycle of capitalism. The *gender script* interpellates citizens as belonging to a gender binary (as either male or female) and places them on a lifelong trajectory of, respectively, masculine or feminine order toward heteronormative monogamous relationships and conjugal arrangements. With the onset of neoliberalism, issues of homonormative monogamy (e.g., same-sex marriage, gays in the military) and their mainstream constituents, middle-class gays and lesbians, have also been increasingly incorporated into the normative economy of gender-sexual citizenship in liberal social life (Duggan 2002; Puar 2007). Finally, the *life script* nurtures a civil and proprietary citizen-subject in a depoliticized and unbridled pursuit of life, liberty, and happiness.

While they are not the only examples, these major subscripts craft and shape a stagnant "lifecycle" of liberal citizenship in prescribing a relatively fixed social, political, and moral order. Specifically, they perpetuate a repetitive circuit of a standardized male or female subject who works and consumes, saves and invests, and pays taxes in the productive cycle of capitalism as an honest and law-abiding citizen-worker, and who periodically participates in an orderly manner in the business of governing and deliberating through the bureaucratic representative matrix within an imagined national community.

To fully attain the rights, protection, and merited valuation conferred by citizenship, subjects must participate within the parameters set by the script that binds them in place—whether in national place (one nation-state), gender place (gender binary, monogamy, monosexuality), political place (representative/deliberative bureaucracy), economic place (law-abiding worker or entrepreneur in capitalism), or life place (civil, orderly, and proprietary). This standardized citizenship script is thus cultural not in ethnocultural terms but in the ideological-cultural sense, wherein a cultural hegemony of citizenship is articulated and interpellated in the sphere of everyday discourse and institutions as common sense and materialized into a way of life.[3] The script is thus not merely cultural but material, as it is linked to material rewards, entitlements, and protections and is lived by human subjects.[4] It is also inflected by biopolitical calculation, since it induces and fosters particular modes of individual corporeal bodies and mass social bodies toward the normative reproduction of liberal social life.[5] Notably, the governing subscripts are elastic in accordance with new social situations and political calculations, as well as in their regional and transnational dissemination. Their shifting realignments, even when they appear to be mobilized by democratic social change, are embedded in regenerating this cycle of liberal citizenship in its constellating realms of the political, the economic, the gender binary, and life itself.[6]

To further substantiate our understanding of the cultural script of liberal citizenship, it would be helpful to see it as embodying genres of ideology, hegemony, and discourse on a moving continuum. Mark Stoddart, in a critical essay, indicates that the concepts of ideology, hegemony, and discourse have been used to explain how "the social production and dissemination of knowledge secures our consent to systematic social inequity" (2007, 192). While varying critical theoretical accounts have pointed to tension between these perspectives, Stoddart argues, "these approaches are not mutually contradictory options for understanding social power . . . [and] we might usefully locate them along a continuum" (193). He writes, "This continuum allows us to visualize the ongoing tension between critical theory's attention to political praxis, oppression and domination, on one hand; and poststructuralism's attention to complexity, fragmentation, and the microstructures of power, on the other. While theories of discourse emerge prior to ideology theory, in a temporal sense, the continuum allows us to visualize the continuity between these concepts. In other words, theories of discourse rarely act as a total negation of the notion of ideology. Instead, discourse, hegemony and ideology are intertwined with each other" (193).

While I take insights from Stoddart, because Gramsci's notion of hegemony improves on the economic determinism of Marxian ideology to provide a more open-ended account of ideological struggles in the multidimensional arenas of class, race, gender, and sexuality (Hall 1996a, 1996b), I deemphasize Marx's class-based ideological analysis and focus on hegemony and discourse in my description of the citizenship script. Through Gramsci's notion of hegemony, I argue that the liberal citizenship script is naturalized as common sense via its ideological and material appeal to acquire the massive consent of citizen-subjects. Because such consent needs to be manufactured, built, and won, it also presents the possibility of disruption and change. In addition to hegemony, the script is further enriched and made elastic by the elements of what Foucault calls discourses and technologies in its concrete applications in different contexts. This discursive and technological element of the liberal script makes it capable of rendering its effects even when it does not achieve hegemonic status in certain non-Western regions. For instance, in socialist China, the liberal script does not have hegemonic status as a political institution, but it nonetheless exerts discursive and technological effects in innumerable other ways, whether through the local governing regimes of special market zones (Ong 2006) or through popular media and public culture (Rofel 2007).

Thus, even if the development of neoliberalism in global regions is uneven, its forces and effects have generated a transnational reach across borders, to the extent that competing scripts in non-Western regions have to negotiate with neoliberal imperatives and undergo dynamic struggles of contestation, alliance, and accommodation. And the very fact that competing local scripts in places such as Palestine have to negotiate with neoliberalism shows the script's *aspiring* hegemonic power (see chapter 5).

It should be further noted that, as a cultural-material product of European capitalist modernity, the different realms of lives embodied in the traveling liberal citizenship script are inescapably racialized and thoroughly contaminated by the civilizing engineering of whiteness/Westernness. In the United States, for instance, national citizenship has never been a purely neutral institution; rather, it is systemically and invisibly processed by the symbolic and material structuring of whiteness (McIntosh 1990; Lipsitz 1998; Banet-Weiser 1999; Delgado and Stefancic 2001; Jung et al. 2011).[7] This deeply affects the extent to which a white/Western, capitalistic, heteropatriarchal, and bourgeois civil-institutional worldview informs the disseminated ethos of a globalized liberal citizenship script beyond the sovereign boundaries of liberal democracies. As such, despite varying configurations of citizenship as an institutional and material way of life in different nation-states, all are undergirded by the same historical-structural source: an invisible system of ideological interpellation and biopolitical instrumentalization.

As Barry Hindess observes, to the extent that modern citizenship structures a biopolitical regime vis-à-vis the internal populations in advanced liberal states, it further informs the relations between states in an overarching "supranational regime of population management" (2005, 243). Specifically, while European states during the colonial era sought to bring non-Western populations into the modern system of states through imperial discipline and direct domination, the decolonization process has subjected newly independent states to a regulatory regime of market interactions (i.e., international trade in goods and services) supervised by powerful Western states and supranational agencies (247). Postcolonial states have to demonstrate their fitness within the international system by participating in various international arrangements, embracing the market mechanism, and subjecting themselves to regulation by international financial agencies (250). Hindess thus argues that liberalism is crafted through a "positive project of government" that uses "market interactions to civilize and to regulate the conduct both of states themselves and of those within the particular populations under their authority" (251). This supranational governmental project orients postcolonial states toward a modern liberal world order, while their own populations are molded into the European institution of citizenship (247, 256).

Hindess's observation helps draw out an important inference that the liberal script of citizenship is disseminated in non-Western states in an *aspiring* convergence toward the white/Western liberal world order (although such convergence is "patchy and incomplete," as Ferguson reminds us). In the

words of Ien Ang, this "white/Western hegemony is . . . the systemic conse-
quence of a global historical development over the last 500 years—the expansion of European capitalist modernity throughout the world, resulting in the
subsumption of all 'other' peoples to its economic, political and ideological
logic and mode of operation. . . . In other words, whether we like it or not,
the contemporary world system is a *product* of white/Western hegemony, and
we are all, in our differential subjectivities and positionings, implicated in it"
(1995, 65; emphasis in original). The historical and structural entrenchment
of the contemporary world system—and its embodied global citizenship—
in the modern liberal world order suggests the inevitable collusion of overwhelming numbers of global citizen-subjects in reproducing white/Western
hegemony as they go about their daily routines and enact the liberal democratic script in everyday life. As human subjects born into capitalist modernity, we continuously perform the white/Western liberal citizenship script
to survive.

To be sure, such global dissemination of liberal citizenship never proceeds
through a uniform process. It takes on contingent and differential configurations. Inderpal Grewal has examined how the power of the United States
enables the dissemination of the ideal of "America" beyond its sovereign borders and diffuses the promise of democratic citizenship through consumer
practices. As she notes, however, this transnational dispersion of "becoming
American" is never "fully formed or stable," but "changeable, contingent,
and historical" (Grewal 2005, 8), creating and enabling "new American subjects in diverse sites" (7). Similarly, the globalized cultural script of liberal
citizenship molds different types of liberal citizen-subjects in varied sites;
this durable and elastic texture suggests the seeming invincibility of the
script in capturing a standardized and yet adjustable version of transnational
capitalist democratic life, which is, again, buttressed by the "historically and
systematically imposed structure" of white/Western hegemony (Ang, 66).

In a sense, one may say that there is "no outside" to the aspirations, forces,
and effects of this liberal citizenship lifecycle and, albeit to varying degrees
and in different ways, we may be inescapably complicit in its reproduction.
Such aspirations, forces, and effects can be felt even in places that are marginalized and disconnected from the global economy, as shown in Ferguson's
discussion of African "yearnings for cultural convergence" with "development" and "modernity." From a gendered perspective, Evelyn Nakano Glenn
has also examined the "yearnings for lightness" among African and African
diasporic women, specifically their growing consumption of skin-lightening

products manufactured and marketed by transnational pharmaceutical and cosmetic corporations (2008, 284–86). My point about this "no outside" is that, because local cultures in different regions and places also need to jostle with neoliberal imperatives and effects, it is more and more unlikely for human subjects to remain untouched by this malleable script. For subjects to demand social justice, they may need to appropriate the script rather than seek spaces outside it to make change happen.

As Ferguson argues, it is doubtful that we can "run history backward" to a time *before* neoliberalism (2009, 169), but we can work to engender different "uses of neoliberalism," appropriating neoliberal moves for progressive ends (174). In fact, while Ferguson attempts to detach purity from contamination in his creative redirection of progressive politics, his own discussion of how advocates for the Basic Income Grant (BIG) in South Africa (i.e., a modest monthly payment to all citizens as a direct assistance to the poor) employ neoliberal rationales—such as combating dependency, building up human capital, increasing productivity, and encouraging entrepreneurship—to justify the program (Ferguson 2009) actually shows their inevitable immersion in contamination, rather than their flight from it, in serving the ends of justice. Appropriating neoliberal programs for the ends of progressive politics does not immunize such politics from recapitulating neoliberal logics or activating a neoliberal course of events, but we may, as Ferguson suggests, reorient this neoliberal direction in engendering more progressive kinds of effects.

Ultimately, understanding human subjects as always operating inside the moving continuum of the liberal script need not be seen as succumbing to a fatalistic or nihilistic logic. Rather, it actually opens up a horizon for us to see this painful and shadowy contamination as the perpetual tunnel we need to go through to continuously rediscover the purity of social transformation. Since any cultural resistance and political contestation will be filtered, inflected, and circumscribed by the script, the transformative process is likely to be nonlinear and complex. Ingenious citizenship, however, might just show us that the more inventive we are in disrupting and appropriating the script, the more transformative the effects will be.

Appropriating Liberal Citizenship:
Oppositional, Negotiated, Interstitial,
and Subcultural Resistance

Indeed, to the extent that liberal citizenship embodies a hegemonic cultural script, it has been unable to bring closure to subversion and contestation. By virtue of the fact that it brings a life of normality into existence, the script requires a domain of abjection to allow normative citizens to emerge. The abject, being externalized by the script of proper citizenship while also being wretchedly attached to it, nonetheless perpetually intercept and appropriate the script in creating and expanding their own liminal spaces of survival and belonging in elastic and durable fashion. The potentiality of change is thus also already immanent to the formation of the script, as it contains hidden fissures and gaps in its embellished design that it is unable to delete. The citizenship script, being so multidimensional, has pluralized the layers of dissident practices and discourses improvised by the abject in those interstitial spaces that are not captured by the investigative frame of democratic agency. These subtle acts, signaling ingenious agency of the abject, who must act to survive in the marginal interstices of liberal social life, persistently appropriate the given citizenship script via an ambiguous and dissonant dynamic. I argue that this appropriation of the cultural script of liberal citizenship takes on a four-pronged frame, erupting in ways that are mutually oppositional, negotiated, interstitial, and subcultural.

Below, I provide an explication of these concepts and illustrate their agentic manifestation in quotidian social life. For illustration, I invoke *In Service and Servitude*, Christine Chin's ethnography about foreign domestic workers in Malaysia (Chin 1998). Chin describes conditions for such workers in the context of the Malaysian "modernity project" driven by neoliberalism. The Malaysian New Economic Policy was implemented during the years of 1971 and 1990 to achieve two objectives: (1) to eradicate poverty through export-oriented development; and (2) to "redress . . . interethnic inequalities [between Malays and non-Malays] held over from British colonial rule" by instituting "a quota system for Malays in most areas of social life, e.g., education, employment, and banking/finance" (Chin, 2).

With both the New Economic Policy and the National Development Policy of 1991–2000 (which furthers the free movement of transnational capital), Chin argues, the Malaysian state elites devised strategies to mobilize the middle classes in support of the shift toward modernity, placing an emphasis on "what Pierre Bourdieu called the 'pursuit of distinction,' in which the consumption of goods and services are seen as a key way to construct identities and lifestyles that distinguish them from the lower or working classes" (12). Such strategies involved an idealized "modern Malaysian middle-class family in which men . . . remain the main wage-earners while women assume the responsibility for performing housework or supervising servants" (13). What encompasses this modernity project is a nationalized pursuit of the "good life," wherein "utility becomes the principal legitimating moral criterion . . . revolv[ing] around an emphasis on more efficient ways to generate, accumulate, and utilize material wealth" (10).

In this state-led economic restructuring, middle-class consumption of goods and services—including foreign domestic workers' labor—comes to stand in for "symbols of personal and national progress" (Chin, 15). It has resulted in "a transnational 'trade in maids,' in which migrant women are 'exported and imported,' and bought and sold, like consumer goods" (15). In this shared vision of modernity, "the mistreatment and abuse of Filipina and Indonesian domestic workers are rationalized as valid and moral because the women are not considered and treated as human beings" (16). As a result, abject conditions become rampant, routine, and legitimized:

> Benefits accrued to the state and the middle classes . . . [are] perceived to far outweigh the negative aspects of employer-servant relations. In a multiethnic context, the official policy of restricting foreign female domestic workers' movement in public space is justified to ensure social order. Domestic employment agencies and employers are complicit . . . in denying domestic workers rest days to prevent them from being exposed to criminal elements beyond the home. Employers who provide foreign domestic workers with board and lodging in addition to wages expect and insist that servants earn their keep by working longer hours, and sleeping and eating less. (16)

Employers and society at large remain largely silent regarding this condition of servitude. Chin writes, "The interests of the state elite and the Malaysian middle classes have converged in a way that perpetuates the silence, since the plights of many domestic workers are deemed inconsequential to the modernity project" (16). In Malaysia, migrant domestic labor "has become an integral component in the state elite's strategy of garnering consent for export-oriented development" (16).

It is within this historical and political economic context that I shift attention to a flashing instance of ingenious agency staged by a foreign domestic worker in a Malaysian household. Chin describes myriad acts improvised by domestic workers "that challenge or renegotiate employer-employee relations" (128). These resistant acts can best be understood in the context of the workers' dehumanized status as controllable and consumable objects. For instance, many workers' "free" time was severely restricted, as "some women were given one day off a month while others had two rest days or even none at all" (24).

In one incident that Chin chronicles, Lita, a Filipina servant who considered "the embassy ineffective in resolving employer-employee disputes," used her bodily fluids to contaminate her employer's property to change her employer's abusive behavior (Chin, 159–60). One day, having been driven to exhaustion by her employer, Lita deliberately chose not to wear sanitary pads during her menstrual cycle and left trails of blood all over the house. While demanding that Lita clean up her blood, the employer nonetheless also instructed her to stop her work and go back to her room and rest. The employer stated to Chin, "Aiyah! No more blood on my floor and bedroom please. So dirty. Better let her rest, take it easy" (160). Perceiving this as uncivilized and backward behavior from the worker, the employer protested (in a racist fashion), "Bun Mui [literally, Filipina mui-tsai, or girl slave] are as dumb as the Indonesian ones" (160). However, Chin saw Lita smiling at her "as if to congratulate . . . [her] for having solved her puzzle," and observed that the employer had failed to decipher that Lita had "successfully redefined the conditions" in which she worked (160).

How does one make sense of such an act—a tactic that compels the employer to change exploitative behavior but also demeans the worker? This act is not derived from the heroic democratic agency so celebrated in mainstream political thought. In fact, given the Malaysian state's prohibition of "all categories of migrant or 'guest' workers from participating in organized labor," foreign domestic workers "cannot act in ways that we have come to expect of workers who express their grievances via formal political channels . . . by participating in collective action such as strikes" (Chin, 128).

At the same time, Lita's act was certainly risky, as there was no way to know that the employer would react as she did rather than summarily dismiss her. But what should be teased out here is that, despite the challenges and obstacles, Lita's act of creative and yet self-demeaning resistance momentarily interrupted a dehumanizing state of exploitation and circuitously claimed for her a certain measure of material and symbolic benefits (i.e., rest, a break, dignity) in the workplace.

In Malaysia's modernity project, the domain of abjection in domestic labor does not simply describe a foreign population excluded from Malaysian citizenship; rather, migrant domestic workers play a crucial part in enhancing and solidifying the normative citizenry in the state's neoliberal transition. Abjection and normality are thus mutually constitutive, for "the state elite and the middle classes' pursuit of . . . national and personal progress" (Chin, 166), as normality (i.e., "middle class-hood"), is in part defined and produced through the employment of the abject (i.e., foreign domestic workers) as its constitutive outside. The middle classes' consumption of "abject" Filipina and Indonesian domestic labor becomes a key way to constitute themselves as the norm, as citizens and subjects. For migrant domestic workers such as Lita, their contestation of the liberal citizenship script that produces their (immanent) abject existence does not crystallize into a direct defiance. Instead, it manifests itself in the subtle and roundabout disruption exemplified by the four-pronged frame.

Theresa Martinez has articulated the processing of what she calls "oppositional culture" by subordinate groups that draws on nonmainstream cultural resources to resist systematic subjugation and oppression (Martinez 1997). As Martinez asserts, being oppositional does not necessarily equate to direct confrontation; it can embody a much wider and more complex spectrum of resistance. She writes, "The development of counterstances, or resistant stances to domination, is never a simple, straightforward process for subordinated groups. The relationship between dominant and subordinate groups encourages, enforces, fosters and even coerces a full continuum of moves, countermoves, negotiations, protests, submissions, struggles, neutralities, alliances, accommodations, and resistances. In sum, complex and contradictory relations emerge which result in a web of interactions which make 'resistance' itself a contested arena of discourse" (269).

This conception can be used to understand the quotidian acts of abject subjects as oppositional staging in inventive and protean ways. For instance, Lita's deliberate act of not wearing sanitary pads during her menstrual cycle and leaving trails of blood in her employer's house constitutes a subtle (rather than openly confrontational) countermove that refuses abusive and exploitative treatment. Instead of directly communicating her grievances to her employers or claiming justice through formal institutional channels, Lita feigned "stupidity" or "backwardness" and used that charge covertly to improve her labor conditions. This act is oppositional to Malaysia's liberal citizenship script, which suspends the "political life" of foreign workers, by enabling Lita to exercise her "right" to be political, albeit in a nonstraight-forward fashion. In sum, oppositional appropriations of the liberal citizenship script sidestep the binary frame of accommodation versus resistance and manifest "endless ambiguities" in configuring the ingenious agency of the abject (Lears 1985, 593).

Borrowing from Stuart Hall, such oppositional positioning is "negotiated"—that is, it is neither hegemonic in following the dominant order of citizenship nor emancipatory in directly rejecting the script, but modifies and readjusts the script to fit one's specific circumstances (Hall 1980). Lita's act exemplifies this quality, as she neither directly refuses the liberal citizenship order that impairs her biological-political being nor quietly accepts her victimization, but instead amends given relations determined by the script to negotiate for a limited measure of dignity.

In addition, negotiation necessarily implies a transaction, and as such, ingenious agency never coheres into a pure and sacred form of struggle and resistance. It is always already dipped in complicity and contamination, given its subtle bargaining with liberal hegemony. While "complicity" describes the ways in which a political agent's acts of resistance both reproduce and benefit from the existing structure of liberal economy (Moallem 2006), "contamination" suggests that the acts of disruption in question are not claimed outside the existing structure of hierarchy and inequality but are produced *inside* it and thus polluted and circumscribed by it (Cheah 2006). Complicity and contamination help define the mode of negotiation, and they characterize essentially all forms of subordinate resistance within liberal citizenship. As Jacques Derrida argues, there is always something "dirty" about negotiation because "something is being trafficked" (2002, 13). Yet if one does not negotiate, Derrida continues, "the thing will be even more impure" (14). It is precisely this impure negotiation "in the name of purity" (14) that enables agentic change and movement by abject subjects trapped in liminal intervals.

In Lita's instance, her act momentarily fissures the liberal script of citizenship without fully exploding it. Her resistance stops short of a total negation of the system because of her need to still make a living through the instrumental transaction of her bodily labor. Her act disrupts liberal normativity while recuperating it in the same instant, marking its complicity and contamination in the existing power structure. For Lita, these limits speak to her embodied location as a migrant domestic worker, whose abject livelihood (and possibly that of her family) depends on those in relatively privileged and normative positions in the liberal world order. Because her being as a human subject is both abjectified and sustained by liberal citizenship, she may only negotiate with this given economy—thus trafficking in its cyclical reproduction of hierarchy and inequality—to ameliorate her abjection, rather than completely negating the chain of survival of which she is a part. In Derrida's language, Lita's negotiation can be understood as "impurity in the name of purity"—seeking to purify things by an imperfect and impure means.

Negotiation underscores how abject resistance rarely takes on a pure form of negation or refusal, but almost always renders a transactional quality in its subversive disruption in hegemonic liberal lifecycle (García Canclini 2001, 139; Yúdice 2001, xxxv). As Ang asserts, the contemporary world system as a product of white/Western hegemony "is a historically and systematically imposed structure which cannot yet, if ever, be superseded," and we are differentially implicated in the cyclical reproduction of the modern liberal order (66). She writes, "Complicity, in other words, is a structural inevitability which we can only come to terms with by recognizing it as determining the limits of political possibilities, not as something we can work to undo (by consciousness-raising, for example)" (66; emphasis in original). The given economy of European capitalist modernity means that marginalized peoples "are left with two options: either enter the game or be excluded" (67). Abject subjects such as Lita must first "enter the game"—that is, negotiate—in order to rupture the domineering cycle of the liberal citizenship script. As Ang concludes, "Any resistance to this overwhelming hegemony can therefore only ever take place from a position always-already 'contaminated' by white/ Western practices, and can therefore only hope to carve out spaces of relative autonomy and freedom within the interstices of white/Western hegemony" (67–68; emphasis in original).

All this should not be understood in a pessimistic way; rather, it points to spaces of hope for abject subjects and social activists in using negotiation to expand the possibility of livelihood in liberal citizenship. In fact, considering the overwhelming historical and political force of Malaysia's neoliberal modernity project, in which Lita is situated as a disposable laborer, it is crucial to look at how she seizes the contaminated space of the household as an instrumental channel to ingeniously disrupt the normality of Malaysian citizenship. There is value, even in complicity and contamination, such that Lita can be read as "working with" these limits to improve her status and remold existing relations between normality and abjection. Instead of refuting these limits, in this book I consider what lessons they may actually bear for strategies of activist intervention.

Ang's last comment on resistance as occurring within and through interstices points to the third mode of appropriation of the liberal citizenship script: the quotidian practices improvised by the abject are "interstitial" in the sense that they are not immediately visible or legible within existing institutions or knowledge frames of citizenship. The abject make appeals through neither juridical institutions nor activist politics. Rather, like what James Scott calls "hidden transcripts" (Scott 1990), they maneuver interstitially as contingent and unpredictable ruses, emerging through cracks and loopholes while appropriating and subverting the bourgeois citizenship script like "a guerrilla warfare of the interstices," where "opposition is not only responsive, but creative" (Lavie and Swedenburg 1996, 165). Given their subtle and hidden character, these interstitial acts can also manifest in ways that may be perceived as unlawful and irresponsible. Fitting this description, Lita's act not only erupts unexpectedly; it can also be seen by many as demeaning and debasing.

Note that describing interstitiality as an essential component of ingenious agency is not to take a celebratory tone regarding these acts. It is, rather, to acknowledge—given that the transparent mode of democratic agency is largely inaccessible or ineffective for those subjects who are marginalized and remaindered by liberal citizenship—that abject subjects must often resort to interstitial methods (i.e., to move furtively under the surveilling eye of normative citizenship) to reanimate their agency and acquire livable spaces.

Finally, interstitial, erratic ruses are not merely singular or isolated eruptions. Rather, one may further underline the appropriation of liberal citizenship in the form of what Dick Hebdige has articulated as "subcultural" contestation, in which subjects take existing mundane cultural artifacts—in our case, the citizenship script—and appropriate and reuse them to fashion a new way of being vis-à-vis the bourgeois public order (Hebdige 1979). Conceived through the notion of bricolage, Hebdige defines subcultures as "cultures of conspicuous consumption," involving the uses and reuses of various cultural products and artifacts; through this process, a subcultural style "reveals its 'secret' identity and communicates its forbidden meanings" (103). Borrowing from Hebdige, it is in the notion of reusing and appropriating cultural artifacts (i.e., scripts of citizenship) rather than following the normative convention of what a "citizen" is or ought to be that we may come to theorize abject subjects' ingenious acts as the formation of a subcultural style of citizenship. When

Lita uses her bodily fluids to regain rest and dignity, her appropriation of the script that defines her as abject interrupts the "normalization" of citizenship in Malaysia's modernity discourse, signifying "gestures, movements toward a speech which offends the 'silent majority,' which challenges the principle of unity and cohesion, which contradicts the myth of consensus" (Hebdige, 18).

The descriptive of subculture also underscores dissident stances not as momentary ruptures, but as sustained and permeating practices that are repeated and replicated by a collective body to the extent that a subcultural script of citizenship—an oppositional subhabitus—is subtly inscribed vis-à-vis the dominant liberal construction. Lita's act is only one among the manifold and heterogeneous acts and practices staged by foreign domestic workers in Malaysia (as well as in any other states and localities) that may be read as reuse and appropriation of the liberal script that denies them citizenship rights. This subcultural script of citizenship forms an oppositional subhabitus as it is collectively enacted and improvised—albeit in different forms and manifestations—by domestic workers contesting for inclusion, belonging, and livability in different regions governed by liberal citizenship. And this oppositional subhabitus can be said to acquire the qualities of what Asef Bayat refers to as "social nonmovements," which exert power through "the similar practices that a 'big number' of subjects simultaneously perform" (2010, 21).

To the extent that the oppositional subhabitus mimics the "original" script of citizenship, the spaces of "rights" it appropriates are not officially protected or guaranteed. The subcultural style of citizenship is thus essentially an improvisation of what I have called nonexistent citizenship. Some might dismiss the importance of such informal citizenship, perceiving it as merely a "failed copy," a "faint copy," or "a negative image of someone else's positivity" (Ferguson 2006, 16–17). But it is more appropriate to see the unceasing stream of subcultural appropriations as constituting what Bayat describes as the "quiet encroachment of the ordinary" that engenders change in infinitesimal and polymorphous ways (2010, 56). Such subcultural formations of nonexistent citizenship "keep creeping in, insisting on an ongoing relationship between" the normal and the abject (Ferguson 2006, 17). They constitute "not simply a negative space, a space of absence, . . . [but] a likeness, an inseparable other-who-is-also-oneself to whom one is bound" (17). Most important, by rewriting the normative script to create nonexistent spaces of inclusion, belonging, and citizenship, this oppositional subhabitus signals critical scholars and social activists to *also* invent fluid and unconventional ways to reconfigure the liberal script to collectively reshape and remold existing abjectifying relations in their respective locations and contexts.

In all, the four-pronged frame—oppositional, negotiated, interstitial, and subcultural—crafts and articulates the dynamic qualities of ingenious appropriation of liberal citizenship by abject subjects. It demonstrates a subtle and ambiguous agency that cannot be understood in any linear or binary fashion. This ingenious agency of the abject persistently disrupts the stagnant life-cycle of liberal citizenship while reanimating and extending these subjects' precarious citizenship from the very margins of abjection and creating liminal spaces of inclusion and belonging.

In the next part of the book, "Episodes," I trace a series of enactments of ingenious citizenship improvised by abject subjects. As I argue, if democratic agency is not established a priori as the only (proper) way to enact citizenship, it follows that we actually have more acting citizens than we realize—whether they are formal citizens, aliens, or nationals of other sovereign states and localities (liberal democratic or otherwise), doing the work of revising and rewriting the habitual and yet elastic script of liberal citizenship. It also implies that subtle change and movement are already happening in every instant of the quotidian. What are the possibilities opened up by ingenious citizenship? What are its limits? To what lessons about social transformation may such ingenious improvisations point us, even in their complicity and contamination? I take up these questions in the next four chapters.

Part II

Episodes

2. Migrant Domestic Workers, Hidden Tactics, and Appropriating Political Citizenship

Perpetual Ingenuity and Complicity in Social Change

The Help, a novel by Kathryn Stockett published in 2009 about the life of black maids in the racially segregated, pre–Civil Rights South, became a national sensation in the literary world after selling millions of copies and spending more than one hundred weeks on the *New York Times* bestseller list.[1] In 2011, the runaway bestseller further ventured into the cinematic market and made a splash in Hollywood: the movie version, produced by DreamWorks and distributed by Disney, shot its way to box office success and garnered several Oscar nominations.[2] While both fictional and nonfictional works on black domestics have previously been produced by black writers (see, e.g., Childress 1986; Neeley 1993; Clark-Lewis 1996), The Help is unusual not only in that it was written by a white author, but also because none of the previous works reached the level of national popularity or were adapted to films and warranted such levels of corporate investment and promotion. Anyone familiar with the story knows that the novel and film focus attention on the subject of race and racism through the portrayal of the plight of black maids in the South. Yet I wish to underscore how two underexamined elements of The Help—the depiction of ingenious agency in its content and its popularity as a cultural product in a capitalist economy, a popularity subsequently used as an instrumental conduit for social activism—offer previously unrecognized lessons about improving labor conditions in domestic work.

Set in Jackson, Mississippi, in the early 1960s, *The Help* (Stockett 2009) centers on two black maids and friends, Aibileen and Minny, who work for white Southern families, and a young, white female college graduate named Skeeter who is searching for her lost nanny. Through writing a housekeeping advice column for a local newspaper, Skeeter gradually comes to learn about how racism pervades black domestic workers' lives. She then secretly collaborates with Aibileen and Minny, writing a book about black maids' alienation and marginalization in their own voices. Themes of revenge, punishment, and fear permeate the novel, as the reader learns how black maids must observe the "rules" set in the South and by white women, including using separate black bathrooms only, not dining with the white employer's family, not talking back when scolded, keeping their real selves hidden, and appearing submissive and subservient at all times.

Yet this setting of racial oppression is also portrayed as a breeding ground for a series of subversive acts by the subordinate subjects. For instance, Aibileen feigns illness to get an afternoon break to grieve the anniversary of her son's death. On another occasion, Aibileen helps out Minny, who is fired by her employer, by lying to a housewife who is new in town and urgently needs a maid that her boss has recommended Minny for the job. During the process of collaborating on the book project that uncovers the pervasive mistreatment of black maids in Jackson, Skeeter and Aibileen (and, later, Minny) must conduct clandestine meetings to circumvent the "integration violation" that prohibits the intermingling of white and black people behind closed doors. Then, when the book is published, Skeeter surreptitiously delivers copies of the book to Aibileen's church, pretending they are donated clothes in a box so that their oppositional staging will not be discovered. In what is perhaps the most striking scene, Minny takes a special chocolate pie as a peace offering to Hilly Holbrook, the wealthy and influential white woman who has just fired her and attempted to ruin her reputation by spreading rumors that she is a thief. As Hilly pleasurably consumes slices of the pie, she offers to take Minny back as a maid but with a pay cut. Minny refuses and tells Hilly to "eat . . . my . . . shit," gesturing to Hilly that she has added a "real special" ingredient to the pie: her shit. This last instance of the maid's boldly informing the employer that she has just gobbled up bodily waste achieves a dramatic effect for the reader and audience, but such open disclosure is certainly more fictional than real. Considering the historical background of the Jim Crow

South, where racial brutality and lynching of blacks were not uncommon, a maid could hardly escape such a "treasonous" act unscathed.[3] In fact, in the context of contemporary life, it is also extremely unlikely for a domestic worker to inform the employer of her subversive acts against the employer's abusive and exploitative treatment, for the reprisal from those in power can deal a disastrous blow to the worker's precarious material livelihood.

Still, taken as a whole, the largely hidden acts of resistance staged by the maids in The Help are unique in that they draw connections to what I have articulated as the eruption of ingenious agency by abject subjects. For instance, Minny's act of baking her feces in the pie is especially comparable to the actions of Lita, the Filipina domestic worker in Malaysia, who uses her bodily fluids to contaminate her employer's possessions. Both unconventional acts illustrate the unpredictable and inventive agency of two depoliticized subjects who are not supposed to participate politically to acquire inclusion and dignity in their respective locations: Minny as a quasi-citizen living in racial segregation in the pre–Civil Rights United States, and Lita as a foreign domestic worker without citizenship status to leverage for state protection in modern, liberal Malaysia.

Switching time and space, had Minny, Aibileen, and other black maids in The Help been working as foreign domestic workers in contemporary Malaysia, like Lita, they might very likely have engaged in the multitude of subversive acts chronicled in Christine Chin's critical ethnography. For example, Mira, told by her employer to continue to work and wash the plates faster, even though she has a fever, suddenly feels dizzy and drops the plates, forcing the employer to ask her to rest (Chin 1998, 155). Ruth, in response to her employer's verbal abuse in the kitchen, brings the soup bowls to the table one at a time (rather than all at once) during mealtime to embarrass the employer in front of her friends and guests, thus inducing the employer to speak to her in a nicer and kinder manner (156). And an anonymous domestic servant refuses to put on a Band-Aid after accidentally cutting her finger, leaving bloodstains all over the clothes that she is ironing and leading the employer to ease her demands on the worker (159).

Improvisational acts such as these are thus not unusual or without precursors. Instead, accepted literature resonates with tactical resistance across locations by subordinate classes that do not possess enough power to effect substantive change through formal political institutions. In Weapons of the Weak, a study on the South Asian peasantry, James Scott speaks of acts of "foot dragging, dissimulation, desertion, false compliance, pilfering, feigned ignorance, slander, arson, sabotage" (1985, xvi). Similarly, in *Race Rebels*, an examination of the black working class in the urban South, Robin D. G. Kelley adds theft, absenteeism, cursing, graffiti, slowdowns, leaving work early, quitting, "pan-toting" (household domestics taking home leftovers), and singing in unison in the factory to the dynamic repertoire of black resistance (1994, 17–34). For these subjects, as for domestic workers, ingenious agency enables them to create a contingent and momentary change—if not a shift of power, at least some breathing room—in their immediate confinement. Such change is improvised constantly in the abject spaces of the quotidian, whether as portrayed in Stockett's fictional work or in real life.

In addition to this element of ingenious agency, *The Help* is unique for being an exceptionally successful popular cultural product in a capitalist economy. While one might marvel that a novel and film about black maids would capture the popular imagination and garner so much attention, I would argue that such popularity is due in no small part to the plot's underplaying of racism and depoliticization of structural inequality, which existed both before and well beyond the Civil Rights era. In fact, the Association of Black Women Historians has chastised the work for its distorted presentation of black dialect, stereotypical portrayals of black women reflected in the Mammy figure, lack of attention to the struggles of Civil Rights activism, and trivialized account of the hardship of domestic work devoid of "sexual harassment as well as physical and verbal abuse in the homes of white employers."[4] Not only do the novel and film reflect a relatively "soft and beautiful view of Jim Crow,"[5] they offer its mainstream white audience a glimpse into "historical" racial injury through safe entertainment delivered in a heartwarming tone, selling a comfortingly progressive story of racial justice suitable for contemporary "post-racial" liberal America. The text's setting in the pre–Civil Rights South and its singular focus on blatant and explicit racial segregation and discrimination—which the predominant population of U.S. citizens, from adults to children, already intuitively associate with "evil"—make the black maids all the easier for the reader and audience to identify and sympathize with. As Mary Romero, a pioneering scholar on domestic work, critically notes, the mainstream media coverage of domestic workers "has brought increased attention to the existence of these workers, but not necessarily to their working conditions" (2012, 54). The novel and film would meet a different kind of reception had they touched on the complicated global reality of corporate outsourcing, sweatshops, and pervasive exploitation of manual laborers, including domestic workers.

It is all the more significant, then, that the National Domestic Workers Alliance (NDWA), a major organization in the United States that aims to improve the labor conditions of domestic workers, including nannies, housekeepers, and caregivers for the disabled and the elderly, endorsed the film and used its popularity to publicize the lived conditions of contemporary (predominantly migrant) domestic workers and to enlist support for its policy campaigns addressing domestic workers' rights.[6] The racial justice activist Rinku Sen captures the significance of this move as a strategic intervention to further an unfinished struggle, writing:

> There is a danger embedded in stories of triumph over segregationists, especially a story as prettily presented as this one. Viewers develop little appreciation for the grit of struggle, imagine that the era was less horrifying than it really was, and thus imagine that ending such practices was both more easily achieved and more permanently effective than the struggle's reality. NDWA's intervention around "The Help" created a chance that viewers would walk away inspired to take action on the unfinished justice agenda of the Civil Rights Movement, rather than crowing about how much things have changed for the better.[7]

Romero echoes, "The media efforts of the . . . NDWA appropriate this 'feel good' story about race and inequality in order to reposition domestic workers at the center of the story and to recognize the fullness of their experiences" (2012, 56).

Adding to Sen's and Romero's forceful positioning of the NDWA in the Oscar buzz around The Help, I wish to highlight another key underlying element in the organization's political intervention—that is, the NDWA's complicity in reproducing the instrumental chain of global racial and class inequality. As indicated in chapter 1, while Lita's oppositional improvisation interrupts liberal normativity, it also sustains the given material structure, marking complicity in the same system she contests. The same can be said about Minny and Aibileen in The Help, whose acts of resistance culminate in the publication of their stories of unjust treatment and create ruptures in the cycle of racial repression. Nonetheless, they are not able to transcend the systemic structure of white privilege. And because their employment (whether in domestic work or otherwise) is embedded in the same institutional structure of whiteness, their contestations, like Lita's, are negotiated rather than emancipatory, reproducing the same power structure they disrupt. The NDWA is no exception: by using the wide popularity and high visibility of the film to mobilize its political cause and generate social change in the realm of domestic work, not only is it complicit in helping the film relay a softer and lighter view of racial injustice and violence (acceptable to mainstream America), it further reinscribes the capitalist chain of the global media and entertainment industry, which depends on a variety of low-wage manual labor for its profitable reproduction. After all, Disney, the distributor of the movie, has received no shortage of accusations regarding sweatshop practices and worker abuse in Third World countries.[8] What we find here, then, is a parallel between the domestic workers' ingenious acts and the NDWA's democratic activism in being complicit with the given liberal economy, and its embodied hierarchy and inequality, to create disruption and change.

I make this observation not to negate the political objective and efforts of the NDWA but, rather, to accentuate that such complicity in the instrumental structure of the liberal economy actually constitutes an inevitable and yet creative conduit for generating a complex process of social transformation, whether for individual abject subjects or for the activist organizations that act on their behalf. What The Help offers, then, both in its content and its crystallization into a cultural phenomenon that later was deployed as a launch pad for addressing social struggle in domestic work, is not so much its animated lesson about the country's "past" racism (a lesson that might be considered largely redundant given present history curricula in public and private schools), but rather an indirect lesson on the ineradicable layers of ingenuity and complicity that are always present in the vicissitudes of social change.

My intent in analyzing The Help is not to use it to illustrate life for domestic workers per se. And although I begin my discussion with a mainstream Hollywood film, I do not consider films and ethnographies equivalent. Rather, given this book's critical reinterpretation of social change, my goal here— unlike that in an ethnography—is to extrapolate unexamined political insights from popular media to foreground the theoretical lessons in this chapter in a simple and revealing way. This reading strategy is similar to The Queer Art of Failure, in which Judith Halberstam uses the method of "low theory" to extrapolate insights and lessons of radical utopia from animated children's films (Halberstam 2011). But, as illustrated above, my objective of critical contextualization does not stop at analyzing popular culture but advances to demonstrate how these cinematic insights are both *substantiated* and *complicated* in the actual contexts of everyday worker resistance and movement struggles. For instance, as I have noted, Minny's ingenious act in the film resembles that of Lita and many other domestic workers in Malaysia, although her confrontational revelation of the act to her employer is unrealistic when situated in the historical and material contexts of domestic labor. Similarly, the very fact that the NDWA uses the popularity of the film to enlist public support for domestic workers' cause further demonstrates a "dark" pragmatic element of complicity with global capitalism in the real-life struggles of migrant laborers that contradicts the romantic script and harmonious closure of the film.

But for all The Help's faults and insufficiencies as a cinematic representation of domestic labor, the ingenious agency it depicts, along with the story's popularity, nonetheless pinpoint a "nondemocratic" lesson on the perpetual presence of ingenuity and complicity in the generation of social change. This lesson has largely been made invisible in Western political thought, and even more critical strands of philosophical rumination on undocumented migrants and refugees have not been immune to this oversight. As I argue, this limitation can be centrally traced to the ways in which existing political theory continually appeals to and recapitulates a linear ideal of democratic agency rooted in the founding Western political script. As I have noted, any script of citizenship always produces mutually constitutive "normal" (proper) citizens and "abject" subjects. By conceiving proper citizens as those who embody democratic agency and participate publicly in a political community, these political philosophical works—even when acting in sympathy or in concert with undocumented migrants and refugees—unwittingly reproduce as abject nonstatus subjects who are unable or unwilling to act in this democratic manner. A doubling abjection is thus at work: the undocumented migrants and refugees are abjected not only in their lived material conditions but also in their presumed lack of the (normal) political agency that defines democratic citizens in the political script. Such doubled abjection preempts any consideration of the lived horizon of the abject as embodying potential social change, given their remote distance from the standard ideal of democratic citizenship.

One prominent example in this regard is the work of the critical philosopher Giorgio Agamben, whose enigmatic treatise on the intersection of sovereign power, juridical power, and biopower in Homo Sacer has emerged as a seminal text that crucially informs the dehumanized condition of irregular migrants (Agamben 1998). In gesturing to the condition of the modern concentration camp as a paradigmatic case of what he calls "bare life"— human subjects reduced to a naked depoliticized state without official status or juridical rights—Agamben identifies a similar form of totalitarian power operating in the juridical realm of contemporary liberal democracies. Critical migration scholars have taken up and extended Agamben's formulation to address the plight of global refugees and unauthorized migrants, who live in an indefinite and suspended state of noncitizenship, as a form of bare life (Rajaram and Grundy-Warr 2004; Salter 2008). The move in paralleling *Homo Sacer*'s characterization of the juridico-political space of "camp" with the geopolitical condition of undocumented migration corresponds with Agamben's call to examine the ways in which a massive number of human subjects in our age have all "appear[ed] virtually as *homines sacri*" (Agamben 1998, 111).

Agamben's transhistorical call notwithstanding, to what extent is the space of "camp" an adequate depiction of the social condition of undocumented migrants? Consider the workspace of households in which female migrants labor as domestic workers: these spaces relate to the camp, since labor laws and regulations are indefinitely suspended, and undocumented workers are seemingly reduced to a state of exploited bare life. However, the conception of the camp lacks a dynamic account of power relations to address the ingenious agency of migrant subjects as they negotiate their daily workspace and the subtle configuration of social change this agency generates. Significantly, what begins for Agamben as a space of interstitiality posited in camp—a zone between life and death, inside and outside—ultimately slides into an immobile binary between the political beings of citizens and the excluded bodies of bare life. Yet if the space of camp is interstitial in nature, what preempts the possibility of the abject manifesting an agency that is also cunning and clandestine in character? What if differently situated contexts— especially in spaces such as camp-like working households—actually call for a different gauge of agency and change that do not go by the linear constitution of democratic subjectivity?

Reflecting on the myriad creative acts staged by the fictional characters of Aibileen and Minny, as well as by real-life foreign domestic workers in Malaysia, reveals the ways in which these quasi-citizens and undocumented subjects, though without formal status and rights, leverage their "inclusive" status in working households to bargain and exchange for informal measures of dignity and belonging. Instead of reflecting Agamben's binary formulation of pure bare life and full citizenship, they cleverly and skillfully negotiate and mediate these two extreme ends of the political and nonpolitical in carving out their own spaces of survival and appropriating political life from the very margins of abjection. They can be understood as improvising interstitial spaces of what I call nonexistent citizenship that neither fall into the desperate void of bare life nor neatly align with the universal trajectory of democratic citizenship.

This oversight, I argue, can be traced to the inheritance and reinscription of the cultural script of political agency in Agamben's work. Specifically, by following the lineage of Western political thought from Aristotle to Hannah Arendt that demarcates spheres of *bios* (political life) and *zoē* (natural life), Agamben has not interrogated the scripted and ritualistic contents of *bios* that already predefine who counts as acting citizens by way of *how they participate* in political life. In its conception, the *bios* formulates the proper way to enact and perform political life along the same paths by which I have characterized democratic agency—public, visible, audible, legible, and collective—since citizens "make politics" by engaging in deliberation about common affairs.[9] This induces exclusion, not merely of juridico-political status (i.e., *who* are the citizens of a democracy?), but also of the cultural script of citizenship itself (i.e., *how* should subjects participate to be citizens in a democracy?). Analytically, Agamben's distinction between "an endowed citizenship life" and "a naked life without citizenship" in liberal democracies stays at the level of juridico-political status without touching on the cultural content of democratic citizenship. Devoid of a deeper structural critique regarding how the cultural script of the liberal *bios* has ushered in a standardized political life-cycle that assumes a priori the proper parameters of citizenship and precludes "other" subtle and nondemocratic ways to enter such political life, Agamben's recapitulation of democratic citizenship already delimits bare life (representatives of which may act politically via clever and clandestine means precisely because of their nonstatus) to the apolitical realm of noncitizenship. As such, his conception of bare life actually reinforces the gap between the normal and the abject in the political script by trapping undocumented migrants or refugees in their wretchedly apolitical (or insufficiently political) condition, which in turn accentuates the (privileged) constitution of the normal—that is, the citizenly, the democratic, and the properly political.

To be sure, this is neither to deny the existing sociopolitical disparity between normative citizens and unauthorized migrants and refugees nor to celebrate the unauthorized migrants' and refugees' creative resistance as liberatory. Rather, what is critical to note here is the absence of the lessons of ingenious agency in Agamben's interpretation of irregular migrants and bare life. Specifically, while Agamben keenly underscores the looming presence of the massive structure of dehumanization, his formulation of the totally victimized state of bare life makes invisible the ingenious agency of abject subjects and the subtle traces of social change such agency engenders.

To push this observation further, the uninterrogated script of *bios* is so pervasive in critical political theorizing that even critics of Agamben, who point to spaces of political resistance by marginalized subjects in suspended zones of exception, have merely reversed the order of political life and bare life while maintaining this very binary distinction. In particular, these critics have problematized Agamben's thesis and its connection to unauthorized migration by pointing to refugee anti-deportation campaigns and migrant worker protests as counterexamples of "noncitizen citizenship" that defy the image he presents of camp as bodies of victims. Yet while chronicling such resistant acts constitutes an urgent political intervention that counters the state of abjection, this line of critique, painting citizenship as consisting solely of visible political acts, actually reinscribes the same qualities of the political spelled out in the script of *bios*—resulting in a linear conception of migrant subjectivity that limits the purview of social change to the one-dimensional path of democratic agency. To link this once again to the indirect lesson of *The Help*: this linear conception makes invisible the surprising ingenuity and inevitable complicity present in any critical staging of social change.

From Agamben to his critics, what has been lost in the archive of bare life is thus how undocumented subjects, remaindered by the liberal script of *bios*, can nonetheless be read as appropriating this script in their own ways, seeking to shed their abjection and reinsert themselves (even if liminally) into political life. In this chapter, I investigate how migrant domestic workers without formal status and access to "proper" democratic participation can be seen as deploying *hidden tactics* vis-à-vis their employers to appropriate the political script of liberal citizenship. For this reason, they are not representatives of the depoliticized bare life that has often been assumed in political thought but, rather, full of ingenious political life in their own clever and inventive ways.

My conception of hidden tactics borrows from Michel de Certeau's distinction between strategy and tactics: while strategy refers to the discipline of the dominant political-social-economic rationality, an institutional entity of will and power, tactic refers to the art of the weak, which finds cracks and holes in the surveillance of dominant power and subverts it (de Certeau 1984, 34–39). Through the concept of tactics, de Certeau traces the ways in which subordinate subjects lacking the means and resources to put up a direct challenge to the dominant social order resort to hidden, subtle, and devious practices to detour around the surveillance apparatuses in obtaining their desired ends. Tactics take advantage of opportunities and make use of circumstances and occasions, operating "in isolated actions, blow by blow" (37). Similarly, as I argue, the hidden tactics mounted by migrant domestic workers in households demonstrate their ingenious appropriation of the political in the everyday.

Certainly, this improvisation of ingenious citizenship is not a "voluntary" act freed from structural constraints. Neither is it detached from the neoliberal technologies of power that utilize and subjugate the bodies of migrant workers. As Pheng Cheah cautions, any emergence of humanity or opening of freedom is inescapably inscribed within an already contaminated instrumental force field of human relations undergirded by "the very nature of economic development within the structure of capitalist accumulation" (2006, 259). In fact, as Rhacel Salazar Parreñas indicates in her ethnographic work, some migrant Filipina domestic workers also hire domestic workers in their home country and pay them a much lower wage than what they themselves earn abroad, thus "maintain[ing] unequal relations with less-privileged women in the Philippines" (2001, 77). However resistant their tactics, migrant domestic workers may still be entangled in complicit relations of normality and abjection to other female low-wage workers, in a systemic material cycle from which there is little escape.

Yet within limited terrain, migrant domestic workers' tactical appropriation of *bios* does signal ambiguous and nonlinear social change in the unseen spaces of liberal citizenship. It is precisely through its complicity and contamination in the liberal economy that ingenious citizenship opens up an interstitial space between political life and bare life that conceals a greater repertoire of agency than both Agamben and his critics realize—an agency that is not unidirectional but roundabout and circuitous. Ultimately, the underlying limits migrant domestic workers must participate in, complicit with the given economy, to improvise informal spaces of equity and dignity also provide further lessons for immigrant and labor rights activists. They suggest that domestic workers' movements must also work within given contextual limits—embedding themselves in webs of complicity and contamination rather than seeking to transcend them—to create ever more fluid room for appropriation among their constituents.

Agamben, Suspended Zones of Exception, and the Script of *Bios*

In *Homo Sacer*, the camp designates a space in which inmates are neither living as political subjects endowed with juridical protections nor declared dead or outside the rule of law (Agamben 1998). Camp dwellers are stripped of political rights and reduced to a biological minimum, a state of "suspended life and suspended death" (Butler 2004a, 67). In Agamben's conception, deprivation of political life accentuates the dehumanized existence of bare life.

As a state of exception, the camp signifies an external space while remaining immanent and attached to the juridico-political order (Isin and Rygiel 2007, 183). In Agamben's words, "The exception does not subtract itself from the rule; rather, the rule, suspending itself, gives rise to the exception and, maintaining itself in relation to the exception, first constitutes itself as a rule" (1998, 18). Inside the camp, the norm and the exception are indistinguishable: the exception is found to be part of the rule, and sovereign power is both legal and outside the law, both "outside and inside the juridical order" (15). In "legally" suspending the validity of the law, sovereignty interjects normalcy and exceptionality, defining its power through interstitiality in constituting the camp, where "exclusion and inclusion, outside and inside, bios and zoē, right and fact, enter into a zone of indistinction" (9).

For Agamben, this interstitial zone signifies a breakdown of "subjective right and juridical protection" (1998, 170). In a space of abjection where laws are completely suspended, anything becomes possible, and the subjects caught within the camp are "so completely deprived of their rights and prerogatives that no act committed against them could appear any longer as a crime" (171). Furthermore, the zone of bare life is not only juxtaposed against the democratic order but is necessary for its continuing function. The normalcy of biopolitical life depends on the fringe elements of bare life to signify itself as the norm. Sovereignty and biopower are inextricable: "Sovereignty is the ability of the sovereign to step outside the law in order to (re)establish the biopolitical regularity or normalcy of life necessary for law itself, the juridical order, to function" (Hannah 2008, 59). Sovereignty perpetuates interstitial zones in maintaining the normalcy of the body politic.

As Agamben argues, rather than being bound to a determinate time and place, the camp has transformed into "the political space of modernity" and become "the *nomos* of the modern" (1998, 166–80; 2000, 39–40). One sees "camps" metamorphosed into all sorts of sites in everyday life, manifest in inner cities, gated communities, airports, and the indefinite detention of "enemy combatants" at Guantánamo Bay (Agamben 1998, 174–75; 2000, 41; Rajaram and Grundy-Warr 2004, 39; Walters 2008, 187). Critical migration scholars have further seized on Agamben's thesis to theorize the materialization of camps at state borders and refugee detention centers (Rajaram and Grundy-Warr 2004; Salter 2008). Two elements in particular in Agamben's concept compellingly inform the social condition of undocumented workers and refugees: the immanence of interstitiality and the depoliticized state of bare life.[10]

First, Agamben's depiction of the interstitial is salient to the situation of refugees and migrant workers, who are neither fully recognized as citizens nor completely excluded as strangers. As William Walters notes, in embodying an "in-between space," the camp constitutes an "ambiguous, grey zone between the inside and the outside, the social condition of being neither fully excluded nor fully recognized" that resonates with conditions for border-crossing refugees and migrants (2008, 187–88). Moreover, the interstitiality of irregular migration is immanent to the liberal biopolitical order. As Prem Kumar Rajaram and Carl Grundy-Warr point out, "The refugee or other irregular migrant, the detritus or remainder, is integral to the sovereign law that encompasses the interiorized humanity" (2004, 35). They write,

> The encounter with an excess . . . is both a threat to the regular order and integral for its continuation. It is a threat to the order because it reminds of [sic] the ruses undertaken to confine human beings to a politicized life within the nation-state. And it is integral to the continuation of the system of the nation-state because its unruliness serves to define the norm. . . . [The sovereign law] maintains a ruse of inside/outside while at the same time creating the ambiguous system of the nation-state that depends on the appropriation of the ostensibly excluded in order to maintain the inside. (36; emphasis in original)

Building on Rajaram and Grundy-Warr, the remainder is integral to sovereign power not only juridically or politically, but also economically: the exception of undocumented labor is immanent and integral to the normalcy of neoliberal economy. Sovereign power simultaneously adopts labor laws to regulate the market while willfully withdrawing itself from subcontracted sweatshops, export processing zones, and the informal economy, which hire undocumented immigrants to sustain and reproduce hypercapitalist order. Migrant workers are not simply excluded: they are deliberately sought after and tolerated by the capitalist regime to play a critical part as disposable, compliant labor of the state operation (thus *inside*), while their membership is deliberately left suspended as "undocumented" workers with no official sanction to participate politically in the state as citizens (thus *outside*). Anne McNevin argues that undocumented immigrants are "immanent outsiders" who are "incorporated into the political community as economic participants but denied the status of insiders" (2006, 141). Undocumented labor is left in an exceptional state of interstitiality, yet constitutes an immanent and productive part of neoliberal economy and biopolitical citizenry.

Second, the depoliticized state of bare life further illustrates the suspended condition of refugees and the undocumented, who lack institutional-political recourse to citizenship. Rajaram and Grundy-Warr point out that the concept of *homo sacer*, in signifying "a life that could be killed with impunity," fits refugees whose a-territorial or extra-territorial form of existence subjugates them to "'inhuman' treatment by aid workers because of their lack of 'access to legal remedies' or . . . indefinite detention" (39). Refugees are trapped in "an abject condition of speechlessness which leaves them with little or no remit to challenge often ill-intentioned depictions (as well as occasional brutality or violence)" (37). Similarly, nonstatus migrant workers constitute a docile labor force marked by the biological minimum and political quietude. Both refugees and undocumented workers thus constitute the "no longer human" on Agamben's spectrum, which distinguishes the depoliticized remainder from the politicized human being (Rajaram and Grundy-Warr, 35). The "no longer human" lives in a "netherworld," a "nondomain," a "space of illegality," and above all, a "space of nonexistence . . . [that] divides the legal and the illegal, the legitimate and the illegitimate, the overt and the clandestine" (Coutin 2003, 172).

Agamben's "camp" thus provides a compelling framework for migration studies that generally result in two conclusions: (1) unauthorized migrants, as subjects who are neither citizens nor strangers, are deliberately left in an exceptional state of irregularity to constitute a productive part of the neoliberal economy; and (2) irregular migrants are reduced to the state of homo sacer, without official status to demand juridical protections of citizenship or human rights. Living on the edges of sovereign *bios*, there is seemingly no political life to be observed in the undocumented.

Yet despite the powerful parallel between the camp and undocumented migration, it is notable that what begins for Agamben (and his migration studies followers) as an open-ended space of interstitiality posited in sovereignty (i.e., camp, border, detention center) in the end slides into an immobile closure when it comes to the undocumented, who are forced to scramble between a rigid binary of political life (legality, rights, citizenship) and bare life (illegality, no rights, nonparticipation). Such bipolar mapping invites questioning, as one wonders whether it accurately accounts for the complex and intricate power relations in refugee and immigrant struggles in various locations.

As I remarked earlier, in dramatizing the distinction between political life and bare life, Agamben does not question whether the classic lineage of Western political thought predefines and prescribes a democratic notion of the "political" as constitutive of citizenship. Yet in existing liberal democracies, the script of *bios* not only largely defines citizens as belonging to singular national status (at birth as *ius sanguinis* or *ius soli*, or through naturalization), it further embodies proper political life through public, visible, audible, legible, and collective civic participation in a political community. Proper political life is identified within predetermined parameters that include voting, lobbying, and campaigning through the representative matrix; serving on a jury; deliberating in a town hall meeting; or assembling peacefully and protesting collectively without causing public disturbance.

If these are the fundamental terms of the script that make an act *count* as proper participation in democratic political life—which requires not only judicial status but also a certain level of political currency, knowledge, education, or material and collective resources if such participation is to be meaningful or effective, not to mention the very willingness to risk publicly politicizing oneself in the face of threats of deportation—then it certainly is difficult to imagine those inhabiting bare life, who likely lack some or all of these implicit prerequisites to engage in liberal representative politics, as anything other than depoliticized vulnerability remote from endowed citizenship. As such, the depoliticized state of bare life (and its abjection) is declared not only because of the nonstatus of undocumented subjects, but also because their clandestine acts of resistance and nondemocratic ways of political participation—perceived as illegible, unlawful, and irresponsible—are already precluded from entering the authoritative realm of "proper citizenship" in the founding script of *bios*.

Thus, while Agamben intends to bring out the abject aspect of bare life as a critique of liberal political life, his reliance on the founding citizenship script to accentuate the binary existence between citizens and aliens only reinforces, rather than destabilizes, existing relations of normality and abjection. While he critically demonstrates how the exception of liberal rule is necessary to the normative functioning of the democratic order, he does not bring the same intricate perspective to bear on political agency—that is, seeing how the script of *bios* produces an abject domain of "deviant" political acts that formulates "a constitutive outside to [the democratic agency of] the subject . . . as its own founding repudiation" (Butler 1993, 3).

In the end, Agamben's analytical vision forestalls a serious inquiry into how mass abject subjects may resort to innumerable avenues outside formal political channels to obtain and appropriate limited measures of political power. While the borderland of unauthorized migration certainly embodies a juridical nonspace that one "cannot celebrate" (Coutin, 172), the Agambian account, which conceives political life as being constituted by a set of formal criteria and ritualistic qualities stipulated in the *bios*, also forecloses the investigative opening of a complex and ambiguous terrain of political life and social change within the juridical space of nonexistence.

Resurrecting the Political (Repeating the Script of *Bios*)

Critics have sought to problematize Agamben's declaration of the death of political life for the abject and its connection to unauthorized migration. Walters notes that one major problem in Agamben's thought concerns his generalization of camp as materializing everywhere, to the exclusion of location or agency (187–88). If the camp captures the *nomos* of the modern, it overrides analysis of alternative sites of escape and resistance, while the abject, whether as inmates, the poor, or migrants, "are rarely agents in their own right" but, instead, are constructed "as passive, almost helpless beings" (188). These critics aim to document episodes in which undocumented subjects refuse the status of bare life and counter the abjection of camp via moments of political insurgency.

Engin Isin and Kim Rygiel propose an alternative conception of "abject spaces," which includes zones, frontiers, and camps in all of their "material, experiential, and diverse forms" (2007, 184). Beyond Agamben's account, which essentializes camp into a space of victimization, abject spaces implicate "spaces of politics" that intertwine abjection and resistance, involving "different strategies to reduce people to abject inexistence, not only creating varying conditions of rightlessness but also making different logics and acts of resistance possible" (185). Here, Isin and Rygiel accentuate the possibility of the enactment of rights by those without rights. They refer to Jacques

Rancière's critique of Agamben for assuming that "the rights *belong* to defi-nite or permanent subjects" (i.e., citizens), with the implication that those without rights cannot act but must be saved by others, as in humanitarian intervention where charity is given to the poor (Rancière 2004, 306–7, emphasis in original; see also Isin and Rygiel, 186). For Rancière, democracy is about "the power of those who have no qualification for exercising power" (2004, 304). McNevin sums up: "Resistance occurs as outsiders attempt to recast their identity as politically legitimate subjects of justice" (138).

Inside Isin and Rygiel's abject spaces, immanent outsiders have enacted themselves as political by exercising rights they do not have, thereby turning bare life into political life (2007, 186). Scholars have described these political stagings widely, as "insurgent citizenship" (Isin 2002), "acts of citizenship" (Isin and Nielsen 2008a), "noncitizen citizenship" (Gordon 2005), "democratic cosmopolitanism" (Honig 2001), and "abject cosmopolitanism" (Nyers 2003). For instance, Isin and Rygiel point to refugees' acts of suturing their mouths in protest against state asylum laws and setting boats on fire to avoid being sent to offshore detention centers (193). They also find acts of resistance in the "sanctuary city" movements across Europe and Canada, where state law is suspended to provide hospitality to aliens, as well as "Don't Ask, Don't Tell" campaigns in the United States that forbid city workers from inquiring into a person's immigration status to ensure universal access to social services (198–99).

In his study of the anti-deportation campaigns by the refugee group Action Committee of Non-Status Algerians (CASS) in Montreal, Peter Nyers further cites political acts such as regular assemblies, weekly information pickets, delegation visits to immigration offices, public demonstrations and marches, and leafleting against deportations at airports (2003, 1083). Through these public and collective demonstrations, undocumented subjects mark themselves as visible and audible and write themselves into a status of recognition. McNevin echoes this view in her study of the *sans-papiers* (people without legal documents) in France, finding insurgent citizenship in acts of "church occupations, hunger strikes, demonstrations and petitions" by asylum seekers (135). In the United States, Jennifer Gordon has looked at how immigrants working in the low-wage tier of the service industry in New York organize into collective legal aid groups, deliberate with legislators, and draft laws to end sweatshops, noting that these noncitizens are demonstrating the true meaning of democratic citizenship (Gordon 2005).

Stripped of its shell of status and linked to political acts, citizenship becomes the keyword in theorizing and activating the agency of political refugees and migrant workers in battling against the abject conditions legitimated by sovereign states. These public acts of citizenship constitute an urgent political intervention that grounds a refusal of the abject "to remain fugitive, underground, and hyper-exploited" (Walters, 194). The division between the politicized human being and the depoliticized remainder is thus not as clear-cut as Agamben assumes, for "politics lies precisely in that moment wherein one becomes a political subject by enacting or claiming 'the rights one does not have' rather than in some already given status with rights" (Isin and Rygiel, 186). Here, critics of Agamben powerfully resurrect moments of the political in bare life.

But this critical turning point also invites further questioning. In reconceiving representatives of bare life as political beings by way of public and collective acts that break through the confines of camp, does this line of inquiry not also recapitulate Agamben's immobile binary between the political life of citizenship and the depoliticized state of bare life? The only difference is that the latter (depoliticized remainder) can now also transform and elevate into the former (politicized humans). Do we assume that the mass of the abject, those who have not enacted themselves as political, fall straight into the abyss of bare life and victimhood? In fact, if sovereign power has placed the undocumented in an "ambiguous, grey zone between the inside and outside, . . . neither fully excluded nor fully recognized" (Walters, 187–88), why is it an automatic assumption that the agency of the undocumented must be ostentatiously political or transparently counterhegemonic?

In gesturing to spaces of democratic politics in suspended zones of exception, critics of Agamben thus unwittingly reaffirm his binary order of *bios* versus homo sacer, which signifies the former as privileged/endowed and the latter as lamented/despaired. In doing so, they further entrench the script of *bios* that predefines how subjects should act or participate in politics in being or becoming citizens—that is, publicly, legibly, collectively, and "respectably." To be clear, such democratic stagings are both necessary and desirable. However, when they are implicitly valorized as the only (proper) way to enact citizenship and political life, they have the deleterious effect of reinforcing a conception of many irregular migrants as representing purely bare life when a great mass of them keep quiet and are not seen publicly claiming their rights. As such, unauthorized migrants are conceived as bearing political agency only in the exceptional moments of their public and collective acts, but not in the quotidian, complex, and subtle ways they navigate the interstitiality of their lives. Thus far, existing critiques of Agamben have yet to extend his analysis of the interstitiality of sovereign power to also probe the corresponding interstitial agency of the abject.[11] What has been absent in this archive of bare life—both in its reification (by Agamben) and its refusal (by critics of Agamben)—is how undocumented subjects remaindered by the script of *bios* can nonetheless be read as appropriating this script in their own cunning and original ways.

Ingenious Citizenship: Hidden Tactics in the Household

Informal and clandestine labor sites, such as households, where undocumented female immigrants work as domestics may be conceived of as Agambian camps—or, better, as Isin and Rygiel's abject spaces, which intertwine abjection and resistance. As Cheah articulates, the labor power of human life is attached to the rational-technological regulation and reproduction of sovereign states' economic apparatuses, with formal citizens organized into a *bios*, "a system of means and ends in which the contribution of each member is reciprocated with benefits and rewards that are not merely monetary" (208). By remaindering foreign domestic workers from the formal social fabric of sovereign states, however, "What we have is a form of governmental regulation without the welfare of the *bios*," as these abjected subjects "are viewed in terms of sheer technical utility: as mere means to the ends of others, without any ends of their own that need to be taken into account in the state's calculations" (208). Here, Cheah makes an important distinction: whereas formal liberal citizens are also embedded in instrumental exchange and subject to utilitarian configuration in capitalism, they are at least accorded certain ends in life (i.e., values, benefits, rights) that are not purely monetary. Foreign domestic workers, by contrast, are divested of consideration of those ends and treated strictly in terms of their laboring-functional utility because of their exclusion from membership in the script of *bios*.

The abjection of migrant domestic workers as a form of Agamben's depoliticized bare life, without ends of their own, can be seen in both laws and work conditions. As Evelyn Nakano Glenn points out, women's household labor historically has been relegated to the "private" arena, defined by dependence and lack of freedom, away from the "public" realm of citizenship and rights. In capitalist cultures where "earning" is considered an obligation of citizens and where social rights (e.g., unemployment insurance, health provisions, retirement pensions) are distributed accordingly, "unpaid family caregivers were seen as carrying out strictly private responsibilities and not as fulfilling broader citizenship responsibilities" (2007, 49).

This logic has been extended to paid domestic service, where domestic workers were historically "denied recognition as real workers" and "explicitly excluded from legislation that granted entitlements and protections to other types of workers" (Glenn 2007, 55). For example, within the United States, while the provisions of minimum wages and overtime pay stipulated in the Fair Labor Standards Act have now been applied to domestic service, exceptions remain (e.g., live-in domestics are not covered by overtime law), and they do not cover all types of domestic work (e.g., "babysitters" and "companions" for the sick and elderly). Domestics also continue to be subject to various exclusions from "public" citizenship, from the right to unionize under the National Labor Relations Act and the right to labor in safe and healthful working conditions under the Occupational Safety and Health Act to the right against employment discrimination based on race, color, religion, sex, national origin, disability, and age under Title VII of the Civil Rights Act of 1964.[12] As paid domestic service is now disproportionately performed by female migrants who lack citizenship status, their abjection is made more acute as the provisions of existing workers' compensation laws have continued to leave suspended the uncertainty of coverage for undocumented workers (Gonzales 2008). As Glenn argues, migrant care workers from the global South laboring in their destination countries are predominantly "denied rights and protections" (2007, 56).

Domestic work thus operates in an "exceptional" underground economy in the absence of explicit and determinate labor laws and regulations (Romero 1992, 120). To cite Agamben's phrase, "anything becomes possible" in these personalized hierarchical relations, because employers have great leeway in determining work conditions "by setting wages, establishing job descriptions, and determining the work structure," and workers are at the mercy of employers to either accept the job or to quit (Romero 1992, 120). In both laws and work conditions, undocumented domestic workers are thus excluded from the script of bios, since they lack the official status required to gain formal recognition and rights. As Cheah argues, the dehumanization of migrant domestic labor has its basis in the structural conditions of postindustrial capitalist biopower, which, in urging the joining of middle-class educated women into the hyperdevelopmental production apparatus of the professional and service industries, must transfer the burden of labor elsewhere by importing female migrant workers whose bodies can be temporarily used "as tools or means in the employer's quest for economic advancement and the larger project of national development" (204). Simultaneously, foreign workers are "barred from becoming part of the permanent population" because they do not carry any extra value to the host states beyond their extractable and disposable "low-skill" labor (202).

For these subjects, who cannot even participate in the civic institutions of the state regime, radical collective acts in countering their subordinate condition—or simply requesting employers to observe the terms of existing contracts or reporting abuse—often invite further threats of deportation, blacklisting by employment agencies, and suspension of economic livelihood (Chin 1998, 128; Cheah 2006, 221–22; Constable 2007, 119). How, then, do we conceive the apparently "apolitical" subordinates who are bound by bare necessity and unable to enter the public script of *bios* as enacting citizenship in the "private" sphere of home?

As I would argue, the remaindering of migrant workers from the *bios* should not be seen as pure exclusion in a strict sense. Sovereign states do not simply exclude undocumented subjects; rather, they actively *include* them as an immanent part of their biopolitical order—as disposable and exploitable labor—to foster and optimize their own sovereign production of liberal citizenship. This echoes Agamben's view that bare life is not simply remaindered from the democratic juridical order but necessary for its continuing production of normalcy. Importantly, this abject "inclusion" of migrant workers that formal citizens depend on in their day-to-day life provides the instrumental basis for workers to tactically bargain. By virtue of being a constitutive outside to the normative population that includes them as laborers, the abject domain of migrant domestic workers already crystallizes as an immanent disruption within the political script of liberal citizenship that episodically and yet continually destabilizes the abjectifying labor relations.

The contaminated space of working households that monitor, police, and discipline migrant workers' bodies has thus become an instrumental channel and contested site seized by domestic workers to leverage their inclusion and humanity. While foreign domestic workers may be viewed as sheer utility (i.e., means) in the eyes of sovereign states or domestic employers, they have nonetheless used their bodily utility to acquire liminal spaces of political citizenship (i.e., ends). Operating in modes that constitute neither open collective participation nor silent inaction, migrant domestic workers stage hidden tactics that lurk beneath a façade of loyalty, civility, and law-abiding behavior and refrain from turbulent open confrontation in the usual routines of domestic work.

Migrant domestic workers have improvised such hidden tactics in different ways. In fact, the traveling liberal script operates via competing scripts in different local and regional contexts, rendering complex forms of work conditions and abject circumstances both *across* and *within* varied sites. Thus, one should not assume that such hidden tactics are wielded with universal and equivalent effects across local social and political conditions: "Local forms of xenophobia, occupational and gender stereotypes, attitudes about ethnic, racial, and cultural differences, as well as local laws and government policies, all contribute to the difficulties faced by foreign domestic workers in their day-to-day lives" (Constable 2007, xix).

Parreñas has further pointed to the issue of the "care chain" or the "international division of reproductive labor," wherein "a privileged woman pays a migrant woman to perform her housework, and she in turn passes on her own household work to a woman left behind in her country of origin." (2012, 269). Since "the economic value of care work diminishes as it gets passed along" (269), such trans-local inequalities between the migrant domestic worker abroad and the local domestic worker who works for the former complicate the performative and material connotations of creative resistance for both subjects in their linked contexts. As Monisha Das Gupta similarly indicates, migrant domestic workers from a seemingly ethnically homogeneous group (such as South Asians) may "come from a range of socioeconomic backgrounds," with some holding "higher education or professional degrees and white-collar jobs in their home countries" or coming from "reasonably well-off families," while others are "poor rural women whose poverty had forced them to work since childhood and had kept them out of school" (2006, 216). And while most scholarly analyses on domestic work have focused on heterosexual women, one may further consider the circumstances occupied by men (Parreñas 2012) or queer subjects (Manalansan 2006).

Local conditions are also constantly changing rather than static. In the preface to the second edition of *Maid to Order in Hong Kong*, Nicole Constable notes that the single most important change since she first conducted research in the area in the mid-1990s is the dramatic increase of Indonesian domestic workers, which is catching up with the population of predominantly Filipina domestic workers (2007, vii). This is partly linked to "the imagination of employers" (x) who view Indonesian domestics "as 'cheaper and more docile' than Filipinas" (211). The social and cultural differences between Filipinas and Indonesians affect their discrepant work conditions and treatment: "Whereas most Filipinas are Roman Catholic, . . . most Indonesians are Muslim. On the whole Filipinas are also older, more likely to be married, and more highly educated than Indonesian domestic workers. Filipinas have also been in Hong Kong longer and have had more opportunity to develop support networks. Such differences are no doubt related to the greater problems faced by Indonesian domestic workers, including higher rates of underpayment than among Filipinas and much higher rates of overcharging by employment recruitment agencies" (x–xi).

In fact, Constable points out, "Indonesians face unique problems when their employers prohibit them from wearing modest dress (hijab) while at home, forbid them from participating in the daily rituals of Muslim prayer, or require them to cook pork" (xi). To what extent these religious aspects and their less advantageous positions relative to their Filipina counterparts condition Indonesian domestic workers' dissent and accommodation vis-à-vis their employers is worthy of investigation. What is clear here is that these changing local circumstances add variability to the experiences among foreign domestic workers even within the same locality.

Furthermore, as Constable argues, foreign domestic workers "should not be reduced to fixed 'types'" (xviii). She writes, "Their views might fluctuate in the course of a day, or shift over the years with their work conditions and experiences" (xviii). Those who "often appeared extremely passive . . . were not as innocent as they sometimes appeared" (xviii), and while the more activist-oriented "were adamantly fighting for social change . . . their confidence sometimes wavered, and at times they wondered out loud about romantic fairy-tale endings" (xviii).

These varied local conditions and contexts all suggest that one may not take migrant domestic workers' subversive contestations to any singular conclusion, as if they are universal in their political trajectories, connotations, and effects. While being cognizant of these discrepancies and differences, what I wish to extrapolate from the following heterogeneous acts staged by migrant domestic workers is their shared political ingenuity in disturbing and unsettling disseminated liberal political life in their respective conditions. As I shall suggest, this ingenious appropriation of nonexistent citizenship from varied sites harbors critical lessons for domestic workers' rights activism as it is practiced globally.

To begin, as Parreñas's ethnographic study of Filipina domestic workers in

Rome and Los Angeles indicates, in addition to physical labor, domestic work is governed by the familial script of "deference and maternalism," wherein workers are expected to carry out the emotional work of deference by being spoken to by employers as subordinates, engaging in ingratiating behavior, performing tasks in a lively manner, and constantly putting on a smiling face in "reflecting the idealized, pleasant environment of the home" (2001, 171). In exchange, employers respond through maternalism, acting "protective" and "nurturing" to the "childlike" domestic workers and sometimes even treating them as "one of the family" (170–71). Like practices of gift giving, the family analogy, however benevolent, has a coercive effect on the domestic workers by extracting "unpaid physical and emotional labor" (Romero 1992, 124), thereby "obliterat[ing] their legal status as a worker, and their own obligations and responsibilities as members of their own family" (Stasiulus and Bakan 2003, 142).

Yet in the interstitial space where governmental regulation is suspended, domestic workers have precisely leveraged their informal status as "family members" to negotiate better labor conditions with their employers: not being ordered around constantly, given the option not to wear a uniform, allowed to have visitors and partners spend the night, given the time to rest and ease their pace, offered snacks and invited to sit down and chat, obtaining advance payment to take care of a family emergency, or securing employers' sponsoring of legalization or permit to stay (Parreñas 2001, 181–88). This can be read as what Scott calls "calculated conformity" (Scott 1985), whereby domestic workers subjugate themselves to the familial script to protect their own positions within the household and, where possible, subtly exchange the employers' purchase of deference for limited benefits and uncodified rights as laboring members of the family—and, by extension, the sovereign national economy, the *bios*.

Filipina domestics in such sites have also used emotive appeals to employers through occasional departures from the familial script. In place of rational deliberation and open campaigning for public citizenship, their contestations often involve tactical deployment of "chicanery, cajolery, and negotiation" (Parreñas 2001, 188). Hence, mixing work ethic, efficient home care, a pleasant attitude, and deference with occasional projections of anger, silence, crying, talking back, or frowning has enabled domestic workers to send covert signals to employers regarding mistreatment and on occasion be offered a raise in wages, extra money for shopping, gifts, or an apology from employers in return (188–91).[13] In their study of West Indian and Filipina domestic workers in Canada, Daiva Stasiulus and Abigail Bakan point out further strategies devised by many live-in workers whereby, while neither subjecting themselves to a paternalistic script nor risking open confrontation with employers, they draw boundaries and secure an autonomous living space by "co-rent[ing] small apartments with other domestic workers, . . . cook[ing] their own food, and socializ[ing] during their days off" (2003, 142). In this way and many others, domestic workers manipulate varying degrees of conformity and emotive eruptions to procure limited inclusion, belonging, and dignified personhood.

Field research on Indonesian and Filipina domestic workers in postcolonial states and regions has similarly unveiled a wide array of dissident and oppositional practices, spontaneous or planned. For example, Chin's study in Malaysia indicates that in response to the unpaid labor extracted by employers, some foreign domestic workers "consistently use their employers' telephones to call friends and/or families overseas," without their employers detecting, "by gradually raising the charges on monthly statements from the telephone company" (155). In one instance, a Filipina domestic worker took advantage of her employer's attachment to her (because she took such good care of the baby) by informing the employer that her wrist was swollen from ironing and that her doctor in the Philippines had told her that it would get worse if she used her hand too much. The employer then hired another woman to iron three times a week, thus freeing up the Filipina worker from ironing responsibilities (155–56). The other episodes staged by migrant domestic workers in Malaysia discussed at the beginning of this chapter—"accidentally" dropping plates while washing dishes, bringing out soup bowls one at a time to embarrass an employer in front of guests, and leaving bloodstains from injured fingers on clothing—also involve leveraging one's "inclusion" in the household to negotiate better treatment in the workspace of the home.

Constable's research in Hong Kong further demonstrates how domestic workers attempt to take control of their labor conditions through similar tactics and manipulation of rules. Struggling over a lack of food in the household, they might take the initiative in teaching their employers not to be selfish by buying and putting their own food in the kitchen, thus embarrassing employers into providing an adequate quantity and quality of food or into giving workers a food allowance beyond their salary (Constable, 173–74). Sometimes such struggles involve negotiation over the timing of a bath: in response to employers' demands that workers take baths at given times, one worker recommends "taking a 'fake' bath in the evening: run the water and

wet the towel to 'fool' the employer, then take another in the morning, after the employer has left the house" (175). Another interesting phenomenon
documented by Constable, also noted by domestic work scholars who conduct research in other regions, is the use of mobile phones by domestic workers to "[facilitate] (often subtle) communication and support networks, . . .
[allowing them] to control the complex and challenging processes of recruitment and employment" in a highly isolated workplace (214; see also Lan
2006, 179–80; Perez 2014, 18–19).

Neither civil nor radical, these hidden tactical ruses allow foreign domestic workers to bypass the inert state of bare life while gaining dignity, respect,
and limited material sustenance and generate maneuverable spaces to acquire certain ends of their own rather than being treated as disposable means
to the ends of others. Their subtle contestations chronicle ingenious appropriations of political life: they are *oppositional* in character in their refusal of
silence and abjection; *negotiated* in neither directly rebelling against the liberal
order nor completely submitting to a bare state of exploitation; *interstitial* in
interweaving the habitual household scripts of familial civility with contingent disruptions that compel employers to respond to injustice (even if they
do not recognize it as such) and modify their behavior; and, finally, *subcultural*
in reusing the political script of liberal citizenship by detouring around conventional political deliberation and legislation while devising subtle and hidden "political" expressions. They are also subcultural in the sense that, rather
than being isolated individual acts, they are staged and written by a collective body of migrant domestic workers laboring in multitudinous households
across a range of liberal and postcolonial states and localities. In fact, these
acts constitute not only defensive survival strategies but also what Asef Bayat
calls the quiet but aggressive "encroachment of the ordinary," wherein domestic workers exert "the art of presence" in households, with "the courage
and creativity to . . . circumvent constraints, utilizing what is available and
discovering new spaces within which to make themselves heard, seen, felt,
and realized" (2010, 26). In so doing, they secretly enact change by remolding
existing relations between normality and abjection in disparate locations. In
all, migrant domestic workers' hidden tactics can be read as piecing together
episodes of ingenious citizenship that are as momentary and ephemeral as
they are perpetual and durational.

The Value of Limits:
From Ingenious Citizenship to Nonexistent Rights

The foregoing discussion aims not to celebrate ingenious citizenship as much as to illuminate its status of abjection as well as its deeper lessons for social contestation. To be sure, such resistance has not revamped, and will not revamp, the material-ideological structure that sustains workers' subordination; it may even backfire or reinforce the public's negative perceptions of foreign domestic workers (Chin, 163–64). Ingenious citizenship is attached to and inscribed within what Cheah articulates as the inhuman force field of the instrumentalization of human relations configured by the technology of global capitalism. It is situated *inside* the structural normalcy of neoliberal economy and the subjugating habitus of exploitation (Cheah 2006). Scott comments soberly that it is unlikely that the members of the subordinate class can significantly improve their lot through quotidian transgressions; rather, many of them are likely to "lose out, as have millions . . . before them" (1985, 27). Chin conveys a similar sentiment, concluding that "the fate of informal assemblages appears precarious" (164). Or, as Parreñas indicates, the average migrant worker "does not come to realize her world through the understanding of larger systems such as patriarchy and global capitalism" (2001, 33). They are more concerned with their immediate situations, and their "immediate struggles" can recuperate and sustain even as they resist the power structure (253).

But could these limits of ingenious citizenship also point to their invaluable lesson? As I emphasized in chapter 1, through its mode of negotiation, ingenious citizenship is necessarily complicit with and contaminated in the given liberal structural order that it itself contests. Yet it also is precisely this complicit contamination that opens up an interstitial space for migrant domestic workers to maneuver limited measures of inclusion and belonging. At the very moment that the abject is declared politically dead by Agamben, domestic workers are seen taking other routes via the fissures and interstices of their everyday work life to edit and revise the given political script, thus secretly and slowly extending and reanimating their own political life. Rather than spelling the end of citizenship for the abject, the interstitial character of sovereign power that deprives undocumented subjects of political agency that Agamben so deftly characterizes has also—through the very interstices, in-betweens, and neither/nors—produced more "citizens" than it recognizes. Between political life and bare life, there exists a milieu of inventive practices where immanent outsiders mimic sovereign power through nego- tiation and subversion and navigate their interstitiality inside and outside the normative script of citizenship in a way that is not directly counterhegemonic or transparently democratic.

Instead of concluding that the hidden tactics staged by migrant domestic workers are ultimately futile, I suggest they may actually signal the lesson that domestic workers' movements and organizations also need to work within their own given limits in varying contexts and locations. Further, they may need to enact politics in original, inventive, and not strictly democratic ways in order to generate and expand accessible and maneuverable spaces of political citizenship for their constituents.

Such lessons are especially crucial in light of the success of recent do- mestic worker campaigns, which have achieved significant victories, both in the United States and internationally, through a democratic framework of rights-based strategies. As I argue here, while these victories are indis- pensable to the welfare of domestic workers, it is under-investigated whether such strategies are universally effective regardless of local complexity and differences. I am not suggesting that existing rights-based movements are not being creative in advocating for domestic workers. To the contrary, as I articulate below, even while they actively push and campaign for domes- tic workers' rights, many domestic workers' organizations have inventively mixed their democratic politics with a necessary dose of ingenious agency, using their complicity and contamination in the given economy to negotiate an official recognition of rights.

Where the issue arises, however, is that contemporary rights-based move- ments have generally followed the historical trajectory of domestic work ac- tivism that positions ingenious agency in a secondary or supplementary role in relation to democratic collective resistance. This preempts the opening up of a different political horizon that does not always take the democratic claiming of rights as the go-to tool in engendering social transformation. By repositioning ingenious agency at the front and center of domestic work- ers' movement struggles, I wish to point to the myriad ways in which cer- tain local conditions and contexts actually call for an *even more* extensive and fluid incorporation of ingenious agency into local organizations' advocacy strategies—including deemphasizing rights claims or even dropping the focus on rights.

The democratic emphasis on rights should first be considered in the historical context and trajectory of domestic workers' movements; battling the public misperception of domestic work as lacking economic value, focusing on
its recognition as "real" labor entitled to official regulation and protection.
Not only does historical slavery contribute to this misperception—as Sheila
Bapat notes, "Early codes regulating indentured servitude in the United
States reveal that both slave and nonslave domestic labor were legally deemed
to have no economic value" (2014, 30)—but the very nature of domestic work
as being reproductive labor confined to the private sphere further divorces
it from economic valuation (17–18). A report issued by the NDWA captures
this public conception of domestic labor: "no durable goods or consumer
products have been created or distributed; neither the flow of capital nor the
accumulation of profits has been directly served."[14] As such, "Labor rights
considered normal in the formal economy (e.g., minimum wage, days off,
vacation, and fixed working hours) are not viewed as necessary or even appropriate in the context of work in a private household" (Chuang 2010, 1641).

Thus, as Bapat chronicles, despite the early efforts by domestic worker
union activism from 1870 to 1940 that made real gains in better wages and
working conditions—including an attempt by the Young Women's Christian
Association to upgrade the feudal mistress-maid relationship into a "modern business contractual relationship" (Shah and Seville 2012, 421)—both
domestic and agricultural workers (many of whom were African American) were excluded from most of the New Deal labor protections, as well
as from the National Labor Relations Act and the Fair Labor Standards Act
during the first half of the twentieth century (Bapat, 49–57). It was not until
1974—thanks in part to the domestic workers' advocacy in the late 1960s and
1970s by organizations such as the California Homemakers Association and
the National Domestic Workers Union—did the U.S. Congress finally amend
the Fair Labor Standards Act "to include domestic workers within minimum
wage protections," although it came with certain restrictions (58). And even
then, domestic workers' activism continued to face resistance from the U.S.
labor movement in obtaining further changes to state or federal policy, because labor unions "did not see the struggle of domestic workers as part of
the 'real' labor movement and . . . worked to 'maintain unequal rates of pay'
for women" (60).

This historical context and environment has shaped the political trajectory of domestic work activism. In seeking the recognition of domestic work as valuable labor "worthy of compensation or labor protections" (Bapat, 19), the movements generally proceed through the process of *revelation* (of the plight of domestic work), *critique* (of inequality and injustice), and *enacting democratic agency* (via the claiming of rights). Given that many domestic workers are trapped in conditions of "loneliness; lack of dignity and respect; lack of job security, health benefits, and sick days; and employers' failure to comply with withholding-tax laws," collective organizations that focus on rights, respect, and dignity play a crucial role in helping "[draw] the women together, and . . . provide a basis for solidarity" (Hondagneu-Sotelo 2001, 227).

One notable phenomenon in late capitalism is that social change in domestic work is "no longer driven by behemoth legislation like the NLRA but by smaller-scale, group-based advocacy" (Bapat, 16). Importantly, these smaller-scale organizations that were founded in the late 1980s and early 1990s—such as the Mujeres Unidas y Activas in San Francisco and the Domestic Workers' Association (DWA) of the Coalition for Humane Immigrant Rights of Los Angeles—do not operate like labor unions but incorporate elements of ingenious agency into their democratic organizing. For instance, as Premilla Nadasen, a scholar on the history of domestic workers' organizing, remarks, "Our meetings are nothing like any labor union you can imagine. There's women of all ages, and there's always child care, food—and singing—at domestic workers' meetings" (quoted in Bapat, 129). Grace Chang adds, "DWA members focus on 'expressive or cultural events, with self-help seminars and consciousness-raising' around common issues they face" (2000, 202). They "see all of the women in the group as leaders rather than selecting individual spokeswomen, and rely on all members to do outreach in their daily lives and within their direct communities" (202). The ingenuity of domestic workers' activism is perhaps best exemplified when the DWA created a comic book, *Super Doméstica*, for free distribution, which "featured the story of a housekeeper who successfully learns to negotiate with her demanding employer, and the cover image [of a domestic worker superhero] became an important icon in Latino civil rights marches and labor protests in Southern California" (Hondagneu-Sotelo, 224).

By infusing ingenious agency into their collective acts of resistance, these organizations serve an indispensable function in helping bring immigrant workers together. However, it should also be noted that these organizations tend to position ingenious agency as an "evolutionary" stepping stone that could help politicize the workers en route to the eventual collective attainment of democratic agency rather than as a direct political tool in itself to create social change. In other words, where ingenious agency emerges within these collective movements, it plays a cheerleading role that is used to strengthen or mobilize democratic campaigns; it is not placed at the front and center of political struggles. In this way, when it comes to contributing lessons for democracy, it is still the collective democratic acts that constitute the strongest link—the absence of which would greatly diminish the connections between immigrant workers' ingenious agency and social change.

I would like us to consider, however, that while such evolutionary ways of relating to ingenious agency served a critical purpose at that historical juncture in molding domestic workers' political consciousness and democratic actions, it might be imperative that we not stop there or insist on returning to the past—for it might only get us so far—but must advance it further to adapt to the neoliberal politics of our time. Looking at the movements historically may thus further point us to the need to devise more fluid and varied conceptions of collective movements for the present and future beyond an exclusively democratic horizon.

Ingenious Pathways to Nonexistent Rights

Such subordination of ingenious agency to the larger democratic goals of the movements has nonetheless continued to influence domestic workers' rights activism in the early twenty-first century. Consider two prominent recent examples of political victories for domestic workers that harbor elements of ingenious agency within a predominantly democratic frame. First, in 2010 the NDWA achieved a historic victory in getting the first Domestic Workers Bill of Rights, recognizing domestic workers "as real workers under state labor law," passed into law in the State of New York.[15] Some of the key provisions specified in the law include state minimum wage, overtime pay, days of rest, sick leave, paid vacation, protection against discrimination and sexual harassment, worker's compensation insurance, and protection against retaliation by employers for filed complaints.[16] The NDWA has subsequently won passage of a similar Domestic Workers Bill of Rights in Hawaii and—after two vetoes—in California. Campaigns are ongoing in the states of Illinois, Massachusetts, and Connecticut as of this writing.

Second, in 2013, the Domestic Workers Convention (also known as C189), adopted by the International Labor Organization (ILO) two years earlier, went into effect and marked the first international human rights document to set global labor standards for domestic work "after decades of struggles by domestic workers' organizations for recognition, rights and respect."[17] After the historic and overwhelming vote for the convention, domestic workers and their supporters "unfurled a banner from the balcony of the grand United Nations Assembly Hall in Geneva, Switzerland" that read "C189— Congratulations! Now comes the domestic work of governments: RATIFY— IMPLEMENT."[18] Rights for domestic workers stipulated in the convention include entitlement to a minimum wage; freedom of association and right to collective bargaining; daily and weekly rest hours; elimination of forced or compulsory labor; freedom from abuse, harassment, and violence; the right to keep possession of their travel and identity documents; and freedom to reside outside their working households.[19]

Together, these formal democratic measures provide essential labor rights for domestic workers, recognizing them as rightful citizen-workers who deserve dignified material treatment and social acknowledgement in their manual labor. Considering the contexts in which many domestic workers labor, this official recognition is transformative at both the local governmental and global intergovernmental levels. In California, for instance, the Domestic Workers Bill of Rights "will finally provide overtime pay to an estimated 200,000 California housekeepers, child care providers and caregivers when they work more than nine hours in a day or forty-five hours a week."[20] Such measures make inroads into the scripted terrain of liberal political life by unsettling and remolding (without transcending) the existing relations between formal citizens and foreign domestic workers, further expanding the contestable and appropriable spaces of citizenship life for the latter.

At the same time, we should not construe these rights as constituting a transcendent victory that triumphs *over* neoliberal globalization. Rather, they formulate provisional reforms that domestic workers can utilize to negotiate and appropriate a more expansive spectrum of political citizenship *within* a capitalist economy. These labor rights expand the appropriable spaces of citizenship for domestic workers by professionalizing their corporeal bodies and labor status, even as they use and invest in these same laboring bodies to sustain the continual reproduction of liberal citizenship by engulfing them in the bureaucratic-contractual arrangement of U.S. capitalist sovereignty. As Cheah argues, "Human rights are generated as concrete rights at the level of bodily needs and materialized through institutional practices as part of a complex of processes by which global capitalism continually sustains and reproduces itself through the production of human subjects with rights. . . . Rights are not, in the original instance, entitlements of intersubjectively constituted rational social agents but *violent gifts*, the necessary nexuses within immanent global force relations that produce the identities of their claimants. Yet they are the only way for the disenfranchised to mobilize" (172; emphasis added).

The rights that are gained by domestic workers, as "violent gifts," do not occupy a transcendent position above and beyond the instrumental field of liberal economy, but come from an already contaminated source that safeguards their biological welfare while etching their bodies even more closely into the organic configuration of global capitalism. Capitalist *bios* requires the biological sustenance of such bodies for its continuing reproduction. The use value of domestic labor is instrumentally exchanged for a set of citizenship or human rights that would, in turn, preserve and enhance this use value.

In fact, the progressive spirit of the NDWA's democratic politics notwithstanding, its campaign operation has had to cleverly use the racialized commerce of domestic labor in forging alliances with relevant consumer groups and local governments in leveraging their constituents' rights. For instance, through its "Caring Across Generations" campaign, the NDWA is collaborating with elderly and disabled home-care employers in seeking to both "improve access to care and support services . . . [and] create a path to citizenship for domestic and home care workers."[21] As Nancy Perez argues, however, it matters whose bodies are doing the serving and whose are being served: given the "age wave," in which a predominant number of senior white Americans will be needing care and that care work is provided by mostly Mexican, Central American, and Filipino migrant women, the resolution provided by the NDWA cannot easily reconcile and smooth over the corporeal disparity in the market for intimate care (Perez 2011). She writes, "Caregiving also includes emotional support for aging citizens who are having difficulty with memory loss or other medical symptoms due to disease or trauma. This last one can be difficult for many workers, more so than the physical aspects of caregiving, as they are asked to exert 'care' and 'love' in the midst of undergoing traumas themselves pertaining to migration, displacement, or economic struggle" (2011, 3).

Perez thus critically lays bare the limits embedded in the NDWA's Caring Across Generations campaign from the perspective of racial justice. Yet this same observation also implies that, for the NDWA to propose a citizenship path (i.e., entrance into the *bios*) for migrant domestic workers, its democratic campaign has to traffic instrumentally in the unequal racialized corporeal relations to attain its desired ends of immigration and labor justice in the given economy.

This racialized biopolitical bargain and instrumental calculation constitutes the very terrain in liberal economy where migrant workers' rights and inclusion are contested and negotiated. California's Governor Jerry Brown, in his prior veto of the bill of domestic workers' rights advocated by the NDWA in his state in 2012, gestures to this calculation in this way: "I am very concerned, about domestic workers and that they be treated right, I am also concerned about retired teachers, and retired janitors and ordinary people who have to take care of their mother or father or their aunt or their uncle, and they need someone to come in. . . . If you're going to double (those rates), you are going to say that a lot of people have to go to nursing homes. So I want to study that."[22]

Without visibly signifying "race," Brown's allusion to "the effect of increased costs [that] could burden the disabled and elderly and their families" by the Domestic Workers Bill of Rights nonetheless underlines an implicitly racialized commerce of domestic labor that jostles between (white) disabled/elderly people's (and their children's) economic possessions and biological well-being and (brown) migrant domestic/care workers' bodily labor and citizenship conditions.[23] The repeated references by the NDWA to winning "respect" and "dignity" for workers are constructed and predicated on this racialized commerce and instrumental exchange—a bargain that it cannot avoid, but must negotiate.

My point here is not to signal the political futility of NDWA's democratic politics but, rather, to emphasize that any progressive social movements are inevitably limited by their complicity and contamination in the given material economy and as such can generate only negotiated and compromised (rather than transcending) effects. Yet the illumination of these immanent limits also speaks to the most essential contribution of the NDWA: this complicit contamination can be seen as being creatively and resourcefully employed by the organization to tap into the instrumental field of the liberal economy to generate appropriable spaces for migrant domestic workers. Like the individual domestic workers who use the limited tools they possess to create change in their immediate surroundings, the political reforms launched by the NDWA should be read as *ingeniously* using the limited instruments and resources available in the contaminated global economy to create more opportunities for contingent and nonlinear social change.

This deployment of ingenious agency, however, is never explicitly stated by the NDWA (perhaps necessarily so), and like its predecessors, its political script is still centrally written within the expected frame of democratic agency. In fact, as a member of the International Domestic Workers Federation, the NDWA has been part of the global democratic effort to enact the ILO Convention, which sets international human rights standards on domestic labor. The question arises whether this universal claim of human rights—a direct and contestatory appeal to democratic purity (respect, dignity, labor justice) to overcome capitalist contamination (corporate greed, economic inequality, state complicity)—can be readily applied to other regional, cultural, and political contexts. Might these other contexts require an even more protean and versatile incorporation of ingenious agency into the advocacy strategies of local domestic workers' organizations in order to win broad support for their initiatives and achieve the actual realization of political citizenship for foreign domestic workers? Indeed, if the NDWA's Caring Across Generations campaign instantiates that even its democratic politics has to make creative compromise with neoliberal contamination in given contexts, it suggests that any universalizing rights-based strategies also need to be flexibly adjusted in accordance with differing local conditions.

This is not to say that we should give up on rights activism (which would become another problematic sort of universalism); rather, I am suggesting that social movements should heed the lesson of domestic workers' ingenious citizenship at the individual level to do their advocacy work unrestricted by the universal prescription of rights-based strategies. If the NDWA has productively demonstrated its flexibility in shifting between democratic rights campaigns and ingenious politics, then my suggestion here is that such flexibility might need to be stretched even further in other local contexts.

As Aihwa Ong argues, "Labor tactics and rebellions tend to be highly context-specific, and they do not easily coalesce into a global mass movement or multitude, with its promise of global citizenship" (2006, 21). As of this writing, fifteen countries have ratified the Domestic Workers Convention; however, a large number of states (well over a hundred) remain that have not ratified it. We can certainly expect that the prudent push for the ratification of the convention by local and international domestic workers' organizations will compel more states to follow suit. But what do we do with those states that may not budge (at least, not in the immediate future), and how do we help domestic workers laboring in those states? Can discourses of "rights, recognition, and respect" trump all local scripts and their interaction with the disseminating neoliberal instrumental logics of different contexts? As Ong points out, "The United Nations lacks the power to enforce its many instruments of human rights, and it is highly susceptible to the influence of leading nations to initiate humanitarian interventions" (17). In fact, as early as December 1990, the United Nations had already passed the International Convention on the Protection of the Rights of All Migrant Workers and Members of Their Families, but the forty-seven states that have ratified it as of 2014 remain primarily migrant-sending states in the global South. No migrant-receiving states in North America or Western Europe have ratified the convention.

Taking stock of the actually existing matrix of human rights politics, I suggest that, if neoliberalism is the winning political imperative for the time being, then it might be useful to employ that imperative (and not necessarily the imperative of rights) to win over other scripts and logics on behalf of domestic workers in concrete circumstances. Borrowing Ong's term, I point toward a context-specific politics that takes insights from domestic workers' improvisations of nonexistent citizenship to innovatively and circuitously expand nonexistent rights via neoliberal logics in localities where formal rights claims may not be effective.

Ong's work has documented instances of such a scenario in Malaysia, indicating that "while NGOs [nongovernmental organizations] may formally invoke UN [United Nations] conventions to claim rights for migrant women and their families, their interventions respond directly to the *specific conditions* in the space configured by labor markets, biopolitics, and divergent moral economies" (2006, 210; emphasis added). Given the strong belief of Southeast Asian countries and their populations that "it is legitimate for the state to discriminate against aliens in favor of its own citizens" (212), NGOs in Malaysia do not demand that foreign maids be granted citizenship or human rights; rather, they resort to an alternative strategy that fuses considerations of local ethical regimes with business instrumentality, seeking to demand "moral legitimacy and market access" in their ethical-political intervention (210).

Thus, on one hand, NGOs make appeals to "basic cultural values about the moral worthiness of women's bodies, . . . [focusing] on *biowelfare*, an ethical claim that skirts the issue of political rights by focusing on the sheer survival of foreign female workers" (Ong 2006, 212; emphasis in original). As Ong writes, "Only by invoking cultural understanding and compassion, not abstract human rights discourse, can the moral legitimacy of alien women's biosecurity be persuasive to the host society" (212). She explains,

The biowelfare of foreign domestic workers, as "women at risk," is an even more fundamental claim on Asian ethics. The bodily integrity of women, the female body confronted with potential violence, is something that can elicit greater moral sympathy from Asian society than demands for gender or migrant rights. . . . In the absence of enforced laws requiring maids to have rest days, feminist NGOs are now insisting on employers' moral obligations to let their domestic helpers have days off for "rest and relaxation" or to attend to religious services. The language avoids demanding "worker rights," stressing instead the moral and health benefits from time off, since the foreign worker should not be treated like a slave-like thing. After all, migrant women and foreign maids are frequently also mothers and nurses, life-givers and life-nurturers that are cherished in Asian traditions. (212)

On the other hand, NGOs further link "the demand for a healthy migrant body to a kind of neoliberal calculation," claiming for foreign maids their right to "free competition in regional labor markets" (214). That is, in order for foreign domestic workers to become "truly free economic agents" in the current economy (213), NGOs argue, they "should enjoy freedom of residence, employment, and family life, that is, the conditions of social reproduction that are enjoyed by foreign professionals in Asia . . . [They] should have the right to reside in the host society, to bring their families, and to change jobs or find other lines of work" (214). NGOs emphasize "the economic benefits to the host society" from this professional and respectful treatment of domestic workers, indicating that "health security and market flexibility will ensure that the foreign servant class continues to be available to affluent Asians, but under better material, moral, and economic terms" (214). What we see in these NGOs' advocacy work is thus an encapsulation of nonexistent rights for migrant domestic workers (e.g., biological welfare, legal residence, market access, unrestricted mobility to and from home country) through an inventive and clever "alignment of gendered biological security and neoliberal logic" (214) in a particular local milieu.

Cheah points to similar processes in Singapore, noting that some church-based NGOs seek to humanize the conditions of foreign domestic workers without deploying the language of human rights "by convincing employers, agents, and the Singapore state that the humane treatment of foreign workers will lead to better and more efficient service, cause fewer 'social problems,' and improve Singapore's international public image" (247). He writes,

For instance, although Father Luciano believes that "one of the aims of pastoral care is to make the maids aware of their rights and how to exercise them through all the legal means prescribed by the Ministry of Manpower in cooperation with the Philippine embassy," his public appeal to employers to allow their domestic help to attend Christmas celebrations was based not on the right to have a day of leave but instead on the reasoning that "this will surely reduce their loneliness . . . and they will be able to serve you better in the future." (247)

This kind of appeal to social and economic harmony is different from the contestatory bargaining style of union organizing. These NGOs recognize that "because the Singapore state views the outright assertion of human rights as antagonistic, it is an ineffective way of safeguarding humanity" (248). Bridget Lew, the director of a Catholic NGO commissioned to serve the needs of Filipina domestic workers, indicates that her organization primarily works in a consultative manner, operating as a liaison that consults the government, the Ministry of Manpower, and the embassies for "all parties . . . to reach an amicable solution in the interest of all parties" (quoted in Cheah, 247). As Cheah reflects, "The means deployed are precisely the strategies of business management: networking and liaising beyond the church . . . [with] secular bodies . . . to convince all parties, including the migrant worker, that a humane outcome will serve their economic self-interest" (248). He concludes forcefully, "Rights related to minimum employment conditions for domestic helpers are not enforceable because they do not have state recognition. Insofar as these techniques achieve the same result without formal state codification of such rights, they are a de facto actualization of labor rights in a concrete situation" (248).

Ong and Cheah provide important insights that international domestic work activism needs to reach beyond the blind spots of democratic agency configured in universal human rights strategies to more effectively address the needs and improve the livelihoods of domestic workers living in differing local contexts. These local conditions constitute the gaps and fissures that are unreachable by any universally or linearly conceived strategy and can be addressed only through roundabout means. Such a nonlinear take on cultural and political resistance defies any neat provisional blueprint, for the appropriate strategies necessarily vary from context to context.

To give another example of the direction of this argument, as Constable notes, while certain domestic work literatures have advocated for "the 'professionalization' of household work" through a standard contract, in Hong Kong, Filipina domestic workers' attempts to professionalize their occupation have not been liberating but have translated to "ever more rigid forms of discipline," including "adhering to stricter timetables and adopting more efficient and 'modern' work methods" (197). Specifically, they self-impose a professional discourse that is "aimed at transforming demeaning aspects of domestic work" and upgrading their status as professional helpers, "but in so doing, it also imposes discipline and docility" by generating a submissive embodiment of "the ideal domestic worker desired by employer and agencies" (198). Here, Constable's observation usefully illustrates the limits of a universalistic prescription of formalization to address domestic workers' woes in a particular context, underlining how professionalization might not always bring benefits and might even engender new dilemmas for workers.

At the same time, Constable's conclusion can be further extended, for while professionalization may not bring about the kind of democratic transformation indicated by its advocates in every situation, it may nonetheless be taken up by NGOs in a reverse, neoliberal direction as leverage for the welfare of domestic workers in certain contexts. For example, they might use "professional development" programs to train domestic workers in important practical and household management skills "to build . . . [their] confidence on the job" and equip them with "effective interviewing techniques" and negotiation strategies, thus helping them secure employment and higher wages.[24] Such measures need not be understood as conforming to liberal normativity; rather, like domestic workers' hidden tactics, these reuses of neoliberal scripts by NGOs can be read as prudently oppositional, negotiated, interstitial, and subcultural in formulating a fluid and polymorphous style of social activism.

This is also to say that rights-based strategies that construe workers' rights as purely oppositional vis-à-vis the interests of privileged entrepreneurs and consumers (Das Gupta 2006) need to be flexibly and shrewdly reconceived. Ingenious citizenship offers us the lesson that in certain circumstances, domestic workers' activism may actually need to work through negotiated and interstitial spaces to reposition foreign maids as nascent entrepreneurs and seek alliance and support from consumers via the mainstream media and other commercial outlets. The NDWA's appropriation of The Help and its Caring Across Generations campaign are potent examples that use consumerism to raise awareness about working conditions in domestic labor and leverage domestic workers' rights. I suspect that in certain states in the United States that are resistant to democratic change through the passage of the Domestic Workers Bill of Rights, the NDWA may need to resort to even stronger entrepreneurial and consumerist appeals to gain de facto recognition, respect, and rights for migrant domestic workers.

In the end, the flashes of ingenious agency shown by foreign domestic workers inform us of the value of limits: they signal to immigration and labor rights advocates that the given liberal landscape can be cunningly and resourcefully reconfigured to strengthen domestic workers' appropriation of basic provisions of political life (i.e., dignity, respect, inclusion, and rights) in a tactful, savvy fashion. This might entail resorting to business management logics, nondemocratic channels, and even non–rights-based ethics and discourses in differing local circumstances. Such insights have been absent in the political work of Agamben and his critics because of their subscription and attachment to democratic agency in the Western founding script of *bios*. By untethering itself from the universal prescription of democratic agency, social movement activism can constitute an ever more vital and creative force in helping bolster domestic workers' disruption and appropriation of the political script, making it easier for them to acquire a wider spectrum of de facto citizenship rights and better their material lives. Such is also the indirect lesson rendered via *The Help* at the opening of this chapter: ingenuity and complicity are perpetual, indispensable elements in the generation of social change.

3. Global Sex Workers, Calculated Abjection, and Appropriating Economic Citizenship

Using Bread to Earn Roses in Neoliberal Times

Based on the Justice for Janitors campaign of 1990, organized by the Service Employees International Union in Los Angeles, the film *Bread and Roses* (2000) tells the story of Maya, an undocumented immigrant from Mexico who crosses the border with smugglers to reunite with her sister Rosa in Los Angeles.[1] During the course of her stay working as a janitor at a downtown building alongside Rosa, Maya becomes involved in the Justice for Janitors campaign against the janitors' nonunionized cleaning company, which has cut wages and withheld health insurance and benefits over the years. Desperately needing the money that would allow her diabetic husband to undergo surgery, Rosa betrays her fellow workers by giving their manager, Perez, information about the campaign, resulting in the firing of several workers. Furious over her sister's action, Maya confronts Rosa, who in anger and devastation reveals her past use of sex work to support their family:

Maya: You're a fucking traitor, Rosa. You're a fucking traitor, sis.
Rosa: You do, don't you? You think that? Even when I was supporting everybody? Sending money to you and mamá? . . . Did you guys ever wonder . . . how did Rosa manage to send the money? . . . Rosa kept

your mouths pretty full. You know how I did it? Turning tricks. I was a hooker. What do you think about that?

Maya [*suddenly in agony*]: I didn't know . . .

Rosa: I was turning tricks, honey. So that you guys didn't starve. For five fucking years in Tijuana. Every single night. Just about every single night. "Suck their dicks, Rosa. Fuck, Rosa. Fuck. Fuck." . . . "Come on, because your family is starving." Huh? "Suck their dicks." Right? "Come on, come on!" *O la le, o la le.* Sounds awful, huh? Disgusting? What do you think? Nobody asked me, huh? My dad leaves, and who gets screwed? Who gets screwed? Rosa. Let Rosa start fucking everybody.

Maya [*covering face with her hands in disbelief*]: I didn't know, Rosa.

Rosa: . . . My husband gets sick, and I have to fuck . . . Let Rosa pick up all the pieces, right? [*Crying.*] She has to be doing everything all the time, as if Rosa were an idiot, fucking everybody, right? So you had something to eat! . . . I've put up with it all my fucking life! I've been keeping it here, in my own gut . . . Do you know how I got you your job? . . . You know what I did? Yes, honey, I had to fuck Perez.

Maya: Don't joke about that!

Rosa: I fucked him for you! I fucked him for you! Because I'm tired. Tired! All my life. My husband gets sick, I go fuck. My dad leaves, I go fuck. . . . You want a job? I go fuck. All the time!

Maya: Goddamn it, I didn't know!

Rosa [*crying*]: I have a husband! I have two kids! And what? And I'm a fucking whore, right? That's what I am! . . . My own daughter, my baby asks me where her dad is. What am I going to tell her, Maya? I didn't even remember his face. I didn't know who the fuck is her father. "You were born in a brothel, honey." You're right, Maya. I am a fucking traitor. A traitor who is lying to herself, to my own family, to my baby girl.

Maya's shock, pain, and disbelief on learning of her sister's prostitution provides a contrast in the film: the compassionate and daring Maya on the path of social justice and the progressive labor movement, and the equally bold but experienced and psychically wounded Rosa, who has "learned" the hard way that a subordinate migrant woman has to extract the very last bit of her body and soul to keep surviving, including selling others out. The film depicts the struggles and eventual triumph of the janitors' labor uprising through two sisters' divergent paths: while Rosa demonstrates the harsh reality of personal and familial survival as a female immigrant manual laborer in a capitalist economy, Maya exemplifies courage and vision, mobilizing her coworkers to learn about and agitate for labor rights regardless of the potential risks for her own well-being. If Rosa represents "bread" (practicality and survival), Maya can be said to symbolize "roses" (aspiration for equality and justice). Through the internal conflicts of these two characters, the film revivifies the political message inspired by female immigrant textile workers in U.S. union strikes around the turn of the twentieth century: "Yes, it is bread we fight for, but we fight for roses, too!" That is to say, we need to survive, but we want respect and dignity, too.

The relatively positive and celebratory presentation of Maya and the negative but sympathetic depiction of Rosa in the film parallel the social contrast between abject subjects such as domestic workers and sex workers in liberal citizenship. Specifically, if foreign domestic workers (or undocumented janitorial workers like Maya) are abjected due to their nonstatus, their occupation in the "lawful" realm of domestic labor may nonetheless redeem them worthy of dignified status and accord them certain labor rights inaccessible to migrant subjects in "illicit" trades (such as Rosa, the former sex worker). In fact, Maya's political acts, being visible and counterhegemonic, recall the meritorious vision of democratic citizenship enacted by nonstatus subjects seen in chapter 2 (referred to, for example, as "noncitizen citizenship," "acts of citizenship," and "democratic cosmopolitanism"). Maya's exemplary democratic actions place her in a normalized position in relation to Rosa, who is portrayed in the unappealing light of secrecy, betrayal, and the willful contamination of her body and soul. The representation of Rosa's acts—whether the hidden sex acts of prostitution (as a "whore"), the secretive sexual liaisons with the company manager Perez (as an adulterer), or the manipulative acts of selling out her coworkers (as a traitor)—silently stations her in shame and dishonor as the anomalous other to the immigrant labor movement. Both characters can be considered abject subjects in relation to liberal citizenship, yet an implicit distinction is made in the film between the deserving democratic citizen (Maya) and the scheming and calculating other (Rosa).

However, in the fleeting scene presented above, the powerful dialogue enacted through Rosa's emotional disclosure of her past also creates an opportunity for further thinking and alternative reading. Although Maya's visible acts mobilizing her coworkers in fighting for labor rights and human dignity take center stage throughout the film, her heroic and honorable embodiment of democratic agency is temporarily subdued in this scene by Rosa's revelation of her "ignoble" acts of prostitution—"getting screwed," "sucking dicks," and "fucking the manager." And while the darkness of prostitution bleeds through Rosa's deceitful act of betrayal, the audience is also shown how this unordinary practice is committed with the purpose of providing financial support to her struggling immigrant family (including getting Maya, the incarnation of a democratic citizen, a job). Despite the fact that the dialogue depicts Rosa's once abject life as a sex worker in Tijuana, could prostitution demonstrate her agency in purposefully using the "shameful" abjection of her body to earn an economic livelihood, allowing her to acquire limited degrees of normality in relation to liberal citizenship?

After all, sex work is the pivotal practice that has enabled the attainment of "economic citizenship" of Rosa and her family across the transnational border of North America. However dishonorable and emotionally and physically draining, it provides Rosa with the means to make a living by herself, send remittances back home to Mexico, and form a heterosexual nuclear family with a white husband and two kids. In short, sex work provides Rosa with an instrumental springboard to launch an economically viable life, allowing her and her children—immigrants and minorities—to chase the "American dream." If sex work is abjection, is it not also strategically calculated and, in fact, inventively deployed by Rosa (within her limiting conditions) to bargain for something material in return? Does she not devise and appropriate liminal spaces of inclusion and belonging within the toil of capitalist citizenship?

Situating Rosa as a subordinate, female migrant subject in this larger context of liberal citizenship enables a rereading of her subjectivity that may be prematurely foreclosed by the filmic script: perhaps her practice of prostitution does not simply stay at the level of survival, as it may first appear. Rather, it may also be read as resituating the metaphoric relations between "bread" and "roses" by specifically using bread to earn roses. Although sex work abjectifies her, it allows Rosa to unsettle and reorient the given relations of normality and abjection in exchange for a semblance of "normal" life within capitalist citizenship (and this capitalist script is simultaneously disrupted by her crafty means of appropriation). Reading the film sideways through the character of Rosa may disclose the relationship between bread and roses not as exogenous entities (i.e., practicality on the one hand, justice on the other), but as endogenously intertwined and constituted (i.e., justice as earned through money, practicality, and instrumentality).

This burgeoning and yet unrealized lesson in Bread and Roses is taken to a more explicit expression when sex workers in other venues specifically employ the liberal language of the "free market"—that is, offering their bodily features and sex acts as special goods and services available for capitalist monetary exchange—to normalize and legitimize their subjectivity (i.e., humanity, respect, dignity). In doing so, they can be described as crafting their subjectivity to embody that of a business entrepreneur to obtain measures of economic inclusion and gender equity within liberal citizenship.

For example, the episode "In Bed with a Los Angeles Prostitute" on the popular Internet program *The Skyy John Show* features an interview with a black escort named Raven. In it, Raven describes herself as the daughter of a cop; she wears a T-shirt with the words "For Rent: $300 Buy the Hour" on the front, and "Inquire with me . . . Also, inquire about my COPS special!" on the back.[2] Raven's reference to being "the daughter of a cop" accompanied by the sign of her sexual body being available for rent explicitly blurs the boundary between normality and abjection. In fact, she is deliberately marketing the *abjection* of her normality (i.e., having come from a "normal" background) as a distinctively "valuable" and "enticing" good or service she could offer to her potential clients. The monetary sign on her T-shirt abjectifies her humanity (i.e., signaling to men that they may "rent" her body as a means to an end), but it also validates and normalizes this very humanity. After all, she is the one, the entrepreneurial *subject*, who controls and negotiates the monetary terms of this abjection in the amount and in ways that are acceptable to her.

Explaining to the show's host that she does not mind kissing a client because "he is buying my time," Raven states, "The determination of a good woman who is going to be good at this is based on how good of a slut she was before this. And I was a really good slut."[3] The deliberate abjection of her subjectivity (as a "slut") in the commodification of her body is exchanged for the appropriation of liberal economic citizenship. She comments, "And I realize that it's a very profitable way to make money."[4] Moreover, in deploying this strategic abjection, Raven is aware that her sexuality is racialized by the men, as she describes the bulk of her clients being Jewish and Japanese (the latter group surprises her, since she "never thought that Japanese men were attracted to black women"). Through her engagement in illicit sexual labor, Raven can be read as instrumentally using racialized bodily abjection to both disrupt and appropriate the cultural script of liberal economy. Her narrative of prostitution ruptures the proper capitalist rituals while also following their logic and trajectory in circuitous and roundabout ways to obtain desired economic ends. As Raven remarks, she did not get to finish college, although she was a major in "business administration" and is now "right in the business."

When the show's host jokingly comments, "But they didn't have this in mind, I'm sure," she responds, "I don't care . . . My body, my business."[5]

Notably, both Bread and Roses and The Skyy John Show harbor fragments that not only signal hidden linkages between abject subjects in discrepant locations, but also allow us to understand these contrasting relations as shifting and contingent rather than fixed and absolute. In the former, as noted earlier, the apparent contrast between Maya and Rosa parallels the distinction migrant domestic workers in real life sometimes draw between themselves and migrant women who engage in prostitution, articulating a discursive boundary that sets themselves up as "normal" and "deserving" citizen-workers and abjectifies migrant prostitutes as "illicit" and "improper" others (Chin 1998, 161). However, in the final scene, when Maya is deported for an act of robbery (committed to help a friend in financial need), and Rosa is seen sorrowfully running after her bus and waving goodbye to her, the film shifts and upends these two migrant subjects' relations to liberal citizenship. Maya is now the more abjectified (as both an "illegal immigrant" and a "criminal") being sent back to Mexico, while Rosa, with her "normalized" earnings, stable home, and nuclear family, gets to stay in the host country to continue chasing the American dream.

In The Skyy John Show, Raven also suggests a hierarchical dynamic internal to the sex industry that signals the reproduction of normality and abjection among sex workers. On the one hand, she criticizes how many escort agencies will not take black girls because they are not booked as often and will not make a lot of money, thus underlining a critical understanding that black escorts are situated in more abject positions in relation to white escorts. On the other hand, she also puts her occupation as an indoor worker in a more normalized position by abjectifying sex workers who work the streets, agreeing with some male clients' reviews of street sex workers on a website that "there is a lack of hygiene there; the women stank."[6] Like domestic workers, then, sex workers like Raven are similarly implicated in reinscribing a liberal structural order that continually reproduces contingent relations between normality and abjection both among themselves and toward other abject subjects.

While these complicit reproductions of inequality and shifting relations to abjection may seem utterly confining, they also suggest that the cultural script of liberal economic citizenship is not totally fixed but contains gaps that allow it to be reshaped, harboring the possibility for global sex workers to redirect their abjection through strategic disruption and appropriation.

These contingent relations may well constitute and embody the dynamic openings of social change.

The discussion above foreshadows the discussion in this chapter. Focusing on female sex work to narrow the scope of my argument, I wish to illustrate instances in which global sex workers reconfigure the metaphoric relations between bread (practicality, survival) and roses (democracy, equality, justice) by using practical means to generate openings of social transformation in the neoliberal context. Female prostitution conjures up the popular degraded image of contamination of body and soul—a body devoured by misogynist lust and a soul saturated in objectifying instrumentality. It is tempting, in the name of humanism and social justice, to seek to eliminate and transcend such inhumane abjection and to lift the "fallen" subject above the depths of contamination. Applying the examples of Rosa and Raven, however, addresses the sphere of social change: in the unending capitalist lifecycle, the contaminated field of prostitution may constitute a critical site for abject subjects to audaciously improvise more inhabitable spaces via the hegemonic script of liberal economic citizenship. Specifically, if what is transacted in sex work is the "contamination" of women's sexuality, then this abjection can be calculatingly offered and exchanged for sex workers to gain limited degrees of "purity"—for example, by improvising spaces of financial independence, economic inclusion, and dignified (entrepreneur or consumer) subjectivity.

When considering strategies to achieve gender and economic equality, it is crucial to consider what kind of strategies may expand appropriable, livable spaces for those female subjects remaindered by the liberal economic script and which approaches may tear down those spaces and solidify the script, deepening their abjection. If sex workers can enact themselves politically in animated ways and thus insert themselves into liberal economic life, upsetting the given abjectifying relations inscribed by the script, then social justice advocates in this arena may take their lead in innovatively generating more expansive spaces of economic citizenship for women in global sex commerce.

As Philippa Levine argues, prostitution is relegated to the zone of the abject, as it has always been seen as "work's mirror image, profit without honor" (2003, 191). And as Foucault further articulates, the bourgeois detachment of work from "illicit" sexuality is not only a question of moral values and ethics but is rooted in economics, for capitalism requires "proper" sexual arrangements as an integral part of its productive regeneration (Foucault 1978). The expected sexual propriety and repression of capitalist labor are intimately tied to the biopolitical mode of production itself (Evans 1993, 15–16). Improper sexual exchange in the form of prostitution, which interferes with the biopolitical reproduction of capitalist life, is relegated to the edges of liberal social life and slated for the exceptional powers of state criminalization and regulation. It is not considered a fully legitimate means to acquire an integral economic embodiment. At the same time, prostitution is not simply remaindered but functions as a "constitutive outside" to the normal. Specifically, it provides a sexual "outlet" for those male subjects who cannot or choose not to constrain their "excessive" sexuality within the capitalist confinement of heteronormative monogamy to fulfill their sexual desire in the shadow of the normal. A contributing factor exists in that men are less compelled by patriarchal ideology than women to restrain their sexuality.

As I argue in this chapter, however, prostitutes do not stay in a fixed state of abjection in relation to the normal. In fact, many female subjects who participate in the sex industry can be understood as purposefully and creatively reclaiming prostitution as an agentic instrument. This disruption is instigated by their deployment of ingenious agency as they strategically inhabit and embody abjection in order to reinsert themselves into normality in capitalist life. I use the narrative frame of *calculated abjection* to describe the ways in which sex workers deliberately and intentionally subject themselves to sexual abjection and dishonor in exchange for economic benefits while appropriating more livable and inhabitable spaces. In this context, what distinguishes global sex work is its mimicking of the globalized liberal script in reducing citizenship to the bottom line or moneymaking activity, though with a deviance: through the explicitly objectified and commodified use of one's private body parts and sexual organs (i.e., calculated abjection) in the public sphere of work. As such, sex work can be understood as simultaneously disrupting and appropriating liberal hegemony by subverting and redrawing "the link between profit and social approbation" (Levine, 184). It embodies "the paradox of using stigmatized work to realize social advancement" and, as such, is an inventive and scheming venture, turning sexual abjection into "a calculated maneuver to fulfill economic ambitions" (Katsulis 2008, 58). This very ploy to use abjection to lift oneself out of abjection describes the political *ingenuity* of global sex work.

One question arises here: considering that prostitution has existed since ancient human history, what is original and inventive about its contemporary enactment? Indeed, prostitution has served different purposes at different points and contexts in human history, showing its elasticity as an agentic instrument that can be adapted for varying objectives. For instance, Shannon Bell has traced the meanings of the prostitute body in ancient Greece as sexual, sacred, and healing through sophist *hetairae*, Diotima, and Aspasia, who occupy central roles in informing the texts of Socrates, Plato, and Pericles and who destabilize the Western philosophical foundation from within. She further elucidates how the postmodern erotic and political performance by North American sex worker artists engenders the dynamic of sacred carnival to unsettle modern and feminist preconceptions of the prostitute body, simultaneously dissolving and unifying the dichotomies of "whore and madonna," "feminist and slut," "good girl and bad girl," "sacred and profane," and "abuse and empowerment" (Bell 1994).

In her study of Caribbean prostitution, Kamala Kempadoo further traces the political agency of prostitutes to the historical antislavery resistance against European colonization of the sixteenth century and later (Kempadoo 1999). As Kempadoo points out, sexual alliances were craftily used by slave women to achieve emancipation and freedom from oppression. They exploited the colonial masters' exotic fantasies and sexual demands in exchange for money "to purchase their own or their children's freedom, or . . . in exchange for manumission" (8). As she writes, some "'exchanged sexual favors [with soldiers] for bullets and gunpowder' . . . to support slave revolts, to break the crushing bonds of slavery for both women and men" (8). Thus, in the colonial context, "Caribbean prostitution [is] not only . . . a form of masculine oppression and exploitation or . . . a survival strategy in time of economic hardship but also . . . a strategy of resistance to racialized relations of power and dominance" (9).

Taking cues from these works, I wish to stress in the current investigation the creative ways in which global prostitution is being adapted by abject subjects to renegotiate and redirect their abjection vis-à-vis the economic script of liberal citizenship, which continually adjusts itself in accordance with new social alignments and biopolitical calculations. In other words, abject subjects are dealing with a constantly shifting social environment, since the liberal economic script does not remain entirely stable but undergoes changing configurations, creating differential opportunities and constraints for them. The most prominent (and infamous) adjustment in the economic script is the neoliberal turn since the 1970s, which intensively disseminates market logic to all social institutional domains, encompassing both state and civil society (Brown 2005; Somers 2008). The preeminence of market logic hitherto frames the ideal citizen as a self-managing entrepreneur, a "flexible homo economicus" (Ong 2003, 9). In doing so, the script thus reconfigures and complicates relations of normality and abjection. For instance, an abject subject who undertakes entrepreneurial dispositions may become relatively "normalized" through her endeavor, while others who are incapable of adopting entrepreneurial subjectivity may be remaindered and excluded even further.

I call these shifting and fluid relations around the centrality of the market logic *neoliberal abjection*, which imposes new constraints and opens new possibilities for differently situated citizen-subjects. As I will identify and analyze, global sex workers can be interpreted as having devised two "strategies of normalization" to tap into this shifting field of neoliberal abjection: (1) reinventing themselves as "subcultural entrepreneurs" by appropriating and reusing the neoliberal logic of market, entrepreneurialism, and consumerism to normalize and remake their livelihood; and (2) taking advantage of the migration channels opened up by neoliberal globalization to invest in multiple long-term relationships with foreign clients, whether to expand existing sources of earnings or to strategize heterosexual matrimony and stability.

Calculated abjection underlies such strategies of inclusion in liberal economic life. I should note that these are not the *only* strategies. They are, instead, two examples that I investigate and illustrate. In fact, these two strategies correspond to the different modes of ingenious agency signaled by the two characters introduced at the opening of this chapter: Raven, who remakes herself as a business entrepreneur, normalizing what she does with market language and capitalist contractual agreement, and Rosa, who migrates to do sex work, with her endeavors consummated in heterosexual marriage and a nuclear family that normalize her pursuit of the so-called American dream.

The purpose of investigating these strategies is not to laud their success—which is uncertain and, in fact, for some sex workers may prove elusive. Rather, what I wish to emphasize are the calculation and ingenuity that propel the emergence and eruption of these acts and practices even within sex workers' limiting conditions—and the lessons they signal for generating larger scales of social change in global sex commerce. I argue that calculated abjection imparts valuable lessons for sex work activism in our present neoliberal times. In fact, there is no such thing as "free" justice; rather, one has to offer something of instrumental value to *earn* it. What this implies is that social justice advocacy in this arena cannot simply hinge on a universal framework of human rights, but must instead deploy an instrumental exchange as the critical pivot in creatively and resourcefully expanding appropriable spaces of economic life for sex workers. In many instances, the official recognition of human rights will not be granted to global sex workers purely for humane reasons of justice and equality. As such, sex work activists need to take critical lessons from the instrumental abjection of sex work at the individual level in using sex workers' status as commodities, entrepreneurs, or consumers in their collective advocacy on behalf of their constituents—thus transforming the contestatory stance of sex workers' rights movements into a fluid constellation of *commodity activism*.

Before proceeding with my analysis, I wish to remark on my terminology. For the present discussion, I will use the terms "prostitution" and "sex work" interchangeably—the former as a specific form of commercial sex, and the latter as a broader category that encompasses a wider variety of bodily services, such as erotic dancing and hostess work at nightclubs. While prostitution will be the central reference of my analysis, I incorporate other types of sex work when relevant for discussion. Using both terms also helps acknowledge both the distinctiveness and the protean boundaries of different types of sex work.[7] In addition, while recent studies on sex work have provided commanding insights into both transgender and male prostitutes (Kulick 1998; Katsulis 2008), as indicated earlier, I will limit the following discussion to female subjects to narrow the political scope of my claims and avoid overgeneralization in my current investigation. Finally, I would like to point out that my discussion herein should not be taken to suggest that *all* sex workers are able to or choose to act in the way that I discuss or that these strategies of calculated abjection centrally define these sex workers' essential humanity. Instead, I am focusing on *specific* aspects of *some* sex workers' modes of negotiation within the sex trade as an illustration of their ingenious agency to study how the artful ways they enact themselves politically may point us toward innovative ways of staging transformative change in sex work.

Antitrafficking Assemblages: Reproducing the Liberal Economic Script amid the Neoliberal Abjection of Laboring Female Bodies

In *Migration, Agency and Citizenship in Sex Trafficking*, her critical ethnographic study of migrant sex workers in Italy, Rutvica Andrijasevic begins by telling the story of Liudmila, a woman from Moldova who agreed to a three-month contract with an agent to perform street prostitution in Italy (Andrijasevic 2010). In exchange, the agent would organize the travel to help her cross the border without documents. Two points are worth observing in this story. First, after a period of time working on the streets, Liudmila decided to quit sex work and stay in Italy. Since Italy provides residence permits for "victims of trafficking," the nongovernmental organizations (NGOs) that Liudmila consulted suggested she press charges against the agent to be eligible for the residence permit—even though she had been informed of what she would be doing before her travel. Second, sex work is only one of the numerous jobs Liudmila has held in her life trajectory: she worked first as a secretary at a supermarket in Moldova, then as a migrant street sex worker in Italy, and finally as bar staff at a pub. Liudmila saw the job at the pub "as a much better opportunity than working in a factory packing Easter baskets. . . . Alternatively, she could take up caring and cleaning for the elderly, but she was not fond of that idea and found that job too demanding and tiring" (Andrijasevic, xi).

These two observations in Liudmila's story complicate the narrative of "sex trafficking" that has become the hegemonic frame in approaching global prostitution. As Andrijasevic defines it, sex trafficking is "commonly understood as a process by means of which people are purposely recruited by use of force or deception for forced labor or exploitation in the sex sector" (1). The first observation about the "victims of trafficking" status indicates that both the Italian state and NGOs share a vested interest in depicting the migrant prostitute as a forced victim and signifying that only a victim is worthy of sovereign protection and entitlement to legal status. The trafficking paradigm assumes victimhood as the only venue for a migrant prostitute to be recognized as a normal subject worthy of humane treatment. Without absolving the third parties of responsibility, the fact that migrant women such as Liudmila take the advice to press charges against these parties even when they were not deceived underlines their action as, at least partly, a calculated ploy to attain residency.

The second observation on the range of options of work available to Liudmila points to migrant prostitution not as the most demoralizing work imaginable, but as merely one of the temporary stops in the working trajectory that enables her livelihood. As a migrant woman from an Eastern European, non–European Union state, she faces not an exceptional sexual abjection in trafficking but normative labor abjection in global capitalism. By placing emphasis on forced victimhood in global prostitution, the mainstream discourse of sex trafficking takes focus away from the core abjections of liberal economic life, which already use subordinate female bodies for exploitation according to their racialized, classed, gendered, and sexualized labor values throughout the commercial exchange of global capitalism.

As I argue here, to the extent that the United States at the turn of the twenty-first century becomes progressively involved in combating terrorism and human trafficking as the "two greatest threats to democracy" (Parreñas 2008, 135), the discursive regime of sex trafficking it has spawned globally should be seen as not merely a moral, anticrime, or human rights stance. Instead, this treatment should be viewed as an essential measure of its bio-political effort to sustain and reproduce capitalist democracy predicated on a proper heteronormative and homonormative gender/sexual order that remainders prostitution to the edges of scripted economic citizenship. In *Terrorist Assemblages*, Jasbir Puar has traced how the allying biopolitical forces of neoliberalism, Western sexual exceptionalism, and the global ascendancy of whiteness enfold mainstream queer subjects into liberal life in the U.S. war on terror (Puar 2007). Similarly, I will trace the biopolitical formation of "antitrafficking assemblages," which build a complicit alliance of differently ideologically positioned social actors and forces in seeking the elimination of prostitution to reproduce the cultural-material script of liberal economic citizenship. In this light, the U.S. passage of the Victims of Trafficking and Violence Protection Act of 2000 and the subsequent President's Emergency Plan for AIDS Relief of 2003, which together initiated the U.S. global war on trafficking, should be read not merely as reflecting a conservative culture of "benevolent paternalism" (Parreñas 2008, 135), but also as mirroring a larger biopolitical context of neoliberal governmentality that has fueled the gentri-fication of urban social life in the global North in recent decades. What is sig-nificant about this U.S. antitrafficking alliance, then, is its reinforcement of the liberal economic citizenship script, which re-engenders and intensifies the distinction between the *normal* (civil and law-abiding workers and entre-preneurs) and the *abject* (subjects engaging in the "immoral" and "illicit" sex trade). Because such assemblages have not made sex work disappear but, rather, have driven it into clandestine indoor venues and online commercial sex markets (Bernstein 2007), what results is not the elimination of sexual abjection but a fluid and protean formation of neoliberal abjection.

In her study on the commercial sex scenes in three global cities—San Francisco, Stockholm, and Amsterdam—Elizabeth Bernstein situates a con-temporary shifting coordination of prostitution within a broader trend of postindustrial economic and cultural transformations. As she observes, in postindustrial cities across North America and Western Europe, one witnesses how "municipal politicians strategize about the best means to eliminate the eyesore of street prostitution while encouraging the development of corporate 'gentleman's clubs'" (Bernstein 2007, 7). Using the Tenderloin district in San Francisco as an example, Bernstein points to the transformation of the neighborhood in the 1990s, as small-scale erotic massage parlors were shut down or targeted for closure while "large scale, commercialized sexual services and individually run, off-street operations in the city's residential periphery [exploded and] drew relatively little attention from the police" (31). This dwindling of street prostitution and booming of the corporate sex industry, she argues, needs to be understood in relation to "shifting patterns of urban geography" in the neoliberal postindustrial economy, in particular the development trend toward gentrification (26).

If under liberalism the three central spheres of state, civil society, and market maintain their relative boundaries and distinctions, under neoliberalism, such boundaries and distinctions have become increasingly porous and blurred. Drawing on Foucault's notion of governmentality, Wendy Brown has argued that what is particularly "new" about neoliberalism is that it progressively formulates itself as not merely a capitalist economic logic but a political rationality, a mode of governance that involves "*extending and disseminating market values to all institutions and social action*" (2005, 40; emphasis in original). The market not only occupies a distinctive institutional sphere but becomes the organizing and regulating principle of state and civil society, as "all dimensions of human life are cast in terms of a market rationality" (40). This neoliberal political rationality is what drives the urban gentrification process that enjoins state, market, and civil society forces in transforming physically deteriorated urban neighborhoods into booming business districts with high real estate values while displacing working-class minority inhabitants, older and smaller shops, and other "disorderly" elements (i.e., homeless people, drug addicts, prostitutes) that form a remaindered bloc of alterity to the neoliberal alliance of prosperity.

In San Francisco's Tenderloin district, the municipal government gathered force in the 1990s with "quality of life" campaigns organized by middle-class neighborhood residents and business owners to drive prostitution away from bourgeois-street visibility (Bernstein, 61). In 1992, the police again made a rigorous effort to get rid of the street industry, especially after the corporate implementation of "Project Hollywood." They did so out of a "growing *structural* imperative to intervene in the women's lives, an imperative derived from the more general restructuring of the welfare state away from social services and toward heightened police control and surveillance" (65; emphasis in original). The heightened policing was enforced as a governing technology to preserve, enhance, and reproduce the neoliberal way of life. Bernstein quotes Michael, a small business owner from the neighborhood group Save Our Streets, as saying, "We're upset not because it's illegal or immoral, but because it disturbs our lives" (37). Even if Michael and other business operators personally do not have a problem with prostitution per se, the phrase "it disturbs our lives" underlines an implicit economic logic: a fear of visible commercial sex acts upsetting bourgeois hetero-family norms and alienating customers, thereby bringing down business profits and property values. In the collusion between the municipal government and the residential and business "quality of life" campaign, it is *life*—the liberal economic lifecycle—that is seen as threatened and disrupted by the visible blight of the "dishonorable" and "contaminated" sexual moneymaking activity of prostitution.

What is perhaps the most explicit illustration and intriguing development in the neoliberal ascendancy of urban gentrification is the entanglement of queerness in the biopolitical promotion of quality of life. Dereka Rushbrook, for instance, argues that global entrepreneurial cities have now increasingly marketed normative "queer space" as a marker of ethnic and sexual diversity and tolerance, which comes to stand in as perceived quality of life by businesses, residents, and tourists. As gay neighborhoods experience private growth and gentrification, they are in turn "appropriated by the state" through governmental promotion of the global cities as being gay-friendly and "queer-lite" in hopes of attracting upscale tourists and visitors (both homosexual and heterosexual), and revenues and capital (Rushbrook 2002, 187). Rushbrook notes that the "gay index," which reflects "concentration of unmarried same-sex partners living in metropolitan areas" is now found to be "the best predictor of the presence of high-tech businesses in U.S. cities" (189). The process of "glocalization" reimages local gentrified queer sites in merging them seamlessly with global high-tech, financial, and service industries (187), thus folding commodifiable queerness into the profitable cycle of neoliberal citizenship.

Woven into liberal domesticity, consumption, and property making, white bourgeois queerness has in fact evolved into a vanguard in preserving this cultural-material script, which gives life to its normative reproduction against other encroaching deviants, such as street prostitutes, who would unsettle the lucrative liberal order. Becki Ross's discussion of the "antihooker" campaign in Vancouver's West End neighborhood from 1975 to 1985 provides just such an illustration. Responding to the increasingly visible presence of the street sex trade, the community organization Concerned Residents of the West End (CROWE), composed of gay men and white middle-class residents and business owners, took to the streets under the leadership of a gay man named Phil Gordon to crack down on "sex deviance" (Ross 2010, 250). Portraying street prostitution as a "blight on urban life" and "intent on transforming the port town into a 'world-class city,'" CROWE worked with "Vancouver's city politicians, provincial legislators, residents' groups, business owners, realtors, and police force . . . [in forming] a powerful network with a single-minded mandate to criminalize prostitution and purge prostitutes from the West End" (251). As Ross articulates, the urban alliance to clean up street prostitution in 1980s neoliberal Vancouver was about "consolidating bourgeois whiteness through coercive boundary control and the assertion of respectability" (257). The contentious queer desire to eliminate street prostitution to allow for an unfettered enactment of citizens' right to property "unencumbered by . . . the 'depressed values' of a 'de facto red light district'" (258) reflects a biopolitical investment in the reproduction of liberal economic citizenship.

Neoliberal governmentality in urban gentrification brings about a significant political realignment that absorbs queerness into a campaign to foster and reproduce the liberal economic script. It simultaneously anchors feminist antiprostitution activists as complicit subjects in reifying the abjection of prostitution to legitimize the normative cycle of honest, law-abiding commercial production and consumption. As Bernstein points out, sovereign intervention in prostitution in Western Europe and the United States has increasingly sought to criminalize sexual demand by penalizing not only prostitutes but also their customers (115). The creation of "John Schools" as diversion and reeducation programs for clients who solicit prostitutes has emerged as a neoliberal disciplinary technology to clean up the streets. While painting the johns as "aggressors against family, community, and . . . business" (136), the program is geared toward a small subgroup of clients—heterosexual men of color from less affluent and nonprofessional backgrounds who shop the streets, where women tend to charge lower fees for sexual services than do indoor sex workers (135).[8] In contrast, johns who are white and relatively wealthy and who purchase sex indoors or online are generally left alone (135).

In fact, the institutional personnel who staff John Schools—from the director, district attorney, neighborhood residents and shopkeepers, and media representatives who report on the spectacle to the licensed marriage and family counselor—are solidly white, middle-class professionals. Bernstein writes, "'John Schools' are the outcome of an alliance between feminist antiprostitution activists, organized groups of predominantly middle-class community residents and shopkeepers . . ., and politicians and big businesses with interests in gentrifying neighborhoods such as San Francisco's Tenderloin and Mission districts. Although the three groups indicated have disparate ideological and material agendas, as part of their agenda to eliminate street prostitution as a whole, they have joined forces to target the male patrons of prostitution's most public domain" (140). The participation of antiprostitution feminists in an institutional establishment that features bourgeois "pro-family" and "pro-business" actors in "educating" the racialized other on civilized sexual propriety accentuates a political bloc formed to preserve the white/Western liberal order.

In addition to these local urban programs, feminist NGOs such as the Coalition Against Trafficking in Women and the National Organization for Women have similarly "campaigned for federal legislation to penalize prostitutes' customers" (Bernstein, 183). Just like urban renewal alliances that bond myriad ideological forces and material interests to weed out street prostitution, these NGOs "have . . . been joined in their efforts by right-wing and religious activists from Concerned Women for America, the National Association of Evangelicals, and the Southern Baptist Convention" (183). Bernstein continues, "Male demand for sexual services has been identified by a broad-based coalition of social actors as the principal engine behind the 'traffic in women,' culminating in the criminalization of 'prostitute use' by the U.S. military, the foregrounding of demand at the Beijing+10 meetings of the United Nations Commission on the Status of Women, and the incorporation of a program to reduce demand for commercial sex acts as a core element of the Trafficking Victims' Protection Reauthorization Act passed by the U.S. Congress" (183).

Indeed, the endorsers of the Victims of Trafficking and Violence Protection Act are similarly composed, including "the women's organization Equality NOW, the conservative women's groups Beverly LeHaye Institute and Concerned Women for America, the conservative group Family Research Council, and the Religious Action Center of Reformed Judaism and the National Association of Evangelicals" (Parreñas 2008, 135). Here, one must wonder what kind of citizenship is being reproduced by this messy assemblage of antitrafficking forces as it focuses on the most "visible" abjection of women's bodily labor—prostitution rather than, say, domestic work, garment sweat-shop, or electronic assembly—while criminalizing a specific area of male demand among working-class people of color.

This collusion among the neoliberal state, corporate business, religious conservatives, and antiprostitution feminists can further be read in light of the proliferation and normalization of the sex trade in indoor corporate establishments and online commerce, which pump voluminous profits into the capitalist engine *behind* the visible campaign of the war on trafficking. It should first be denoted that, while designed to combat trafficking and forced sex acts, both the Victims of Trafficking and Violence Protection Act and the President's Emergency Plan for AIDS Relief also target voluntary prostitution. Congressman Christopher Smith, one of the authors of the Victims of Trafficking and Violence Protection Act, has stated that it "emphatically rejects the principle that commercial sex should be regarded as a legitimate form of 'work'" (Parreñas 2008, 163). The objective of the law is thus "the elimination of international sex trafficking and domestic prostitution, both broadly defined to include consensual adult sex work" (Bernstein 2007, 238n51). The President's Emergency Plan for AIDS Relief, launched by President George W. Bush, also requires all NGOs that receive aid from the U.S. Agency for International Development for programs combating HIV/AIDS "to formally pledge their opposition to prostitution and trafficking into sex work." One restriction specifically "bars the use of federal monies toward activities that promote or support the legalization or practice of prostitution."[9] But even as the U.S. liberal antitrafficking paradigm opposes prostitution across the board, in actual practice it is selectively administered. In Bernstein's words, "Contemporary campaigns against prostitution are chiefly concerned with cleaning up the gritty underbelly of an industry that is in practice left alone so long as it remains behind closed doors. Attempts to eradicate the most 'problematic' segments of the industry implicitly serve to legitimize the *un-problematic* parts which remain" (140; emphasis in original).

In fact, while street prostitution composed predominantly of working-class women has been the principal target of policing and crackdowns, the adult sex industry as a whole has metamorphosed in recent decades into a privatized, indoor, and online commerce that is largely left alone by sovereign power and "subjectively normalized for sex workers and clients alike" (Bernstein, 7). Significantly, the burgeoning of sex commerce, which enacts its transactions in increasingly fluid and multifaceted forms, occupies a critical node in the global chain of liberal economy. Bernstein writes,

By all accounts, the sex industry has far exceeded its prior bounds to become a multifaceted, multibillion dollar industry, produced by and itself
producing developments in other sectors of the global economy, such as
hotel chains, tourism, long-distance telephone carriers, cable companies,
and information technology, and creating burgeoning profits for right-
and left-wing entrepreneurs alike. . . . What is new in the current economy is the scale of the profits being generated, the diversification of the
modes in which sexuality is transacted, and the increasingly businesslike
and even corporatized structure of many profiteers. (13–14)

While street prostitution is demonized, certain forms of sex commerce that
are "discreet" are accommodated and receive "almost no police intervention"
(Ross, 252–53). In postindustrial cities, one thus witnesses a broad pattern
of selective excision of prostitution: "the removal of economically disenfranchised and racially marginalized streetwalkers and their customers from gentrifying city centers; the de facto tolerance of a small tier of predominantly
white and relatively privileged indoor clients and workers; and the driving of
illegal migrant sex workers further underground" (Bernstein, 146).

In this light, not only does the U.S. antitrafficking campaign fail to eliminate the sexual abjection of prostitution, it should also be seen as emanating
from the same neoliberal trajectory of urban gentrification in removing the
most visible and shameful blight—street prostitution, trafficking, forced
sexual labor—from contaminating the normative reproduction of "honorable" liberal citizenship. What is at stake in antitrafficking and antiprostitution measures is thus not only a moral stance of benevolent paternalism
that stifles women's transgression and mobility (Levine 2003; Parreñas 2008),
but an inherent validation of the cultural-material order of the liberal citizenship lifecycle. As urban gentrification continues unabated, and feminist
antiprostitution organizations that seek the elimination of sexual abjection
never address the core abjections of capitalist life that that commodify female corporeality as a motor of capitalism's late-modern regeneration, what
is preserved is the cultural script of liberal economic citizenship.[10]

From the local urban redevelopment alliance to the U.S. war on trafficking, antitrafficking assemblages constitute a biopolitical machine to remove
visible "taint" (sexual abjection/dishonorable transaction) that disrupts the
cyclical democratic reproduction of liberal economic citizenship, while discreet indoor entrepreneurial sexual commerce that is attached profitably to
other neoliberal commercial sectors is sustained and expanded. Despite the

claim by feminist organizations that they oppose "a violation of human intimacy" in sexual trafficking (Bernstein, 181), antitrafficking assemblages that seek to eliminate the contamination of prostitution only collude in—rather than transcend—the neoliberal cycle that produces the commercial abjection of female laboring bodies as its constitutive embodiment.

But this analysis does not simply stop at underlining a grim conclusion of the cyclical reproduction of liberal economy and the abjection of women's labor. Rather, what is also central for us to take away from antitrafficking assemblages is that their concerted effort to end the sexual abjection of prostitution has transferred into a fluid and protean abjection in the realm of sex commerce that conforms to neoliberal logics. This neoliberal abjection reproduces relations of normality and abjection among sex workers in ways that are not fixed and absolute but shifting and contingent, and this realignment is especially oriented toward market logic in reallocating differential status, recognition, and privileges. And as I intimated at the beginning of this chapter, these shifting and contingent relations to normality and abjection may be reexamined as potentially generating and multiplying openings for sex workers to unsettle and reorient any such given relations.

To elaborate on my point here, as Aihwa Ong argues, neoliberalism is a malleable technology of governing that can be deployed to exclude *as well as* to include human subjects according to its market logic. Neoliberal governmentality not only "marks out excludable subjects who are denied protections," it may also morph into "a positive decision to include selected populations and spaces as targets of 'calculative choices and value-orientation'" (Ong 2006, 5). Building on this observation, contemporary sex workers are brought into the neoliberal realm of biopolitical calculations in discrepant ways, as some are "included" (normalized abjection) while others are "excluded" (further abjectified).

For instance, professionalized sex workers who have acquired the educational capital, entrepreneurial savvy, and technological know-how to move into corporate nightclubs, escort services, and online sex commerce can be understood as being incorporated into the normalized spectrum of neoliberal subjectivity. In contrast, others who rely on prostitution as a kind of "survival sex" on the street—petty sexual exchange for "small amounts of money, for drugs, or for a place to stay" (Bernstein, 45–46)—become a further abjectified population excluded from neoliberal logic. Neoliberalism thus abjectifies sex workers in different ways and to different degrees according to their respective market values, profitability, and orientation to the neoliberal logic.

Placing my earlier discussion about Raven, the black escort, in this larger context: her standing in a less privileged/normalized position to white escorts and in a more privileged/normalized position to street prostitutes and migrant brothel sex workers illustrates the complicit entanglement of these women within the webs of neoliberal abjection.

But if this contingent reproduction of inequality accentuates the seeming elasticity of neoliberal abjection in caricaturing the corporeal bodies of female sexual labor, such elasticity may also be seized by global sex workers to tap into this shifting field and remold existing abjectifying relations. In fact, by virtue of the verity that the liberal economic script sustains a domain of abjection as its constitutive outside, it is bound to be disrupted by abject subjects, who possess a crafty and audacious agency that flows in many directions, and that is unforeseen and cannot be captured by the enforcers and preservers of the script.

Calculated Abjection as Strategy of Normalization: Using Commercial Sex Acts to Appropriate Global Economic Citizenship

"If I leave, will you help me to find a job, a house, to get documents?" . . . "Why do you bother me if you know that there is nothing you can do." I also know what is good and what is bad but it is not the same thing to know and to be able to do what one wishes for.
—Kateryna, Eastern European migrant sex worker in Italy, describing her conversation with clients who have advised her to leave prostitution (quoted in Andrijasevic 2010, 88)

What you see is completely an act! The only reason that you think everything works so well between us is because I am pretending. And the only reason that I am willing to pretend is because you pay me.
—Rita, sex worker in Sweden, responding to clients who propose marriage to her (quoted in Bernstein 2007, 46)

Now I have become a bad girl [anyway], I want to make good money of it.
—Thai sex worker in Switzerland (quoted in Sereewat 1985, 18)

Progressive theorists from different critical trajectories have previously sought transcendence of the contaminated prostitute body (Pateman 1988; MacKinnon 1989; Dworkin 1997; Bishop and Robinson 1998). This body of literature offers insights into the latent gender and capitalist power structure, which systematizes men's dominance and women's subordination in prostitution but is often masked as neutral, normal, and standard. Advancing the view that in the realms of gender and sexuality, democratic social change necessitates a vision of the female body that rises above and is untainted by capitalist instrumental relations, these theorists argue that prostitution embodies women's degradation and commodified alienation that must be transcended through elimination.

Despite their contributions, the implicit ideological positioning and unquestioned assumption of monogamous heterosexuality as a more "civilized" gender relation than "barbaric" prostitution unwittingly colludes in reifying the heteronormative, monogamous foundations of liberal economic citizenship. In fact, considering the cultural-material effects of the antitrafficking assemblages mentioned earlier, it prompts caution about the ways in which the progressive attempt to transcend the "degraded" prostitute body through antiprostitution efforts may end up engendering neoliberal policies that deepen the economic, sexual, and racial abjection of women situated in relatively marginalized conditions. Moreover, this progressive account inherently assumes a normative vision of democratic agency that obstructs recognition of the artful and roundabout modes of resistance improvised by many prostitutes as they specifically reuse and appropriate capitalist instrumentality to generate change in liberal economic citizenship.

As noted earlier, I refer to this inventive agency as calculated abjection, a term that describes the myriad ways in which global sex workers instrumentally turn the racialized and sexualized abjection of their own bodies to politicized economic use. The narratives by the three sex workers quoted at the beginning of this section provide a general delineation of this circuitous political dynamic. The East European migrant sex worker Kateryna underscores the necessity of detouring away from doing "what is good" (i.e., "moral, virtuous") to doing "what is bad" (i.e., "immoral, tainted") to enable women like her to survive in the liberal economic lifecycle—"to find a job, a house, to get documents." In other words, abjection of oneself is deployed to gain normality. The Swedish sex worker Rita, describing prostitution as "completely an act," further articulates the calculated nature of constructing intimate pleasure in sex commerce. Her narrative also suggests that sex work must traffic in complicity with heteronormative masculinity ("willing to pretend"—sexual objectification) and capitalist logic ("because you pay me") to acquire economic inclusion for its performing subjects. Finally, the

Thai sex worker's narrative delineates a cyclical intertwinement of abjection ("I have become a bad girl") and calculation ("I want to make good money of it") in which abjection becomes a *calculation* and such calculation is abject in essence.

The calculated abjection performed by women with limited resources describes ingenious agency within liberal economic life conditions. As Saba Mahmood suggests, agency is not "a synonym for resistance to relations of domination, but . . . a capacity for action that historically specific relations of subordination enable and create" (2001, 203). Rather than waiting passively to remain abjected and excluded, here is an agency that informs and enables women to "enter the game" (rather than refusing or transcending the game; see Ang 1995, 67) "by using the very terms of one's subjection" (Shimizu 2007, 273).

Here, I discuss two such strategies women in global sex work have devised to disrupt and appropriate the economic script of liberal citizenship in order to regain entry into liberal normativity, engendering spaces of nonexistent citizenship via sex acts. My analysis draws on examples from three realms of sex work: domestic sex commerce (domestic-based sex workers engage in sexual exchange with domestic-based clients within national territorial boundaries), transnational sex tourism (domestic-based sex workers engage in sexual exchange with foreign tourists), and migrant sex work (women who migrate across borders to engage in sex work). Again, the point of my analysis is not to celebrate calculated abjection as a liberatory way to act, but rather to underscore these sex workers' ingenious agency as they appropriate and negotiate with the disseminated liberal economic script from their own situated contexts. I do not intend my discussion to be a generalization of what *all* female sex workers are doing across these three broad realms, or a statement that they deploy calculated abjection to equal effect or success regardless of their locations. In fact, the sex work industry is distinguished both by the diversity of its participants (e.g., races, classes, genders, sexual orientations, nationalities, physical appearance, geographic locations, cultural contexts, with or without dependents) and the hierarchy of its structure (e.g., escorts/ call girls, clubs/brothels, window prostitution, street work; Chapkis 1997). These different social locations all affect the varying degrees of autonomy and choice for women in prostitution and sex work and disrupt any homogeneous narrative of their enactment of ingenious agency. The improvisations of strategies are constrained, and sometimes enhanced, in different ways by sex workers' situated contexts.

To index a few examples of these discrepant contexts and locations (and their accompanied privileges and disadvantages) by focusing on the factor of racial difference, sex workers of color in North America need to deal with a pattern of issues that tend not to affect white sex workers: racist attitudes from customers and management, white customers who have sex with them but would not interact with them as peers, a higher likelihood of being arrested and jailed, pressure to fit into an industry dominated by idolized imagery of "blondes with big boobs," and lower wages than their white counterparts (Aarens et al. 1997, 197, 206–7; Chapkis 1997, 207–9). A similar racialized hierarchy exists within global sex commerce, where "color and 'race' define a woman's sexual capital" (Kempadoo 1998b, 131). As Kempadoo observes,

> The brown or black woman is regarded as a desirable, tantalizing, erotic subject, suitable for temporary or non-marital sexual intercourse—the ideal "outside" woman—and rarely seen as a candidate for a long-term commitment, an equal partner, or as a future mother. . . . White sex workers invariably work in safer, higher paid, and more comfortable environments; brown women—Mulatas, Asians, Latinas—form a middle class; and Black women are still conspicuously overrepresented in the poorest and most dangerous sectors of the trade, particularly street work. Whiteness continues to represent the hegemonic ideal of physical and sexual attractiveness and desirability, and white sexual labor is most valued within the global sex industry. (1998a, 10–11)

In Western metropolises, native white sex workers are more likely to establish a degree of "equality" with their clients by filling the role of "confidential partner with communication skills," while foreign, Third World women are primarily defined by their bodies and erotic services (Spanger 2002, 132). In the Caribbean, light-skinned mulatto (mixed African-European) women are more valued and privileged than women of Afro-Caribbean descent; Kempadoo, imitating Fanon, calls this phenomenon "Black Bodies, White Faces," because it synthesizes the racialized fantasy of "the promiscuous and physically desirable Black female body and 'delicate' facial features . . . of the White Euro-American woman" (1998b, 131).

Such structural differences, indexed by racial, colonial, class, and global disparity, thus need to be attended to when considering the political implications of calculated abjection as it manifests in polymorphous forms. However, while I provide an appropriate amount of information regarding contextual differences among subjects in their local conditions, my objective here is not to provide a detailed account of the local background of every case, given the unending spectrum of complexity involved. Rather, by articulating and illustrating these momentary and recurring eruptions of ingenious agency, I wish to emphasize how sex workers have deployed calculated abjection to enable change in their respective locations and, more important, how global sex workers' rights movements may precisely learn from such ingenious strategies of normalization.

Subcultural Entrepreneurs: Appropriating and Reusing the Neoliberal Script of the Market, Entrepreneurialism, and Consumerism

The first strategy of normalization finds sex workers refashioning themselves into "subcultural entrepreneurs" who appropriate and reuse the neoliberal script of the market, entrepreneurialism, and consumerism to legitimize their way of living and expand spaces of economic livelihood. The term "subcultural entrepreneurs" needs to be explicated, for I do not mean that all sex workers are in fact entrepreneurs. While some can be understood as such (e.g., independent call girls or escorts), others may not be (e.g., brothel workers). Rather, I use the term to designate instances in which sex workers can be interpreted as mimicking the entrepreneurial disposition lauded in the neoliberal script of citizenship to create spaces of economic inclusion in circuitous and stealthy ways that destabilize the normative expectations of the script.

As critical scholars have pointed out, in the process of neoliberalization, citizens' subjectivity has been intensively interiorized by the entrepreneurial disposition. Since the 1970s, Ong argues, "the norms of good citizenship in advanced liberal democracies have shifted from an emphasis on duties and obligations to the nation to a stress on becoming autonomous, responsible choice-making subjects who can serve the nation best by becoming 'entrepreneurs of the self'" (2003, 9). This "entrepreneur of the self," in Wendy Brown's words, "figures individuals as rational, calculating creatures whose moral autonomy is measured by their capacity for 'self care'—the ability to provide for their needs and service their own ambitions" (2005, 45). In other words, in the neoliberal context, whether or not we are actually business entrepreneurs, we as citizen-subjects are subjectivized, to different degrees, by the preeminent mode of neoliberal governmentality to govern our personal conduct and social life in accordance with rational entrepreneurial logic.

Without exception, the neoliberal expectation to enact an entrepreneurial disposition affects global sex commerce, as well. However, sex workers are not ordinary "entrepreneurs of the self," for they creatively reconstruct the neoliberal script in their own terms to circuitously reorient themselves to the logic of the market. Specifically, they use their explicitly objectified and commodified corporeal bodies in the public sphere of work to optimize their entrepreneurial skills and enhance their capacity for "self-care." In fact, given that their corporeal bodies are the immediate goods transacted, many sex workers are literally *entrepreneurs of the self*, as their bodies constitute the commodities and capital with which they operate.

In this sense, sex workers can be understood as subcultural entrepreneurs. Dick Hebdige's notion of "subcultures" as "cultures of conspicuous consumption" (1979, 103) is useful here. As Hebdige defines it, a subcultural style emerges when its participants consume, use, and remix an assemblage of existing cultural products and artifacts, turning them into bricolage. In the words of Dana Polan, "Culture can be empowering not only in its use value, but also its reuse" (1993, 39). It is by calculatingly turning bodily abjection into empowering entrepreneurial capital that women in global sex work can be interpreted as reusing the economic script of liberal citizenship to interrupt liberal normativity.

Bernstein's ethnographic research on sex workers in San Francisco helps demonstrate this in both streetwalking (working-class, controlled by pimps) and indoor sex commerce (middle-class, self-employed). Obviously, there is a disparity in these two locations, since streetwalkers come predominantly from lower socioeconomic backgrounds and are deprived of the dominant currency of social, economic, and cultural capital. Nonetheless, they "cultivate their bodies as value-producing instruments" and turn them into money-procuring capital (Bernstein, 42). This demonstration of bodily capital is an explicit instantiation of calculated abjection that uses women's objectification to negotiate economic livelihood in capitalist life. Streetwalkers do so by mimicking the capitalist work logic; some street sex workers note the importance of "having a regular work schedule," such as working an average of 5.2 days per week (Weinberg, Shaver, and Williams 1999, 511; Bernstein, 48).

This calculated abjection does not suggest selling a woman's whole body and spirit, but is strategically crafted. As Susan Edwards argues, prostitution does not result in a complete unveiling of the sex worker's interior self, but rather produces a "carefully circumscribed" transparency in the erotic performance (1993, 98). She writes: "Prostitute women care less about the genitals and breasts, and much more about the mouth, the lips, the kiss, and tenderness, for them the truest meaning and expression of intimacy" (98). Street workers simultaneously cross permissible boundaries by displaying their private body parts for public consumption *and* affirm the closure of such boundaries by refusing mouth-to-mouth kiss as "occupational strategies for enforcing the separation between public and private selves" (Bernstein, 49). Again, such strategies are not always successful; Bernstein describes a Swedish sex worker who expresses the difficulty of maintaining a strict public/private boundary when having sex with her husband (46). Practices by some women to adopt "working names" or put on "uniforms" can also be read as strategies for navigating the commercial necessity of being public with one's private parts while hiding one's "true self" (49). This resonates with the practices of some Afro-Caribbean migrant sex workers, who deliberately abjectify their bodies by imposing on themselves a racially exotic and misogynistic stereotype of "mulatto babe" or "chocolate brown," thus highlighting their sexuality to attract more clients while artfully hiding their "real identity behind the stereotype" (Spanger, 130–32).

Calculated abjection is also intensely taken up by indoor escort services, which are composed predominantly of self-employed middle-class women. Given their relatively privileged socioeconomic locations, they are able to capitalize prodigiously on their resources to renovate their economic spaces of inclusion and belonging. As Bernstein observes, postindustrial transformation brings about a recreational sexual ethic predicated on *bounded authenticity*, or "emotionally bounded erotic exchange" (6). In contrast to the impersonal and Taylorized "sexual release" of street prostitution, this new recreational sexual culture provides access to authentic personal erotic connection within a professionalized space demarcated by the rational basis of market exchange (127). It is also accentuated by its normalizing visibility in the proliferation of intimate services offered (e.g., local escorts, fetish specialists, erotic masseuses, tantra sexuality experts), as well as its accessibility through online commerce.

One of the most notable phenomena of indoor escorts is a type of service known as the "Girlfriend Experience," which allows clients to reserve and interact erotically with sex workers as lovers at a personal and intimate level. One ad, for instance, features a black woman named Ava, who describes herself in this way: "Sexy gray eyes, long brown curly hair, smooth chocolate skin, full luscious lips. Pretty face, curvy body with a dynamite personality to match . . . I offer a true girlfriend experience without the headache. My measurements are real and so am I. . . . Please reserve ahead. . . . *Check out my re-views on TheEroticReview!*" (Bernstein, 129). By strategically intertwining bodily objectification and racialized sexuality with the humanizing touch of being the client's "girlfriend," the ad blurs the boundary between abjection and normality, creating an interstitial space for the sex worker to be objectified while remaining human. In fact, by positioning Ava as a girlfriend available for rent, the ad stages her as an entrepreneurial *subject* who dictates and controls the kind and range of services offered and the monetary terms of this transactional abjection in ways that would be considered "normalizing" to her as the operator of her own business. While indoor sex workers cannot escape and must negotiate the instrumental objectification of their sexuality— as demonstrated by the "restaurant-style 'reviews' of their services" on client websites that evaluate their appearance and performance on a numeric rating scale (94, 221n36)—it is also their complicity in this instrumental objectification that allows them to refashion themselves as being "entrepreneurs of the self" in the neoliberal script.

Similarly, consider Elina Penttinen's study of Russian and Baltic migrant sex workers in Finland, where women perform the role of an objectified exotic "Eastern girl" to make their livelihood (2008, 87). As much as this position is a product of the Western imagination, Penttinen notes, it is "not only useful but a necessary condition for the subject" (88), for it "enables her to cross the border and 'have a job'" (87). Penttinen writes:

> The position of the Eastern girl can be characterized as that of an abject. . . .
> The abject does enable for the man to enact his subjectivity by being able
> to buy her time, body and services, but she also takes advantage of this
> performance of the erotic other. She instrumentalizes that position only
> to express that that is not what she is "really," she does not tell anything
> of herself, she only expresses out loud those things that he wants to hear
> and what is expected from her as the erotic other. From this performance
> she can make her business. (xv)

While the commercial transaction of ethnicized sexuality seems to reduce human corporeality to objectified and priced body parts, such abject objectification has also been slyly reused by these East European migrant sex workers as they refashion neoliberal entrepreneurial subjectivity by "adopting the principles of efficiency and maximization of profits" (Penttinen, 70), ultimately negotiating an emergent space of dignity that transiently humanizes their corporeal being. As an illustration, Penttinen recounts a meeting with migrant prostitutes at a sex bar during her fieldwork: the women identify themselves as "businesswomen," and when they learn that her male research assistant is not there to buy any service, "they excuse themselves saying, they have a business to run" (78). In another scene, she describes the transaction between a woman and potential client: "She takes out her notepad and writes numbers on the paper. He nods, or shakes his head, and she continues. They arrive at an agreement and she smiles confirmingly almost like a car sales- man, smiling in a way that says, 'It is expensive but I assure you, you made a very good choice'" (86). These migrant sex workers have learned to incor- porate the neoliberal market logic of "maximum profit for minimum time" into their work ritual (88). While this incorporation is an abject mimicking, since "it represents forms of self-discipline and subjection to the dominat- ing discourses of the market" in offering the commercial use/service of their body (88), it nonetheless positions migrant sex workers as negotiating busi- nesswomen who can be read as reusing the scripts of the market and entre- preneurialism to their benefit.

Being subcultural entrepreneurs also sometimes involves making invest- ments in the refashioning of capital and commodity—that is, the racialized/ sexed body—through the purposeful use of neoliberal consumerism. Lisa Law's critical ethnography of transnational sex tourism in Cebu in the Philip- pines illustrates these instances (Law 2000). Problematizing predominant interpretations that view the neocolonial economy of sex tourism through a singular lens of domination, Law describes local bars where Filipina erotic dancers and prostitutes meet white, Western men in racialized and sexual- ized encounters as a "third space," an ambivalent space of negotiation. In such space, "a 'submissive' Filipina may be striving for self-actualization," and "a 'voyeuristic' Western customer may be humbled by an awareness that his masculinity is yoked to his pocket book" (Law, 48). What I want to emphasize here is not that such disruption of the Western voyeuristic gaze is sufficiently empowering. Instead, I want to emphasize the ways in which these women can be understood as artfully staging a calculating, entrepre- neurial subjectivity that disrupts colonial normativity while creating spaces of economic inclusion.

Law points out that "dancers in Cebu are aware of, and perform, their status as objects (of Western desire) and subjects (immoral Filipinas)" (60). In the case of a dancer, Cora, who underwent breast implants, Law notes that this is "one example of how the bodies of Filipina bar women . . . become marked through the selective incorporation of features of an imagined Western sexuality" (51). She argues, "These practices [plastic surgery, cosmetics, weight-loss pills] are often interpreted by middle-class Filipinos as a purely Western influence—large breasts and skinny bodies are not highly valued in the Philippines . . . but they could also be read as the psychological dynamics of resistance which allow women to retain control of their bodies" (51). In fact, while these dancers' employment in the sex industry necessitates their "becoming modern," their dancing styles and entertaining costumes remain distinctively Filipino. Law writes, "It is precisely this hybridity—exotic otherness and a sexualized modernity—that male customers are often attracted to" (51–52). The everyday acts and practices by the Filipina dancers are not directed at transcending the white/"other" divide; rather, they are dipped in what Ien Ang calls the "structural inevitability" of complicity in European capitalist modernity (1995, 66)—and they instrumentalize this complicity to optimize their financial well-being. This willful immersion in the Western masculine imagination of the racialized-sexualized "other" should be seen, again, as calculated abjection, a strategic negotiation with the dominant colonial imagery of sexuality to expand spaces of economic livelihood in globalized liberal citizenship.

One may understand these neoliberal consumerist practices of female bodily reconstructions as being another resource incorporated by sex workers into their medley of subcultural entrepreneurship. They refashion their body image in accordance with dominant cultural aesthetics as a calculated maneuver, using racialized objectification to "hook" clients and increase earnings. Such neoliberal consumerist practices are intimately connected to the larger scheme of procuring earnings to provide "basic needs for themselves and their children, . . . to send their family to college, to invest in small business ventures, to save money toward home ownership, or to acquire luxury goods and social status" (Katsulis, 39). While this demonstrates the power of neoliberal citizenship to subsume the abject zone of global sex commerce to its logic of rationality, it simultaneously demonstrates its incessant appropriation by sex workers in different locations to ameliorate their abjection and increase their economic normality.

Plotting (Western) Heteronormative Romance: Capitalizing on Neoliberal Migration Channels in Long-Term Relationships with Clients

In addition to refashioning themselves as subcultural entrepreneurs by normalizing their "deviant" and "dishonorable" work through market language, monetary contractual agreements, and investments in feminine consumerism, many sex workers devise a second strategy: capitalizing on the migration channels opened by neoliberal globalization to invest in long-term relationships with foreign clients. This strategy is exercised in the courses of transnational sex tourism and migrant sex work when women exploit white/colonial fantasy and heteronormative romance to either generate multiple sources of income or plan a strategy of monogamous conjugal-economic stability.

Hence, as documented in Law's study, calculated abjection can extend to acts of non-use of condoms by some Filipina bar women when they have sex with foreign customers, strategically planning on having a baby to solidify a long-term relationship with them (Law, 53–55). The avoidance of condoms in prostitution is often seen as a demand made by male clients vis-à-vis sex workers in vulnerable positions (such as undocumented migrant street prostitutes) who are unable to negotiate safe sex, thereby intensifying women's abjection. However, Law places this issue in the transnational sex tourist context of Cebu, indicating that such a practice does not necessarily equate to disempowerment in sex work but is deliberately calculated by the bar dancers in this instance. She writes, "It has more to do with Filipino conceptions *of bahala na*—. . . 'risk-taking in the face of the proverbial cloud of uncertainty and the possibility of failure.' . . . Many women employed in these establishments are looking for a future husband, and the use of condoms in these instances—that is, with a prospective husband—is seen to impede the achievement of intimacy, and ultimately, an opportunity to exit the industry" (53).

Here, what appears to be an abject practice in prostitution is calculatingly reused and appropriated by the Filipina bar dancers to fit their specific circumstances. In fact, sexual abjection, romantic dreams, and economic desires are intricately intertwined in this case, culminating in the yearning for heterosexual matrimony as the basis of long-term conjugal-economic stability. As Celine Parreñas Shimizu argues, to deny these complex desires of prostitutes is to "totalize them into a victim identity without the contradiction of projecting fantasy on the johns as the johns project fantasy upon them" (2007, 221). While this illustrates ideological complicity in the heteronormative foundation of the capitalist lifecycle, one may nonetheless read such acts and practices from the positions of Filipina sex workers as redeploying their corporeal abjection in an unequal global economy.

As Denise Brennan's study on Caribbean sex tourism in Sosúa in the Dominican Republic also illustrates, while European sex tourists may see Dominican sex workers as sexual commodities for erotic pleasure, Dominican sex workers see these clients as "potential dupes, walking visas, means by which the women might leave the island, and poverty, behind" (2002, 156). They "feign love" in establishing long-term transnational relationships with the sex tourists and invest in the possibility of economic success, romance, visas, and eventual settlement in Europe (159). Brennan asserts that women in Sosúa choose sex work not simply as a "survival strategy" that solves short-term economic problems, but also as a "strategy of advancement" that will change their lives in the long term (1999, 17). Even when such romantic dreams fail to materialize or come with unhappy endings, these women's designing acts can nonetheless be read as an attempt "to take advantage of the global linkages that exploit them" (18).

The attempt to appropriate economic inclusion through calculated romance in sex tourism is also demonstrated in the transnational correspondence between local sex workers and their foreign clients. In a study of the personal letters exchanged between Thai girls engaging in tourist-oriented prostitution and their *farang* (foreign tourist) boyfriends, Erik Cohen shows that, while sex tourism may involve sexual exploitation of local women, once the Western tourists leave, the Thai sex workers are particularly adroit at manipulating absent clients who desire to extend their liaison beyond their departure "and may be in a position of dominance in the 'relationship-at-a-distance'" (1986, 115). As Cohen explains, in spite of facing the dilemma between believing a girl's genuine attraction to him and doubting her sincerity and seriousness, the farang is eager to continue the relationship by correspondence after his sojourn in Thailand draws to an end. For him, the "relationship grows in importance and intensity *after* the separation" (119; emphasis in original). And the Thai girl, "even if she is not genuinely attracted to the *farang*, usually consents to extend their relationship by correspondence. To have a remote *farang* boy-friend is a source of potential financial and emotional support, and offers a possible counter-balance to the uncertainties and fortuitousness of her daily existence. Indeed older girls often purposely nurse a series of such liaisons with different men, and then derive their main support from remittances, rather than from regular work in prostitution" (116).

Limited in their English proficiency, the Thai prostitutes hire "scribes" to serve as language brokers and translators in composing letters for them. Compared with the intense yearning and emotional tone in the farangs' letters, the girls' responses, except in rare cases when they take the relationships seriously, usually follow a standard format:

> Thus, one girl who maintains a wide correspondence with several men was observed giving brief instructions to a scribe, adding: "Put on a lot of sugar, he likes sweet." . . . The more experienced scribes develop with time a standard scheme for letters, to whomever they may be addressed, in which the following topics are touched upon: a polite inquiry about the boy-friend's health, some details about the girl, her children or parents, a declaration of love and continued faithfulness, a report on her current (mostly financial) problems, an overt or covert supplication for support, and the expression of the hope for a reunion. Consequently the girls' letters, supposedly a most personal and intimate form of communication, tend in fact to become routinized and very much like one another. But while a girl may keep in touch with several *farangs*, the *farang* typically corresponds with only one girl, and is not in a position to notice the standard character of the letters he receives. (Cohen, 119)

In this snapshot, the fantasy for a stable, long-term relationship with his beloved exotic girlfriend in the "Orient" of a well-to-do but remote Western man is appropriated by the Thai prostitute to devise and expand material spaces of economic livelihood.

Using personal correspondence to procure financial support has not faded with the passing of time; it has taken on new forms in our contemporary information age—via the Internet and email—and is replicated in many sex-tourism sites. Kimberly Kay Hoang notes that sex workers in Vietnam engage in an "expressive emotional labor," by which they emphasize their condition as victimized and poor and "use their emotions as a form of currency, to induce feelings of sympathy and love through a series of lies designed to sustain and advance their standard of living" (2010, 166). She brings up the case of Hanh, a bar woman who is married to William, an American man and former client who regularly communicated with her online and sent her money. They married when he returned to Vietnam and had a baby girl together. However, Hanh continues to work in the sex industry, not only to support her ex-husband and their children, but also as a backup plan in case her relocation to the United States with William does not materialize. Hanh later engaged in a commercial sexual liaison with an Australian man, Matthew, with whom she also maintained ties through email after he returned to his home country. Hoang observes, "Hanh developed multiple scenarios of crisis, including stories of her having heart problems, the desire to open her own clothing shop, debts she owed to the Mafia, and an alleged ailing child. Matthew sent her nearly $2,000 over the course of one month to help her with these crisis situations. Women like Hanh are able to capitalize on the location of the country as poor and Third World in the global order to create an imaginative fantasy, making their clients feel like heroic saviors to their poverty" (174).

Here, sex workers in Vietnam again participate in, appeal to, and use colonial imagery—not strictly of the exotic sexualized racial woman, but also of the victimized Third World woman—to evoke love, sympathy, and savior-like masculinity from their Western clients "to obtain multiple remittances, advance their standard of living, and migrate abroad" (Hoang, 175). Such sex work practices at once recapitulate the white/Western structure of global capitalism *and* disrupt and reconfigure the embedded power relations between Western clients and non-Western sex workers relative to the global distribution of rights, inclusion, and belonging.

Andrijasevic's research on Eastern European migrant sex workers in Italy also shows how the "victim" position is purposefully plotted by some women vis-à-vis other men as a strategy of normalization (Andrijasevic 2010). She identifies various types of resources migrant women accrue to enable them to escape confinement and exploitation by third parties and to either prostitute on their own or exit sex work altogether: the third parties themselves, the police, peer workers, and clients. Of clients in particular, she notes, their role of being a helper or protector is intricately linked to Western masculinity. Acts by these clients, who are "male, white, Italian nationals and employed or retired," to save the women, who are the ethnically "other," undocumented, and making a precarious living through stigmatized activity in conditions of confinement—and who have sexually served them—are laden with "Western notions of masculine honor and the capacity to harm or help others" (Andrijasevic, 85). As Andrijasevic indicates, "A number of clients who facilitated respondents' exit from prostitution later (or before) became their boyfriends but kept on buying sex from other prostitutes and assisted them in leaving prostitution too" (85). One may read this masculine bestowing of sympathy and protection in a similar light as the practice by Western clients in sex tourism of sending remittances to Third World sex workers. Yet by placing themselves on the receiving end of a Western savior romance and colonial love saga as "victims," Eastern European migrant prostitutes have also expanded their spaces of maneuvering for liminal economic inclusion, as clients take it on themselves to convince third parties to return the women's passports or open a bank account to keep "safe" the women's earnings (85).

This deliberate self-inscription of victimized identity is further shown in migrant prostitutes' complicit reinforcement of the forced–voluntary binary in the official state trafficking discourse in order to normalize their status, like Liudmila, described earlier. As Andrijasevic observes, many of her respondents attempt to form romantic relationships with their Italian clients, who are in stable economic positions, to upgrade their social status and integrate themselves into Italian society. Even though prostitution was a foreseen part of their migratory trajectory when they traveled across borders, the women dissociate from being "voluntary" sex workers and describe themselves as being "forced" onto the streets. As Andrijasevic is careful to differentiate, dissimilar to the way "force" is defined in the United Nations protocol as coercion or deception, her informants use "force" as indicating "an economic pressure or need" (113). By emphasizing that they do not "choose" to work on the street but do so out of economic need (for themselves or their families), they disidentify from "being a whore inside" (91). As such, they could be repositioned by their prospective boyfriends "not as . . . participant[s] in an 'abnormal' sphere but instead as entitled to inhabit 'normality'" (90). By taking on the status of forced victim, the sex worker unlocks the possibilities of heterosexual romance, seeing herself as "able to fall in love, engage in a relationship, be welcomed at her boyfriend's house and finally leave prostitution" (91). In this instance, Eastern European migrant sex workers can thus be read as purposefully plotting the role of the abject victim, rather than that of a willful perpetrator, to win their Western boyfriends' sympathy and love. Such abjection is thus calculated to purify and normalize the self and increase the chances of heteronormative economic advancement within liberal citizenship.

Commodity Activism: Neoliberal Abjection,
Rather than Rights, as the Pivot of Activist Intervention

What lessons has this investigation of the manifold ways of deploying calculated abjection heralded? As underlined in the analysis of sex workers as subcultural entrepreneurs, their improvisation can be understood as *subcultural* because it appropriates and reuses the neoliberal script to fashion a dissident way to be economic citizens in the varying geographic locales of global sex commerce. But all of these heterogeneous modes of disruption also capture other essential dynamics of ingenious citizenship: they are *oppositional* in that the women resist a fated totality of economic subordination; *negotiated* because they do not directly refuse scripted economic citizenship but, instead, adjust the script to fit their immediate circumstances; and *interstitial* because they emerge contingently and unpredictably to generate stealthy blows to the bourgeois script in maneuvering limited spaces of survival.

These ingenious acts suggest that the contamination of sex workers' bodies in global capitalism actually constitutes the site of a contingent and complex figuration of social change, enabling sex workers to place themselves in relatively normalized and inclusive positions in liberal economic life. At the same time, it is critical to acknowledge that, as such normalization and inclusion are cyclically intertwined with neoliberal abjection, their search for normality is never complete and can also place other abject subjects in even further abjectified positions. For instance, within transnational sex tourism, those who are able to devise a long-term strategy to diversify their pool of clients, save money, and purchase their own homes are also more capable of normalizing their status than those who harbor romantic dreams about foreign clients but end up disillusioned with short-lived transnational relationships (Brennan 1999). Within migrant sex work, Eastern European street prostitutes who eventually marry Italian boyfriends to form a heteronormative family are in a more advantageous position to mitigate their abjection. This normalizing state may be inaccessible to undocumented Mexican sex workers in the United States, who may be pressured to engage in unsafe sex with clients to pay off debts or to send remittances back home, all the while battling racialized immigration law enforcement.

Without trying to show the internal disparity among global sex workers in any exhaustive or determinist fashion, this nonetheless demonstrates that sex acts of calculated abjection do not produce global ingenious citizens in a homogeneous way. Rather, these acts generate diverse effects depending on the abject subjects' respective social locations. As critical research on intersectionality has informed us, social markers such as race, class, legal status, age, sexuality, disability, residence in the global economy, and so on can all significantly complicate the ways in which subjects experience the lived effects of citizenship and their actual realization of rights and inclusion (Crenshaw 1991; Cho et al. 2013). The same goes for abject subjects' improvisations of ingenious citizenship, which are subject to even greater degrees of precariousness, since such nonexistent citizenship is not formalized and enforced in public laws and policies.

At the same time, the polyvalent schemes of ingenious citizenship improvised by global sex workers may have precisely demonstrated the lesson that sex workers' rights movements cannot strictly predicate advocacy on the legal codification of rights, but may need to pursue alternative strategies in more fluid and inventive ways in the current political conjuncture of neoliberal abjection. Like the historical configuration of domestic work activism, this political emphasis on rights has its roots in the historical trajectory of the modern prostitutes' rights movement, which, as Gregor Gall documents, started in the United States in 1973 with the creation of Call Off Your Old Tired Ethics (COYOTE) and its "associated-cum-parent organizations," the National Task Force on Prostitution (NTFP) and the International Committee for Prostitutes' Rights (ICPR). Gall observes, "COYOTE . . . , the US-based NTFP . . . and the Amsterdam-based ICPR . . . were created to repeal existing prostitution law, empower prostitutes to bargain with their employers, educate the public on prostitution, end stigmatization and campaign for health provision" (2006, 47). While he argues that these initial organizations acted more like pressure groups than like trade unions (6–8), what is important to underline is that, regardless of the political forms they assume, these collective organizations persistently focus on the recognition of sex workers as humans, and sex workers' rights as human rights.

This central theme runs throughout the movements from the 1980s to the present, evidenced by key literatures on the subject—from Gail Pheterson's *A Vindication of the Rights of Whores* that anthologizes the proceedings of the World Whores' Congresses that adopted the World Charter for Prostitutes' Rights in the mid-1980s (Pheterson 1989a), Kamala Kempadoo and Jo Doezema's *Global Sex Workers: Rights, Resistance, and Redefinition* in 1998 that contests the First-World character of the movements and provides critiques and perspectives from a Third-World vantage point (Kempadoo and Doezema 1998), to the two documents drafted and presented at the European Conference on

Sex Work, Human Rights, Labor and Migration in 2005, the *Declaration on the Rights of Sex Workers in Europe* and the *Sex Workers in Europe Manifesto*.[11] Recent sex work awareness campaigns that resort to public service announcements to empower sex workers to assert their professional identity, "I Am a Sex Worker," similarly represent these women as genuine human subjects bearing consciousness, agency, and rights claims.[12]

As I argue, given the historical-ideological context of the overwhelming "whore stigma" and dehumanizing treatment of sex workers (Pheterson 1993), such rights-based discourse that focuses on the recognition of sex workers as whole people constitutes a crucial rhetorical and political move. At the same time, we may want to be keenly aware of how such articulation of rights and a continuing insistence on returning to the "human" may only promote the movements to a certain distance (e.g., partial rather than full human rights recognition). We need still more fluid and varied strategies to advance the movements further in gaining economic citizenship for sex workers in de facto ways. In fact, like domestic work activism, sex workers' rights movements have displayed flashes of ingenious agency—such as deploying the discourse, "Good girls go to heaven, bad girls go everywhere"—to empower and bring their constituents together (Pheterson 1989a). But again, such agency is largely subordinate to the prevailing democratic rights frame of the movements and not centrally utilized as a direct tool in the workers' struggles for social transformation.

Rather than denying the value of rights-based politics, my aim here is to signal a more expansive repertoire of "strategies of normalization" by which sex work activism may rekindle and reuse ingenious agency at the front and center of its movement struggles to generate nonexistent rights for sex workers in varying ways at a collective level. Such strategies are especially critical in light of the massive number of locations where prostitution remains criminalized and prohibited, or tolerated and semi-legalized, without recognition as a legitimate occupation that entitles sex workers to the same kinds of rights and benefits accorded other citizen-workers. Location matters when considering whether a universal rights-based strategy may apply in differing geopolitical contexts. It may be impractical, for instance, to expect prostitutes in Vietnam to go to the streets demanding their rights as "sex workers." To engender a broader spectrum of social change in the global arena of sex commerce, sex work activism may need to absorb insights from calculated abjection, learning that rights may not come freely and directly from democratic activism, but need to be *earned* in creative ways by appropriating and reusing the shifting field of neoliberal abjection. Even in countries where prostitution is legalized or decriminalized, sex work activism may still benefit from these non–rights-based strategies to further improve and enhance the working conditions of constituents, given the persisting social stigmatization of sexual labor, especially for those situated in more marginalized positions such as street, migrant, or transgender sex work.

To be more specific, I suggest that in certain circumstances, sex workers' rights movements may consider shifting their focus to, or engaging in a greater incorporation of, what I call the strategy of *commodity activism*. What distinguishes commodity activism from sex workers' rights movements is that it uses neoliberal abjection rather than human rights as the pivot of activist intervention, repositioning sex workers as commodities, entrepreneurs, and consumers and advancing their welfare through the reuse of the liberal script of business rules and ethics. This more expansive approach, beyond the singular route of human rights, points to more flexible objectives in which activist intervention can be initiated in global sex commerce.

The Existing Democratic Frame: Global Sex Workers' Rights Movements

In contrast to domestic work activism, which has been able to secure the adoption of the International Labor Organization's Domestic Workers Convention stipulating international labor standards, sex work activism has faced an even more challenging battle in the arena of international human rights. Traditionally, prostitutes are considered victims of trafficking rather than "sex workers" who bear positive rights claims. Although international legal documents and rights organizations have generally distinguished between "forced" and "voluntary" prostitution, Doezema observes that they are more interested in condemning forced prostitution and saving its innocent victims than in affirming and promoting prostitutes' rights (1998, 41). While recent developments have pointed in a more progressive direction, as new United Nations reports recommend "the decriminalization of pimping, brothel-keeping and the purchase of sex," anti–sex-trafficking groups are mobilizing an international protest to derail such efforts.[13] As Doezema notes, the absence of sex workers' rights in actual human rights practices perpetuates a false division between forced innocent victims (madonnas) and guilty voluntary transgressors (whores) who deserve to suffer. In short, no "normal" person would choose prostitution unless forced into it by another person or by poverty (42–44).

While none of the current international human rights documents explicitly legitimize prostitution as work, sex workers' rights advocates have pointed to language in certain documents that can be interpreted as recognizing sex workers' rights as human rights.[14] In fact, sex work activists have drawn from, while expanding on, existing international law instruments to draft their own human rights documents. It should be acknowledged that, as with sex workers themselves, a disparity remains between sex workers' rights movements in the First World and those in the Third World. Many Third World sex workers have contested that their perspectives and voices are not adequately reflected and represented in the supposedly "international" rights instruments (Kempadoo 1998a).[15] For this reason, I present a sample of the rights claims advocated by sex workers in the First World and Third World, respectively. What I wish to accentuate here, however, are the ways in which the collective movements across regions have staged their rights claims through a predominantly democratic frame.

Let us look at these rights claims. In the First World, the foundational World Charter for Prostitutes' Rights in 1985 and the more recent Declaration on the Rights of Sex Workers in Europe in 2005 have articulated sex workers' rights as human rights.[16] They include the right to work and freely choose one's job; the right to life, liberty, and personal safety (free from harassment and abuse by employers, clients, and police); the right to peaceful assembly and to form unions; the right to health insurance, sick leave, retirement benefits, vacation pay, and workplace safety and hygiene; the right to independent and confidential public health services for all people, including sex workers; the right to education and job training programs for those who wish to leave the industry; the right to educational programs to change social attitudes that stigmatize prostitutes; and the right to freedom of movement and residence (International Committee for Prostitutes' Rights 1989; Andrijasevic et al. 2012).[17]

As further documented in Kempadoo and Doezema's important volume, *Global Sex Workers*, although they are not part of the Western-centered international prostitutes' rights movement, sex workers' rights groups in South and Central America, Asia, and South Africa have also generated inventive activist strategies by claiming a historical heritage of sex worker resistance in antislavery and anticolonial struggles in their homelands, while articulating a citizen's right to initiate, use, and sell sex outside of marriage, love, and desire in accordance with their particular cultural contexts and social locations. For example, the Association of Autonomous Women Workers in Ecuador employs strikes and lockdowns to press issues of police abuse, exploitation by brothel and club management, and workers' health and labor conditions. The group draws political inspiration from "the Latin spirit of dance and music as well as . . . the spirit of the women and . . . their particular life histories and . . . struggles" (Abad et al. 1998, 174). South Africa's Sex Worker Education and Advocacy Taskforce (SWEAT) focuses on legal and civil discrimination against sex workers and advocates democracy for sex work through legal reforms in accordance with the World Charter for Prostitutes' Rights (Petzer and Issacs 1998). It publishes a monthly newsletter that facilitates communication among sex workers, including an "Ugly Mugs" list that blacklists dangerous and violent clients. It further provides "training of mainstream medical healthcare workers, police, legal professionals and medical healthcare personnel" on awareness of the needs of sex workers from a sex workers' rights perspective (Petzer and Issacs, 195). Combating both the whore stigma and economic deprivation, La Únion Unica of Mexico emphasizes the need for labor laws that would provide sex workers with "social security, low-income housing, medical assistance, and tax rights like other workers," in addition to undertaking health projects (Colimoro 1998, 197).

In all, the legalization and decriminalization campaigns advanced by the global sex workers' rights movements operate through the motor of democratic agency in advancing the visions of justice, liberty, and equality for their constituents, who are framed as legitimate laborers with claims to citizenship and human rights. Notably, however, these movements and organizations do not seek to transcend the cyclical forces of oppression, but rather aim to humanize intimate labor within an existing inhuman economy in order to ameliorate sex workers' abjection and expand liberal spaces of inclusion and belonging. In fact, similar to domestic work activism, global sex workers' rights movements mix their democratic politics with an element of ingenious agency that incorporates neoliberal logic in advocating for women in prostitution. As we have seen, women's erotic bodily labor in global sex commerce relies on calculated abjection—that is, capitalist marketization, sexual objectification, and colonial racialization—as instrumental conduits to turn sex work into a not just legitimate but profitable enterprise. Sex workers' rights movements thus do not seek to upend these highly oppressive forces (i.e., capitalism, misogyny, colonial racialization), on which global sex work is predicated, but to "imbibe" such dynamics and work artfully through them. The rights claims the movements make thus act as complementary conduits rather than as antagonistic suppressants to capitalist objectification and racialized sexualization within the liberal economy of instrumental exchange. By anchoring sex workers' ingenious citizenship, these rights claims can be seen as using "calculated abjection" to maximize spaces of dignity and humanity for sex workers in the midst of global capitalist contamination. In doing so, these movements and organizations formulate a kind of ingenious resistance that *reuses* existing structures and resources to fashion a disruption of liberal hegemony.

It is precisely for this reason that Penttinen has critiqued the "non-radical" nature of the movements:

> In this respect the sex workers' rights movements, which emphasize the profitability of sex work and present it as such a rational choice as opposed to other forms of labor and which ground the arguments in individualist freedoms to earn money through commodification of sexuality, do not seem radical at all. Indeed, they are not a form of resistance nor are they in any way counter-hegemonic to the dominating discourse of the neoliberalist world economy. Instead, they follow the principles of marketization and consumerism by arguing for the commodification of the private or personal and thus bringing it into the gaze of power. . . . This project seems to be more involved with discovering who we are as subjects according to the dominating logic of marketization than with refusing who we are. (17)

However, this limited horizon of resistance can open up once we go beyond the notion of resistance as being strictly about anti-subordination and instead view it as oppositional in multifaceted and nonlinear ways. Like the National Domestic Workers Alliance discussed in the previous chapter, global sex workers' rights movements do not adopt a totalizing stance of the politics of the "anti" (Ferguson 2011, 62). Instead, they conduct their democratic politics with "a full continuum of moves, countermoves, negotiations, protests, submissions, struggles, neutralities, alliances, accommodations, and resistances" (Martinez 1997, 269). In fact, by seeking to formally normalize sex workers, these rights claims potentially destabilize the existing relations embedded in the economic script and reconfigure power relations on the existing neoliberal terrain. While such a list of rights may appear conventional, they are unusual when applied to sex workers, and even in their limits and complicities, create unexpected ways to envision renewed human relations that narrow, rather than widen, the gulf between the normal and the abject.

Despite these potential contributions, however, the issue remains that these rights claims are not enforceable without state recognition. Furthermore, when the language of democratic rights occupies the center of such movements' formal mode of operation, their universalizing application may unwittingly become inflexible baggage that prevents a broader and deeper advancement of sex workers' welfare through other, nondemocratic means in certain contexts and circumstances where non–rights-based discourses may have stronger appeal. In fact, to the extent that sex workers' rights movements have positioned the role of their constituents as laborers and articulated their demands as claims of labor citizenship and human rights, I wish to point to ways in which a refashioning of sex workers' status as commodities, entrepreneurs, or consumers may occasionally gain them de facto measures of rights in the concrete context of neoliberal abjection.

The Ingenious Constellation of Commodity Activism: Sex Workers as Commodities, Entrepreneurs, and Consumers

I borrow the term "commodity activism" from the title of a volume edited by Sarah Banet-Weiser and Roopali Mukherjee (Banet-Weiser and Mukherjee 2012a). The main thrust of the compilation volume is that political activism and cultural resistance need to be radically reconceived in the neoliberal moment, for "realms of culture and society once considered 'outside' the official economy are [now being] harnessed, reshaped, and made legible in economic terms" (Banet-Weiser and Mukherjee 2012b, 1). One of these realms is social activism. As Banet-Weiser and Mukherjee articulate, not only is social activism increasingly "shifting shape into a marketable commodity" in the contemporary cultural economy, but the act of *doing* activism needs to be situated "in a sociocultural context increasingly defined by neoliberal ideas about self-reliance, entrepreneurial individualism, and economic responsibility" (2). Marita Sturken thus argues in the volume, "Clearly, activism is not what it used to be. Resistance was never what it was understood to be. And capitalism is always reinventing itself. The power of capitalism as a global force has always been in its capacity as a system to adapt, incorporate, and expand. Yet the prevailing sense that capitalism is undergoing a new phase in relationship to activism and resistance is palpable" (2012, x). In this constantly changing configuration of capitalism, I suggest that sex work activism cannot remain in a fixed universal position undergirded by a strictly democratic notion of citizenship and human rights. Rather, it needs to "creatively play different, more flexible and constantly changing games" (Bayat 2010, 24) in order to cohere into a more viable and potent political force.

Without mapping out step by step how such "constantly changing games" should be played, I offer several tentative directions on how sex work activism can reinvent itself by reconceiving workers as commodities, entrepreneurs, or consumers to negotiate more effectively for their inclusion, equality, and nonexistent rights. These propositions should not be interpreted in any fixed or rigid way, but can be flexibly adjusted, recombined, and reused in different locations and contexts. In fact, since the disseminated neoliberal script is bound to interact with local scripts, sex work activism must disrupt and appropriate neoliberal logic in varying fashions based on local circumstances. My articulations here are better understood as a brainstorming of ideas aimed at stimulating ongoing experimentation and formulation of strategies rather than as a user's manual. My belief in the necessity of these alternative strategies hinges on my conviction that in the global field of neoliberal abjection, we need a more flexible mode of political engagement that directly engages the logics and discourses of neoliberalism to stage the most creative disruption and potent appropriation of livable spaces for global sex workers.

First, while there is no shortage of discussion regarding how we have all become "human commodities" in late modernity, what is especially notable about the nature of sex work is that sex workers proffer their sexual bodies directly as commodities for rent. As Raven articulates in the opening pages of this chapter, she is not so much "selling" her body as "renting" it out for a specified period of time. Instead of always framing workers as humans with rights who are entitled to humane treatment, I propose that in certain contexts it may be effective to reposition workers as rental commodities (similar to car rental or bowling rental) with stipulated business rules and policies to ensure proper treatment by clients and law enforcement. This alternative activist approach takes lessons from calculated abjection: it deliberately reframes the workers in the abject status of business commodities in order to leverage how third parties should treat these commodities within commercial, legal, and ethical bounds. That is to say, while rental commodities do not have rights, both consumers who have paid access to the rental products (i.e., johns) and outside parties who regulate the commerce (i.e., the police) are prohibited from violating or damaging the products; doing otherwise would make them subject to fines or other punitive measures and even potential lawsuits by management (i.e., brothels, sex clubs, escort agencies, pimps). This deliberate objectification of sex workers as rental commodities seeks to obtain their "freedom from violence" vis-à-vis clients and the police by using instrumental business logics and ethics where they possess stronger force and authority than the language of human rights. It deviously and circuitously employs the hegemonic logic of the liberal economic script to obtain nonexistent (human) rights for sex workers as commodities.

In addition, sex work advocacy may also precisely leverage the business discourse of rental commodity to compel better treatment of workers from management. Rental products need to undergo regular maintenance to ensure their longevity and durability; similarly, it is better for management to nourish its commodities (i.e., sex workers) regularly—in the form of higher wages, health insurance, sick leave, vacation pay, workplace safety and hygiene, and other benefits—to ensure their optimal performance over the long run. This investment in commodities may also give management stronger incentives to devise and enforce "rental agreements" with clients in stronger terms to protect the financial value of their rental property. Furthermore, specifically for those who work in transnational sex tourism and migrant sex work, I suggest that the discourses of commodities can be invoked to advocate for "free movement" across borders to further generate and expand appropriable spaces in liberal economic citizenship. For instance, since commodities have been granted greater cross-border access than human subjects in global capitalism, if the time is ripe, the commodity discourse could be presented to sovereign states (maybe beginning at a limited regional level) to demand the free movement of uncoerced and non-trafficked sex-worker commodities across borders (subject to potential duties or other forms of excise taxes).

Although some may consider it dehumanizing to explicitly position workers as commodified objects in activist discourse, it should be pointed out that, as we saw, many sex workers are already actively commodifying themselves in their day-to-day work while hiding their true selves/subjectivities behind their projected commercial personalities and images. If calculated abjection is an embedded part of the instrumental exchange of sex work, there is no reason not to extend such calculated logic to activist intervention if it can be effective in gaining material benefits for workers, thus humanizing them in indirect but practical ways.

Second, this subtle humanizing strategy need not be limited to identifying sex workers as material objects, but can be further achieved by positioning sex workers as entrepreneurs who are in financial control of their own sexed bodies as commodities. Taking insights from these subcultural entrepreneurs, sex work activism can appropriate the logics of markets and entrepreneurialism to demand both publicly and privately funded grants to provide access to education and job training programs for prospective or current sex workers to enhance their entrepreneurial and business management skills. Arguments can be made that such programs would benefit at-risk minority women, helping them to become economically independent through creative entrepreneurship (in whatever they do, including sex commerce) and reduce dependence on welfare. By emphasizing that the overarching goals are individual financial success and national prosperity, the advocacy of such programs can be understood as an inventive way to gain "entrepreneur citizenship" for women in prostitution and sex work. Such entrepreneurial discourse, which recognizes sex workers as autonomous agents seeking the maximization of utilities and profits, can also be used to negotiate freedom in choosing places of work and business.

Third, activist intervention can be further undertaken through the realm of consumerism. One way, of course, is to promote the production of films and television programs that facilitate and enhance greater understanding and acceptance of sex work among consumers of media and popular culture. An even more inventive technique, however, is to position sex workers as consumers, too. Given the large number of sex workers across all regions of the globe—and their relatively high earnings compared with female manual laborers in other sectors—they formulate a formidable bloc that consumes products such as lingerie, cosmetics, plastic and reconstructive surgery, condoms, sex toys and products, mobile phones and information technology, motel and hotel services, and more. There are ways in which sex work activism can use sex workers' collective purchasing power to leverage discounts, fundraising, mutual advertisements, and other forms of support from these linked commercial industries—whether for sex workers' own businesses or for activist movements. The same argument can be made to governments: that is, by using sex workers' purchasing power to negotiate with officials to support the legalization and decriminalization of sex work in order to strengthen this consuming power and, in turn, enhance the profits of linked commercial chains and stimulate greater business development (as well as tax revenues). In fact, appeals to financial autonomy and national prosperity derived from the utility value of sex workers as both entrepreneurs and consumers may also be used to support their greater cross-border mobility in the transnational circuits of sex work.

Again, all of these propositions can be adapted or combined with other discourses, logics, ethics, and tactics in different contexts and circumstances. What is important to note is that, together, they point to ways in which universalizing rights-based strategies may be bypassed, deemphasized, or complemented to gain greater degrees of inclusion, equity, and rights for global sex workers. This constellation of commodity activism, informed by the ingenious agency of calculated abjection, suggests more protean forms of political and cultural resistance—being fluidly oppositional, negotiated, interstitial, and subcultural—in current conditions of neoliberal abjection, which exert new constraints as well as open new possibilities for social justice struggles.

This ingenious frame of commodity activism shows that, as indicated earlier, the ideal aspiration for roses (i.e., justice, equality, democracy) needs to be realized and earned through the material offer and exchange of bread (i.e., via the instrumental appeals of commodities, entrepreneurship, and consumerism). In the neoliberal moment, we can no longer imagine justice as a kind of "free" delivery that will come about purely through sustained democratic action and popular struggle. Neither can it be conceived as being achievable in a universal way based on the ideal of human rights across all locations and contexts. In many instances, as Lynn Comella points out, "Money not only greases the wheels of social change but keeps those wheels spinning" (2012, 249). The hopeful sign here is that while the commodity activism of global sex work would certainly recoup and reinforce the capitalist underpinnings of liberal citizenship, it also bears the potential to inject it "with new meaning and social value" (249) by constantly recrafting the existing power relations between normality and abjection.

4. Trans People, Morphing Technologies, and Appropriating Gendered Citizenship

Twisting Sex/Gender within the Citizenship Script

In her autobiography, Donita Ganzon provides detailed sketches of her life trajectory as a Filipina transgender migrant who underwent a sex change operation from man to woman in the United States (Ganzon 2008). She obtained U.S. citizenship as a woman in 1987. Nevertheless, she became the subject of a legal case over the immigration status of married transsexuals, in which her Filipino husband, Jiffy Javenella, was denied U.S. permanent residency because the Department of Homeland Security refused to recognize Ganzon's sex change operation and the couple's "heterosexual" marital status. Ganzon's statements in media interviews during the proceedings bring to light the abjection of trans people, whose gender transformation ruptures the binary category of "man" and "woman" scripted in liberal citizenship.[1] Ganzon presents an immigrant subject who revels in her relocation to the United States, opening the door to her sex change operation. Then she suddenly finds herself declared "abject" in relation to American liberal citizenship precisely because of her "aberrant" gender status and "un-heterosexual" marriage. In fact, if women in transnational sex tourism and migrant sex work have sought to normalize themselves through heterosexual matrimony with Western men, Ganzon is denied this "inclusive" heteronormalization because of the perceived ambiguity, or even "false presentation," of her female gender identification.

In spite of this sovereign misrecognition, I wish to direct attention to several fragments in Ganzon's memoir that illustrate the intricate twists in her negotiation with liberal gender life, and the renewed spaces of inclusion and belonging that are generated through her gender transition. In the autobiography, Ganzon tells of her past of growing up in the Philippines as an effeminate boy and then as a gay man. A breakup with a European American boyfriend after she moved to the United States to work as a nurse in her early thirties left her in a state of depression and eventually awakened her desire to become a woman, something that she felt had been missing in her life. Upon consulting with doctors and surgeons, she started the process of transgendering to transform her physical appearance and body shape, including purchasing and putting on feminine clothing, weekly electrolysis sessions, and hormonal therapies. Seven months into her gender transition, she presented her new gendered outlook at her workplace: "That summer in 1979, wearing a billowing black silk skirt with a loose silk gray blouse, . . . my 23 inches waist—accented by a black thin snake skin leather belt, and a matching Veneta Bottega bag, a Charles Jordan black stiletto shoes (size 6), I worriedly entered the hospital. I was tense, yet was oozing with sexual pride; I felt steamy and—quite confident that I would get more positive than negative response" (Ganzon, 151). After undergoing the eventual sex change operation, she notes, "I was glowing from the inside. . . . Men were drooling over me."[2]

Ganzon's euphoria following her gender alteration is bolstered by her feeling of being a "properly" gendered woman who fits into heteronormativity and whose female body image and "straight" sexual orientation can be accepted by mainstream society. As she writes, *"The truth of the matter was I wanted to be a full woman and no in between"* (151; emphasis in original). Although after the sex change she "noticed bewildered looks from people searching for a flaw," she declares, "They couldn't find any."[3] The potent force of abjection that could visit her as a transsexual is assuaged by her exhibition of, and disposition toward, gender normativity.

In fact, what is implied here is Ganzon's assumption of a "proper" kind of mind and body for men and women, respectively. Her agency in shaping her mind and body according to given gender definitions is implicated in the hegemonic script of liberal gender citizenship, which assigns normality and abjection differentially to citizen-subjects depending on their conformity to or deviation from the scripted binary of "man" and "woman." Thus, when Ganzon states, "I had been a gay man, lived a straight life in college, was forced to screw a prostitute in Vietnam, and had a me-nage a trois [sic] (compelled by a male lover/boyfriend to perform cunnilingus while he watched)—and now, I am finally a woman. My life is more than full" (175), this feeling of "fullness" (*normality* as opposed to *abjection*) is enabled by her following the heteronormative life trajectory of the liberal citizenship script.

But if this description seems to reflect a linear "assimilation" trajectory, a deeper look into Ganzon's life reveals more complex turns and negotiations in her gender transition. Although her transition was a "public fact" to her immediate circles (and to the staff in the medical infrastructure who assisted with her sex change), these flashing scenes of her transgendering were by and large concealed and hidden from public view (until, of course, the publication of her autobiography). In fact, desiring to live as a "full woman" while also fearing prejudice, ridicule, and rejection, Ganzon mentions in her memoir how she had to be discretionary in revealing her transsexual identity in the early stages of her transgender life, whether at work, having casual sex, or meeting new friends and lovers (Ganzon 2008). As such, Ganzon's agency in morphing her gender is not strictly linear but full of subtle, nonstraightforward, and roundabout twists. This circuitous agency can further be considered in light of the fact that while she stepped forward as a spokesperson for queer rights when allying with the activist organization Embracing the Movement for Pinays and Queers (EMPAQ) during the proceedings of the legal case, she nonetheless reinscribes heteronormativity in her public statements: "And my husband is in shame and in fear. ... He's embarrassed because people might think he's gay. He's not gay; he's straight. He fell in love with me because I am a woman."[4] And again in her autobiography: "Between fame and fortune versus having a happy married life I would choose the latter anytime. I think having a husband and a happy family would be the acme. I am not giving up in finding the right person. Will I ever have a little semblance of the so called normal life?" (205). If Ganzon's transsexuality defies the hegemonic citizenship script that determines one's gender life based on biological sex, her aspiration for the *normal*—being a "full woman," finding the "right husband," and having a "happy family"—also deviates from the trajectory of queer activist movement that does not subscribe to the mainstream ideal of gender normativity.

Without losing sight of the limitations and contradictions embedded in her gender narrative and transformation, it is nonetheless notable that Ganzon, as a trans person, uses elements in her surroundings to contrive more inhabitable spaces for herself. These autobiographical fragments illustrate Ganzon's nonlinear agency in remodeling her gender identification to fit into the standard frame of heterosexual womanhood. This allows her to live a normative gender life in liberal America and, *in fact*, enables her to claim a citizen's (hegemonic monogamous) right to marriage in the first place—which non-normative, nonmonogamous trans people who disidentify from straight men or women would not be able to claim. In addition, she flexibly resorts to democratic agency by joining a queer activist movement when facing an obstacle in her path to becoming a married heterosexual woman, realizing that collective political effort is required to further expand livable spaces for transgender immigrants such as herself. Ultimately, it is her simultaneous transgression of, and complicity with, the gender citizenship script that allows Ganzon to be thankful for the liberal life she has: "I thank the Lord Almighty for bringing me to America. I was availed of the advances in modern medicine and surgical technique. It was destiny that brought me to the United States" (Ganzon, 149–50).

In their study "Transsexuals' Embodiment of Womanhood," Douglas Schrock and his colleagues' discussion of an informant, Marzie, who holds feminist values and has reservations about using cosmetic redecoration to "feminize" herself in her transition from a man to a woman (Schrock et al. 2005), evokes a similar reflection. Marzie narrates her struggle:

> I've always identified with women coming from a feminist perspective. And so I've always kind of rejected things that oppress women; you know, the way women are traditionally treated in society. A lot of this clothing and makeup are things that I've always thought were ridiculous. . . . I think [clothing and makeup] become harmful when they are something that you are forced to do or you have to do in order to be accepted, to fit into what society expects of you. . . . I'm hoping that I don't have to do that. But I'm not certain, you know. I'm wondering if I do have to start wearing a lot of makeup and dressing in more traditionally feminine ways and try to get people to think of me as female. (Schrock et al., 326)

Despite her reservations, Marzie indicates that she has endured the physical pain and financial cost of undergoing procedures of electrolysis and hormonal injections (Schrock et al., 327–28).

On the surface, this instance underlines a feminist transwoman's complicity in capitalist consumerist practices as she remodels her body in a particularly gendered—read *feminine*—way. But I would like us not to rush to reading Marzie's experience as merely a reinscription of gender normativity. To begin with, we as citizen-subjects are also implicated to different degrees in our own gendered ways and, by virtue of our outward dressing and clothes, complicit in reproducing the gender technology of capitalist consumerism. In fact, all of us, transsexual or not, were subject to constant social monitoring and supervision throughout childhood that kept us in conformity with the gender binary (e.g., picking up on and internalizing gender cues through toys, colors, hairstyle, clothing, occupation, food, and manners), and we could even receive discipline and punishment for crossing the gender line. Yet the effects of monitoring, supervision, discipline, and punishment are especially acute for transsexuals and transgender people compared with normative gendered people. Transsexuals' autobiographies often chronicle an intense state of mental distress and psychological pain during childhood as a result of thinking they had some serious defect, not knowing whether they were boys or girls, and having to pretend to be someone they were not (Bornstein 1995; Prosser 1998).

Such pain does not describe a "natural" state of psychopathology, but rather underlines the material and political force of hegemonic liberal socialization, which determines and marks gender-variant subjects, forcing them to "become abject" (Rose 1999, 253). Their somatic feeling of "gender dislocation" is portrayed as deriving from a mentally disordered state of the gender script, when it is the normalizing force of the script that abjectifies their gender variance. In light of this hegemonic force of abjection, we may reread Marzie's feminized embodiment as using complicity in a regenerative way, because it enables her to fashion a normative gendered self within the scripted life of liberal citizenship.

In another related example, Cymene Howe, Susanna Zaraysky, and Lois Lorentzen describe how Mexican male-to-female transgender sex workers travel from Guadalajara to San Francisco in pursuit of stronger earning potential so they can help their families back home in Mexico and "build capital in order to start their own small businesses" (Howe et al. 2008, 37). Two things are notable in this study. First, like Ganzon and Marzie, these migrant trans subjects attempt to settle into the feminine gender role in liberal citizenship. Not only have many pursued cosmetic surgery "to appear more physically feminine both for clients and for their own sense of self" (35), they also harbor plans to normalize their occupations in accordance with the gender script. The authors note, "Leticia's plan, for example, was 'to get out of this business [sex work] and open a beauty salon.' Other women wanted to open their own dressmaking or seamstress businesses in Mexico, enterprises commonly associated with women and therefore 'feminizing'" (37). Second, however, while many desired a sex change operation, none in the study had undergone the procedure. This is not only because of the expense of the operation, but also because many of their clients specifically desire penetration by feminine-looking transwomen with male genitalia (35). As a market strategy for their sexual labor, they thus continue to preserve their male genitalia and gender ambiguity (35).

Here, these migrant transgender sex workers can be understood as strategic and creative as they reconstruct and recode their gender identification and sexual bodies, thus devising heterogeneous ways to attain livable spaces in liberal citizenship. By feminizing their physical appearance and embodiment while retaining the male sexual organ, they at once reinforce and subvert the gender binary. In fact, they move fluidly between "ordinary women" in one context and "women with male genitalia" in another to re-create inhabitable spaces in the liberal gender script.

In all three instances, such trans subjects are not simply reiterating the given script of liberal gender life. Rather, in their appropriation of the gender script to create renewed spaces of normalized inclusion, they twist and stretch it—to different degrees and in different ways—beyond its conventional definition to make it inclusive of different kinds of gender-variant subjects. In so doing, they destabilize existing relations, creating varying degrees of mutable sex and amorphous gender within this very script.[5]

These vignettes highlight the ways in which the everyday practices of transgendering can be understood as disrupting and appropriating (without being able to transcend) the gender script of liberal citizenship. Such appropriation is undoubtedly complicit in reinscribing the gender power structure, yet it is also precisely this *creative* and *fluid* complicity that makes possible the reanimation of precarious citizenship.

As we have come to learn since childhood, the gender script of liberal citizenship configures normative reproduction by assigning citizen-subjects to binary gender poles—what I term M and F—since birth and placing them on a lifelong trajectory of masculine and feminine order toward monogamous heterosexual relationship and conjugal arrangement. As Foucault argues, the gender system in liberal society does not express a "natural" fact of life; rather, it is predicated on economic logics, for the advent of capitalism requires a stable, gendered bourgeois structure and sexual arrangement to enable its productive regeneration (Foucault 1978). Precisely because liberal citizenship cannot encompass the copious and protean forms of gender expression and sexual ways of life immanent to the human condition, it must, via its script, exercise cultural-material powers of surveillance, discipline, and punishment to enforce consent and compel conformity. Patricia Gagné and Richard Tewksbury thus write:

> While some believe gender is rooted in our biological make-up, as a system it receives constant surveillance and is policed continually through social interactions that socialize new members of society and sanction those who violate the rules. It exists at both individual and group levels, where women and men "do gender" and others decode, interpret, and categorize individuals based upon presented gender cues. At the organizational level gender exists to categorize individuals and assign them meanings and roles. At the institutional level (e.g., in the economy, family, religion, law, politics, and medicine), gender determines individuals' roles, statuses, rights, and responsibilities. Western industrial and post-industrial cultures share the ideological presumption that gender will correlate with the sex assigned at birth. Individuals who seek to challenge this binary system of gender through enactments of androgynous gender or by crossing gender boundaries, including masculine women and feminine men, are likely to be stigmatized, ostracized, and labeled mentally ill. (1998, 81)

As Dan Irving argues, such gender socialization and surveillance does not solely correspond to the liberal sex/gender regime but emanates from the regime's "integral links . . . [with] exploitative economic relations of production as mutually constitutive systems of domination" (2013, 16). It is through "the intersectional relations of power among heteronormative gender roles, sexuality, and the demands of capitalist (re)productive regimes of accumulation" (16) that the liberal script assigns citizen-subjects into dual zones of normality and abjection based on their conformity to, or deviation from, scripted gender life.

Yet precisely because of the embedded economic element of liberal gender citizenship, these relations are not stable and fixed but are contingent and shifting, depending on each citizen-subject's orientation toward this economic component in different contexts. For instance, as Irving has illustrated, the discursive constructions of transsexuality in early medical studies of transsexuality, as well as in transsexuals' autobiographies, frame the legitimacy of transgender people based on their being "normal" and productive members of capitalist society (Irving 2013). While Irving is critical of this trend toward trans-normativity, I wish to suggest that precisely such complicity with liberal normativity may be utilized to generate and expand spheres of trans disruption in the unstable field of liberal gender citizenship. Rather than seeing such liberal complicity as *only* reinforcing the assimilatory imperative, I urge us to recognize the endogenous intertwining of purity and contamination in any process of social change in order to open up a different view, wherein trans activism absorbs and incorporates this liberal complicity into its arsenal to disrupt and transform liberal gender citizenship in complex and nonlinear ways.

To venture that trans people and trans activism make inventive and flexible use of complicity to generate social change is undoubtedly controversial in the current state of trans theory and politics. In contrast to domestic and sex workers, transgender underlines a human category that is not attached to work or occupational status in capitalist economy. Thus, there is a strong imperative, as Paisley Currah and his colleagues indicate in their important volume, *Transgender Rights*, to engage in an intellectual dialogue and political approach regarding human rights that "does *not* situate trans people as a means to an end . . . but considers the well-being of trans people as an end in itself" (Currah et al. 2006, xxii; emphasis in original). Recent critical trans theorizing, in fact, advocates for a nonnegotiable stance toward even a rights-based framework precisely because of its inevitable complicity in recuperating the capitalist machinery of instrumentalization and commodification as well as the liberal discourse of property, value, and worth vis-à-vis transgender subjects (Spade 2011; Beauchamp 2013; Irving 2013; Snorton and Haritaworn 2013; Stryker and Aizura 2013).

Yet, despite this potent line of critique, I wish to ask: What if even here, where the corporeal human subject becomes transgendered, there can be no escape from instrumental participation in the normative script of liberal citizenship? And what if trans politics, rather than seeking oppositional flight from this complicit contamination, might actually need to head into it with the kind of savvy, shrewdness, and creativity displayed in the process of transgendering?

While Judith Halberstam has previously located the transgender body in a radical queer temporality and space that generates its own subcultural life distinct from, and in opposition to, heteronormativity (Halberstam 2005), in this chapter I advance an alternative figuration of political change that views both individual transgendering practices and collective trans politics as actually requiring complicity with the gender binary in order to create renewed gender-sexual spaces *beside* heteronormativity. Critical trans disruption thus does not necessarily lie in a transcendent space that is nowhere or beyond the gender binary, but rather emerges artfully *through* its entanglement with the binary forces to improvise more livable spaces for the polymorphous trans subjects in the lived gender script.

As I argue, such politics become conceivable when we consider how contemporary trans corporeal embodiment hinges on *morphing technologies*—which are inextricably attached to, and inevitably reinscribe, the liberal gender script—to generate and expand its gender becoming. Borrowing from the concept of morphing (a computer-mediated digital metamorphosis that continuously transforms one image or shape into another), I use morphing technologies to refer to a variety of practices and programs that assist in transforming one's gender identification and presentation across gender boundaries. Broadly conceived, these technologies include learning to talk, sit, stand, and walk like the opposite gender; donning masculine or feminine clothing, makeup, and cosmetics; undergoing psychotherapy for "gender identity disorder"; remaking the body through electrolysis, hormonal treatment, silicone injections, and sex reassignment surgery; changing one's gender status on official documents, such as birth certificate, passport, and driver's license; and revising and reinscribing gender roles in intimate relationships. As I will address below, although the idea of morphing technologies may seem similar to Judith Butler's conception of performative repetition, there is one key difference: while morphing signals and accentuates the inevitability of making creative use of complicity in the heteronormative capitalist economy to expand social change in the gender realm, repetition ultimately devolves into a position against complicity in a search for purity. And I suggest that trans activism, rather than operating on the premise of refuting complicity, incorporates the complicit logics of morphing technologies to stage trans metamorphosis vis-à-vis the liberal gender script in the larger social realm.

To lead to this alternative conception of trans politics, I build on Gagné and Tewksbury's conception of "the transgender individual . . . [as] an active agent in the establishment of an alternative gender identity. . . . [and] the presentation of alternative gender as an act of everyday resistance" (1998, 82) in interpreting practices of transgendering as a creative process of twisting and appropriating the given liberal gender script via morphing technologies. In the midst of the division within the trans community between those who wish to fit into the "ordinary" male–female binary and those who desire to dismantle the dualistic system of gender, I want to emphasize the commonality of diverse trans subjects' quotidian practices in disrupting and appropriating the liberal gender script, albeit in different ways. Ultimately, I argue that trans activist strategies fluidly absorb and mediate complicity without a preconceived universal framework—sometimes in conjunction with rights, sometimes not—to generate ever more livable gender spaces.

Before pursuing my analysis, I wish to specify my terminology, which has been a contentious issue for the transgender population as it implicates contrasting representations of identity and platforms of political and social interventions. As Tam Sanger points out, "A major site of dispute is the naming of transpeople as either 'transsexual' or 'transgender.' Transsexual is a label most often associated with those who place themselves unproblematically within the gender binary of female/male, with transgender describing a more complex relationship with gender norms" (2008, 42). Sanger uses the term "transpeople" to refer broadly to individuals "whose gender identity does not match that assigned at birth. This could mean being assigned a female gender but identifying as male, or vice versa. It could also involve being assigned either male or female and identifying as neither or both" (42). I follow Sanger's conceptualization by using the term trans people (or trans subjects). However, since the term "transgender" is now commonly used as an umbrella term "inclusive of all and any gender variance" (Valentine 2007, 33),[6] for stylistic reasons I will also use "transgender people" or "transgender subjects" interchangeably with "trans people" throughout my discussion. For the present analysis, my primary reference for trans people in this chapter are MTFs (male-to-female transwomen) and FTMs (female-to-male transmen) in Western postindustrial contexts. Acknowledging the internal trans debate concerning "MTF" and "FTM," I use the terms to designate a general sense of gender location in transitioning, without committing to the idea that the binary poles hold an essentialist or determinist meaning for every subject in transition.[7]

In fact, one overlooked issue in this debate on trans terminology is the inherently "contaminated" character of these very terms within European capitalist modernity, which inextricably circumscribes the aspiring transformative effects of trans politics. David Valentine has argued that despite the collectivity and inclusivity of "transgender," the use of the term in now extensively "institutionalized contexts cannot account for the experiences of the most socially vulnerable gender-variant people" (2007, 14). He points specifically to the "poor, black, and disenfranchised" gender-variant individuals who do not understand themselves in the category of transgender and are potentially "left out of an imagined future of justice and freedom frequently understood as enabled by this category" (6). Similarly, Susan Stryker argues, "The Eurocentric whiteness of transgender's theorization within the academy . . . can hardly be denied," and can "become another index of a Northern and Western conceptual imperialism that threatens to overwhelm, subsume, and refigure specific sex/gender/sexuality configurations in colonized locations" (2013, 552). As Stryker suggests, it is important that we acknowledge and analyze "the sometimes oppressive ways in which 'transgender whiteness' functions, or how conceptual categories derived from social experience within the United States impinge upon and interact with sex/gender/sexuality/ identity configurations rooted in other socio-cultural formations" (552).

But this critical reflection on terminology also offers complementary lessons on social change in the same mien. First, just as there are limits to the universality of the term "transgender," there will be limits to any universalizing trans political strategy—whether conceived in terms of human rights or radical emancipation—when applied to different locations and contexts. Second, like morphing technologies, "transgender" as a term, in spite of its limits, can be seen as being deployed through creative complicity, operating within limiting conditions to help expand and reanimate anew trans people's livable spaces. In this light, it points to the limits of a kind of trans politics that is rooted in visions of absolute purity, and signals the necessary, inventive invocation of complicity in generating change.

The Corporeal Practice of Transgendering:
From Performativity to Morphing Technologies

The notion of morphing is often attributed to computer software: digital morphing creates a transformative effect in changing the appearance or shape of an object into another, sometimes in a seamless sequence. While the ideas behind morphing have been around for several centuries (Wolf 2000, 84), and metamorphic shape-shifters can be found in creation myths from many cultures (Kinder 2000, 63–64), in the digital age morphing is inextricably linked to the corporate realm of mass entertainment, being used in films, animations, television programs, commercials, music videos, and magazines. Through commercial morphing, "We have had our fill of cars turning into tigers, of human bodies going liquid and transforming into inanimate objects, of men changing into women, Caucasians into Asians or Africans or Latinos, dogs into cats, razor-thin models into busty Marilyn Monroes" (Sobchack 2000a, 131–32). Indeed, since commercial morphing predominantly portrays effortless and pleasurable dissolving of boundaries of the body and self, it raises important questions on the corporeal mutability of identity and subjectivity.

Critical media scholars have taken commercial morphing to task—most notably, in Vivian Sobchack's edited volume, *Meta-Morphing: Visual Transformation and the Culture of Quick-Change*, wherein cultural theorists critique a domestication of racial history and depoliticization of racial and gender inequality behind the glossy, postmodern presentation of fluid bodies, shifting shapes, and free-floating identities (Sobchack 2000b). As Scott Bukatman argues, "Morphing presents racial identity only to neutralize it" (2000, 237). Through "a celebration of endlessly transmutable surface, [it] becomes a sign only of itself, hardly even alluding to the complexities of history and ethnic culture behind its digital gloss" (240). Sobchack echoes this skepticism, arguing that morphing "represents and enacts human transformation, metamorphoses, mutability outside of human time, labor, struggle, and power, seemingly transcending structures of hierarchy and succession" (2000a, 151), and harbors an "untenable myth of a heterogeneity that can be homogenized easily, without labor, without struggle, without violence, without pain" (152).

These cultural theorists rightly indict digital morphing for its historical and political emptiness. In fact, the commercial presentation of morphing images hollows out the pain and travail involved in real-life and real-body morphing such as transgendering. Such somatic transformation from the initial feeling of gender dislocation to the "passing" ritual of psychotherapeutic interview and to the actual bodily reconstructive procedure takes more than a split second of cosmetic donning or cybernetic morphing. For trans people, corporeal morphing inside the hegemonic sex/gender system embodies significant political struggles and material consequences.

At the same time, I also wish to supplement these cultural critics' insights by noting that trans people *do* nonetheless need to resort to varying forms of commercial (albeit nondigital) morphing technologies—such as clothing, makeup, cosmetics, electrolysis, hormonal treatment, silicone injection, sex reassignment surgery—built by the same heteronormative capitalist industry to obtain corporeal embodiment, claim gendered citizenship status, and even achieve economic survival (e.g., the Mexican transgender migrants who engage in sex work discussed earlier). The very remediation of pain and violence for trans people thus requires, and is enabled by, a complicit negotiation with capitalism. This consumptive complicity in the bodily reconstructive industry governed by heteronormative capitalism entails the inevitable reinscription of the gender binary, yet it also provides the instrumental conduit by which they reclaim their precarious citizenship when no other means are possible or available.

Trans people's corporeal use of morphing technologies can thus be understood as being driven by an ingenious agency that assembles and acts on the gendered technologies available (however limited by heteronormative capitalism) to ameliorate their abjection and normalize their humanity and livelihood. It is by way of their original and skillful use of an assemblage of morphing technologies—practices, programs, and policies that help transform one's gender identification and embodiment—that transgender subjects appropriate the gender script and disrupt the scripted relations in the ongoing transformation and metamorphosis of their trans selves.

While normative men and women may also resort to certain aspects of such gendered technologies in fitting into masculinity and femininity in liberal life, it is important to note that these technologies take on additional significance for trans people who come from, to different degrees and in varying ways, a nonnormative, abjected position in the gender script. The material contexts and consequences of morphing vary between normative gendered subjects and trans people (which are further complicated by the intersectional effects of race, class, legal status, disability, and location in the global economy). For instance, Stryker and Aren Aizura point to the wide range of issues facing transgender subjects: "Through the operations of employment and housing discrimination, lack of access to health care and social services, and the persistence of both state-sanctioned and unchecked popular violence against many gender-variant individuals, transgender populations are disproportionately incarcerated, living in poverty, and unable to access higher education. These differences in opportunity and vulnerability map starkly onto the intersections of structural racism, gender inequality, and neoliberal economics: trans women of color are far more likely to be poor, to be incarcerated, and to be the victims of street violence" (2013, 6).

While we all have the capacity to morph, transgendering presents conditions of abjection in ways that are particular to trans people (even while they also intersect other conditions of precarity shared by varying segments of normative gendered people). At the same time, it is also within these abject conditions that morphing becomes a way for trans people to improvise and appropriate more livable spaces and destabilize the given relations in liberal citizenship.

To say that we all have the capacity to morph may at first glance seem similar to Butler's notion of performativity, by which she argues that "gender is in no way a stable identity . . . [but is] instituted through a *stylized repetition of acts*" (1988, 519; emphasis in original). As Butler argues, gender is constructed through a mimed, repetitive performance of dominant conventions and through this repetition establishes the appearance of the "realness" of gender. However, this performativity also represents the very possibility of subverting the norms of gender, because we could perform differently (Butler 1990, 1993). Butler points specifically to drag queens as an example of subverting the stableness of gender identity and exposing the tenuous foundation of gender "naturalness" or "reality" (1990, 174–75). Based on this framework, morphing technologies (such as those adopted by drag queens) can be considered a set of instruments that enable our gender repetition and thereby subsumed into Butler's performative theory.

But despite the apparent parallel in illustrating how human subjects "perform" or "morph" gender in everyday life, crucial differences remain in the implied *political* aims and approaches between the two concepts. Specifically, while Butler does not envision gender performativity to be radically free-willed, "a set of free-floating attributes" (1990, 33), by seeking to expose the imitative structure of hegemonic gender—that is, there is no "being" behind the deed or "no gender identity behind the expressions of gender" (33)—her performative thesis ultimately tries to dissuade us from complicity in reinscribing this gender "realness." As such, in ways that are similar to my earlier critique of James Scott's work (see the introduction to this volume), Butler's theorization of queer performativity ends up running away from contamination rather than actively engaging and making ingenious use of it. In contrast, by emphasizing morphing technologies' inextricable connection to heteronormative capitalism, I use those technologies to suggest that complicity with liberal gender citizenship is actually a key to strengthening queer disruption and trans social change.

This distinction, in fact, is particularly evident in Butler's commentary on transsexuality, as its body narratives simultaneously demonstrate the performative thesis *and* contradict her preferred mode of queer performance. In the preface to the 1999 edition of *Gender Trouble*, Butler remarks on the subversive implications of transsexuality:

> Indeed, if we shift the example from drag to transsexuality, then it is no longer possible to derive a judgment about stable anatomy from the clothes that cover and articulate the body. That body may be preoperative, transitional, or postoperative; even "seeing" the body may not answer the question: for *what are the categories through which one sees?* . . . When such categories come into question, the *reality* of gender is also put into crisis: it becomes unclear how to distinguish the real from the unreal. And this is the occasion in which we come to understand that what we take to be "real," what we invoke as the naturalized knowledge of gender is, in fact, a changeable and revisable reality. (1999, xxii–xxiii; emphasis in original)

Butler's reading emphasizes trans people's transgression of the gender binary—that is, their efforts to carve out spaces of purity from the contaminated structure of gender normativity. Without disputing this insight, it is also true that many trans people remodel their gender identification to inhabit the normative frame of heterosexual manhood or womanhood (as exemplified in the case of Ganzon). As Susan Bordo points out, Butler cannot explain why dualist gender binary norms are reconstituted even in drag performance—for example, the drag star Chili Pepper "felt drag queens could help teach women how to be 'real women'" (Bordo 1992, 177). In the case of transsexuals, Butler is similarly unable to account for the fact that some transsexuals feel like the "opposite" gender beginning at an early age. Subversive drag/transgender performance can establish the reification of the gender binary, or, conversely, drag/transgender performance hinges on this binary reification to enable its regeneration of gender life in the cultural script of liberal citizenship. By emphasizing that gender is not dictated by nature or internal disposition but is socially constructed and performatively constituted, Butler can only displace transsexual narratives of somatic dislocation and desire for sexed embodiment that do not explicitly signal gender subversion in the direction that she favors (i.e., purity rather than contamination).

This symptom carriers forward in *Bodies that Matter*, in which Butler examines the ambiguity of the transsexual body and is troubled by its aspiration for "realness." As Jay Prosser notes, from *Gender Trouble* to *Bodies that Matter*, Butler moves from "using the transgendered subject [drag queen] to 'trouble' the naturalization of heterosexuality and sex to using the transsexual subject . . .

to mark the limits of the trouble the subject in transition can effect" (Prosser 1998, 6). Specifically, in her reading of the life of the Latina MTF sex worker Venus Xtravaganza, who was murdered during the filming of the documentary *Paris Is Burning*, Butler locates Venus's potential subversion in her possession of a penis despite her desire to become a "complete" woman (Prosser, 45–55). Butler, in fact, takes Venus's transgression and deviance from the norm—signified by her incomplete transition in possessing female bodily attributes and male genitalia—to be the cause of her murder and death (presumably committed by a client in a hotel room where Venus was engaged in sex work to earn money for her sex change operation). However, while Butler sees value in the subversive transgression of the transsexual body, she is ambivalent that such transgression is motivated not by an oppositional stance but by a hegemonic desire to fit into the "normative framework of heterosexuality" (Butler 1993, 133). For Butler, Venus thus demonstrates the limits of the transsexual sex change: performing the denaturalization of sex/gender can still work to sustain heteronormative arrangements. Prosser writes, "Venus's fantasy . . . of becoming 'real' . . . and her corporeal progress in realizing this fantasy mark her out from the drag ball performers [in the film] who 'do' realness and who 'resist transsexuality'" (48). In other words, instead of disrupting and troubling the gender binary, transsexuality in fact reinscribes and reiterates heteronormativity. As Prosser argues, ironically for Butler, it is in Venus's death, when her "realness" is revealed as "fake," that "Venus holds out . . . the promise of queer subversion" (49). Had Venus completed her transition in acquiring a vagina and becoming a "full" woman, she "would cancel out this potential and succumb to the embrace of hegemonic naturalization" (49).

In the end, by mapping a purifying framework onto transsexuality, Butler's performative theory misrecognizes the inextricable element of contamination in the corporeal practice of transgendering that many trans subjects require to envision and attain, however imperfectly, their ideal spaces of purity. Departing from the idea of performativity, I use morphing technologies to foreground the inevitable contamination of transgendering in the heteronormative capitalist structures as an inextricable route for trans people to settle into normalizing gendered spaces (thus assuaging their abjection), and to further "imagine an embodied elsewhere" (thus recoding other gendered possibilities and regenerating other inhabitable spaces in the given script; see Hayward 2008, 72). If performative repetition ultimately slides into a position that escapes or repels liberal complicity in its vision of transformative politics, this foregrounding emphasis on morphing technologies signals an innovative engagement, negotiation, and reuse of such complicity to expand the spheres of social change.

Morphing In, Morphing Out:
Appropriating Liberal Gendered Citizenship

Infused in trans people's everyday practices, from self-identity construction to sexual practices and intimate relations, the adoption of morphing technologies can be seen as a deployment of ingenious agency that creates renewed spaces of livelihood and nonexistent citizenship for trans subjects. Here I distinguish between two interpenetrating modes of morphing adopted and deployed by trans people to disrupt and appropriate the gender citizenship script: morphing in (when practices of transgendering move toward the opposite gender pole and *morph into* the binary category of M or F) and morphing out (when practices of transgendering improvise spaces of neither man nor woman and neither gay nor straight, thus *morphing out* of the conventional trajectory of M or F). The former disrupts the gender script of citizenship by forcing the binary categories M and F to be inclusive of subjects born with the "opposite" biological body, thereby stretching and expanding the original meanings of the categories of man and woman; the latter challenges the fundamental binary system of citizenship, stipulating that a citizen has a right to travel to gender/sexual destinations other than those labeled M or F. The former signifies a trajectory of corporeal remodeling more or less congruent with the dominant gender binary; the latter signifies attempts to create alternative gendered identities, sexual practices, and amorous relations other than those accorded to heteronormative men or women.

I speak of these two modes as interpenetrating to accentuate their dialectical intricacy—that is, morphing in, as much it implies assimilating into the normative gender script, also expands and reconfigures the conventional definitions assigned to M or F; and morphing out, to the extent that it seemingly carves out alternative spaces beside M or F, remains implicated in heteronormative gender life. In other words, morphing in is stretched and expanded by ingredients of morphing out, and morphing out is restrained and encumbered by elements of morphing in. Together, these jostling desires and practices formulate invigorating ways to shift a transgender subject's life trajectory from M to F or from F to M, as well as from M or F to yet other gendered possibilities, thus reconfiguring the boundaries set by the gender script and enhancing the vitality of appropriable spaces in liberal gender citizenship.

Morphing into M or F

While the predominant idea of transsexuality follows the trajectory of "man becoming woman" or "woman becoming man," the very fact that one has to remodel the body to take on the opposite gender means that the subject is already different from and, in fact, destabilizes the dominant definition of man or woman. As such, transgendering through morphing in can be seen as "challeng[ing] the assumption that gender is congruent with the sex assigned at birth" (Gagné and Tewksbury, 83). But precisely because morphing in slides into the category of M or F, its disruptive effects also "simultaneously and inadvertently" reinforce the gender binary "as an institution" (83). In this way, echoing Gagné and Tewksbury's assessment of transgenderism, morphing in both challenges and reasserts the binary gender system (81). What I wish to accentuate here, however, is the ingenious agency embodied in morphing in that signals subtle twists and nonlinear enactments in appropriating the gender life of liberal citizenship. Transgendering does not constitute a straightforward journey of either assimilation or emancipation. Rather, it highlights a complexly negotiated venture.[8]

The feeling of being oppositely gendered experienced by many trans people in early childhood and adolescence determines their subjectivity into an abject zone of existence in the liberal gender script. Gagné, Tewksbury, and Deanna McGaughey comment on their interviews with sixty-five MTFs: "After an initial period of confusion about sex and gender, most children recognized that cross-dressing and feminine behavior were deviant and, therefore, they tried to repress it and keep it secret. This suggests that as children begin to understand the mental binary gender system, they become ashamed of feminine or transgendered feelings, learn to hide their behaviors, and become confused about who they are and how they fit into the world" (Gagné et al. 1997, 488). Sanger's study in the United Kingdom makes explicit such struggle through the statement provided by Liz, a transwoman: "Anything that I'd ever done that would have sorta given an insight into my inner self my parents would've said things like 'oh you don't do that' or 'boys don't do that' or 'don't do that, that's sissy' and things like that, so you developed even ways from the earliest of age to disguise how you felt inside" (Sanger, 46).

Yet this inability to express and present their "true" feelings or sense of gender publicly does not simply signal a passive state of suppression; rather, the very act of "disguising" one's gendered self during childhood and adolescence transfers into an improvisational agency in remaking one's gendered body and subjectivity to enact trans becoming. For instance, one preoperative transsexual informant in the study by Gagné and colleagues recalls her childhood memory of "wearing her mother's panty hose and shoes at age eight or nine," then progressively "putting the entire ensemble together" when going into adolescence: "I used to borrow [wigs and clothes]. . . . I would put this stuff on when [my parents] were gone and I went running around the house, and it just felt that I was relieved. A great burden was lifted off me. I felt like I'm fine now" (Gagné et al. 1997, 489). In another study conducted by Gagné and Tewksbury, a postoperative MTF's early practices of transgendering similarly "exemplified the hidden resistance . . . [of the] search for identity":

> As I got older, throughout elementary school, I really started to get the wrath of the peers at school. I certainly would not tell anybody about my feelings or express my desires. . . . It was like I was cross-dressing and I really didn't understand and I knew I was alone in the world. . . . Then The Mike Douglas Show had somebody on there [who] had a sex change operation. . . . And it was at that point in time that I realized that other people had my problem and there was a solution to it. From that day forward, I knew I had to have [sex reassignment surgery]. (87–88)

As both accounts demonstrate, the transsexual informants in their early years secretly experimented with and improvised ways of being transgender. These practices do not transcend the given script, but involve negotiation with the liberal lifecycle to create liminal change. They interstitially use mass consumerist products built by the heteronormative capitalist industry to aid their corporeal transformation.

This interstitial negotiation further extends to the stage of psychotherapy during adulthood, a necessary step for those seeking transition through hormonal treatment and sex reassignment surgery. Prior to the publication in 2013 of the fifth edition of the Diagnostic and Statistical Manual of Mental Disorders (DSM-V), which declassifies transsexuality as a mental disorder (renamed a condition of "gender dysphoria," a state of emotional distress), trans people in the United States needed to provide the psychotherapist with the symptomatic narrative of "gender identity disorder" as prescribed under the

DSM-IV, such as feeling "trapped in the wrong body" and wanting to be the opposite sex from early childhood, thus demonstrating gender "realness" in order to convince the medical authority to prescribe treatment. The labeling and classification of transsexuality as a psychiatric disorder has been a contested issue within the trans community: while those seeking its removal from the DSM-IV point to its stigmatizing effects and reification of gender normativity, others argue that such medical diagnosis is necessary to gain access to hormones and sex reassignment surgery (as well as to insurance coverage). What I wish to emphasize here is how the medical-psychotherapeutic model has been strategically used by trans people as another instantiation of morphing technologies.

Transgender patients deliberately play into stereotypical gender roles in order to gain access to the bodily reconstructive procedures that can more fully remodel their bodies in line with their desired gender identity. A transgender informant in Sally Hines's study in the United Kingdom illustrates this process in her narrative: "'Cos you want what they've got to give you and so you quickly learn the script . . . for what you should say and not say. And I think people buy into that, people do say these things that the doctors need to hear to tick off on the form to make you eligible" (Hines 2009, 89). In such scenarios, transgender patients manifest characteristics of "knowing the answers before the questions are asked" and "being less honest about their personal histories" by repeatedly rehearsing the "wrong body" narrative (88). Crucially, as Hines argues, what is critical to acknowledge here is that "the self-conscious repetition of this narrative can be read as an agency driven process whereby trans people employ knowledge as power . . . as . . . [this] rehearsed narrative . . . is consciously repeated as a means to an end" (89–90). Indeed, performing this ritual demonstrates ingenious agency, since trans people cleverly "[present] textbook cases and [develop] ideal medical profiles" in front of medical professionals (Valentine, 265n13) to appropriate the liberal gender script in their ongoing gender metamorphosis. In this regard, the heteronormative establishment of medical psychotherapy actually does the work of facilitating the corporeal opening of mutable sex and amorphous gender. At the same time, because of its complicity in the binary gender system, it simultaneously circumscribes the extent of trans metamorphosis within the given gender script.

This aspect of creating liminal change in the sex/gender system continues when transgender individuals engage in laborious and creative work to retrain, redecorate, and remake the body as they "come out" to enact and affirm their morphed gender identity publicly. Schrock and his colleagues' study on MTFs' embodiment of womanhood demonstrates this process. As they note, "Trans-embodiment is more work intensive for male-to-female transsexuals than it is for female-to-male transsexuals—largely because gender norms surrounding appearance, demeanor, and the body are more stringent for women" (Schrock et al., 321). While biological women also undergo the process of gender socialization to perform their gender in a feminine way, this gendered relearning is unique for transwomen, who have been "trained" to enact their gender since birth in a masculine way, imparting to them a regenerative capacity to ameliorate the force of abjection and resettle into normalizing spaces of gender citizenship.

For instance, retraining the body involves "overcoming habits of moving and speaking like men" through practice and self-monitoring. Many MTFs secretly study women they know (lovers, coworkers, friends) "to not only retrain their demeanor and voice . . . but also take women's perspectives" (Schrock et al., 321). Kris, an interviewee who is a veteran of the Vietnam War, states:

> With the three wives I had, I studied them. I mean I studied them. It wasn't just observation. I watched how they did things. How they held a cigarette, how they sat, how they walked, how they gestured . . . picking up a fork, the way a woman drives a car. Men don't realize it, but everything is so different. . . . A woman holds a cigarette out toward the end of her fingers, and a male holds a cigarette down here [near the knuckles]. . . . When a woman drives a car, both hands are not on the sides; they're at the top [and] the thumbs are always above the steering wheel. . . . If you start listening, when [women] end a sentence, they go up. The voice inflection will always go up. And when you do that, it softens your voice. (322)

Karen, another respondent, also underlines the interstitial character of her transgendering by hiding her transsexuality from her wife and teenage daughter while learning to imitate feminine demeanor when watching television with them: "Women touch more. They are more intimate with each other. They are not afraid of showing emotion. They smile more. They are not afraid to express vulnerability. . . . Basically, learning how to sit, gestures, the tilt of the head, smile, touching you" (322).

In addition to retraining the body, redecorating the body involves financial investment in the purchase of women's clothing, shoes, and makeup to discipline the body. Another participant, Joyce, indicates that "she often had to make a 'conscious effort' to not 'sit with [her] legs spread' but that wearing long skirts 'reinforces it a lot more'" (Schrock et al., 324). Others would "[invite] makeup professionals to support group meetings for discussion and demonstration, participating in Mary Kay makeup parties for trans women, . . . exchanging decorative information and techniques on transgender e-mail lists" (325). As Schrock and his colleagues argue, while special cosmetic knowledge enhances transwomen's ability to pass (thus shielding them from potential harassment and violence), it also subjects them "to profit-seeking cultural 'experts'" (325). Morphing in for these MTFs implies the filtering of one's body "through the hegemonic male gaze" (being conscious of their receding hairline, body weight, and body shape); as a result, these transwomen become "the objects of their own objectification" (327). The creation of a morphed gender life is built through a negotiated complicity with "the [cosmetic] profiteers and promoters of gender differentiation" (325).

Similarly, when it comes to remaking the body, it is by participating in the bodily reconstructive procedures of electrolysis and hormonal treatment, which are steeped in heteronormative capitalism. While it may seem that transwomen are trapped by biological significations and gender stereotypes, one may relook at this as a negotiation with the liberal gender script whereby enacting "changes in their physical bodies [gives] them permission and opportunities to further feminize their subjectivities" (Schrock et al., 329), thus facilitating their transgendering and appropriation of the gender script. For instance, Marzie in the study comments on how taking hormone pills not only reshapes her body but also pulls her subjectivity more in line with the feminine gender pole:

> I felt a lot more emotional, a lot more in touch with my feelings. And I was able to express my feelings a lot better. . . . It seems like I get more depressed, more easily, more often than I did before. . . . My interests have changed a lot. It used to be that when I go into a bookstore, I'd go to the science and computer section or whatever, and—in the last couple years I've been getting a lot more into nature, like growing plants and things—and so no matter when I go to the book store, first I go and check out the gardening books. . . . I'm definitely very much more into relationships. You know, I mean connecting with people and being in nature, and not at all into technology. (329)

It is critical to note, however, that morphing in does not necessarily slide into the stereotypical, heteronormative notion of man or woman. In many instances, it creates new meanings, subjectivities, and embodiments that are not traditionally understood as M or F, thus reconfiguring the script in even more substantial ways. As Jason Cromwell, an FTM scholar, recounts, "All my young life I knew I was a boy." His lack of male genitalia never convinced him otherwise (1999, 4). He argues, "Most female-bodied transpeople have always had the self-concept of being male and/or man, although the degree differs." For reasons that include financial constraints, health, medical eligibility, low success rate of phalloplasty, self-identification, and politics, many FTMs "choose to live . . . as men with vaginas," thereby destabilizing the heteronormative myth that one has to have a penis to be a man (107). One FTM informant in Cromwell's study put it this way: "If I didn't have the label transsexual I'd probably think of myself as a man with a female body. I belong to neither sex, yet I'm both: I have a beard and a deep voice, I've had a mastectomy but I still have a vagina. I don't have a problem with that, neither does my wife, but society does" (105).

In this narrative, the respondent's reference to himself as a "man" and to his partner as "wife" suggests a process of morphing into conventional gender roles, but his absence of male genitals and being a husband with a vagina also suggests an improvisational challenge to the liberal script of gender binary. Resonating with the experiences of the migrant transgender sex workers who maintain their male genitals discussed earlier in this chapter, FTMs who live as men with vaginas move creatively between "ordinary men" in the general public context and "men with female genitalia" in their own comfortable private lives.

In fact, some FTMs specifically vary their gendered presentations depending on social contexts. Henry Rubin remarks in a study of FTMs, "If their status as men is challenged, they will choose to appear as stereotypically male as possible and behave like the most 'manly' of men. Their behavior may be hostile, oppressive, and even violent in ways that deny recognition to women and other men. Conversely, if they are recognizable as men, they will feel comfortable enough to deviate from the dominant types of manly presentation and behavior" (2003, 165). This nuanced and contextualized reading shows that the way trans people present themselves may have much to do with their sense of social comfort and recognition in any given context, suggesting that they inventively appropriate, negotiate, and deploy rules of gender.

Consider, thus, the case of Louise, a transwoman in Sanger's study who does not identity as fully female but is happy to be perceived that way because it allows her to be more readily accepted and avoid uncomfortable questioning by others: "Only I need to know that I'm not entirely straight (laughs) and only I need to know that I'm not entirely female, but I don't think anyone is really, I think if anyone says they're entirely one or the other they're probably misunderstood, and I think [there's] just some kind of balance somewhere between. Yeah I think I'm 90% female most of the time" (Sanger, 47). Although such silence may be perceived as perpetuating a gender binary, one may also read Louise as interstitially and creatively negotiating with the given gender script to appropriate liminal inclusion and belonging. What has also been demonstrated here thus far is that, as indicated earlier, morphing in does not suggest a straight assimilation into the normative gender script, but contains fissuring elements of morphing out that expand and reconfigure the conventional definitions assigned to M or F.

In all, these transgendering practices and narratives show the inventive ways in which, in their respective contexts and limiting conditions, trans people resiliently fashion a different way to be gendered citizens that is simultaneously assimilatory and disruptive with regard to the liberal gender script. They resort to morphing technologies to facilitate their gender transformation, manifesting a designing agency that makes use of its complicity with heteronormativity and the capitalist structure to normalize their humanity even in the midst of abjectifying forces.

Morphing out of M or F

Although morphing in creates dissonance in liberal gender life, its tendency toward settling into the gender binary does not characterize other trans people who are dissatisfied with the either M or F option. Many, in fact, seek to morph out of binary genders by reassembling and reconfiguring existing gender categories to improvise spaces of neither man nor woman and neither gay nor straight. In doing so, they challenge the fundamental binary system of liberal gender. Importantly, as I conjectured earlier, to the extent that morphing out is facilitated by the same heteronormative morphing technologies, its embodiment of gender and sexual plurality is not likely to signify the end of gender. Instead, it is likely to regenerate and innovate interstitial spaces beside (rather than beyond) the gender binary. As Anne Fausto-Sterling notes, "Gender variation [does not] mean the concept of gender would disappear entirely" (2000, 108). Binary genders do not vanish nor are rendered meaningless, but are reappropriated and rearranged. Morphing out thus translates not into "undoing" gender (Butler 2004b) but into a recoding, in C. Jacob Hale's words, wherein "the dominant cultural gender categorizations are not ignored but reorganized" (quoted in Cromwell 1999, 134). As I illustrate here, trans people's attempts to morph out of M or F cannot be completely disentangled from heteronormative gender life; they remain restrained by elements of morphing in. Morphing out thus does not signify a liminal space of radical transcendence; rather, like morphing in, it is enacted in the shadow of the gender script of liberal citizenship.

To begin, certain informants in Sanger's study openly reveal a fluid sense of self that identifies with neither strictly men nor women. Sam, who identifies as genderqueer, comments, "I'd really like everyone to just be able to, if someone doesn't feel male, female, feels both, feels something else, it would be nice if there was some representation of that. Or alternatively there was no representation of gender and everyone was just a person. That would be nice" (Sanger, 48). Lisa, who identifies as a non-trans woman, also narrates, "Depending on what mood I'll tick whatever, I'll tick female and male sometimes, but there's more female" (48). Although she feels comfortable with her female identity, Lisa refuses to be reined in by scripted femininity: "In terms of where I am in that spectrum I'm not . . . that sort of clear-cut, one pole or the other. I'm very, very sort of borderline sort of genderqueer kind of stuff, particularly through knowing people that are way more so" (48). Similarly, Marina, another genderqueer respondent, states, "I now identify as somewhere in between, somewhere . . . just neither female or male, or both. Neither or both is how I identify" (49).

Although their narratives and practices seemingly place the trans subjects outside the gender binary, they are actually negotiated within the liberal gender script. For instance, the trans subjects' claims to being "neither-nor" or "both" still use M and F as the central referents, and their trans embodiments, assisted by morphing technologies, manifest varying degrees and elements of masculinity and femininity. As Sanger argues, "This identification outside the gender binary is still positioned with respect to the categories of male and female, underlining the impossibility of discounting this discourse altogether, . . . [and implicating] a more contingent relationship" (49). Thus, as Pat Califia observes, despite her claim to be living outside the rules of gender, the transgender writer Kate Bornstein still retrains, redecorates, and remakes her body in a feminine way (Califia 1997, 259). This is not to say that Bornstein's gendered subjectivity is not fluid. Rather, it suggests that her morphing out is inevitably implicated in, and circumscribed by, the hegemonic gender script. The same goes for other trans and genderqueer subjects who may switch between masculine and feminine self-presentations or who combine both gendered outlooks in their self-embodiment: given that their morphing out requires the reuse and appropriation of morphing technologies produced in heteronormative capitalism (e.g., masculine or feminine dress and adornment), their protean transformation constantly resignifies the gender binary in the very act of destabilizing this binary.

Morphing out thus does not shift a trans subject's gender embodiment to a limitless beyond. Rather, it is filtered through the heteronormative script of gender life and may only result in compromised effects. Yet I wish to emphasize here again that it is also precisely this creative reuse of the heteronormative binary that provides the basis for trans people to disrupt and appropriate the gender script in staging their morphing out.

Thus, as discussed earlier, FTMs with vaginas who live as heterosexual husbands can be understood as participating in a scripted gender role at the same time that they also destabilize the phallocentric equation of manhood with penis that predicates the gender requirements of liberal citizenship. In short, they morph out even in their complicity with resignifying the heteronormative binary. Consider the cases of FTMs who go through pregnancy with their female reproductive organs while insisting on gender identification as men, not women. For instance, one trans man in Rubin's study, Matthew, looks at his attachment to the newborn he gave birth to in "the way a father would" (Rubin 2003, 123). The self-description as a "father" suggests a specific gender role taken on by Matthew in the way he understands his parental identification and relates to his child, but his corporeal embodiment as an FTM also confounds the definitions of female pregnancy and paternal gender role, creating gendered destinations beside the conventionally conceived trajectory of M or F. Desires to morph out of the gender binary are thus continually pulled in by tendencies to morph into that binary; and yet, through this dialectical interpenetration, trans people re-create liminal spaces of inclusion and belonging beside the given gender binary.

What is especially interesting in the improvisation of this not-yet-existing citizenship is the interstitial regeneration of plural sexualities. The diverse spectrum of trans folks does not follow heteronormative gender roles by blending into straight heterosexuality: they may self-identify as straight, gay, lesbian, bisexual, queer, or engage in sex or relationships with other trans people. They may see themselves as both sexes and neither and incorporate their born-sexed body parts or prior gender traits into their new roles. As Butler puts it,

> One can become a transman and want boys (and become a male homosexual), or one can become a transman and want girls (and become a heterosexual), or one can become a transman and undergo a set of shifts in sexual orientation that constitute a very specific life history and narrative. . . . Shifts in sexual persuasion can be in response to particular partners, so that lives, trans or not, don't always emerge as coherently heterosexual or homosexual, and the very meaning and lived experience of bisexuality can also shift through time, forming a particular history that reflects certain kinds of experiences rather than others. (2006, 278–79)

Thus, while in the psychiatrist Robert Stoller's "diagnostic criteria" FTMs are attracted only to the conventionally feminine—heterosexual women desiring pregnancy and motherhood (Stoller 1975, 224)—this is by no means the only location or identity FTMs adopt. For example, Justin M., an FTM informant in Cromwell's study, disassociates with heterosexual masculinity and identifies as a "feminine gay man" (Cromwell, 130). And while many may think that FTMs, having chosen the path of becoming a man, would have no use for their vagina and strongly desire a penis, this is not necessarily the case. As Cromwell points out, many "derive pleasure from genitalia, including vaginal penetration." He cites two informants:

> Rich: I am one of those who "enjoy my cunt" but still see myself as male. I do not identify as a lesbian or a dyke. I am a sexual being and will be sexual with the organs I have.

> Mark Craig: I'll use the equipment I've got. To me, that's a sign of strength, of my manhood. (Cromwell, 131)

FTMs creatively improvise sexualities that cannot be contained within heteromasculine territorial borders and redefine notions of maleness and manhood in the process. It is also crucial to highlight the interstitial quality of such sexual practices of morphing out, as they are enacted without others' knowing. It is not known to the public that an FTM engages in sex as a man with vagina. These ingenious sexual acts story trans people's "hidden transcripts" (Scott 1990), which maneuver interstitially through cracks and loopholes in hegemonic gender.

This interstitiality is further delineated in other trans folks' narrations of sexual encounters. Marina, who considers herself a genderqueer, states:

> I've very clearly had straight women attracted to me because they thought I was a boy, and conversely I've had gay men attracted to me thinking I was a man, and I like that androgyny, definitely thrive on that. . . . On one hand on a superficial level I actually thrive on just letting people be confused and I want them to stay confused. I don't want them to just only see me one way or the other way. On a deeper level I also, I don't want to be explaining myself all the time, because it's more than just one thing. (Sanger, 49)

Nataf, a transman in Cromwell's study, also describes his plural sexuality in this way:

> With a heterosexual man I can be their best nightmare fantasy in the shape of a boy hustler. With a heterosexual woman I can be a pretty hetero male; or if I perceive her as a fag hag, I can be a faggot with bi tendencies. With a lesbian top femme I can be a high heel worshipping boy bottom or a third sex butch, a lesbian man. With a gay man I can be a cock worshipping catamite or a fisting top. With gender ambiguous bi men and women and sexually ambiguous transgendered people maybe I can just be myself. (Cromwell, 134)

Through their "private" sexual practices and amorous relations, trans people thus continually explore and experiment with different possibilities of doing gender and sex, interstitially morphing the original copy of M or F into something else in their everyday lives.

Yet again, even such interstitial sexual plurality (morphing out) is not necessarily detached from entanglement with the reproduction of heteronormative gender. For instance, in her examination of the intimate space of trans-femme relationships, Jane Ward points to the ways in which queer celebration of the oppositional identity of FTMs overlooks the "gender labor" in which their femme partners engage to bolster and validate their trans masculinity (Ward 2010). By invoking the term "gender labor," Ward examines the ways in which certain trans intimate relationships reinscribe conventional gender roles to assist trans people in realizing their gender transformation and morphing out. As Ward argues, while there has been much discussion of the "defiant self-making" and politics of refusal in queer studies, there is "little attention to the ways in which queer forms of 'undoing' and fluidity remain reliant on the normative genders and feminized forms of care work that queer politics rejects" (92n12). For Ward, certain queer celebration of "utopic 'ways of life'" is often aligned with adventurous masculine subjectivity (mobility, independence, risk taking) that disavows ways of life associated with mundane femininity, such as reproductivity, caretaking, shopping, and homemaking (81–82). Within the home sphere, femmes are subject to this same dichotomized, hierarchical position by having to "validate and celebrate their [FTM] partners' masculinity and to suppress the complexity of their own gender and sexual subjectivity in the service of this goal" (79). Given such experiences, femmes often describe "the trans-femme erotic script as a site of negotiation, confusion, and hard work" (88). The morphing out in these FTM-femme relationships thus traffics in the reiteration of heteronormativity as the binary gender script "is reproduced through routinized forms of care work" (81). Reinscription of the gender binary in these instances shows the ways in which the gender script of liberal citizenship is negotiated and revised rather than transcended.

I use Ward's study not to generalize all trans-femme relationships, but as an example to delineate the ways in which the bolstering of trans people's gender identities and sexual subjectivities may sometimes rely on selective participation in, and appropriation of, the heteronormative gender script, though they are still creative and improvisational as they collectively carve transgressive spaces from relationships unrecognized by liberal citizenship. In fact, it may be best to describe such intimate endeavors of morphing out as instigating an open and moving journey without a foreclosed future. On the whole, the morphing out of sexual and intimate relations may be conceived as what Eve Kosofsky Sedgwick describes as "daring surmise and cognitive rupture, followed by moments of experiential reflection, forward projection, trial and error, and reality testing of such surmise" (1997, 238). Each episode of morphing out constitutes an identification with "the growing edge of a self," in Sedgwick's words, as it carves out a "new site of provisional meaning-consolidation . . . [where] many new paths and itineraries evidently become visible. . . . Their existence could never have been guessed from the place from which one began" (238). It is within limits, complicities, and continuing innovation that practices of transgendering refigure the contingent and unknown futurity of gender life.

In the end, while the perpetual return and replication of morphing out in appropriating the liberal gender script undoubtedly inscribes these transgendering practices as subcultural, this subcultural expansion and enhancement differs from Halberstam's formulation of transgender subculture as a singular and external queer temporality and space in radical distinction from heteronormativity (Halberstam 2005). Rather, as I have illustrated here, trans people's morphing out is precisely enabled and facilitated through its implication and selective participation in the normative gender binary (embedded in various morphing technologies). It works *inside* and *through* the liberal script in appropriating a dissident gender life and creating renewed gendersexual spaces *beside* heteronormativity. Like a gender bricolage, transgendering through morphing out rearranges and recodes the original normative product (M and F), creating new subcultural meanings without being able to fully displace the reifications of the original copy.

Activist Reorientation: Morphing in and out of Rights

To the extent that morphing technologies are produced *within*, rather than outside, the script of liberal citizenship, trans people are thus inevitably implicated in replicating the heteronormative production of the gender binary even in their acts of crossing the boundaries of gender. However, given the liberal suspension of gender variance in the zone of abjection, such complicity with the hegemonic sex/gender system can be read as a creative and resourceful way for trans people to produce a circuitous dynamic of change in their own lives and the larger society. Together, morphing in and morphing out produce forms of ingenious citizenship in their own creative and audacious ways: they take on *negotiated* forms as they continuously revise and reconfigure the gender script by enlisting and reassembling the heteronormative ingredients of the gender binary. They are *interstitial*, because they emerge guilefully and surprisingly, whether through scenes of passing as the other gender at psychotherapy sessions or through devising plural sexualities in their intimate relationships without public knowledge. They underline a *subcultural* gendered existence in which subjects shape their own right to exist as differently gendered citizens. Finally, they are *oppositional* to the liberal gender script, not in a simple or direct way, but because they entail a complex and contradictory disruption that makes flexible use of what Theresa Martinez describes as a strategic spectrum of submissions, neutralities, alliances, accommodations, and protests (1997, 269).

As with hidden tactics and calculated abjection, this does not suggest that trans people's adoption of morphing technologies produces equal effects across different locations and contexts. First, given the signification of the gender binary in the liberal citizenship script, it necessarily compresses any official recognition of transgender life toward the binary gender trajectory. As such, those who morph in are more likely to ameliorate their abjection and normalize their status in relation to those who morph out. For instance, Hines comments on the passage of the Gender Recognition Act of 2005 in the United Kingdom, which allows trans people to change their gender status on birth certificates and to marry:

> The law now allows for movement across the binary of male/female, but the spectrum in-between male and female, such as transgendered, inter-sexed, bigendered, and androgynous, remain[s] outside current frameworks of citizenship. . . . [A]n understanding of gender as intertextual and precarious is at odds with current concepts of citizenship. . . . In this way, people who rebuff the gender binary by refusing neatly to dovetail gender presentation and gender identity (e.g., bigendered trans people, butch trans lesbians, camp trans men, cross-dressers, and drag kings and queens) continue to be excluded from the rights and recognition of citizenship. In rejecting the surgical route, then, transgender people fall outside the domain of the "deserving citizen." (96)

The liberal gender citizenship script is opened up only to the extent that such opening is predicated on a gender binary model that does not recognize "the diversity of new (trans) masculinities and femininities as they are variously constructed and experienced" (96). In this way, trans people who morph into M or F (such as Ganzon, who embodies straight heterosexual womanhood) become relatively *normalized* as deserving liberal citizens in relation to those who morph out of the gender binary and remain relatively *abjected* (such as genderqueer people, who identify with neither men nor women).

Second, such relations are further compounded by intersectional dynamics such as gender, race, and class. For instance, in interviews with twenty-nine FTMs in Southern California, the sociologist Kristen Schilt examines how her respondents report receiving more social status and respect, as well as promotion and economic opportunities, after transitioning to the male gender, thus providing an "outsider-within" perspective and awareness of the "patriarchal dividend" derived from the subordination of women (Schilt 2006). As Schilt argues, this masculine differential further intersects with race and body structure: "Tall, white FTMs see more advantages than short FTMs and FTMs of color" (465).

Ingenious citizenship is thus inextricably implicated in reproducing inequality and abjection even as it produces more appropriable gender/sexual spaces for differently situated trans subjects. As I have argued, such imperfection cannot be transcended in the script of liberal citizenship. But the point is not that we should sit idly by and do nothing beyond observing trans folks' quotidian improvisations. Instead, these limits push us to consider a more important question: what lesson might trans people's everyday enactments of ingenious citizenship, enabled through morphing technologies, offer us on political activism?

As I wish to suggest, trans people's participation in morphing technologies signals a needed political reorientation of trans activism: an ingenious approach that fluidly mediates, incorporates, and utilizes complicity with heteronormative capitalism in expanding maneuverable and livable gender/sexual spaces for trans people in different contexts and circumstances. Following practices of transgendering that employ liberal complicity to morph into, and out of, M or F, we need an elastic kind of trans activism that deploys liberal complicity to morph into different shapes and forms without a preconceived political framework. I envision such an activist approach as morphing "in and out of rights"; that is, flexibly alternating between *morphing into* rights and *morphing out* of rights. It may morph out of the logics/discourses of rights in order to gain de facto rights, just as it may morph into the regimes of rights in order to expand spaces of cultural transformation beyond the codification of rights. For instance, trans activism can employ non–rights-based rationales (e.g., business interests) to advocate for the dignified treatment of trans people; at the same time, it can also seek official recognition of transgenderism (e.g., official documents, public school education) via instrumental appeals to destabilize cultural assumptions of gender binary in public spaces. Whether rights should be invoked—and how they should be used—are flexibly determined depending on contexts rather than settled in advance.

Such a fluid conception of trans politics has yet to be fully conceived and explored in the historical and present trajectory of trans activism, which has been predominantly configured by democratic agency. As noted earlier, transgender is distinct from domestic and sex workers in that it embodies a human category that is detached from work or occupation identity in capitalism. As such, while the democratic orientation of collective transgender resistance finds parallels in domestic workers' and sex workers' rights movements, tension exists within trans activism on whether rights discourse can advance the humane recognition and status of trans people or will actually constrain and undermine their emancipation by trapping them within a liberal capitalist configuration.

As Stryker documents, like its counterparts in domestic and sex work, the beginning of transgender activism grows out of the historical context of the population's abject social existence: "Since the late nineteenth century, people whom we would now call transgendered have advocated legal and social reforms that would ameliorate the kinds of oppression and discrimination they have suffered as a result of their difference from the way most people understand their own gender."[9] In the United States, transgender advocacy began to gain momentum in the 1950s with the publicity given to Christine Jorgensen, whose so-called sex-change operation in 1952 "made her an international celebrity and brought transgender issues to widespread attention." During this period, the transgender activist Virginia Prince "founded the first peer support and advocacy groups for male cross-dressers in the United States" in the 1950s and early 1960s. In 1952, Stryker notes, "Prince and . . . other transgender people in Southern California launched *Transvestia: The Journal of the American Society for Equality in Dress*," marking "the beginning of the transgender rights movement in the United States." In the late 1960s, transgender "street queens" such as Marsha P. Johnson and Sylvia Rivera worked closely with gay community advocates in instigating the Stonewall Riots, "which are generally regarded as the origin of the contemporary GLBTQ rights movement."[10]

Importantly, while the democratic orientation of transgender advocacy has been largely shaped (and constrained) by the rights-based framework within the liberal political imaginary, a contesting discursive configuration gained increasing prominence with the emergence of militant queer activism in the late 1980s and early 1990s. At this juncture, "Militant groups such as ACT UP (AIDS Coalition to Unleash Power) and Queer Nation crafted a highly visible, playfully ironic, angry style of media-oriented, direct-action politics that proved congenial to a new generation of transgender activists. The first transgender activist group to embrace the new queer politics was Transgender Nation, founded in 1992 as an offshoot of Queer Nation's San Francisco chapter."[11]

What is critical about this militant shift is that it leads to a radical critique of gender identity categories on which rights discourse is predicated. Thus, Riki Anne Wilchins, a co-founder of Transexual Menace, an activist group that inherited the in-your-face picketing-style political activism of Transgender Nation, argues that transgender politics should seek to detach bodies from their predetermined meaning. As she writes, essentializing trans people into men or women "generally works to our disadvantage . . . [and] places us in the position of pursuing a 'realness' defined on other people's bodies" (Wilchins 1997, 187).

In her foundational essay during this time, "The 'Empire'" Strikes Back: A Posttranssexual Manifesto," Sandy Stone similarly calls on transsexuals to forgo passing as natural members of the binary gender.[12] Calling for a "posttranssexual" genre in rereading and reclaiming transsexuals' intertexual subjectivities, bodies, and histories, she positions transsexuality in a space of political possibility outside and beyond gender binary. Stone writes, "I am suggesting that in the transsexual's erased history we can find a story disruptive to the accepted discourses of gender . . . [T]he transsexual currently occupies a position which is *nowhere*, which is *outside* the binary oppositions of gendered discourse. For a transsexual, as a transsexual, to generate a true, effective and representational counterdiscourse is to speak from *outside* the boundaries of gender, *beyond* the constructed oppositional modes which have been predefined as the only positions from which discourse is possible."[13] Stone's post-transsexual manifesto thus poses a political challenge to any normative passing and compliance with the binary gender regime through which trans rights discourse is constituted.

Further reinforcing this position, Lisa Bower argues that laws, in constructing fixed group categories, are insufficient in understanding the fluid, unstable, and shifting nature of sexual identity, or nonidentity (Bower 1997). Bower advocates that queer subjects shift their forum of contention from "official recognition" by legal institutions toward a "politics of direct address" (such as that of Queer Nation, Queer Nights Out, and Queer Shopping Network), an everyday politics of cultural improvisations that affirm the public visibility of alternative sexual practices and gender identities in different social spheres and institutions. Rejecting liberal tolerance, this politics of direct address demands affirmation and respect by inserting "deviant" identities in the public space to "familiariz[e] mainstream America with 'otherness' in all its varieties" (Bower, 282).

Notably, what accentuates this radical queer/trans resistance is its refusal of complicity with "hegemonic models of gender conformity" (Halberstam 1998, 9). The tension it generates within the movement on whether to seek recognition through rights or liberation from rights continues to shape the dynamics of trans activism in the early twenty-first century. In fact, one can conceive current trans activism as being pursued through two contrasting routes: rights-based politics and a more radical, emancipatory paradigm such as the one envisioned by Dean Spade's "critical trans politics" (Spade 2011).

These two political approaches have provided crucial arguments and discourses in support of their respective formulations in the ongoing struggles for trans justice. Both, however, emanate from the same trajectory of democratic agency that configures transgender activism since its inception. Here I wish to tease out one common, underlying limit in both: their convergence toward the decontaminating ethos I have signaled in previous chapters.

For instance, Currah, while advocating for rights-based politics as an indispensable practical strategy in liberal democracy, nonetheless gestures to a seemingly uncontaminated future when he writes:

> As a movement, however, the ultimate goal of transgender rights does not seem to be to contain gender nonconforming identities and practices within slightly expanded yet still-normative gender constructions and arrangements. . . .
>
> Those working under the trans umbrella are seeking a world in which we have the luxury of disagreeing about gender without worrying about which narrative is more compelling to those who have the power to deny access to social services, to take away children, or to dismiss discrimination claims out of hand. (2006, 24)

Richard Juang, in constructing a democratic formulation of transgender rights based on Charles Taylor's principle of equal recognition, similarly conveys an uncontaminated stance when he argues, "one should not have to 'earn' a conferral of equal value" (2006, 244).

To be sure, what Currah and Juang are also indicating here is that formal rights are inadequate, and "legal recognition of trans people is meaningful only when it is part of a larger cultural transformation" (Currah et al. 2006, xxiii). But what if in liberalism rights are always already encoded as a means to an end, and what if gaining rights and creating larger cultural transformation actually require our ingenious use rather than shunning of the instrumental structure of liberal exchange? As indicated at the beginning of this chapter, the term "transgender" emerged out of the structural-geographic context of Western capitalist modernity. By implication, the very concept of "transgender rights" is generated out of the same contaminated process and, as such, is always already crafted with instrumental and negotiated effects rather than embodying a transcendent position. If we predicate the articulation of transgender rights simply on a critical modality of cultural consciousness-raising, we lose sight of how "the project of consciousness-raising is necessarily part of the same systemic violation" (Cheah 2006, 168). Thus, for instance, while the International Bill of Gender Rights calls for the right to control and change one's own body cosmetically, chemically, or surgically to express a self-defined gender identity,[14] the actual exercise of this human right requires the instrumental invocation of heteronormative capitalism—that is, morphing technologies—for its realization. Similar to the global sex workers' rights movements, transgender rights claims, whether advanced in the realm of hate crimes, employment discrimination, health care, or marriage rights and child custody, must ineluctably traffic in the heteronormative capitalist economy of exchange.

Precisely because of this inevitable complicity, others seek to move beyond the legal strategy of inclusion and recognition to formulate a radical political project rooted in an even stronger conception of purity. For instance, posing the question, "What's wrong with rights?" Spade argues that the "logic of visibility and inclusion" encapsulated in rights-based politics has not significantly altered, let alone eradicated, the multiple axes of structural oppression that systematically harm gender-variant subjects, especially those most marginalized and vulnerable (2011, 81), and in fact produces a politics of normalcy that allows the more privileged to access rights and protections at the expense of others. Cautioning against complicity with instrumentality, Spade specifically warns, "Resistant movements must be careful not to replicate business model approaches" (196).

Spade's indictment of liberal structures is spot on, and one should consider his broader critique in light of his ongoing commitment to providing necessary legal aid to trans subjects as an attorney and trans activist. Still, the larger direction of his argument prompts questioning. It is indeed tempting to conceive of a counterproject of critical trans politics in an emancipatory manner and to articulate a political positioning that is above and beyond complicity in reiterating liberal normativity and structural power relations. But in which ways might such a purifying vision and aspiration, like the human rights framework that it critiques, crystallize into a universal modality that misses a necessary complicity with intricate webs of power and operation—both inside and outside the liberal West?

At this historical conjuncture of global neoliberal politics, it is time for us to consider whether, instead of critiquing, refuting, or transcending inevitable complicity, trans activism needs to shift away from democratic agency

that has inscribed its political configuration since its origin to center ingenious agency in its movement struggles. Morphing technologies offer us
the lesson that trans activism can use the limited but varied resources and
openings available to generate a nonlinear process of social change. Michelle
O'Brien's political tracing of her trans body within the commodity chain of
global capitalism similarly points to this direction. She reflects:

> When I give myself an injection of Delestrogen, I am locating myself and
> am located within global flows of power. I am connected to the complex
> political, economic, and social histories of how these drugs were manu-
> factured and by whom. I am bound within the international trade systems
> that allow those corporations to function, that bring the hormones to my
> door in a brown envelope. I am facing the systems of violence that render
> my body invisible, that make it impossible for many to get drugs at all. By
> taking hormones, I am doing what we all do in various ways: I am par-
> ticipating within the system of transnational capital. These systems are
> racist, classist, sexist, homophobic, and transphobic to their core. . . . And
> yet, all of us are deeply, inexorably dependent on these very structures.
> Quite literally, we need them to keep us alive. (2013, 63)

As O'Brien recognizes, "Our ability to resist . . . is deeply inseparable from
our ongoing connection to these very systems" of violence, oppression, and
exploitation (64). Trans politics thus should not hinge on "a fanatical commitment to purity . . . [or] an attempt at a total refusal to participate or be
complicit in any form of corporate rule," but should instead proceed by "in-
terfacing global capitalism, . . . corrupting, redirecting, and redefining . . .
the . . . system to serve our ends" (63).

The notion of morphing in and out of rights specifically builds on such
insight to configure a fluid political strategy that can morph in its activist
aim and approach in differing locations and contexts. As numerous studies
have documented, gender variance in non-Western regions contains its own
distinctive configurations and particular modes of negotiation in the context
of local scripts, regimes, and mores, which cannot be exclusively understood
through Western concepts or models of gender and sexuality (Johnson 1997;
Kulick 1998; Manalansan 2003; Cabral and Viturro 2006; Najmabadi 2008,
2013). As such, whether rights should be pursued—and how they should
be pursued—must vary in accordance with differing local conditions rather
than determined via a universalizing approach. Consequently, rather than
embracing or refuting rights in advance, morphing in and out of rights for-

mulates an interventionist approach that proceeds in a contingent and fluid relation to rights. Given the transnational dissemination of the liberal script, one thing morphing in and out of rights does cling to is its attachment to liberal complicity in order to use its accrued power to regenerate spaces of purity. Here I provide a few examples to illustrate how such political reorientation of trans politics may be pursued in the U.S. context, with an understanding that this utilization of liberal complicity will vary depending on particular local circumstances.

First, in the arena of work and employment, current legislation in the United States, the Employment Non-Discrimination Act (ENDA), aims to "prohibit discrimination on the basis of sexual orientation and gender identity" to provide protections for LGBT people at their workplace.[15] Like the National Domestic Workers Alliance, which contests for domestic workers' rights, however, I argue that the activist momentum to mobilize democratic support for the bill not only needs to appeal to notions of civil rights and ethical justice, but also needs to enlist the capitalist instrumental logic of liberal citizenship. For instance, recent media commentaries on the bill often appeal to the material benefits of nondiscrimination against LGBT employees for employers and businesses, alluding to the consumerist buying power (and marketable values) that companies cannot overlook. As one commentator puts it, "It's more than unacceptable. It's bad for business."[16] Such support for ENDA has further been framed in terms of "the fight for liberty, equality and the pursuit of happiness"—the founding (capitalist) principle of liberal citizenship.[17]

Rather than condemning this development as purely complicit with normalcy, I suggest that trans activists can actively use such a discourse as a fluid enactment of morphing in and out of rights. That is, it morphs into the official regimes of rights by morphing out of the democratic logic of rights—through the adoption of, and appeal to, business instrumentality. Specifically, it places emphasis on commercial interests rather than democratic principles of social justice as a central consideration for the inclusion and nondiscrimination of trans people. Yet this appeal to business interests also redirects or morphs the discourse back to the legal codification of rights, which can exert culturally transformative effects by crafting broader public spaces to help alleviate the injustice trans people undergo in everyday life.

Second, in the arena of sex change, a brighter future can be conceived by adopting what James Nelson identifies as a shift from the "disciplining" model, which privileges medical-professional authority and pathologizes transsexuality, to an "empowerment" model, which sees transgender patients as consumers of services who hold a predominant say in determining and reconstructing their gender identity through hormonal injection and surgical operation (Nelson 1998). The DSM-V, which reclassifies transsexuality as "gender dysphoria," signals an (albeit imperfect) step toward this sociocultural reconceptualization, enabling a wider range of medical professionals and service providers to see transgendering as *empowering* gender-variant subjects through the consumptive practices of bodily reconstruction. A case may still need to be made that transsexuality is a special kind of gender variance, one requiring medical attention, so that trans subjects can obtain private insurance coverage or public reimbursement for their medical expenses. This political reorientation of activist strategy skips or deemphasizes (thus morphing out of) the rights discourse by centering consumerism as the foundation of corporeal transformation in order to gain de facto rights of gender self-determination.

Third, the consumer discourse can further be invoked to destabilize the public conception of binary gender in terms of public restrooms, whether at public institutions such as schools, libraries, museums, and parks, or private enterprises such as banks, hotels, supermarkets, and restaurants. In these spaces, activists can push for the building of restrooms suited for all genders alongside the traditional M, F, and, in some instances, family restrooms. Given that one (capitalist) argument against such a proposal is the financial costs involved in building more restrooms at these venues, trans activism may appropriate the same financial logic by using a (neoliberal) counterargument to reframe trans people as consumer-citizens in advocating for material incentive and institutional investment in building such facilities. Here again, this approach is an example of morphing out of a direct discourse of rights to obtain a not-yet-existing right to shop and consume (including using public restrooms) without fear, harassment, and violence. For smaller shops or mom-and-pop restaurants that are less able to afford additional restrooms (in terms of costs or space), simply having the existing rooms available for all genders would be a welcome move.

Fourth, concerning official identification documents such as driver's licenses and passports, trans activism may further push for additional categories beside M or F. Leslie Feinberg has previously proposed that "sex categories . . . be removed from all basic identification papers—from driver's licenses to passports—and since the right of each person to define their own sex is so basic, it should be eliminated from birth certificates as well"

(1996, 125). While I concur with Feinberg in spirit, this positioning borders on a transcendent claim that may be less feasible given liberal sovereignty's surveillance logic in using official documentation and category to govern and discipline citizen-subjects (Lyon 2001). Instead, I propose to add at least one (if not more) gender categories on various official or institutional documents. As Stryker and Aizura note, "Nepal and Pakistan recently added third-gender categories to their national identification documents, and Australia is considering an 'X' designation, akin to a 'decline to state' status, on passports" (5). Inscribing a third category beside M and F allows trans subjects to write themselves into the existing liberal gender script as rights-bearing citizens. In fact, the extension and expansion of affirmation action programs to include transgender people hinges on the official existence of these minority categories rather than their removal. The point here is that, to claim rights as citizens or to strengthen trans people's appropriation of liberal citizenship, one cannot argue for "nonidentity," which others cannot recognize, but must stake claims to different and multiple ways of gender expression and identity that, however complex, can be made locatable, translatable, and recognizable as other juridical categories beside M and F (Currah 2001).

Instead of pressing directly for the purity of transgender rights on this proposition, I argue that trans activism can again reframe trans subjects via a consumer-entrepreneur discourse to convince the public that substantive material interests could be gained from supporting this initiative. As shown in the recent decision on gender variance by Pakistan's Supreme Court, while it allows a third gender category on the national identity card, it further stipulates that "transgenders should also be allocated a certain number of government jobs," specifically recommending that "they be appointed as tax collectors to utilize their 'special skills.'"[18] In the words of Shehzadi, a transgender person who was interviewed in a news report, "We knock on the doors of people who haven't paid their taxes. . . . We tell them to pay up, but there are some who don't, so we stand on their doorstep and give them trouble and make a spectacle. Then to stop us attracting attention, they pay." According to the report, "The experiment has been judged something of a success by the local authority, . . . with Shehzadi's team collecting large amounts of unpaid dues."[19]

Similarly, material benefits to the public may also need to be emphasized in the U.S. context. For instance, the "liberal autonomy" argument can be invoked to advocate for more options for gender-variant people to choose from, as part of a larger trajectory of orienting them toward liberal consumer normativity. Such a policy can also be packaged as a way to engineer trans people's entrepreneurial subjectivity, allowing them to reconstruct and innovate gender identity to make the most out of their autonomous, enterprising selves. In sum, such a discursive move morphs out of purity (rights) into contamination (instrumentality) in order to extract spaces of purity out of contamination. And once such "third-gender" spaces are carved out officially, they establish a new terrain on which trans justice struggles can be further staged and expanded.

Finally, since any social movement cannot rely solely on legal strategy or public policy but also thrives in the context of cultural transformation (Currah et al. 2006), transgender activism also entails social awareness and education programs to introduce concepts beside or beyond the gender binary to the larger public. One of the most fertile places to start lies in the realm of education, especially with young children. Critical pedagogy scholars have advocated for a shift in treating children from minority linguistic or dialect-speaking backgrounds as a potential "resource" to enrich the classroom rather than as a "deficit" to be overcome (Delpit 2003). A similar pedagogical approach can be used to introduce topics of gender variance as a resource to enrich and expand students' gendered understanding, awareness, and embodiment. As I have indicated thus far, however, even such cultural transformation cannot rely solely on an idealistic aspiration for justice and equality, but must, again, make use of ingenious agency to instrumentally craft an educational rationale, such as preparing young students to become more informed workers, consumers, and entrepreneurs in a global multicultural economy, where knowledge about cultural-linguistic differences and gender diversity will increase their competitiveness in the cosmopolitan world marketplace.

To be sure, I harbor no illusion that these examples and propositions, even when implemented in the most strenuous and creative manner, will be carried out to perfection in existing liberal life. At the same time, they point to several initial directions in which social change and movement could be generated across spectrums of everyday life to maximize livable spaces for transgender and gender-nonconforming citizen-subjects. In addition, all of these proposals, despite their limits and complicities, destabilize existing relations of normality and abjection without appearing to do so, thus "smoothly" rather than "antagonistically" publicizing and democratizing the recognition of, and access to, mutable sex and amorphous gender within the given citizenship script.

5. Suicide Bombers, Sacrificial Violence, and Appropriating Life Itself

Entangling Suicide Bombing and the Liberal Economy

Before she detonated the explosives strapped to her body in a supermarket in Jerusalem in 2002, killing herself and two Israeli civilians, eighteen-year-old Ayat Akhras was known to her loved ones as an exemplary student and a well-mannered child. As her father describes her, Akhras, who grew up in a Palestinian refugee camp, excelled in studies at school and was engaged to a fiancé, harbored the dream "one day to have her own family and children."[1] Living in the Occupied Territories, which are denied formal state recognition, Akhras had personal aspirations—the pursuit of education, love, and marriage, among other things—that were not so different from the kind of lives lived by Israeli settlers and citizens. The mother of Rachel Levy, the seventeen-year-old Israeli girl who became the victim of Akhras's suicide, states, "This is our routine life, go to the store, go to the mall, just go to the bus. . . . We live in a democratic state, it is free, but I'm not free, by the terror that [Palestinian suicide bombers] bring in here."[2] In fact, the identical age and similar height and complexion of Akhras and Levy—the forensic scientists had difficulty differentiating their dead body parts—strikingly symbolize two tangled human lives torn apart by the unequal, colonialized, binary demarcations of "democratic life" versus "terroristic death."

Yet both were caught in the same script and cycle of liberal citizenship. As an Israeli citizen, Levy was endowed with and *normalized* in relation to the liberal pursuit of life, liberty, and happiness—from which Akhras the Palestinian was indefinitely *abjected*. In fact, given that the lives of both Levy and Akhras (and their respective Israeli and Palestinian compatriots) are linked through the unequal colonial power relations in the Occupied Territories, Akhras and other Palestinians are not only placed in a rejected/excluded outside to the pursuit of liberal citizenship, they are also suspended in an unlivable zone of social life *inside* liberalism, an abjected zone that constitutes liberalism's narcissistic embodiment "as its own founding repudiation" (Butler 1993, 3). In their entangled lives and deaths, the sacrifices of Levy and Akhras symbolize a series of diametrical opposites—democratic life and terroristic death, normality and abjection, and the liberal economy and suicide bombing—as being mutually constitutive and intertwined in their material formations.

These tangled relationships can be further examined in the narrative dialogues between the parents of Akhras and Levy as presented in the documentary *To Die in Jerusalem*. When describing Palestinian life under Israeli occupation, Akhras's father states, "I always teach my daughter to love others, but unfortunately, occupation practices like killings, demolitions, and imprisonments have changed the way boys and girls think. These conditions have forced us and our children to carry out operations. It became a duty to resist the occupation." Her mother adds, "Ayat loved peace, loved children, and learned everything about the Israeli people. But she was often asking me why we weren't in our hometown, like the rest of the world is in their homes. She would've liked to pray in Aqsa Mosque—but that was prohibited. She wanted to visit Yafa—but that was prohibited. Why were we the only people for whom everything is prohibited?"[3]

When Levy's mother comments that her daughter "would never kill someone for nothing," Akhras's mother retorts at various points:

Is living under the occupation peace? You are not living under occupation. We are the oppressed, the imprisoned—with the killings and assassinations! We are the ones living under these conditions. We have become fish in a sealed can.

I invite you to come live with us under occupation conditions, to see how we live. The crimes are beyond description! Killings—bombardments— demolitions! In front of our house. A car with two people inside was attacked by missiles—that made . . . [Akhras] go mad.

For you it's nothing, but for . . . [Akhras's] cause and for her honor, it was something. The U.S., France—when they were occupied, they resisted. My daughter had her own way of resisting. . . . Because your daughter had it all, you were talking from a position of comfort, we were talking from a position of hardship.

How would I love you when you steal our land and country? Give me back my rights and I won't mind if you live in my home! Kids like Ayat don't need me to explain things. They saw what was going on and did what was necessary. Ayat chose her way and took it! I'm saying I want peace. How will peace emerge? Let's join hands and work for peace.

When we have regained our rights, our land, our authority, our government, when we see our children released from prison, our homes rebuilt, then I would go on TV, on the satellite stations, and say we want peace![4]

The themes that emanate from these narratives are suicide bombing's constitutive opposites: normality, democratic life, and the liberal economy. Akhras's parents suggest that their daughter was peace-loving and would have lived a normal (liberal) life if not for the Israeli occupation. The question "Why were we the only people for whom everything is prohibited?" alludes to the denial of fundamental citizenship rights to Palestinians, who are deprived of basic human dignity, movement, liberty, and safety. The reference to "our rights, our land, our authority, our government, our homes" indicates a national population's aspiration for a sovereign state and endowed (democratic) citizenship, including access to earthly and material resources. Finally, the gesture of going on television and satellite stations in delivering messages of peace further suggests awareness of, and participation in, modern communications technology and liberal economy. In suicide bombing, what is often perceived as an opposition to Western civilization is in fact intimately tangled up with facets of liberal citizenship.

Beyond the immediate frame of the documentary, a further view of the entanglement between suicide bombing and liberal economy can be seen in the heteronormative construction of female suicide bombers such as Akhras by both the liberal counterterrorism apparatus and the Palestinian media and militant organizations. While delivering his "Road Map for Peace" speech days after Akhras's suicide bombing, U.S. President George W. Bush stated, "When an 18-year-old Palestinian girl is induced to blow herself up, and in the process kills a 17-year-old Israeli girl, the future, itself, is dying—the future of the Palestinian people and the future of the Israeli people. . . . Terror must be stopped. No nation can negotiate with terrorists. For there is no way to make peace with those whose only goal is death."[5]

On one hand, as V. G. Julie Rajan argues, Bush's speech interpreting the bombing incident as signifying the death of the future is peculiar: "While countless young Palestinian men have also immolated themselves for the Israeli-Palestinian conflict, why is it that the deaths of two young women in particular reflect the dire futures of Palestine and Israel?" (Rajan 2011, 239). To Rajan, this reflects the "prevalent patriarchal views that posit all women as potential mothers of nations, and hence of their nations' futures" (239). Embodying the liberal counterterrorism hegemony, Bush's heteronormative view associates women with purity, harmony, and a loving reproduction that is generative of the futures of nations. Female suicide bombers who wreak violence and deathly destruction can only be explained away by their being less than "normal" women, due to personal frailty, mental problems, sexual abuse, or promiscuity (Banner 2006; Rajan 2011; Sjoberg et al. 2011), constituting the antithesis of and a hindrance to the progress of the (masculine) nation.

However, Akhras was simultaneously extolled for her exemplary femininity and womanhood—embodied in her sacrifice—in Palestinian militant narratives. Along with other female suicide bombers who earned posthumous titles such as "Bride of the South," "Bride of Haifa," or "Bride of Palestine," Akhras was referred to as a "bride of the Heavens" by Saudi Arabia's Ambassador Ghazi al-Qusaybi in an Arabic language newspaper (Rajan, 225–26). As Rajan indicates, this projection of female suicide bombers as brides stresses their sexual purity in offering their piety to the nation. She writes, "Whereas a bride's sexuality may be secured under her husband's authority in everyday life, the metaphorical elevation of the woman bomber to a bride of regions and the nation secures her sexuality under the authority of the Palestinian nation, so that she is married to it. Her mission is, in fact, seen as a wedding, her commitment and loyalty to Palestine" (226). In fact, because Akhras did not consult her parents or fiancée about her decision to martyr herself, her act of sacrificial violence, negating the traditional paths of marriage and motherhood, also led to "rebel and cultural anxieties" about her "transgressive feminine agency" (227). As such, Rajan argues, "Re-casting such women to fit traditional ideologies of femininity reasserts patriarchal control over the women, so that their actions are seen not as the actions of uncontrollable, disobedient, 'improper' women, but as the masculine-authorized actions of 'proper' women" (227). In this way, the focus on the abnormality of female suicide bombers in liberal counterterrorism discourse and the appeal to their model femininity in the Palestinian militant discourse constitute two sides of the same coin: both invoke heteronormativity in their representation of women engaging in political violence for their respective causes.

In her examination of the Islamic *ummat* (an imagined transnational Islamic community), Minoo Moallem has noted the discursive interpenetration between the forces of colonial modernity and religious fundamentalism, indicating that "fundamentalism is not premodern but rather a by-product of the process of modernization" (2005, 13). She writes, "The ummat was represented as uniquely Islamic, yet it was fashioned from identities borrowed from the Western imaginary. . . . Copying in the context of identity formation was already present in relation to one original—that of the Western, imperialist global order. The search for an indigenous original could only lead away from the copy but would necessarily remain linked to the copy. . . . It is this recourse to an Islamic identity and a selective reading of Islam that creates a basis for the emergence of an Islamic nationalism and fundamentalism" (5).

As I argue in this chapter, a similar process happens in the formation of Palestinian suicide bombing: its enactment of sacrificial violence is not uniquely Islamic but contains mirroring parallels and recurring themes found in the Western imaginary of sovereign founding. The sacrificial logic of suicide bombing remains intimately linked to the Western copy. As Moallem puts it, "[Islamic] religion and [Western] reason participate in the same regime of knowledge and power" (2005, 14). It is these complex interpenetrations and appropriations between the suicide bombing apparatus and hegemonic liberal life that lead us to relook at agency in suicide bombing not simply as barbaric or anti-Western but, rather, as intimately entangled with the historical-material cycle of liberal founding, modern economy, and citizenship from which "terrorist" subjects such as Akhras emerge.

While in previous chapters I show how migrant domestic workers, global sex workers, and trans people are varyingly abjected by liberal political, economic, and gender scripts while also seeking to appropriate these scripts to improvise spaces of inclusion and belonging, the act of suicide bombing, in taking lives, renders a common perception that its enactors completely break with the liberal pursuit of life, liberty, and happiness. Its infliction of deathly violence indicates a seeming dissociation from, and catastrophic destruction of, the cycle of liberal citizenship itself. In this respect, migrant domestic workers, global sex workers, and trans people become relatively normalized in relation to suicide bombers who refuse negotiation, opting to liberate themselves outside the earthly pursuit of liberal citizenship.

Yet if the act of suicide bombing is in fact entangled with, and even constitutive of, normality, democratic life, and the liberal economy, then it implies that the bomber rather aspires circuitously *for life*—not merely physical life, but also a life of sovereign (liberal) citizenship that Palestinians under occupation are perpetually and indefinitely denied. This lethal act can be read as an inventive improvisation by abjected bombers and their sponsoring militant organizations to enact themselves politically to destabilize the existing relations of normality and abjection between Israelis and Palestinians, thus ameliorating their abjection and normalizing their dignity and humanity. When life under occupation is pervasively humiliating and hopeless, the act of suicide bombing, even in its limits and complicities, is seized by the abject as a last resort to reanimate hopes for a sovereign citizenship that will give their own lives meaning. If migrant domestic workers, global sex workers, and trans people use the limited tools they have—that is, hidden tactics, calculated abjection, and morphing technologies—to resist and negotiate with the liberal citizenship script, then for suicide bombers, their own corporeal existence is the most effective tool to disrupt and appropriate the script to create a humane life for their Palestinian compatriots and, for many, a sacred afterlife for themselves.

To the extent that suicide bombers are entwined with the liberal lifecycle, they are unable to escape its power; rather, their material existence stands in contingent and shifting relations of abjection to liberal normality and to other abject subjects (even after their death). Thus, their sacrificial acts may in fact enable the local community to cast bombers as venerable martyrs whose noble deeds pave the way for the future sovereign founding of the (liberal) Palestinian state. In the context of what Raja Khalidi calls the "Palestinian national/social contract," which prioritizes aspirations to national self-determination over other internal social problems,[6] suicide bombers can be redeemed by their compatriots as founding martyrs who shed blood for the sovereign right to life, liberty, and the pursuit of happiness encapsulated in liberal citizenship. In this respect, would the future founding of the Palestinian state set in place new configurations of normality and abjection among its citizen-subjects yet again in the liberal citizenship lifecycle (e.g., with domestic workers, sex workers, and trans people in Palestine being the "newly" abject subjects)?

In this final chapter, I examine suicide bombing as a deathly act that unsettles and appropriates the fundamental life script of liberal citizenship, which configures citizens in an innocent and unbridled pursuit of life, liberty, and happiness. Focusing on the Palestinian context under Israeli occupation, where Palestinian subjects have been described by Achille Mbembe as existing under conditions of "living-death" (i.e., a collective living without feel for life; Mbembe 2003), I suggest a rereading of the bombing subjects' sacrificial violence as deploying ingenious agency to destabilize the existing abjectifying relations and regenerate hopes for the collective realization of (liberal) citizenship itself.

The reification of innocent citizenship in liberal national culture is not exclusive to the State of Israel. Instead, it reflects the cultural-material essence of the globalized life script of liberal citizenship crafted by European capitalist modernity and, in recent decades, centrally engineered by the United States and its allies. Cultural theorists such as Lauren Berlant (1997) and Marita Sturken (2007) have examined the ways in which U.S. national culture fashions a liberal script of "infantile" and "tourist" citizens who, in uncritically submitting to the tutelary and pastoral power of the state, are freed up to pursue an unreflective liberal happiness in an "innocent pose and distant position" (Sturken 2007, 10) to the world around them, which is rife with political violence, material inequality, and economic hierarchy. This formation of innocent citizenship involves the liberal sovereignty's active manufacturing of its citizens as oblivious to its own continuous and willful production of normality and abjection in international affairs to sustain and enhance its preeminent geopolitical position, superpower status, and the globalized liberal lifecycle itself. Most insidiously, what is evacuated from this innocent citizenship is the way in which Western liberal democracy (normality) coproduces terrorism (abjection) elsewhere—including the decimation of civilian lives in non-Western regions—to bolster its own ideological and material reproduction.

For instance, reflecting on the attacks on New York of September 11, 2001, Mahmood Mamdani points to the Cold War as the breeding ground of Middle Eastern terrorism, as the United States mobilized Muslims worldwide in a holy war against the Soviet Union's invasion of Afghanistan. He notes, the U.S. Central Intelligence Agency "orchestrat[ed] support for terrorist and proto-terrorist movements around the world . . . [and] . . . cultivat[ed] . . . terrorism in the struggle against regimes it considered pro-Soviet" (2002, 49). Thus, al-Qaeda, led by Osama bin Laden, was born in this context as an ally of the United States in the fight against communism. The alliance was broken once the Russians were defeated, however, as "the Americans abandoned Afghanistan to its fate and the Afghan freedom fighters, mainly Islamic fundamentalists, turned against the United States" (49). Chalmers Johnson further links recent U.S. foreign policies to a neo-imperialism and neocolonialism that seek to buttress its preeminent position in the Middle East by dominating and exploiting weaker states, including securing a stable oil supply for its domestic use and military-industrial complex (Johnson 2004). Rajeev Bhargava identifies how the United States' support for despotic regimes such as Egypt, Pakistan, Morocco, Jordan, and Saudi Arabia for the sake of petroleum or geopolitical interests has thwarted the struggle for democracy by reformers in those regions and given breathing room to militant antagonism (2002, 327–38). Others have further pointed to the U.S. bombing of Iraq in 1991 in the Gulf War and its postwar embargo, which killed half a million Iraqi children, as well as its consistent support for Israel against Palestine as contributing to feelings of humiliation and resentment against the United States on the part of Muslim subjects (Arjomand 2002; Churchill 2003).

Liberal democracy thus profits by trafficking in the realm of terrorism, calculatingly assigning the fate of lives and deaths to further the abjection of the already abjectified and strengthen the normality of the already normalized. While this deathly profiteering by liberalism needs to be fiercely critiqued and protested, I argue that this entanglement also constitutes the frame by which to understand the political agency of those who are abjectified. As we have learned, the abject will not remain where they are but will seek ways to assuage their abjection, and as their lived conditions are created by a historical and geopolitical entanglement they cannot transcend, they will act in ways that appropriate the logic of the liberal life script to stage ruptures of the given power relations.

It is, in fact, this intertwined cultural-material context that enables us to see the contingent and unexpected emergence of suicide bombing as a hybridized product, a creative means improvised by the abject under the historical material condition of living-death to interrupt the democratic life that so "innocently" remainders them. The agency of suicide bombing is thus as cunning as it is inventive, as the abject come up with inconceivable ways to enact themselves politically. I do not mean to gloss over the moral implications of a lethal action that takes the lives of other human subjects. To the contrary, it is precisely a renewed understanding of the bombing acts as being propelled by a designing and audacious agency to create more humane lives among the abject that can lead us to rethink more original and effective ways to create the social change that would help reduce (if not end) instances of suicide bombing.

As I argue in this chapter, the entangled relationship between democratic life and terroristic death (and the entailed improvisational agency of suicide bombing) has so far eluded existing intellectual discourses on non-state political violence—whether by mainstream terrorism research or by the anticolonial inquiry inspired by Frantz Fanon—that limit their purview on the agency in political violence and the horizon of social change. Dominated by the paradigm of sociological positivism and driven by the ethos of etiology, the "scientific" pursuit of mainstream terrorism research in uncovering the causes and patterns of terrorism in avowedly "objective" and "neutral" terms hides an ideological bias that pits the values of liberal capitalist democracy against the contagion of terrorist death. In the modern liberal imagination, non-state terrorist violence is not only perceived as a deviant threat (i.e., it kills civilians or it steals the state monopoly on use of force), but it also constitutes in a deeper sense the very antithesis of a life of democratic citizenship. Being grounded in and attached to *life* itself—the undying, guarded right to life, liberty, and the pursuit of happiness—actually existing democracy can only take self-inflicted death and violence as its negation. Whatever its motive, deathly violence by non-state actors is antidemocratic, and it could never aspire to the realm of the properly political. Deeply entrenched in and profiting from liberal citizenship, mainstream terrorism research functions as part of the hegemonic counterterrorism apparatus that embeds a perpetual binary of democracy is for life–terrorism is for death in its discursive regime, which juxtaposes democracy and terrorism as resolute opposites. From this perspective, no proper agency or social change could possibly be derived from suicide terrorism.

In contrast, by breaking apart the democratic life–terroristic death binary, the Fanonian anticolonial inquiry opens the possibility of looking into deathly violence as an agentic renewal of an abject state of life. To Fanon, violence in liberation struggles is both empirically common, because the dominated are bound to resist, and normatively necessary, to renew a marginal collective's subjectivity (2004, 42). This is not a euphoric celebration of mob violence. As Homi Bhabha argues, "Fanonian violence . . . is part of a struggle for psycho-affective survival and a search for human agency in the midst of the agony of oppression. It does not offer a clear choice between life and death or slavery and freedom, because it confronts the colonial condition of life-in-death" (2004, xxxvi). In the Fanonian formulation, it is in the intolerable interstitial space of living-death where seizing violence allows a collective to feel again the sense of being human and acting politically. Death becomes an empowering instrument to realize a fleeting moment of agency and freedom in a lived condition of unending servitude.

Against the liberal counterterrorism paradigm, anticolonial theory significantly creates a radical opening in reading the political agency in sacrificial violence. Yet by representing deathly violence through the lens of an insurgent life—in the words of Robert Young, "from non-being to being, from being an object to subject" (2001, 295)—the Fanonian inquiry also replicates a linear order of agency that switches the order of the democratic life–terroristic death binary. That is, while it correctly suggests that colonial democracy actually wreaks death and liberation violence can be represented as an agency for life, it does not capture this deadly agency's intricate entanglement with modern liberal life. Thus, it blocks from view the necessary ingenuity and complicity in anticolonial violence such as suicide bombing. As such, it can obscure how the realization of national self-determination may actually hinge on an entangled appropriation of liberal citizenship.

Instead of reconstructing a life–death binary in interpreting non-state violence, I intertwine both in this chapter by exploring how the recurring episodes of suicide bombing in the Palestinian context use death to disrupt and appropriate the life script of liberal citizenship. Because this act of sacrificial violence involves a calculated and instrumental negotiation with liberal citizenship—negotiating the end of one's worldly life for the possibility of liminal renewal in another dimension—this appropriation inevitably delimits and circumscribes whatever freedom, inclusion, and belonging are attained by its enactors. Yet it is precisely from and through this limited realm that Palestinian suicide bombers are enabled to appropriate what they deem noble/sacred spaces of inclusion and belonging for themselves and their fellow compatriots and to project a not-yet-existing, sovereign citizenship life to come in the given liberal economy. As I have suggested throughout previous chapters, what matters for this project is how we may read their momentary and enduring political enactments as instantiations of ingenious agency. Such agency, I suggest, may ultimately hold the key in ending the lethal enactment of sacrificial violence on a collective scale, and has broad implications for transnational democratic movements that work toward political change in Palestine.

A few notes are in order before I pursue my analysis. First, my use of the term "suicide bombing" does not indicate my misrecognition of its problems as a conceptual term. As the term (along with "suicide terrorism," "suicide attack," or "suicide missions") is a Western construction, it already moves the reader/audience to perceive it in a certain direction. Given that bombing participants rarely see their acts as "suicide" and prefer instead terms such as "sacred explosions" or "martyrdom operations" (Hafez 2006a),[7] one wonders why alternative terms such as "sacrificial bombing" or "sacrificial missions" are not being used in media and academia. My decision is thus to retain the term in its common usage to signal a factual phenomenon while accentuating its embedded mode of sacrificial violence in conducting my analysis. Second, while instances of suicide bombing abound in other contexts (e.g., the Hezbollah resistance to the Israeli occupation of Lebanon, the Tamil Tigers' campaigns for succession from the Sri Lankan government, the Chechens' struggles for independence against Russia, and the Iraqi insurgence against the invasion and reconstruction efforts of U.S. coalition forces), I choose to focus my investigation on the Palestinian situation as a case study with potential implications for similar political struggles at other sites.

Finally, while the deathly act is carried out by individual bombers, I suggest that we cannot examine this ingenious agency solely through the bombing subjects. Most bombing operations are part of broader collective movements: they are devised by militant organizations and bolstered by the communal encouragement of other Palestinian civilians. Thus, in contrast to the cases of migrant domestic workers, global sex workers, and trans people, we need to pay attention especially to the ways in which the bombers' ingenious agency is "collaboratively and reciprocally" intertwined with that of their affiliated or sponsoring organizations, which cogenerate the improvised acts (Jean-Klein 2000). Such an approach enables us to understand not only how militant organizations align elements of ingenuity and complicity to individual acts of suicide bombing, but also how the bombing subjects themselves inventively use the available tools and resources in their surroundings to enact themselves politically.

The Modern Sacrificial Economy:
Recurrence and Appropriation of Sacrificial Violence

In this section, I begin by tracing the parallels and recurring themes found in the French Revolution and Palestinian suicide bombing, situating both phenomena in what I call the *modern sacrificial economy*. This refers to the production, reuse, and appropriation of various sacrificial traditions, symbols, and discourses across cultural and geographic contexts in liberal modernity. Through this economy, I examine the ways in which sacrificial violence is instrumentally adapted and reinvented by modern political actors to craft and legitimize political objectives such as sovereign founding, resisting foreign occupation, or achieving other desired geopolitical agendas. My aim here is to show not only that suicide bombing is not grossly exceptional (i.e., solely a Middle Eastern or Islamic phenomenon), but that it is also intricately entangled with liberal modernity.

In *The Headless Republic*, Jesse Goldhammer provides an important look at the founding of modern republics through the lens of sacrifice and bloodshed rather than social contracts and constitutions (Goldhammer 2005). While modern liberals often adopt an attitude toward callous sacrifice and bloodshed "as irrational and barbaric" (3), an unenlightened behavior attributed to Islamic fundamentalism or other "outmoded" non-Western religious fanaticisms, Goldhammer argues that the modern political order is rife with sacrificial origins.

As Goldhammer points out, unlike religious leaders who can readily appeal to a transcendent authority to legitimatize their decisions, modern political founders lack such a divine figure and are in "even greater need . . . for a mechanism that confers sacredness" for their "core principles" (4). Sacrificial violence provides such a mechanism by infusing secular founding with indisputable legitimation and sacred power (8).

In fact, given that Islamic fundamentalism is itself a modern ideology, its resort to sacrificial violence does not suggest signs of perverse antiquity or backwardness; rather, it signals how "the modern world is partly constituted by ancient ideas, such as sacrifice, which have been adapted to novel political conditions" (Goldhammer, 4). What distinguishes the deployment of suicide bombing in the Palestinian context is its simultaneous *parallels* and *convergence* with modern political regimes' sacrificial logic and sacred authority. In this way, liberal democracies and the apparatus of suicide bombing actually mirror each other's appropriation of sacrificial violence.

Indeed, while historical antecedents of sacrificial violence existed within the Islamic context, the fact that these enactments were influenced by strategic considerations underlined their secular and worldly elements even as religion might play a role in fortifying the resolve of the enactors in undertaking such operations. For instance, during the eleventh century, the "assassins," a radical offshoot of the Shiite minority in today's northern Iran, committed their suicide missions with daggers against the ruling Sunni leaders as a strategy to advance their vision of Islam (Reuter 2004, 24–25). In the late twentieth century, one further witnesses the "human wave attacks" in the Iran–Iraq War from 1980 to 1989 in which Iranian youths "ran at the Iraqi positions until they either won the day or were all dead," an act that "caused Iraqi machine gunners to flee" because they could no longer bear the sight of "shoot[ing] children the same age as their own" (35–36).

The secular strategic considerations are shown even more prominently in the emergence of modern-day suicide bombing. "Human bombs" originated in 1983 in Lebanon, when the radical Shiite organization Hezbollah responded to the invasion by Israel, the United States, and France by imitating and transforming Iran's massive human wave attacks into "a precisely controlled, well directed and sparingly used weapon, deploying it to maximum possible effect" (Reuter, 63). As Christoph Reuter argues, this advanced strategy of martyrdom arises out of "a new, coldly rational form of cost-benefit analysis" whereby the weaker force strikes a blow at the enemy with relatively few casualties on its own (58). According to Robert Pape, the success of Hezbollah in driving foreign forces out of Lebanon became "the original source of the global spread of suicide terrorism," as it persuaded militant groups elsewhere (Islamic and secular alike) that "suicide terrorism would be an effective tool for reaching their own goals" (2005, 73). From then on, suicide bombing reached "epidemic proportions, . . . [making] its way to Sri Lanka in 1987 (long before it reached as far as Israel), . . . [and] by the 1990s, it had arrived in Turkey, Kashmir, and Chechnya" (Reuter, 2).

In Palestine, this secularization of martyrdom takes on a specific configuration in its historical and geopolitical context as its use of sacrificial violence is tied to material claims of sovereign statehood and citizenship since coming under Israeli occupation in 1967. As Pape documents, despite the existence of "strikes, protests, and other forms of nonviolent resistance [that] began as early as 1972, . . . most of the Palestinian population preferred to accept the benefits of the economic modernization that occurred under Israeli rule rather than support violent rebellion" (47). However, beginning in 1987, Palestinian resistance grew progressively intense, resulting in "violent (but unarmed) rebellion in the first intifada from 1987 to 1992" (47). Then, after the first year of the Oslo peace process in 1993, militant organizations such as Hamas and Islamic Jihad started to carry out suicide bombing operations (Reuter, 100). But it was not until late 2000, after many setbacks of the Oslo Accords, that the number of suicide missions began to escalate (Human

Rights Watch 2002, 1), marking the beginning of the second *intifada* (Arabic, "shaking off," or "uprising").

As Farhad Khosrokhavar argues, "The meaning of holy death changed" between the two intifadas because of changing perceptions of the realization of a sovereign Palestinian nationhood (2005, 109). During the first intifada, Palestinian resistance combined an optimistic theme of "nation-building with that of self-assertion as a Muslim" (109). The young stone throwers "who were the emblematic figures of the first Intifada . . . testified to the possibility of a Palestinian victory. . . . The self-image of the young people who were challenging Israel's hegemony was basically positive," and the uprising "gave everyone the feeling that they had recovered their honor" (110).

In contrast, the second intifada was permeated with feelings of hopelessness and desperation due to "the setbacks and failure of the Oslo Accords" (Khosrokhavar, 111). In the eyes of many Palestinians, the accords created an inept and corrupt Palestinian Authority (PA) that operated on "nepotism and clientelism" and acted as "the Israeli army's lackeys . . . by arresting Hamas militants and anyone who challenged Fatah's hegemony" (111). Moreover, the number of Jewish settlements kept growing exponentially after the accords, which "not only consumed more land and water, but also required progressive expansion of the Israeli military presence . . ., including more and more checkpoints that made it difficult for Palestinians to travel or even carry out ordinary business" (Pape, 48). Political dissolution, economic desperation, and moral despair led many Palestinian youths to conclude that "building a nation was impossible" in the earthly life, and "martyrdom . . . became a way of totalizing life. . . . In a context where Palestinians did not have the means required to enjoy even elementary forms of citizenship," martyrdom provided "some of the attributes of a non-existent citizenship" (Khosrokhavar, 111).

Palestinians' enactment of sacrificial violence, then, needs to be understood in the context of modernity, where their access to worldly citizenship—land, water, consumer goods, jobs, economic provision, a basic sense of dignity—is persistently thwarted and divested. Khosrokhavar notes that Palestinians regularly watch Israeli television (sometimes in preference to their own) and secretly admire and imbibe the aura of democratic freedom and modern individualism (114–15). In fact, while Palestinian boycotts of consumer goods from Israel have been attempted to compel recognition of their right to self-determination, they "have had little impact" not only because of "the superior quality of Israeli products . . . [compared with] those from the Arab countries and local suppliers," but also because "consuming Israeli products gives Palestinians the feeling that . . . they too are part of a world on [sic] which Israel has an exclusive claim, that they too can live like Israelis and therefore become their equals." In short, "Both Israelis and Palestinians are fully caught up in modernity. . . . They live . . . in a world that is imbued with modern egalitarianism, whereas social relations between the two sides are governed by a neo-colonialist model" (114–15).

As Moallem argues, it is thus important to look at liberal secularism and Islamic fundamentalism not as strictly separate and antagonistic entities but as deeply interpenetrated and intertwined (Moallem 2005). There are fundamentalist elements in liberal secularism, just as there are secular and materialist ingredients in Islamic fundamentalism. Liberal secularism produces "what is in fact a Christianized public space where tradition is reinvented through the framework of Christian tradition . . . [and] integrated into the colonial states themselves" (11). Conversely, Islamic fundamentalism is enabled and influenced by postmodern culture, "where Islamic culture is increasingly commodified and opened to uncertainty, multiplicity, intertextuality, and the collapse of time-space with no foundation" (13). In addition, such fundamentalist discourse makes use of "modern technologies of communication" (90), suggesting its reliance on media, consumer culture, and "the global circulation of images and capital" (120)—the cultural economy of modern liberal secularism—for the dissemination of its messages. Both liberal secularism and Islamic fundamentalism are thus situated within global capitalism, and their interpenetration and mutual appropriation suggest that they each "include a plurality of discourses and practices" and contain "many layers of sedimented ideologies" within them (164).

This observation leads us to look at Palestinian suicide bombing as a contemporary recurrence of sacrificial violence that bears cross-temporal, cross-spatial, and cross-cultural connections to the modern liberal economy. This economy is inevitably linked to the instrumental circuits of capitalism and the liberal political order. Within this economy, one finds interpenetrations, appropriations, and selective borrowing of sacrificial themes across traditions and contexts, not only to deploy such violence as military weapons, but also to craft and bolster political objectives such as sovereign founding and expelling foreign occupiers via a sacred and transcendent aura. Any investigation of agency in suicide bombing must thus situate it within the modern sacrificial economy, which is complicit with the modern liberal order.

A central theme in the enactment of sacrificial violence in both the French

Revolution and the Palestinian situation is the mutual quality of "purity" and "abjection" in their deliverance of sacred power. As Goldhammer observes, in the modern sacrificial exchange, political actors at once transfer the sacred power of the ruling authority to the people through killing, sacrifice, and bloodshed (*abjection*), and attach the violence to a metaphysical promise of communal, national salvation and renewal (*purity*; Goldhammer, 36). Thus, during the French Revolution, sacrificial violence inspired awe and obedience to revolutionary power because it appropriated the legitimacy of the royal authority "rooted in both the pure, elevated, majestic power of the king and the base, polluted, abject power of the executioner" (6). Similarly, in Palestinian suicide bombing, while religious references to God the Almighty, the promised seventy-two "pure" and "clean" virgins awaiting the martyrs in paradise, and aspirations to communal salvation and renewal all accentuate the purity of sacrifice, the deliberate killing of Israeli civilians while taking one's own life in the process underlines the base abjection of this sacred power.

In addition, both events converge on the use of transgressive violence: in the French Revolution, acts of "cannibalism, mutilations, and necrophilia [were] conducted by the revolutionaries against royal bodies" (Goldhammer, 46); in the Palestinian situation, the act of suicide bombing explodes and fragments the bodies of Israeli civilians at populated sites. Goldhammer argues that such transgressive violence "holds the potential to generate a positive sacredness, which mimics the legitimacy of political power . . . [and] transforms the negativity of violence into something socioculturally acceptable" (13). Further, the excess of violence "is indicative of the disintegration of the social boundaries maintained by the monarchy" in the French Revolution (47n49), just as it symbolizes the disintegration of colonial boundaries maintained by Israel in the Occupied Territories. By violating basic human taboos, both the French revolutionaries and Palestinian militants demonstrate "the sublime character of their violence. Acts that so transgress the boundary between culturally acceptable and unacceptable behavior generate a sense of awe that is simultaneously attractive and repulsive" (50). These mutually sublime and barbarian and attractive and repulsive characteristics of transgressive violence allow their enactors to mimic and appropriate the sacred power of the king and the Israeli colonial authority.

Moreover, both events invoke the symbolic use of spilled blood as crucial to their sovereign (re)founding. The French national anthem, *La Marseillaise*, written during the revolution in April 1792, captures this sentiment:

To arms, citizens!
From your battalions,
March on, march on!
May their impure blood
Water our fields.
(Goldhammer, 40)

For the revolutionaries, the abjection of spilling enemies' blood not only serves the purpose of "aveng[ing] their martyred compatriots" and "embolden[ing] their violent actions" (47–48), but it also achieves the symbolic function of replacing the contaminated monarchal order with a sacred and purified republican order. The Palestinian "Declaration of Independence," produced in 1988 during the first intifada, reveals a similar theme: "On this momentous day, the fifteenth day of November 1988, as we stand on the threshold of a new era, we bow our heads in deference and humility to the departed souls of our martyrs and the martyrs of the Arab nation who, by virtue of the pure blood shed by them, have lit the glimmer of this auspicious dawn and who have died so that the homeland might live" (Rajan, 214).

Here, the abject spilling of blood in Palestinian martyrdom fulfills what its participants consider the noble function of expelling the impurity of settler colonial rule and replenishing martyrdom with sacred and sublime power. Commenting on the death of Wafa Idris, the first female Palestinian suicide bomber, the columnist Samiya Sa'ad al-Din coined a similar sentiment from a gendered perspective in the periodical *Al-Akhbar*: "Palestinian women have torn the gender classification out of their birth certificates, declaring that sacrifice for the Palestinian homeland would not be for men alone; on the contrary, all Palestinian women will write the history of the liberation with their blood" (quoted in Rajan, 253).

Furthermore, both phenomena appropriate religious symbols to furnish their worldly violence and earthly political cause with a sacred and redemptive quality. As Goldhammer indicates, French revolutionaries appropriated the idea of Christian martyrdom through a secular translation that "allowed them to transform their own dead into Christ-like sacrificial victims" (37). Terms such as "saint" and "apostle" were often invoked to register the religious quality of revolutionary martyrdom (37–38), with the effect of turning sacrificial violence into a redemption mechanism. He writes, "The secularization of the willingness to die . . . became a quasi-religious duty of subjects and citizens to sacrifice themselves for the good of their countries or fatherlands. This . . . gave rise to the concept of the political martyr who dies . . . for earthly immortality in the historical memory of that political community for whom the self-sacrifice was made" (36).

This quasi-religious element finds recurrence in the Palestinian situation. Although many suicide bombers justify their actions in the name of God and defense of Islam, given that the Qur'an also prohibits suicide, such religious references can be read as a purification mechanism that sacralizes and immortalizes their secular mission (Rajan, 192). The Qur'an is thus selectively interpreted and appropriated to help achieve a secular, earthly cause. As Muhammad Hazza al-Ghoul, a Hamas member who blew himself up on a bus in 2002, killing nineteen Israelis and injuring seventy-four, stated in his will, "How beautiful for the splinters of my bones to be the response that blows up the enemy, not for the love of killing, but so we can live as other people live. . . . We do not sing the songs of death, but recite the hymns of life. . . . We die so that future generations may live" (Hafez 2006a, 72). This statement underscores the immortalizing and religious qualities of suicide bombing while connecting the purpose of the redemptive act to a noble earthly aspiration: the ending of the occupation and sovereign founding of Palestine.

Finally, the sacrifice of one's children to the sovereign political cause signals another parallel theme. Goldhammer indicates that French revolutionaries appropriated the Roman story of Lucius Junius Brutus, who executed his two traitorous sons in the founding of the Roman republic, to affirm their understanding that "citizens must 'be ready to sacrifice everything, up to [their] children, to the happiness of [their] country'" (35). In the Palestinian situation, as Rajan describes, "In some cases, mothers had actively encouraged their children to become suicide bombers; in other cases, they may not have known about their children's missions beforehand, but did eventually vocalize their support for the missions" (255). Rajan documents several instances where Palestinian mothers proclaimed their happiness over their sons' mission on Palestinian television:

Mother A: Praise to Allah! I hold my head high. The honor is mine. I have a son who is a shahid and not only is my son a shahid, but all the shahids are my children, Praise Allah. The honor is mine; the pride is mine.

Mother B: Yes, I did. A mother makes sounds of joy because she wants him to reach Shahada. He became a shahid for Allah Almighty. I wanted the best for him, this is the best for [my son] Shaadi. When he became a shahid, the Shahada was not only for him but also for us, pride for us, honor for us. People started looking at us [saying], "This is the shahid's brother," "This is the shahid's mother," "This is the shahid's sister." The pride was for the whole family, not just for Shaadi.

Mother C: I said: "Praise Allah, my children asked for Shahada," and it is better than the way we will die. (Rajan, 254–55)

Their professed joy over their sons' martyrdom performs a similar function in showing a resolve "to sacrifice everything, up to [their] children" to the militant cause of ending occupation and gaining statehood. In addition, the act of suicide bombing is conferred purity through reference to the Islamic term shahid (holy martyr), which sacralizes the abject act of killing.

In all, the recurring themes of sacrificial violence found in both the French Revolution and Palestinian suicide bombing, cross-temporally and cross-culturally, suggest their common linkage to, and participation in, the modern sacrificial economy. As Goldhammer indicates, liberal regimes continue to possess certain sacred markers suggestive of the founding bloodshed, struggle, and sacrifice that confer on them a venerable status in the present day: in the United States, for example, flag, national anthem, the White House, and the sacred enshrinement of founding constitutional principles such as political equality and freedom (4). Furthermore, in its conduct of international relations and staging of warfare, liberal sovereignty inherits and adapts varying forms of sacrificial violence—whether through the sacrifice of its young soldiers or through the sacrifice of civilians in its targeted non-Western war regions (by casting the latter in the strategic language of "collateral damage")—to sustain and enhance its geopolitical positions and globalized citizenship lifecycle. In the post–9/11 climate, the popular salutation to soldiers and veterans by flight attendants and passengers on commercial airplanes in the United States attests to the everyday invocation of sacrificial violence (although the violent part is never mentioned) critical to the founding and maintenance of the liberal sovereign order, now metamorphosed into the language of "national security."

Despite its apparent antagonism toward Western culture and ideology, the suicide bombing apparatus is nonetheless intertwined and entangled with the modern sacrificial economy in the same globalized liberal lifecycle. As Goldhammer argues, "When Palestinian nationalists undertake martyrdom operations against Israelis for the sake of statehood, and use Islam to justify such sacrifices, they effectively illustrate the same forms of founding violence that have captured the Western imagination for millennia" (196).

As above, that Palestinian militant organizations rely on communications technologies to disseminate their enactment of sacrificial violence attests to their complicit attachment to the liberal economy. As Rajan illustrates, "Suicide martyrs' videotestimonials are disseminated to major television outlets and placed on rebel group websites to celebrate each and every martyr by name. Martyr posters are placed on public walls throughout the [Occupied Territories], and reproductions are available as posters for purchase for every Palestinian. The posters adorn premises ranging from ice cream stores to barber shops—where customers may get haircuts like martyrs" (214–15).

Within liberal modernity, one thus finds appropriation and selective borrowing of sacrificial themes across traditions and contexts to sacralize and legitimize political objectives. Suicide bombing cannot be investigated autonomously apart from the modern sacrificial economy, but must be examined in the context of the complex entanglement between sacrificial violence and liberal modernity. This jarring and dissonant interlacing between liberal life and terroristic death incarnated in suicide bombing suggests that its embodied agency is necessarily intricately and circuitously crafted.

Below, I demonstrate how existing scholarly investigations of suicide bombing capture this non-state violence in a singular and linear mode of death (mainstream terrorism research) or life (anticolonial inquiry) that does not delineate its embedded intertwinement with liberal citizenship. Instead, I argue that only by situating sacrificial violence within the modern sacrificial economy can we tease out the polymorphous twists and turns of improvisational agency embodied in suicide bombing.

Mainstream Terrorism Research:
Consigning Suicide Bombing toward Death

In the years after 9/11, social science literature that makes "scientific" inquiry into suicide terrorism has burgeoned. Unlike commentators who, in the immediate aftermath of 9/11, declared the catastrophe to be outside the understandable discourse of politics or condemned any efforts to understand it as "excusing terror,"[8] these social scientists seek to investigate the root causes of suicide terrorism in an objective and dispassionate way. The opening statement in Diego Gambetta's edited volume *Making Sense of Suicide Missions* is representative of this "scientific" ethos, aiming "to provide the reader with as full and systematic an account of suicide missions . . . as possible, . . . motivated by an intense and dispassionate interest in the explanatory challenge that it poses to social scientists" (Gambetta 2005b, v).

With the intent to provide a "full and systematic" account of suicide terrorism, various approaches emerge in the empirical genre to identify what causes or motivates this deadly phenomenon—to borrow Martha Crenshaw's terms—whether they are "permissive (facilitating) causes" or "direct (instigating) factors" (Crenshaw 1981). At a glance, these studies can be distinguished by the competing factors identified as contributing to the emergence of suicide terrorism: rational strategic choice; religious radicalization and indoctrination; participant altruism; relative economic deprivation; personal crisis; pneumopathology or spiritual disorder; desire for vengeance; and social alienation.[9]

As I argue, in spite of the internal differences that exist among empirical researchers regarding how they gather and interpret the data that lead them to different conclusions, the common effort in operationalizing "suicide terrorism" in mainstream terrorism studies often ends up with a normative ethos of "knowing the enemy, containing the threat" that represents suicide bombing as a mode of death that threatens the liberal order of life. Such an ethos can be examined in two ways. First, while driven by an avowedly "objective" and "neutral" sociological positivism, these studies nonetheless reflect an ideological interest in sustaining a binary of "democracy" (life) versus "terrorism" (death), seeing the latter as a threat to the former's liberal capitalist way of life. Second, whether conceiving terrorism as a threat in the form of a vicious disease (such as cancer or HIV) to be expunged or framing it with the trope of victimization as in the cases of female and child bombers, these "scientific" studies again construct suicide attackers in the realm of death without any meaningful engagement with these abject subjects' inherent political agency. In the end, by detaching suicide terrorism from its tangled linkage to the modern sacrificial economy and the liberal political order, mainstream terrorism scholars dramatize the binary ideological distinctions between liberalism and terrorism. Their research perpetuates the liberal hegemonic status quo while preempting an inquiry into the intimate association between sacrificial violence and the pursuit of liberal citizenship itself.

The "Scientific" Ideology of Sustaining Liberal Democracy: The Perpetual Binary of Democracy (Life) versus Terrorism (Death)

Terrorism studies informed by sociological positivism often juxtapose terrorism as a security threat to democratic national governments, setting up a reductive ideological binary between terroristic death and democratic life. Yet it is not mentioned in these literatures how democratic life sustains and enhances itself through the infliction of violent death on civilian life elsewhere. Pape, for instance, captures mainstream sentiment in *Dying to Win: The Strategic Logic of Suicide Terrorism* by titling his first chapter "The Growing Threat" (Pape 2005). Writing from the vantage point of legislators on Capitol Hill, Pape defines terrorism as "the use of violence by an organization other than a national government to intimidate or frighten a target audience" (9). As he states, excluding state actions from the category of "terrorism" is necessary so that it does not "distract attention from what policy makers would most like to know: how to combat the threat posed by non-state actors to the national security of the United States and its allies" (280n2). Assaf Moghadam similarly positions his effort to understand the causes of suicide attacks "in order to develop policies vital to national and international security" (2006a, 81). But in pointing to foreign occupation as a key motivation of suicide attacks while commenting that "the target state of every modern suicide campaign has been a democracy" (Pape, 45), Pape does not push his observation further in asking why the predominant invading and occupying powers in those contested territories have been liberal democracies in the first place, especially in light of their colonial history. As Johnson reminds us, "'terrorism' is an extremely flexible concept open to abuse" by the political, military, and intellectual establishment, who shift the label to fit the state's geopolitical agendas (121).

Dorit Naaman brings out this unequal intertwining of life and death in her observations regarding the Israeli–Palestinian conflict, commenting that while all Palestinian attacks on Israelis (whether targeting soldiers or civilians) are dubbed terrorist attacks, "dropping a one-ton bomb from an Israeli airplane on a five-story Palestinian house, in which a militant may be present, knowing full well that dozens of civilians will be killed, is hardly ever described in Western media as terrorism" (2007, 939). This uneasy, complex interlayering of life and death for subjects situated in unequal and conflicting locations is preempted by positivist terrorism research in its ideological narration, which performs the binary trope of terrorist "threat" and democratic "security." As noted by scholars such as Mamdani, through its foreign policies the U.S. government has also been complicit with breeding terroristic death to preserve and foster its own democratic life (Mamdani 2002). Democratic life and terroristic death thus have always shared an entangled affinity that contradicts the ideological presumption of mainstream terrorism researchers.

In fact, social scientists' preoccupation with terrorism, while often stated in terms of a security threat to civilian safety, reveals a deeper worry regarding political threats to the liberal way of life. Some researchers perceive democracy as harboring a greater propensity toward civil liberties and freedom, which leads terrorists to exploit it to their own advantage (Pape 2005; Weinberg 2006). Leonard Weinberg goes so far as to suggest that democracy should be considered a root cause of terrorism, since its "open societies and transparent governments" provide the conditions for terrorist operations to grow (2006, 55). Weinberg, of course, is not aligning democracy with terrorism; rather, he is angling for a reactionary argument that being "too democratic" allows terrorists to harm the civil values liberal citizens hold dear. Taking a different position, Louise Richardson cautions against "sacrific[ing] liberal democratic values to secure short-term security" and argues that "the strongest weapons in our arsenal against terrorism are precisely the facets of our society that appeal to the potential recruits for terrorists" (2006, 12). Echoing Richardson, Mia Bloom argues that the challenge is for the liberal state to hold its "high ground," its civil and democratic values, even in the face of atrocious acts by terrorists (2005, 40). Despite their opposition to Weinberg, however, both Richardson and Bloom stand with him in reinforcing the binary between a "democratic" us and "terroristic" them. And whether framing their position in terms of restraining democracy (Weinberg 2006) or reinforcing democracy (Bloom 2005; Richardson 2006), terrorism is nevertheless understood as the antithesis of liberal democracy. The demarcation that marks terrorists as negating the liberal right to life, liberty, and the pursuit of happiness frees terrorism researchers from the political accountability of looking at the lives of suicide bombers as quintessential human life.

This ideological dehumanization in service of protecting the liberal way of life further slides toward the other, as Weinberg and Pape subsequently direct public fears of terrorism toward the subject of illegal immigration. For Weinberg, an "alienated immigrant population" provides an important pool of potential terrorist recruits (52), and the "permeable borders" of democracies allow for easy entry and exit for international terrorists, since "those seeking sanctuary are usually treated humanely even when they express hatred and loathing for the very countries in which they have come to reside" (54–55). In one of his domestic policy proposals, Pape thus calls for the U.S. government to "step up border and immigration controls": "We have substantially increased background checks of immigrants and visa seekers, and these policies should be maintained. The United States should also take stronger measures to control illegal immigration, especially across its most porous border, with Mexico. In 1996 the United States began building a National Border Fence, comparable to the Israeli barriers, covering a fourteen-mile stretch near San Diego. . . . Such measures would make it more difficult for al-Qaeda to continue attacks within the United States" (240). But Pape's proposition is unfounded by his own empirical standard, as no terrorist attack against the United States has ever been conducted by those crossing the U.S.–Mexico border. One wonders whether these "objective" and "neutral" social scientists might have also bought into the popular notion of the dark-skinned and accented English-speaker as the typical terrorist subject.

Pape further proposes withdrawing U.S. troops from the Arabian peninsula without relinquishing political control and diplomatic pressure in the area through "offshore balancing" in order to protect "our core interest in maintaining access to one of the world's key oil-producing regions" (237). What Gambetta poses earlier as "intense and dispassionate interest" in the scientific inquiry of suicide terrorism thus quickly slides into an ideological and material interest in sustaining oil supplies and economic survival for liberal democracy. As several terrorism researchers all call for mobilizing and building allies with moderates in the troubled regions in "our campaigns" against extremist terrorists (Bloom 2005; Richardson 2006; Schweitzer 2006), it also suggests a normative ethos wherein "they" (terrorists and their associated societies) are the troubled ones who need to drastically change the way they behave. Liberal democracy is seen as the form of government to be preserved and protected: we may want to change our policies, such as withdrawing military presence abroad, aligning with foreign moderates, or developing alternative energy sources, but the end goal is to preserve our own capitalist interests and liberal way of life—that is, the script itself. Any radical element is taken as a dangerous threat, and anything moderate is accepted as proliberal and procapitalist.

By othering suicide terrorism as a threat to democracy, mainstream terrorism researchers disguise their ideological preferences and biases in neutral and objective terms. They produce and align themselves as part of *normality* in the liberal script to which the *abject* terrorist is opposed. Noting that the production of human knowledge is never detached from one's own material circumstances, Edward Said has argued, "No one has ever devised a method of detaching the scholar from the circumstances of life, from the fact of his involvement (conscious or unconscious) with a class, a set of beliefs, a social position" (1979, 10). Social scientists' values and beliefs are tied to their money, influence, and property—that is, the "liberal capitalist" world around them. As R. George Kirkpatrick and his colleagues argue, however, "The ideology of 'value-free' science serves as a mask for complicity with the powers that be, [and] 'value-free' science is a value-laden operation" (Kirkpatrick et al. 1980). Thus deeply entrenched in and profiting from the liberal lifecycle, mainstream "scientific" terrorism research becomes part of the hegemonic counterterrorism apparatus, which embeds the perpetual democracy is for life–terrorism is for death binary in its discursive regime.

Threats and Victims versus Agency

Approaching the study of suicide terrorism as a threat not only reveals the hidden ideology of empirical science in sustaining the *normality* of the liberal way of life; it also further denies the possibility of engaging the critical agency behind the threat and connecting that agency to aspirations for life. For example, many researchers perceive terrorism as a vicious disease to be controlled and expunged. Richardson, in the introduction to her collective volume, *The Roots of Terrorism*, narrates the venture of understanding terrorism as the search for a cure for cancer, where "the cure is likely to be almost as complicated as the disease, entailing a combination of alleviating the risk factors, blocking the interactions between them, and building the body's resilience to exposure" (2006, 1–2). Morris Foster and Jesse Butler further adopt a public health model in comparing terrorism to cancer or HIV, arguing that more effective counterterrorism strategies can be developed by applying the biomedical research concept of a "translational pipeline" that critically "links the findings of basic research about the aetiology and epidemiology of the threat to the development of therapeutics and prevention strategies" (2008, 82). Similarly, Yoram Schweitzer portrays suicide attacks as a "global epidemic" (Schweitzer 2006), and Ehud Sprinzak advises democratic citizens to "develop strong terrorism antibodies" (2000, 73).

But to present suicide terrorism in a biomedical disease narrative is to approach the terrorist subjects as if they are without a human "face." In Judith Butler's words, "Those who remain faceless or whose faces are presented to us as so many symbols of evil, authorize us to become senseless before those lives we have eradicated, and whose grievability is indefinitely postponed" (2004a, xviii). Fanon has also indicated that the disease narrative strikes a chord with the colonial civilizing mission, which functions as a form of pesticide as it "destroys parasites, carriers of disease [and] roots out heresy, natural impulses, and evil" (2004, 7). Once the terrorist subjects are framed as diseases or parasites in need of elimination, their subjectivity is effectively dehumanized.[10]

Sometimes the agency of the suicide attacker is deprived not by conceptualizing it as a threatening disease, but through a reverse trope of victimization that describes female and child bombers as susceptible to terrorist manipulation and indoctrination. For example, Ami Pedahzur suggests the personal crises of women, such as being unable to conceive and divorced by a husband, becoming pregnant out of wedlock, or having extramarital affairs, as a cause of their suicide missions (2005, 136–42). To Pedahzur, terrorist organizations exploit the personal pain of such women for their own political gain. Bloom echoes this sentiment, arguing that militant organizations often exploit women's personal grievances as stigmatized widows or rape victims to manipulate them into becoming weapons, reflecting their patriarchal ideals of women's self-sacrifice and self-effacement (165).

Despite being couched in the empirical language of "factors" and "causation," such a probe into the sexual history and mental state of individual suicide bombers becomes a social science tabloid that sensationalizes personal tragedies and victimization. Naaman disputes such gender profiling of Palestinian female suicide bombers, noting that "the logic of such explanations is unfounded. Some of the women were happy, engaged to be married (Ayat Akhras), good students (Dareen Abu Aisheh), professionals (Hanadi Jaridat), and mothers (Reem el Riyashi)" (936). Francine Banner further argues that a psychopathic explanation actually plays into the hands of gender stereotypes when it portrays men as engaged "in terrorism for rational reasons based in altruism, [while] women engage in suicide bombings as a result of 'emotional' problems caused by lack of marital opportunities, infidelity or general frailty" (2006, 242). Banner finds Chechen female bombers to be communal actors rather than passive victims who devote their bodies to a political cause through militant struggle. David Rosen similarly discounts the perception of Palestinian child bombers as brainwashed victims and provides an alternative picture wherein children have been at the forefront of the anti-occupation struggle since the first intifada (Rosen 2005). In Rosen's words, "Children and youth may have been recruited into militant institutions and organizations created by adults, but they pushed and prodded adults into higher levels of activism, rebellion, and terrorism" (93).

Whether treated as vicious threat or exploited victim, the terrorist subject is consigned to the domain of death and written as devoid of proper agency and subjectivity. Embedded materially and ideologically within liberal hegemony, mainstream terrorism research internalizes a normalized understanding of democratic agency in liberal citizenship, which sees suicide attackers as the very negation of liberal life itself. It carves out a perpetual boundary of us versus them that forecloses any understanding of such deathly acts, thus quarantining the abject "disease" of suicide bombing from "contaminating" the normative reproduction of liberal life.

The Anticolonial Inquiry:
Reanimating Suicide Bombing toward Life

Against the prevailing liberal hegemonic view that suicide bombing constitutes the very antithesis of democratic citizenship, Fanon offers another look at sacrificial violence and its potential for rebirthing political life. In his psychoanalytic treatise of colonialism, Black Skin, White Masks, Fanon mentions his conversation with an acquaintance who had recently returned from the Indochina war. Describing the serenity and calmness with which the Vietnamese teenagers rushed toward the colonial French firing squads, the acquaintance told Fanon, "On one occasion . . . we had to shoot from a kneeling position: The soldiers' hands were shaking in the presence of those young 'fanatics' . . . The war that you and I were in was only a game compared to what is going on out there" (Fanon 1994, 227). For Fanon, these youngsters' sacrificial act has nothing to do with the so-called Asiatic attitude toward death. Rather, noting that the Vietnamese soldiers were eyeing the birth of a radical renewal, he writes, "It is for the sake of the present and of the future that they are willing to die" (226–27).

Fanon opens up a critical inquiry into collective violence in emphasizing its moment of "being political"—that is, violence seized by a collective body to capture critical agency and live out subjectivity, even if it requires their own deaths, in an effort to achieve a radical renewal of life conditions, symbolic and/or material. Whether the body actually wins or loses is less important than the fact that they are *acting*, since to act is to initiate a possibility of change. Without ascribing such enactment of sacrificial violence to a universal human history outside differential contexts, it is nonetheless critical to look into the ways in which colonial and geopolitical relations of violent repression and abject subordination enable and create this eruption of deadly agency in certain locations and spaces, especially when what Mbembe calls the necro-condition of living-death becomes part of quotidian life (Mbembe 2003). Although Fanon does not address the political agency in sacrificial violence in connection to citizenship, I argue that his anticolonial inquiry, through the facilitation of Engin Isin's theoretical frame, redefines suicide bombing as "acts of citizenship" that reanimate the living dead toward life.

In the essay, "Theorizing Acts of Citizenship," Isin departs from the conventional conception of citizenship rooted in legal status, formal institutions, and documented rights to instead link it to *acts*—by citizens and noncitizens alike—that entail "a break from habitus" (2008, 18). Calling for a shift from routine to *rupture*, order to *disorder*, and habit to *deviation* in grounding these "acts of citizenship" (20), Isin goes beyond the institutional rules and normalized practices of citizenship to focus on dissident acts by unnamed subjects. To Isin, what matters are not the actors per se, but the *acts* or *deeds* that produce actors as citizens—hence his assertion, "acts produce actors that do not exist before acts" (37). As he notes, a strict focus on the rules, norms, and responsibilities of citizenship "arrive[s] at the scene too late" in accounting for the dissident acts that reconstitute the agency of excluded subjects (37). These acts capture moments of citizenship not by following institutional orders and disciplines, but by rupturing sociohistorical patterns and re-creating scenes of participation (Isin and Nielsen 2008b, 2). This repositioning of citizenship encapsulates stateless subjects or those without formal status into the citizenship game, where they "constitute themselves as citizens or, better still, as those to whom the right to have rights is due" (Isin and Nielsen 2008b, 2).

As Isin asserts, acts of citizenship cannot be reduced to a search for their causes and reasons. "To act," he writes, "always means to enact the unexpected, unpredictable and unknown" (Isin 2008, 27). Hence, "while acts of citizenship involve decisions, those decisions cannot be reduced to calculability, intentionality and responsibility" (38). He argues, "Acts cannot happen without motives, purposes, or reasons, but those cannot be the only grounds of interpreting acts of citizenship. . . . But because they are irreducible to those qualities they can be enacted without subjects being able to articulate reasons for becoming activist citizens (38–39). Not only are acts of citizenship "not necessarily calculable and rational," they "may also be unintentional or affective" (37). The central consideration is not what causes these unpredictable acts, but how these acts embody a renewed political subjectivity that, in turn, renews the scene of participation. Given that marginalized subjects are often written outside the law, their acts may even be unlawful and irresponsible. Hence, he writes, "For acts of citizenship to be acts at all they must call the law into question and, sometimes, break it. Similarly, for acts of citizenship to be acts at all they must call established forms of responsibilization into question and, sometimes, be irresponsible" (39). In emphasizing moments of unconventionality, incalculability, illegality, and irresponsibility, Isin opens up the possibility of reading a multiplicity of dissident acts as acts of citizenship.

To the extent that acts of citizenship are contingent and unpredictable, their insurrection cannot be grasped by habitual modes of norm and obligation. Acts are irreducible to causes, reasons, and patterns—the kind of "scientific" rationale that embodies sociological positivism. Building on Isin, Melanie White further adds to the frame of acts of citizenship by drawing on Henri Bergson's distinction between "pressure" (habit) and "aspiration" (creativity; White 2008). Bergson points out that society embodies tendencies toward both habitual self-preservation and aspiration for change. Applying these dual tendencies to citizenship, White indicates that the habitual instinct of liberal citizenship (e.g., rules, norms, institutions) gears toward obligation and the normal functioning of a "static" society. Obligation is without reason, and "we tend blindly to accept our social obligations without dispute, and consequently obey with habitude" (White, 50).

Since the pressure of habit is so strong, Bergson argues that it is only through the "expression of emotion"—or what he calls the "affective stirring of the soul"—that "the shackles of habit can be disrupted" (White, 51–52). Not a surface agitation, this stirring of the soul is a momentary "upheaval of the depths," a creative emotion organized by aspiration toward openness, movement, and change that "provokes us to dispense with habitual modes of thinking and to embrace profoundly new insights and ideas" (52). Like a mystic, this affective stirring of emotion stirs us to "making a leap of faith" by "opening . . . to the unknown" without "calculating possibilities in advance." White writes, "The mystic helps us to 'see' that we must leap without explicit direction, without knowing where we will end up; in other words, we must embrace the impossibility of knowing the future by simply leaping" (53). This disposition toward leaping and rupture is expressed as a creative act of citizenship, by which subjects "affirm the unpredictable and contingent by provoking encounters that disrupt one's habitual tendencies" and, in so doing, "unleash a creative energy" (52, 54). As White concludes, while the breaking with "habit" is sporadic and temporary, "the effect is to breathe new life into previously static, and potentially stagnant, modes of thought and life" (52).

Here, building on Isin and White, I further illustrate how the phenomenon of suicide bombing in the Palestinian situation, inspired by the Fanonian inquiry into anticolonial violence, can be read as "acts of citizenship" in several important registers: *the affective stirring of the soul* (emotional upheavals in the interstitial space of living-death); *moments of non-habitual and contingent rupture* (unpredictable time, locale, form, and subject of attack); *unlawful and irresponsible aspiration for change* (use of violence that is nonetheless tied to desire for changing the scene of participation); and *the leap of faith that is irreducible to rationality or calculability* (deeds are committed without certainty of future), all of which aim toward a *creative disruption against obligation* (a radical renewal of the static).

Since the Six-Day War of 1967, when Israel occupied the West Bank and Gaza, the Golan Heights, and East Jerusalem, numerous United Nations resolutions have called for the withdrawal of Israeli forces from Palestinian territories. However, Israeli settlements keep expanding, especially since the Oslo peace process in 1993. In December 2001, while calling on Palestinian suicide bombers to stop attacking Israelis, United Nations High Commissioner for Human Rights Mary Robinson pointed to the Israeli government's policies of "collective punishments, such as prolonged siege and closures of the territories and destruction of homes and agricultural land," leading to "increased poverty and a steady economic decline in the West Bank and in Gaza, conditions that fuel desperation and extremism" (Davis 2003, 37). In fact, the current Palestinian situation reflects what Mbembe so vehemently characterizes as the agony of living-death that forms the normative habitus under colonialism.

As Mbembe articulates, *necropower*, or the sovereign power to create death-worlds in late modern colonial condition, involves "the dynamics of territorial fragmentation, the sealing off and expansion of settlements" (2003, 27–28). Although technically not a colony, the land that Palestinians call "home" is made up of fragmented territories without the boundedness of nationhood, where life is arranged and configured by Israeli settlers and military occupation. Going about their daily life amid checkpoints, roadblocks, and surveilling armed soldiers, Palestinians live under a constant preoccupation with death, as death (whether of oneself or others) is immanently inscribed in the quotidian. Mbembe observes, "The *state of siege* is itself a military institution. . . . The besieged villages and towns are sealed off and cut off from the world. . . . Freedom is given to local military commanders to use their discretion as to when and whom to shoot. Movement between the territorial cells requires formal permits. Local civil institutions are systematically destroyed. The besieged population is deprived of their means of income. Invisible killing is added to outright executions" (30; emphasis in original).

The habitual stream of power over death renders a collective living without feel for life. High rates of unemployment, lack of material resources, and persistent surveillance and raids by the Israeli forces create a sense of being trapped in a condition where one constantly feels the pull of insecurity and humiliation and is unable to travel away and escape. Khosrokhavar describes the sense of being "strangled" among Palestinians living in the Gaza Strip:

> More than 80 per cent of the population are unable to leave it, as access to West Bank and Israel is restricted by the Israelis. The rate of unemployment is more than 70 per cent. For these young men, death is a glorious escape from a spatial and economic confinement that is literally suffocating them. In Gaza, it is not simply the daily spectacle of deliberate humiliation that is intolerable, but also the feeling of being strangled in an enclave where life is impossible because there are too many people living in a tiny territory, without any occupation or prospects. (137)

The spatial suffocation of living-death is also illustrated in the case of Jenin, a dismal town in Palestine surrounded by Israeli checkpoints and filled with young prospective suicide bombers. There, one sees panoptical surveillance, with "Israeli soldiers . . . stationed behind sandbags and inside bunkers and towers just outside the town to seal it off and monitor traffic in and out. Israeli tanks seem to emerge from nowhere to block cars on the road, allowing only those deemed suitable to enter Jenin" (Davis 2003, 104).

As Joyce Davis observes, inside Jenin, there is little that "make[s] life more attractive than death" (2003, 104). There are essentially no jobs, and "many have watched their houses destroyed by Israeli bulldozers in retaliation for an attack on a Jewish settlement, and others have seen boys shot down by Israeli soldiers. Most have watched their fathers humiliated at Israeli checkpoints after waiting in lines hours long, trying to bring sick, crying babies to the hospital" (104). Living in a condition in which hate becomes a duty, "young men in Jenin see no future outside of war," outside of fighting the Israelis to regain their land. The militant organizations that sponsor the bombers indicate that there is no need to coerce or cajole anyone to sacrifice oneself for the nation, for "there is a ready cadre of young men, and increasingly of young women, who sign up for such operations" (104–6).

This sociopolitical condition is compounded by the disparity that Palestinians see in their own lived conditions and those of the neighboring Israelis. In interviews with nearly 250 Palestinian suicide bombers, Nasra Hassan found that "none of them were uneducated, desperately poor, simple-minded, or depressed. Many were middle class and, unless they were fugitives, held paying jobs."[11] It is thus not a matter of personal financial distress or objective poverty, but the unequal distribution of material resources between the Israelis and Palestinians under occupation that sustains feelings of injustice and powerlessness. Khosrokhavar notes, "The Palestinian economy's dependency on Israel makes them fragile: they are turned down for jobs commensurate with their qualifications because these are reserved for Israelis or for other nationalities that are not suspected of terrorism" (129). In addition, water, a major issue in the Occupied Territories, is unequally distributed, with Palestinians allotted seven liters per day while Israeli Jewish settlers get 350 liters. The Palestinian American journalist Lamis Andoni points emphatically to "the difference between the lush lands of the settlements, dotted with swimming pools and date palm orchards, and the parched lands of Gaza just across the fence, where water usage is severely restricted, where sewage backs up, and where many families have no drinking water" (1997, 42). Furthermore, the settlers live on the top of hills, enjoy a Western middle-class standard of living, and "overlook the Palestinian villages lower down the slopes" (Khosrokhavar, 118). Khosrokhavar observes, "The symbolic domination (above/below) is mirrored in an economic superiority that stems from Jewishness and not class relations: Israeli Jews are granted rights denied to Palestinians, who are reduced to a form of neo-colonial inferiority within an apartheid-like system" (118–19).

The desire to break out of habitual obligation to the existing apartheid is widely shared among Palestinian subjects. Jamal Nasser, a twenty-two-year-old suicide bomber who blew himself up in 2001, left a note stating:

Who does not feel outrage and is not eager for revenge when participating in funerals for fallen martyrs, especially collective funerals in Nablus . . . and when watching the mourning mothers and wives and children of martyrs on television? . . . And who does not empathize with people whose homes were demolished, and stores destroyed? . . . And who does not feel anger when children are murdered and trees ripped up, and cities shelled, who . . . who . . . who? I marched in their funerals, chanted with the angry crowds, deeply eager for revenge but didn't know how. (Araj 2008, 297)

While this narrative bespeaks the theme of revenge for the mass Palestinian deaths committed by Israeli forces, it portends at a deeper level the desire to unchain oneself and others from the suffocating shackles of suffering under Israeli colonialism.

Without trying to render justice to the whole history of the Palestinian–Israeli conflict, the above description nonetheless points to the material-geographic context of living-death, in which Palestinians are obligated toward a normalized and static submission, and which *affectively stirs their souls* to de-stabilize and break such habitual bonds. In this context, suicide bombing emerges as an unexpected means of expression that conventional forums of citizenship are unable to provide because they "arrive at the scene too late" (especially for Palestinians, who do not even have voice as actual citizens) in accounting for the political agency of subjects under occupation. The violent act constitutes a *moment of contingent rupture* that is unpredictable in its time, locale, and form of attack (whether strapping bombs around the subject's waist, through vehicles such as cars or airplanes, or by some other means). The diverse profiles of the bombers further point to the contingency of the emergence of subjects: one cannot predict where and how a bombing actor will emerge (Hafez 2006b, 172).[12] Moreover, the apparent *unlawfulness and irre-sponsibility* in killing civilians is tied to an aspiration for changing the scene of participation, enabling a *creative disruption against the habitual obligation* of living-death—an ultimate renewal of the static. These qualities activate a reading of Palestinian suicide bombings as lethal eruptions of acts of citizenship.

In this violent manifestation of citizenship, what appears as a negative de-struction of life is in reality oriented toward a positive rebirth—an uncanny renewal, for oneself and for others. As Khosrokhavar notes, the act of suicide bombing oscillates between resignation and self-assertion; it is a realization that one's life is not worth living anymore and a reignited hope that one can attain a drastic rebirth via sacrificial violence (45). By tying the body of the individual bomber to the collective nation, Khosrokhavar argues, the terri-tory of a nation can be seen as a metaphorical dimension of one's body, such that "as he moves around his country, the individual has a feeling of being at home that is experienced inside the body" (135). Nation-state conveys not simply a sense of identity but a metaphoric home where one feels located and embodied. For Palestinians who are denied such a "home" in the earthly life, the body is experienced as being in a constant state of dislocation. The daily searches and raids by Israeli security and the want of material resources in Palestine add to the senses of "fragmentation, mutilation and dismemberment" (135). By exploding in pieces, the suicide bomber "reproduce[s] the image of a Palestinian land that has been shattered by the settlement into fragments" (135). But as his body is blown into thousands of pieces, "his martyrdom will make it intact as is the idealized Palestine in his mind" (135). As Fanon reminds us, "This violent praxis is totalizing since each individual represents a violent link in the great chain, in the almighty body of violence rearing up in reaction to the primary violence of the colonizer" (2004, 50). It is for the re-embodiment of the bomber and his or her compatriots that the mysterious "leap" is taken. In the midst of living-death, one must destroy in order to re-create.

This aspiration for change is coined both religiously and secularly. For instance, some turn to the promised heaven for martyrs designated in the Qur'an as a symbol of renewal. Izzidene al Masri, the Palestinian youth from Jenin who blew himself up inside Jerusalem's Sbarro pizzeria in 2001, thus assured his mother before his mission, "It's the afterlife we should seek, not this life" (Davis 2003, 107–8). As Mohammed Hafez observes, "The last will and testament of the bombers invariably begin or end with Qur'anic verses such as 2:154—'And call not those who are slain in the way of Allah "dead." Nay, they are living, only ye perceive not'" (2006b, 178). Significantly, in the context of living-death, the appeal to religious symbols functions not as the primary engine of sacrificial violence but bolsters the intense desire for renewal. For others, the martyr's deed is enacted to revive the collective spirit of those who continue to exist in the earthly world. The words of the Hamas bomber Hazza al-Ghoul, noted earlier, that "we do not sing the songs of death, but recite the hymns of life. . . . We die so that future generations may live" (Hafez 2006a, 72) instantiates this point. Hiba Daraghmeh, a female suicide bomber who conducted her mission in association with Islamic Jihad in 2003, similarly displayed a renewed spirit when thinking about the act of redemption she was about to offer for her community, informing her family the day before the attack, "I feel that I am a new person. You will be very proud of me" (Hafez 2006b, 176). Either way, the act of suicide bombing seeks a rupture of the static pattern of living-death: to die/destroy in order to live/create. One Islamic Jihad militant thus sums up: "if you want to be a holy martyr, you have to want to live!" (Reuter, 128). The desire to live is not to be taken literally as a desire for physical life, but rather is seeking a drastic reversal of the agony of living-death. Mbembe's musing on suicide bombing advances in this direction: "In that sense, the martyr . . . can be seen as laboring under the sign of the future. . . . The besieged body becomes a piece of metal whose function is, through sacrifice, to bring eternal life into being. The body duplicates itself and, in death, literally and metaphorically escapes the state of siege and occupation" (37).

But just as the "leap" is taken without explicit direction or knowing where one will end up (and thus is incalculable and unpredictable in advance), the certainty of this reversal (ending agony and "bringing eternal life into being") is never guaranteed: *the leap of faith is irreducible to rationality or calculability*. Palestinian suicide bombers commit to the historical rupturing without certainty of future or predictability of outcome—they simply "leap" with the stirring of the soul. By initiating a possibility of change without inevitability of future, suicide bombing constitutes a moment of "being political" in rendering itself as a lethal act of citizenship.

Examining the scenario of Palestinian suicide bombing through the frame of acts of citizenship that reconstruct it as creativity against habitus thus recovers the unlawful and irresponsible bombers as lethal citizens. Rather than conceiving these subjects as a threat to democracy, this anticolonial inquiry repositions them as political agents bearing claims for a radical renewal of life conditions. However, just at the moment when this anticolonial inquiry creates a connection between sacrificial violence and the agency of citizenship, its insistence on viewing the act through the lens of "democratic" renewal also generates its own paradoxes and reaches its own limits. Specifically, by representing the deathly violence of suicide bombing as an insurgent breath of life, it directly reverses the order of the democratic life–terroristic death binary (i.e., colonial democracy actually inflicts death and suicide bombing actually reanimates life) without examining the intricate entanglement of suicide bombing with colonial democratic life. In fact, characterizations such as *the affective stirring of the soul or leap of faith that is irreducible to rationality* carry an implicit assumption that the lethal act of citizenship is somehow pure and untainted (life) and does not replicate or traffic in complicity with liberal instrumentality, norm, or habit (death).

In spite of the iteration of unexpectedness, incalculability, and unpredictability in narrating suicide bombing in this anticolonial inquiry, however, sporadic episodes of suicide bombing are nonetheless tied to the rational, strategic, and predictable apparatus of militant organizations. Pape, for example, has emphasized the strategic logic of suicide terrorism in achieving the political agenda of militant organizations and, by implication, the rationality and predictability of such a venture (Pape 2005). While acts of citizenship are irreducible to instrumentality and calculability, and the absolutism of rationality needs to be questioned, the impression may be rendered that these dissident acts are totally spontaneous and lack strategic planning and calculation. Given that suicide missions often require prior training, planning, and coordination (see Sprinzak 2000; Gambetta 2005a; Hassan 2006), it would be an overstatement to argue that the bombers' "leap of faith" is not in some way tinged with the calculations of an organized campaign that continuously replicates violence. As Lindsey O'Rourke further points out, the use of female suicide bombers by militant organizations is propelled by strategic considerations, given their superior effectiveness (O'Rourke 2009). Hence, even if incidents of suicide bombing cannot be reduced to a purely rational logic, they are nonetheless aided and affected by it. While acts of citizenship are characterized by their unpredictable fracturing, this by no means negates the embedded element of instrumental rationality and orchestrated planning.

Indeed, this is precisely the reason that Isin refuses to consider suicide bombing an act of citizenship (Isin and Finn 2008). While Isin's ideal of "activist citizen" is not the civil and docile kind but is driven and mobilized by acts that impel subjects to usurp "the right to claim rights" (Isin 2009, 381), it is nonetheless imbued with qualities characterized by democratic agency (i.e., public, collective, counterhegemonic, life-sustaining). In spite of the emphasis on contingency, creativity, unlawfulness, and irresponsibility in his anticolonial, democratic frame, Isin's conception of acts of citizenship cannot really fathom acts of sacrificial violence that resort to clandestine methods of ruthless killing and negation of civilian life as belonging to the proper realm of citizenship. Isin and Melissa Finn specifically identify several "undemocratic" features in suicide bombing—*instrumentality, banality,* and *unanswerability*—that make it unqualified as an act of citizenship, thus foreclosing any possible inquiry into the democratic agency of this violent enactment (Isin and Finn 2008). Intriguingly, it is as if the deathly violence of suicide bombing violates an ultimate moral taboo: that a sharp distinction must be drawn between acts of citizenship and acts of callous violence, lest the latter contaminate the purified realm of the former. As a lethal act that takes the destruction of life as its modus operandi, its political life also ceases to be. In the end, though proceeding via radical democratic analysis, Isin and Finn come to a conclusion similar to that of mainstream terrorism research: suicide terrorism aspires toward destructive death rather than democratic life.

But Isin and Finn's analysis is less successful in detaching suicide bombing from the agency of citizenship than it is useful in indicating the inadequacy of enclosing an inquiry into the political agency of sacrificial violence within a strictly democratic frame. This violence furthermore cannot be understood as gesturing only toward life without trafficking in the modern instrumental exchange of sacrificial death. By interpreting suicide bombing as exerting a radical reversal of the colonial condition of living-death and exhuming an aspiration for life renewal, the anticolonial inquiry aided by Isin's conceptual frame voluntarily constructs it as beyond complicity in liberal life, overlooking that such deathly resistance actually takes the modern sacrificial economy as the instrumental basis for its violent enactment. Noting the inevitable entanglement between suicide bombing and liberal citizenship leads us to an alternative framework that joins the two in a different horizon, one that sees suicide bombing as being imbued with ingenious agency in appropriating liberal life itself.

Ingenious Reopening:
Reusing Sacrificial Violence to Appropriate Liberal Life Itself

To the extent that sacrificial violence is not antagonistic to but entangled with the colonial order of liberal citizenship, its embodied agency is necessarily ambiguous. Suicide bombing is thus tied to the agency of citizenship, not in a linearly democratic way, but in an inventive and circuitous way. As noted at the beginning of this chapter, when Akhras's mother asserted the importance of regaining "our rights, our land, our authority, our government, our homes" in the documentary To Die in Jerusalem, she positioned sacrificial violence as a form of political resistance employed to attain a life of sovereign citizenship. But if suicide bombing constitutes political resistance, it is certainly not the democratic political kind, not only because of its act of killing, but also because of its secretive and interstitial qualities—that is, its hidden recruitment, preparation, and operation; its maintenance of silence until the public explosion; its nonverbal way to communicate a political message (except for the post-bombing release of martyr videos); and its staging of civilian deaths at unpredictable moments and sites to evoke fear. In short, suicide bombing is subtle, roundabout, and deceptive, underlined by the secrecy that embodies it.

Such craftiness, however, can be considered improvisational in light of the lack of alternative political forums for Palestinians to express—and for the international community to genuinely *hear* and *address*—their grievances in conditions of living-death. This is especially so as the Palestinians attempted to take democratic political routes before and during the first intifada but did not achieve substantive and effective movement toward ending occupation. Lori Allen, for instance, provides an account of the democratic "popular uprising consisting of grassroots mobilization of all sectors of Palestinian society, including women, youth, and the elderly, who engaged in public demonstrations and nonviolent civil disobedience" against the occupation in the first intifada (2008, 454). As Bader Araj further argues, one needs to consider the ways in which intensifying state repression affects insurgents' choice of tactics and prompts them to resort to more violent means (Araj 2008). Excessive use of force by the Israelis and the bleak prospect for state formation have made Palestinians feel the inadequacy of conventional protest and escalate the severity of their attacks from stone throwing to suicide bombing (Hafez 2006b, 179). Hence, one can argue that it is when their democratic political acts went unanswered that certain Palestinian subjects were motivated to innovate unconventional and unexpected ways to ameliorate their abjection, normalize their humanity, and appropriate nonexistent spaces of citizenship. Their improvisational and nonlinear resistance, as embodied in suicide bombing, sutures the polymorphous dynamics of ingenious agency—oppositional, negotiated, interstitial, and subcultural—vis-à-vis the liberal life script.

As noted earlier, while the focus of the discussion that follows is on individual bombers, I illustrate how the ingenious agency in suicide bombing should be understood as collaboratively and reciprocally inscribed by both the bombing subjects and their affiliated or sponsoring organizations. The militant organizations devise and plan the bombing operations; the bombing subjects then respond to the call and execute them. These organizations inscribe the elements of ingenuity and complicity into the apparatus of suicide bombing, and the bombers take advantage of these existing organizations as resources and channels to enact their ingenious appropriations, thus giving the organizations impetus to continue the repetitions. Their respective agency feeds off each other, and this mutual enactment of ingenious agency is most prominently shown in its negotiated and interstitial qualities.

In addition, as I show, sections of Palestinian civil society are also indirectly but collectively involved in stirring such ingenious enactments through commemorative rituals honoring the martyrs, thereby underscoring the subcultural element of this agentic explosion.

To begin, this deathly appropriation can first be read as *oppositional* to the life script of Israeli liberal citizenship, which forever excludes them and thrives on their abject conditions of living-death. In the testimony of Israeli survivors who suffer severe injuries from suicide bombing, one often hears narratives such as, "I used to be active, to play soccer two or three times a week, I was on teams, I danced" (Human Rights Watch 2002, 11). This type of discourse configures a liberal citizen's right to life, liberty, and the pursuit of happiness that is taken away by the bombing perpetrators. Yet such a right, intimately tied to the material conditions of Israeli citizenship—which proffers bountiful possessions of jobs, lands, houses, swimming pools, playgrounds, and water—is sustained by upholding a geographical distance from and political indifference to the perpetual state of living-death in the Occupied Territories that Israel violently inflicts through blatant killing, militarized siege, armed surveillance, and by building a fortress state that segregates the Palestinian enclaves.[13]

The Palestinian psychologist Iyad Sarraj describes the Palestinian children who came of age during the intifada:

> The words *angry* and *defiant* accurately describe the Palestinian children. . . . They are also tense and vigilant. For many of them, throwing stones directs their anger onto the Israeli soldiers who are considered a legitimate target. . . . These children have learned the language and the meaning of the occupation. . . . Even if every child has not been humiliated by the Israeli soldiers or told that his or her life is worthless, the environment sends this message loud and clear. . . . Children easily perceive the difference between the living conditions in the camps and the newly-built Israeli settlements. These differences make them believe that Jewish settlements deserve big clean playgrounds and swimming pools while their refugee camps have open sewer systems and garbage piled up at every street corner. (quoted in Andoni 1997, 42; emphasis in original)

Resentment, anger, and defiance that come through tensely affective states of trauma, fear, and humiliation craft the crucial essence of acts of suicide bombing, which can be read as an oppositional staging that refuses the continuing abject habitus engineered by liberal citizenship. Countering the liberal dogma that focuses on the earthly accumulation of individual interests and national material well-being (as in "Give me liberty or give me death"), suicide bombing disrupts the citizenship script by temporarily blocking the continuance of liberal life when other nationals are suspended in a space of living-death. In this deathly reinscription, the cultural meaning of citizenship shifts from the individual pursuit of life, liberty, and happiness to one that recognizes national life and death as collectively intertwined with other nationals' life and death: either both live or both die. Suicide bombing thus functions as a perpetual disruption of liberal citizenship in forming an oppositional script of ingenious citizenship.

But the ingenuity of suicide bombing does not stay at the oppositional level; rather, it is further layered through a subtle quality of *negotiation*, as it involves not a negation of life but negotiating the end of one's worldly life for a liminal and noble renewal in another dimension. Eschewing the binary routes of either following or annihilating the liberal life script that outright excludes them, suicide bombers can be read as detouring from the life script in order to improvise both liminal and sacred spaces of inclusion in the midst of living-death. Being denied life, liberty, and the pursuit of happiness in the earthly life and in a perpetual state of dislocation and dismemberment under Israeli occupation, they exchange corporeal death for a measure of renewed individual and collective life, dignity, and freedom. As discussed earlier, the renewal of life and subjectivity in suicide bombing is often projected either in a religiously inflected afterlife ("It's the afterlife we should seek, not this life"; religious intonation) or in a remobilized agency and aspiration for change among the living ("We die so that future generations may live"; secular calling). Either way, both extend the hope for a basic citizenship premise of "life, liberty, and the pursuit of happiness" to an *elsewhere* ("afterlife" or "a revived future generation") and allow the bombers to derive a renewed sense of humanity and belonging (as subjects who "count" in this world) through sacrificial violence.

The fact that one's freedom through suicide bombing can be realized only through desecrated violence that takes the lives of self and others, rather than through direct liberation from servitude, further delimits and circumscribes that freedom. It is freedom in abjection, a *negotiated* freedom taken in abject calculation. Thus, in the commemorative naming of certain streets in Palestine as "Martyrs' Passing," "Martyrs' Street," and "Martyr Square," along with the innumerable martyr posters that are used for remembrance (Allen, 456), the martyrs' names and faces not only symbolize a reanimated (sublime) life and a reignited hope for a not-yet-exiting citizenship life to come among the living; they also serve as a reminder of the actually existing conditions of living-death continuing in present earthly life, underlining the pain and travail of using martyred deaths to negotiate a dignified and normalized life of inclusion.

The negotiated quality of suicide bombing is further demonstrated in that the improvisation of sacrificial violence actually hinges on its complicity and contamination in the liberal lifecycle as the very basis of its deathly enactment. Here it is especially important to consider the coproductive role of militant organizations in crafting this negotiated element. In particular, by using and exploiting the liberal fear of the negation of life as leverage for negotiation, these organizations demonstrate their immersion in liberal modernity and instrumental rationality. Rather than negating or transcending the life script of liberal citizenship, they traffic in and negotiate with the modern liberal order, which acts as a critical conduit in their disruption and appropriation of the life script in claiming an unrecognized inclusion and belonging.

In spite of their transcendent aura of martyrdom, the everyday operations of militant organizations are actually implicated in global capitalist modernity. As already noted, however contingent and unpredictable its occurrence, suicide bombing operates within and through the rational-strategic-instrumental milieu of militant organizations and is always tinged with elements of calculability. For instance, the procedural logistics of the suicide mission—the selection of targets; gathering of intelligence; recruitment and physical and spiritual training; preparation of explosives; transportation of bombers to target areas; and use of videotapes, posters, and public exhibits (Sprinzak 2000, 69)—are pervasively crafted via modern instrumental technologies that bind the mission closely with modern liberal life rather than marking its autonomous transcendent ground. The giving of money from militant organizations to the deceased martyrs' families also resonates with and traffics in a capitalist instrumental exchange that uses material compensation to reward soldierly/sacrificial bravery.

While technology and monetary exchange certainly existed before capitalism, the logistical instrumentality in suicide bombing is indicative of its complex participation in, and selective appropriation of, the modern sacrificial economy, as organizers and participants adapt and reinvent new means to execute sacrificial violence in achieving their political objectives. And although militant organizations devise the logistical operations of suicide bombing, the bombers cannot escape implication in this sacrificial economy. In fact, given that there is no shortage of willing martyrs to be sponsored by militant organizations—best illustrated by the case of female suicide bombers, who usually have no prior ideological-political ties to these organizations (Victor 2003; Reuter 2004)—the bombing subjects can be seen as purposefully and audaciously *reusing* and *appropriating* the organizations' entanglement with the modern sacrificial economy as limited tools and resources to improvise a more noble living space for themselves and fellow Palestinians. A doubling and intricate dynamic of complicity and appropriation is at work in this contemporary enactment of sacrificial violence.

This negotiated appropriation is inevitably *interstitial*. Given the necessity of achieving the political end without the act being detected in advance, suicide bombers must detour around democratic features of being public and collective in the moment of the mission, and instead improvise illegible and guileful blows to the liberal script. Rajan speaks of the surprise factor in a suicide attack:

> Bombers' terror, then, lies in their ability to *deceive* society so easily and consistently, even in a space where society is weary of suicide attacks. The ultimate weapon of suicide attackers is, then, the impression of "normalcy" that they exhibit, the "norms" of the very public that they intend, while simultaneously appropriating their body to affect an entirely unfamiliar identity. The once human body acts in an inhuman way both in its self-immolation but also in the extraordinary way in which it kills—not directly, but indirectly; not in line with common ideas of wars and rules of engagement in typical warfare, but within a seemingly separate, unknown set of rules laid out by an authority that remains elusive and uncontrollable. (16; emphasis in original)

This interstitial quality of suicide bombing in disrupting and appropriating the liberal life script is accentuated through the organizations' use of women as suicide bombers. These women can more easily navigate the liberal surveillance and security system, given stereotypical perceptions of them as occupying "passive or subordinate roles in Muslim culture" (Stone and Pattillo 2011, 163). While female suicide bombers are portrayed in the West as immobile victims of Islamic patriarchy, they can be read as *using* that generalized perception to pierce the normative fabric of liberal democracy. Although Palestinian militant organizations have certainly appropriated women for their political cause, it is critical to note that, like sex workers who reappropriate the masculine gaze to expand their livable spaces, female suicide bombers may also be read as interstitially reappropriating patriarchal cultures—taking advantage of their "attack flexibility" and "surprise factor"—to put themselves in situations where they can act as sacrificial martyrs and political agents.

Moallem has also examined this reappropriation of gendered signs in her delineation of the strategic use of veiling. She asks, "What if the veil, which is depicted in the West as an ultimate signifier of passivity and victimhood, is instead an expression of the desire to hide from the panoptical gaze of modern regimes of power and knowledge? What if the veil is nothing but an occasion for passing, a ruse, a mask, or a site of action by a performing and willing subject?" (2005, 114). This does not suggest that gendered resistance through veiling is autonomous from or transcendent over the regimes of power imposed on the body. As Moallem notes, the veil may also be used as "a means to insert the body into the world of consumer capitalism" as "fashion companies . . . produce dress and various forms of veiling for the global Islamic market" that appeal to Islamic femininity (114, 120). Yet within these hegemonic circuits, spaces exist for marginal subjects to maneuver cultural signs or objects to reverse their immediate situations and affect material change. Reports of male suicide bombers in Afghanistan cross-dressing and disguising themselves in women's burkas in order to pass through security without being searched (Rajan, 128), female suicide bombers in Iraq wearing men's clothing in order to pass unnoticed and stage attacks at a U.S. recruiting center filled with Muslim male military recruits (130), and female bombers in Sri Lanka feigning pregnancy in order to "easily . . . pass through military checkpoints, thereby penetrating social spaces that are less accessible to other suicide bombers" (288) all bolster this argument, accentuating the interstitial enactment of sacrificial resistance. As Rajan argues, while cross-dressers "escalated the anonymous nature of . . . [suicide] bombing, transforming it into something incalculable and disruptive to the US imaginary" (130), women who feign pregnancy deliberately exploit the patriarchal expectation that pregnant women are "morally proper" and would not engage in violence that harms themselves and their unborn child, thus "capitaliz[ing] on that social sympathy to ensure the success of their missions" (288). Like veiling, these practices performed in conjunction with the strategic logic of militant operations make interstitial use of heteronormative gendered signs to enable the bombers' appropriation of liberal life.

Taken together, the oppositional, negotiated, and interstitial appropriations of liberal life inscribe a subcultural script of ingenious citizenship. This subcultural script is not only devised and written by militant organizations and individual bombers but also coproduced by Palestinian civilians, who participate in communal rituals that continuously give new life to an oppositional habitus against occupation. For instance, Hafez points to the importance of everyday ritual and ceremony such as creating posters, websites, and public exhibits to honor and publicize martyred acts in "arousing emotions, deepening commitments, and inculcating the values of collective ethos" (2006a, 67). This elaborate process is worth quoting at length:

> Ritual and ceremony permeate all aspects of preparing "living martyrs" (suicide bombers in waiting) and burying dead ones. The videotapes to record the last will and testament of the bombers and solidify their commitment to martyrdom; the white shrouds that covers the bombers from head to toe to simultaneously symbolize their purity and preparedness for the grave; the headband and banners emblazoned with Quranic verses to decorate the living martyrs' quarters before they declare their intention to go on a mission; the guns and bombs that serve as props for their last photos, to symbolize empowered individuals making a free choice for self-sacrifice for the cause; the mass procession to commemorate the death of the martyr, often featuring other militants dressed as martyrs in waiting and strapped with fake explosive belts; the chants of marchers and loud speakers during burial processions: "With our soul, with our blood, we sacrifice for you o'martyr" (bil rouh, bil damm, nafdika ya shahid); the melodramatic music to celebrate the heroism and sacrifice of the martyrs; the mourning ceremony where the women ululate and distribute candy or sweet coffee to celebrate the martyr's entry into heaven, and where men receive congratulatory handshakes because their sons or daughters have achieved eternal salvation; the posters on a wall, and electronic links on a web site to immortalize the bombers—all these actions are undertaken repeatedly, routinely, and with procedural rigor. (67)

Rather than signs of brainwashing, these communal appeals to religious and nationalist symbols resonate with actors sharing a common identification under occupation. This aspect of intersubjective influence brings to light what Iris Jean-Klein identifies as "cross-subjective self-enactment," whereby "multiple bodies, subjects, and their subjectivities . . . collaboratively and reciprocally [affect] the individual subject" (2000, 101).

Seen in this communal and cross-subjective context, these mass participants' speech acts and communal commemorations help "stir the souls" of potential bombers. Suicide bombing is thus propelled forward as an intimate extension from the communal anticolonial engagement, and its violent eruption in turn remobilizes the agency of the colonized/oppressed community. It is in this larger communal-structural and cross-subjective frame that suicide bombing can be read as instigating reenergizing and renewing effects within the Palestinian community and projecting a sovereign citizenship life within the modern liberal world order.

In all, to the extent that Palestinians in the Occupied Territory remain "impossible citizens" who lack official status and membership rights as subjects of an independent state, these deathly appropriations of dignity, belonging, and sovereign citizenship constitute improvisations of nonexistent citizenship by which the suicide bombers are citizens *otherwise*. While sacrificial violence—unlike other deployments of ingenious agency such as hidden tactics, calculated abjection, and morphing technologies—is not able to generate direct tangible benefits and de facto rights for its enactors, who perish in the lethal acts, I suggest that this rereading of suicide bombing as ingenious citizenship nonetheless opens up a new horizon of social change. As we have seen, the ingenious agency embodied in suicide bombing does not express an antithesis to life and citizenship; rather, it stretches the appropriation of citizenship life to the extreme by giving it a deathly form. The distinction between citizens and terrorists is, then, merely a thin line. If thwarted citizens can become terrorists, then the reverse is also true: by redrawing the scripted contours of liberal citizenship to facilitate and enhance appropriation, prospective bombers can be turned back to living citizens. Indeed, unlike other forms of ingenious agency that I have examined, the enactment of sacrificial violence is something that we would want to end. The way to end it, however, is not to repress or eliminate its ingenious agency, but rather to engage it creatively and fluidly to redirect and reorient it into other forms of manifestation. In fact, contrary to common expectations, it might just take the reuse and reappropriation of the sacrificial logic of suicide bombing to unlock the possibility of social change in the Palestinian situation.

The Sacrificial Violence of Neoliberalism:
Ingenious Agency, Palestinian Statehood, and Reconfiguring
Relations of Normality and Abjection under Colonial Occupation

The recent resolutions adopted by a number of U.S. academic organizations to boycott Israeli universities and academic institutions have sparked intense debate both within and outside academia.[14] Without recounting the whole spectrum of arguments that have emerged from this public dialogue, I wish to note that one prominent element of the debate has been a focus on democratic values and principles from both sides. On one hand, supporters of the resolutions condemn the "restrictions on travel and the forced closure or destruction of schools as a result of Israeli military actions—and [describe] Israeli academic institutions as 'deeply complicit in Israel's violations of international law and human rights and in its denial of the right to education and academic freedom to Palestinians, in addition to their basic rights as guaranteed by international law.'"[15] Emphasizing the democratic process of reaching such resolutions, they argue that the resolutions endorse and honor "the call of Palestinian civil society for a boycott of Israeli academic institutions,"[16] in particular the boycott, divestment, and sanctions (BDS) movement in support of the end of Israeli occupation and colonization, the Palestinian people's right of return and right to self-determination, and "true democracy."[17]

On the other hand, critics of the resolutions point to potential curtailing of academic freedom among Israeli scholars despite the campaign's focus on institutions rather than individuals, and allege the problem of anti-Semitic sentiment by singling out Israel for a boycott when numerous other countries have even worse records of human rights abuses.[18] In short, the discourses of democratic freedom and human rights permeate the debate in such a way that both sides—despite their strongly opposing views—assume democratic agency, humane treatment of subjects, and the inviolable preservation of rights to be the proper way to resolve the Israeli–Palestinian conflict.

What has especially distinguished the discourse of democratic agency in this debate, however, has been a conspicuous absence of discussion of suicide bombing and the development of neoliberal governance in Palestine. Yet in which ways might suicide bombing and the recent neoliberal reforms spearheaded by the Palestinian Authority intimate a trajectory of social change that differs from the model of democratic agency? Despite our impulse to address the calamity of Israeli colonial occupation through democratic agency, the present horizon of social change in the Palestinian situation is unlikely to be contained within an exclusive and universal frame of democracy and human rights. The fact that neoliberalism has taken root both in Israel and Palestine not only suggests the liberal life script's *aspiring* hegemonic power in the region, but also implies that progressive social forces may have to negotiate with, and even be complicit in, the inherently antidemocratic elements of the script in order to transform the conditions of Israeli colonial occupation. To be more specific, if suicide bombers have shown their entanglement with the liberal economy, then their ingenious agency may also point to the lesson of a larger scale of sacrificial entanglement with the violence of the liberal economy to generate even more potent transformation. Sometimes, it may take implicit (and insidious) forms of sacrificial violence—and not necessarily democracy and human rights—to realize aspirations of justice in other dimensions.

It is worth noting that, similar to domestic work, sex work, and transgender rights activism, the BDS campaign practiced by U.S. academic organizations is not confined to democratic agency but also uses elements of ingenious agency. The tactics of boycott involve the use of the consumptive logics of capitalist economy to compel a ruling party or bloc to reconsider and reverse its political course and policies. In this respect, while the gesture may be symbolic, the academic boycott cannot be strictly categorized as an ethical issue, for not only is its method inherently political, but it also resorts to a complicit negotiation with the available tool of consumptive power in market capitalism to achieve its anticolonial aim. There is nothing wrong with such tactics. As Sarah Banet-Weiser and Roopali Mukherjee point out, progressive projects and movements in the United States have historically been launched through the platform and practices of consumption:

> Practicing consumer citizenship was crucial for immigrants, African Americans, and other racialized constituents in the 19th- and 20th-century US as a means to mitigate and challenge racist practices and cultural exclusions. Projecting political aspirations onto commodities and consumption practices, disenfranchised racialized communities organized boycotts of segregated public spaces, collectively invested in independent businesses, and engaged in strategic consumption practices that called into question hegemonic relations of racial power and inequity. . . . The civil rights movement that transformed racial formations in the mid-20th century US was notably organized around issues of consumption and

access—in retail stores, at lunch counters, and on city buses—as a means to enfranchise African Americans. . . . In each instance, tactics of social action engaged with rituals and institutions of commerce and capitalist exchange to demand political freedom and equality. (2012b, 7)

While the temporal and spatial contexts are different, the consumptive politics of an academic boycott against Israel nonetheless resonates in important ways with such antiracist movements in the United States. The BDS campaign is not detached from either politics or market; rather, it embodies a political foray into the instrumental exchange between consumptive power and democratic rights within capitalist commerce.

However, when such uses of consumptive instrumentality are not acknowledged in the BDS campaign, and when the academic boycott is foregrounded and framed as a democratic endeavor in solidarity with Palestinian people's human rights claims, it directs our vision of change toward a particular, untainted transformative direction. What it misses is a political theorization and understanding of the intricate forces of social change that persistently undercut and complicate the democratic trajectory, which might require critical scholars and activists to resort to more fluid and inventive uses of nondemocratic methods to help procure a more humane life for Palestinian subjects. Such lessons, as I illustrate below, can precisely be seen in the PA's efforts to mobilize and enhance its claim of sovereign statehood through the adoption of neoliberal reforms.

On November 29, 2012, the United Nations General Assembly voted overwhelmingly to upgrade Palestine to a nonmember observer state (despite strong opposition by Israel and the United States), thus implicitly recognizing Palestinian statehood. I wish to suggest that this attainment of quasi-statehood is intimately connected to the PA's calculated cultivation of neoliberal reforms.[19] While real independence remains an "elusive dream" in light of the continuing Israeli occupation and construction of settlements,[20] such a move might be seen as "creative" governance that appropriates the sacrificial logic of suicide bombing to redirect its embodied ingenious agency to other manifestations, thus reducing the instances of suicide bombing and reorienting the relations of normality and abjection under Israeli colonial occupation.

Before discussing the neoliberal reforms in Palestine, it is important to first point to the ways in which the development of neoliberalism in Israel has contributed to occupation and settlement construction in the Occupied Territories. As Max Ajl indicates in his analysis of the recent Israeli tent protests initiated by "the university-educated, newly graduated middle class," who demand affordable housing and welfare disbursement from the government, neoliberal policies in Israel since the mid-1970s have led to inflation and the privatization of state enterprises, transferring social wealth and public resources to the hands of the upper class and corporate elite and fracturing Israeli society. In Ajl's description:

> Israeli inflation has led to a redistribution of economic clout from the bottom and middle of Israeli society to its upper echelons. The upper class, welded solidly into transnational capital circuits, is the real beneficiary, behind the veneer of the state and the politicians it pushes into office. . . . Amidst a cartelized economy, prices are pushed higher and higher by the corporations that set prices, while wages do not come close to keeping pace with price increases. . . . The state is not looking out for the interests of the dispossessed. It is looking out for the interests of the possessed: . . . ten large business groups now control 30 percent of the market value of public companies, while 16 control half of the money in the whole country.[21]

To salvage social cohesion in the face of rising inequality (especially among a multiethnic population, many of whom are not Jewish or were not born in Israel), the Israeli elite has sought to "defuse and diffuse" social discontent "through colonization, militarism, and alternative social welfare measures, both material and symbolic, with the common thread of resolving internal Israeli social problems on the backs of the native population: the Palestinians."[22]

Specifically, the Israeli government attempts to address the socioeconomic grievances of the lower class "in the cheapest way possible"—by building settlements on "freshly stolen" Palestinian land. Ajl indicates that "polls show overwhelming Israeli popular support for maintaining the settlements and the occupation of the territories," with the lower class most in favor since the settlements provide affordable housing. By binding its citizens' possessive investment in the occupation and settlements under a nationalist cause, the Israeli elites attempt to divert their attention from the widening gap between rich and poor and ease social discontent. Here is thus the hidden link between the neoliberalism and settler colonialism pursued by Israel: occupation and settlement expansion play the central role of "cementing Israeli social cohesion by letting off lower-class social pressure." Ajl concludes that "occupation and racism are not just a means of social control over a reeling and shattered Palestinian society, but over the Israeli lower classes themselves."[23] One may also add that by allowing Israeli citizens to acquire and accumulate property and profit from the settlements' commercial enterprise, occupation not only serves as a "negative" control mechanism, but also as a "positive" means to sustain and optimize Israeli liberal citizenship.

Based on this observation, it seems a natural democratic impulse for Palestinians to resist neoliberalism, which breeds and reinforces the conditions of the colonial occupation that subjugates and abjectifies them. Yet if neoliberalism has set off a new global phase of capitalism that is duly observed and followed by the international system of states, then the series of neoliberal reforms implemented by the PA can be seen as seeking to carve out a civil-bourgeois path to pursue the agenda of statehood and expand spaces of appropriation of liberal life for Palestinian subjects. As Khalidi notes, the neoliberal turn "has been pursued with vigor by the PA since 2005," as "a new 'entrepreneurial' technocracy has taken the place of PLO [Palestine Liberation Organization] and [Yasser] Arafat-era PA administrators, disinheriting the PLO military cadres whose 'struggle' since the 1960s made the PA self-governance possible."[24] During this process, "The PA embarked on a series of post-intifada, post-Arafat institutional and policy 'reforms' targeting security and rule-of-law measures, enhanced public finance transparency and efficiency, and the provision of improved public services and utilities. In doing so, the PA followed Washington Consensus conventions that severely limit active state intervention in the economy beyond the protection of property rights so as to release the full potentials of the market."[25]

Significantly, such measures are closely tied to aspirations for national sovereign founding, as the PA hopes to use its normative adoption of market fundamentalism to appeal to the international community in lobbying for the cause of Palestinian statehood. Khalidi writes,

> The zeal, indeed exhibitionism, with which the PA pursued these reforms, coupled with the international attention they attracted, implied that the PA needed to successfully navigate the two-year homestretch to freedom through its "state-readiness" program. In line with some of the more dated World Bank notions about good governance, it became commonsense that only by being certified as institutionally ready for statehood by the World Bank, IMF [International Monetary Fund], UN [United Nations] and . . . [others] could parallel political negotiations possibly lead to an

actual Palestinian state. . . . The dedication of the PA to liberalization is undeniable, and earned fulsome praise in 2011 from the international financial institutions.[26]

As Khalidi argues, the economic success of these neoliberal policies is by no means assured, given the laboratory nature of such pursuit "in a distorted, fragmented and occupation-throttled economy" under Israeli colonialism. At the same time, what can be underscored here is the move by the PA to seek certification of its readiness as "a well-functioning state" based on its neoliberal economic performance,[27] for this illustrates an implicit understanding of the inevitable requirement of any postcolonial state to participate as a "good" citizen-state in the international system of liberal order.

In fact, the PA's pursuit of neoliberal reform can be seen as inventively and designingly enacting the prerequisite "ahead of schedule," prior to its sovereign founding, to bolster its national aspirations for self-determination by securing the backing and support of international financial organizations. As Barry Hindess articulates, the decolonization process has not freed postcolonial states from imperial discipline but rather enjoined them in a new regulatory regime of global market mechanisms (i.e., international trading in goods and services) watched over by powerful Western states and supranational financial agencies (2005, 250). That is to say, even an independent Palestinian state would not be able to transcend the given liberal script that modulates the international system of states. While Hindess speaks in the context of post-founding states, it is relevant for the PA, which must seek official entrance to "enter the game" of liberal citizenship. The implicit recognition of Palestinian statehood by the United Nations General Assembly in late 2012 provides evidence of "sovereign progress" in this direction.

In the meantime, neoliberalism has also reengineered Palestinian subjectivity, which makes up the social fabric of everyday life under occupation. Lamenting that "the PA strategy of state-building by policy and in lieu of resistance/liberation encouraged a focus on 'domestic' concerns of 'citizens,' rather than the 'national' concerns of 'militants,'" Khalidi notes, neoliberal ideology has created a Palestinian constituency attuned to "normalcy and risk aversion. . . . [and] willing to resist encroachments upon their material gains and the liberal way of life." He refers to an indebted Palestinian who stated the following in an interview with a *Los Angeles Times* reporter: "Now that I have all the responsibility on me, my main concern is stability. . . . I don't want to see anything happen that might stop my paychecks." Khalidi further describes how other Palestinians exhibit similar subject dispositions toward market fundamentalism: "Many believe in market primacy, define success as working in a bank in Ramallah, think that the poor contribute inadequately to their electricity costs, that drinking an expensive coffee in a Ramallah café is a sign of status, or that kids from refugee camps should be barred from selling their fake CDs in restaurants and night-spots."[28]

In spite of Khalidi's lament about the shifting mentality of Palestinians from "militants" to "citizens," I think that we may actually reread this shift not as a radical break of two diametrical tendencies but rather as reflecting a continuing appropriation of liberal citizenship in differing manifestations. That is, neoliberalism is gradually reorienting and redirecting the ingenious agency of Palestinian subjects under occupation such that they are propelled to appropriate the liberal script of life, liberty, and happiness not through sacrificial violence but through the means of the market.

In this light, to the extent that suicide bombing can be read as reanimating spaces of inclusion and belonging for the Palestinians and hopes for a sovereign citizenship to come, the recent neoliberal reforms and the subsequent attainment of quasi-statehood as a result of such reforms by the PA can be understood as a pragmatic instrument to further strengthen and expand such spaces, thereby reorchestrating how Palestinian subjects appropriate the liberal life script. Given its quasi-sovereign position in world politics, the PA's adoption and appropriation of neoliberal logic can be seen as using an unexpected method among the limited tools and resources it has to disrupt and remold existing relations—specifically, to normalize its status as an "official" state and to assuage the abjection of its citizen-subjects under Israel's settler colonialism.

This observation raises a paradox for critical scholars and social activists committed to the Palestinian cause. While we would undoubtedly like to see the Palestinian people move in the direction of gaining sovereign statehood and ending colonial occupation—and thus be saved from having to resort to sacrificial violence to claim their humanity and citizenship—is neoliberalization of their subjectivity the best possible method and prospect by which to achieve such a goal? The answer is likely no; but this, again, demonstrates to us necessary limits, complicity, and ingenuity in the generation of social change as the PA seeks to tap into and reconfigure the existing international political landscape in order to carve out better spaces of existence for its subjects. Indeed, one should not take the consequences of neoliberal marketization lightly: not only does it imply a *sacrifice* of genuine independence in the

Palestinian people's claims to self-determination, given their government's assimilation to neoliberal logic, but it also portends the kinds of structural-material *violence* within Palestinian society that have been witnessed in so many instances of structural adjustment fixes in the global South (Davis 2006).

The PA, then, is proffering a kind of sacrificial violence in one dimension in exchange for the end of sacrificial violence in another—and in exchange for the ultimate recognition of statehood. In doing so, the PA does not repress or transcend the ingenious agency in suicide bombing; rather, it reuses and appropriates it. It learns that the right to self-determination, statehood, and the potential end of colonial occupation cannot simply be claimed democratically, but must be earned ingeniously. And, under the present international system of liberal order, it must be earned not outside the sacrificial logic, but precisely through the sacrificial violence of adopting the neoliberal imperative—an imperative that perpetuated and emboldened the conditions of Israeli settler colonialism in the first place.

What the PA's campaign for statehood has illustrated for us, then, is a nonlinear lesson of social change, because it uses nondemocratic methods to instigate openings of transformation in the Palestinian situation. But this lesson does not simply end here, with passive acceptance of the PA's current state of neoliberal governance. What it has also taught us is that, instead of indicting the current neoliberal development, it would serve us well to further trace the ways in which neoliberalism is likely to establish new contours of normality and abjection among Israeli and Palestinian subjects in their conjoined life of liberal citizenship. As we have seen, certain segments of populations may become relatively normalized in accordance with market-making and entrepreneurial logics, while others may become further abjectified. And these shifting relations may, in fact, signal new openings of social change, for the further abjectified may link up with newly emerged local activist groups to inventively disrupt any such given formations.

Indeed, such is the open and unknown futurity in Palestine, and the key to how the process will unfold is likely to hinge on how mass subjects' ingenious agency will be rekindled and engaged. In fact, if the PA has reutilized ingenious agency to redraw the contours of appropriation of citizenship in turning prospective bombers into working (though neoliberal) citizens, then it suggests that we may hope for a future in which the newly/further abjectified and their corresponding activist organizations will redeploy this agency in even more innovative fashion, joining the redrawing process to reshape the contours of appropriation in a more, rather than less, justice- and equality-oriented direction. Such direction, again, is not necessarily achievable or reachable through an exclusive frame of democracy and human rights (even though these may serve as a guise). In the end, while ingenious agency has manifested in extreme forms of violence in instances of suicide bombing, that same ingenious agency also, quite unexpectedly, holds the key to ending its own enactment of sacrificial violence—and even, possibly, to transforming itself into multifarious forms of political acts and practices to create a more humane life for Palestinians.

Part III

(Un)Ending

Conclusion. Politics without Politics
Democracy as Meant for Ingenious Appropriation

"Be like Water":
The Warring Stance of Bruce Lee's Jeet Kune Do

In tracing the ways in which the abject can appropriate liberal citizenship, I hope I have shown that there is no shortage of agency to revise and rewrite this global cultural script. This ingenious agency, even in its most unseemly moments, speaks to the perpetual desire of abject subjects to re-create livable spaces of inclusion and belonging, unendingly manifesting in polymorphous episodes of enduring ingenious citizenship. The elimination of this ingenious agency is an impossibility, for those abjected will seek any means suited to their particular situation to negotiate spaces of livelihood in ways they consider "normalizing" to their dignity and humanity. In portraying the formations of ingenious citizenship as arising incessantly to disrupt and appropriate the normative script of citizenship, I also have shown that change and movement are *already happening* in unforeseen and unpredictable ways in the quotidian spaces of liberal social life. This ambiguous and nonlinear process of social change creates spaces of transformation, whether on an individual level, in personal surroundings, or in the larger community, even as it also reinscribes the liberal structural order and reproduces unequal relations of normality and abjection.

Given their need to survive within liberal citizenship, abject subjects need to act in complicity with the given citizenship script even as they disrupt and appropriate it to create spaces of inclusion and belonging for themselves. Their subversive acts thus fracture the script from within, engendering a transactional quality as they subtly bargain and exchange with liberal hegemony for a liminal space of nonexistent citizenship. In this way, the script produces exploitative abjection but also determines a possible field of destabilization, allowing its contours to be elastically reshaped while also restraining the bursting effects of its own organic reconfiguration. It is in this shifting balance between restraint and destabilization that change and movement occur. As shown in each of the episodes of ingenious citizenship, this process holds insights for democratic activism and rights-based politics, demonstrating that any political attempt to attain equality and justice for abject subjects also needs to inventively and audaciously negotiate with the contaminated field of instrumental exchange in liberal citizenship. Most important, these lessons show that purity and contamination are not exogenous opposites; instead, they are endogenous elements that co-generate each other in the contingent vicissitudes of social change.

Such nonlinear insights defy cherished notions about social justice, which has centered on aspirations for purity and decontamination. Social transformation is predicated on unlearning internalized oppression, raising political consciousness, and forging oppositional resistance and strategies. All of these endeavors are indispensable and formulate essential parts of the pedagogical struggle for social change. Yet they also direct us to cling closely to what we believe in most: purity. But what if, when we clench our fists in an attempt to hold on to this purity, it may actually escape our reach? What if, in the actual wars of position within the liberal citizenship script, we might need to let go of what we most revere in order to creatively attain and regenerate it in other ways?

Given the embedded roots of purity in social justice traditions, it is not surprising that contemporary literatures in critical social and political thought, despite varying approaches and contrasting perspectives, and even with advances beyond prior work, continue to be inundated with the ethos and directives of decontamination and purification. In fact, in some of the most sophisticated analyses, recent critical scholarship is even more exacting than its predecessors in surveying and extracting unclean and tainted elements from theoretical propositions or social movements that betray complicity with liberalism. Critiques of complicity abound, but few discuss how we might precisely take, use, or extend this complicity to further the struggles and expand the horizons of social change. Any forged relationship with complicity is taken as a sign of failure. In fact, as reinforcement for their refusal of liberal complicity, some critics have specifically articulated their politics through a negation of a liberal *future* or through an embrace of alternative frames of *failure*.

For instance, the queer theorist Lee Edelman argues that almost all progressive politics contain within them a hope for the future that is incarnated in children, who embody a reproductive futurism that preserves "the absolute privilege of heteronormativity by rendering unthinkable . . . the possibility of a queer resistance to this organizing principle of communal relations" (2004, 2). He proposes instead "the impossible politics of a queer oppositionality" (4) that locates queerness in a space outside the consensus of reproductive futurism, a "space outside the framework within which politics as we know it appears" (3). Signifying the death drive, this queer negativity withholds allegiance to, and complicity with, any fantasy of the future "that's always purchased at our [queer] expense" (4).

From a different angle, Lisa Marie Cacho, taking insights from Derrick Bell's racial realism (Bell 1995), finds issues with the ways in which rights-based movements often reinscribe the dominant grammar and logic of "value," "legibility," and "respectability" in their progressive advocacy, and points toward an unthinkable politics that refuses this practical lure in forming one's political principles and stance (Cacho 2012). Such unthinkable politics "proposes that we begin battles we've already lost," advising that we "take failure for granted," "suspend the need to be practical," and disavow "the logic of survivability" to "practice imagining otherwise": in her words, "to mobilize *against* preserving this way of life or the ways of knowing that this life preserves" (31–33; emphasis in original).

Taking up this politics of failure against the master narrative of success in liberal society, Judith Halberstam further articulates the virtues of "failing, losing, forgetting, unmaking, undoing, unbecoming, not knowing" as a creative style of resistance against the capitalist imperative of merit, effort, and trying (2011, 2). In her words, "Failure preserves some of the wondrous anarchy of childhood" and "poke[s] holes in the toxic positivity of contemporary life," which contains within it "the [liberal] ideology of positive thinking . . . that success depends only upon working hard and failure is always of your own doing" (3).

Although the positions of these critics do not converge in a seamless unity and vary in their faith in the possibility of redemption, their oppositional politics all gesture toward an inviolable purity that needs to be quarantined from the contaminating elements of liberal life. Yet what if this proposed purity—via the politics of "no future" and "failure"—actually requires complicity with the *futuristic* and *successful* transmission of new media and technology to enable its reach and dissemination? That is to say, even *critical* failure might need the fluid rapport of *capitalist* infrastructure and *bourgeois* success in order to render and deliver its far-reaching import. This, once again, signals that an immanent, endogenous relationship between purity and contamination is at work, even in these oppositional politics.

While some critical scholars have pointed to the need for being more strategically flexible in resistance movements, they nonetheless rarely reach the point of letting go of this cherished purity in their theoretical expositions. For example, although Chela Sandoval provides a mobile model of what she calls the "differential oppositional consciousness" that flexibly combines and incorporates liberal (equal rights), revolutionary, supremacist, separatist, and differential approaches, the ideal political subjectivity being conceived is still grounded in, and attached to, a democratizing trajectory of "coalitional consciousness" and "oppositional cosmopolitics" (Sandoval 2000, 181). And while Monisha Das Gupta unmoors rights from citizenship to articulate their fluid political use across local and global contexts, this elasticity is limited, once again, to the oppositional stance of a democratic agency that refuses complicity with neoliberal logics (Das Gupta 2006). Both thus take purity as the foreground of their political imagining in an endeavor to overcome contamination. Yet again, what if this absolute attachment to purity, or the purifying consciousness of democratic agency, is precisely what needs to be surrendered in order to regenerate spaces of purity?

To ask that we let go of purity is not to suggest that we give up on our battle with liberal hegemony in the search for justice; rather, it is to adopt a different warring mentality and stratagem vis-à-vis the liberal cultural script. Here, to extend the insights from the episodes of ingenious citizenship into a concluding lesson, I argue that those lessons culminate in a guiding position, a warring stance that I call a *politics without politics*—connected intimately to the martial artist Bruce Lee's combat philosophy—for progressive activists and social movements.[1] This combat approach teaches us that *whether* and *how* we ought to take up oppositional positioning, democratic agency, and rights-based politics in our resistance need not be assumed a priori, but should entirely depend on their political usefulness in specific locations, contexts, and circumstances.

Although Lee is not known as a political theorist or social activist, I suggest that his unconventional martial arts system provides an engaging theoretical inspiration for the kind of activist combat stance signaled by ingenious citizenship. Space does not permit me to provide a full history of Lee's life and background. However, he is unusual among martial artists, not so much for his fame, charisma, and acting career, but because of his self-devised, eclectic fighting system, which iconoclastically defies traditional martial arts teachings that emphasize unitary and linear forms and styles. While Lee was trained in the famed Wing Chun technique in the early days of his martial arts education in Hong Kong, when he arrived in the United States as an immigrant, a street contest with another martial artist led him to realize that the traditional martial arts emphasis on rigid forms and styles was not necessarily suitable for actual combat. Calling martial artists "the result of three thousand years of propaganda and conditioning," he questions: "When, in a split second, your life is threatened, do you say, 'Let me make sure my hand is on my hip, and my style is 'the' style.' When your life is in danger, do you argue about the method you will adhere to while saving yourself?" (Lee 2011, 24). Thus, he set out to adjust his approach and devise his own combat method and system.

Naming it Jeet Kune Do (JKD), or the Way of the Intercepting Fist, Lee built on his martial arts background to create a distinctive combat philosophy that does not restrict itself to any particular fighting form or style but fluidly incorporates numerous training methods and fighting techniques that can adapt to different combat situations. The motto of JKD is, "Using No Way as Way, Having No Limitation as Limitation." In Lee's words, "Jeet Kune Do favors formlessness so that it can assume all forms and since Jeet Kune Do has no style, it can fit in with all styles. As a result, Jeet Kune Do utilizes all ways and is bound by none and likewise, uses any techniques or means which serve its end" (16). JKD approaches the opponent by seeing what the opponent delivers and then intercepts the attack, appropriates it, and spontaneously uses the logic and force of the attack to exert a counterattack. If we consider social struggles a form of perpetual political combat in liberal life, then the lessons of ingenious citizenship may propel us to learn from the insights of JKD in formulating an eclectic and organic politics—an activist approach that does not limit itself to any preconceived form, style, or method but draws on multifarious political, cultural, and economic tools for different situations, while absorbing the opponent's attack modes into its own politics.

Here is a fluid, ingenious art of fighting without fighting, style without style, method without method, and politics without politics, in which subjects engage in political contestation without any preconceived form or style, but rather operate through formless techniques and polymorphous instruments. Against the background of the fixed stances of oppositional resistance, democratic agency, and rights-based politics, politics without politics sets itself apart by, in Lee's metaphor, *being like water*: it constantly changes forms and shapes as it flows through different landscapes, being protean in adapting to different situations, and utilizing whichever useful tools, methods, and channels are available in the immediate surroundings in its political intervention and movement strategies. As Lee states, "Don't get set into one form, adapt it and build your own, and let it grow, be like water. Empty your mind, be formless, shapeless—like water. Now you put water in a cup, it becomes the cup. You put water into a bottle it becomes the bottle; you put it in a teapot it becomes the teapot. Now water can flow or it can crash. Be water, my friend."[2]

Here Lee caricatures the ultra-adaptability of his combat approach, which is especially critical for a politics of social change that is attuned to locations and contexts. Rather than starting out from a unitary position or universalizing prescription—such as democratic agency and human rights—we need to be like water and adapt our political method in accordance with different geopolitical contexts when advocating for the abject.

Lee further writes, "Adapt what is useful, reject what is useless, and add what is specifically your own"[3]; and "Be empty; have no style or form for the opponent to work on" (23). This liquid-like agency is indispensable for combat, because, as Lee learns, "When you get down to it, real combat is not fixed and is very much 'alive.' The fancy mess (a form of paralysis) solidifies and conditions what was once fluid, and when you look at it realistically, it is nothing but a blind devotion to the systematic uselessness of practicing routines or stunts that lead nowhere" (19). His indictment of traditional martial arts forms that limit themselves to predetermined forms and styles might serve as a caution for social theory and activism that clings to any universal positioning and method: "Stylists, instead of looking directly into the fact, cling to forms (theories) and go on entangling themselves further and further, finally putting themselves into an inextricable snare" (19).

Lee characterizes strict forms and styles as leading to an unproductive entanglement because they sustain binary thinking, which limits their potential strength. To be like water suggests that we negate—and, in fact, stand above—the duality of good versus evil, justice versus injustice, democracy versus antidemocracy, and purity versus contamination. Lee writes, "Wisdom does not consist of trying to wrest the good from the evil but in learning to 'ride' them as a cork adapts itself to the crests and troughs of the waves" (13). In a nonlinear move, he advises: "Let yourself go with the disease, be with it, keep company with it—this is the best way to be rid of it" (13). If we take disease to be a form of contamination, the insight here echoes the thematic of ingenious citizenship: to keep company with (and use) contamination in order to get rid of it. Conversely, we need to let go of purity in order to regenerate it. In Lee's words, "Do not run away; let go. Do not seek, for it will come when least expected" (13). That is to say, instead of running away from contamination, we need to loosen our grip on an absolute outcome of purity. Once we do that, we may realize how purity can come to us in nonlinear and unexpected ways. As Lee argues, "There is no fixed teaching," and what JKD offers is "an appropriate medicine for a particular ailment" (13).

To adapt all of this to the context of social movement activism: there is no one, universal way to obtain social justice and transformation, and we can only apply different methods and approaches under different circumstances and conditions. Like JKD, what politics without politics offers is a situated combat thinking that overcomes our limitations by adapting and using the opponent's strengths to empower our political force. While the following quote may seem graphic, it captures the sentiment and dynamic of politics without politics when practiced in liberal citizenship: "Forget about winning and losing; forget about pride and pain. Let your opponent graze your skin and you smash into his flesh; let him smash into your flesh and you fracture his bones; let him fracture your bones and you take his life! Do not be concerned with your escaping freely—lay your life before him!" (Lee, 16). This again speaks to a warring stance of politics without politics, which does not concern itself with maintaining a strictly purified (democratic) style or approach, but absorbs the opponent's contaminating weaponry to overturn, transform, and regenerate the situation. There is not just one way to use contamination, but many ways; since contamination never stays in one form, utilizing it also takes on many forms.

My arguments in the previous chapters have all tentatively pointed in this direction. Politics without politics thus gives a name to the kind of fluid social justice strategies signaled by ingenious citizenship. Importantly, it also provides a further impetus for critical scholars and social activists to continue innovative efforts to tap into the shifting and protean terrain of liberal life to create transformative change in their respective contexts and locations. In such a way, politics without politics angles social movement activism toward a different conception of the political future.

Ingenious Futurity:
Democracy as Meant for Ingenious Appropriation

By being like water, the formless stance of politics without politics repositions the cultural-political terrain presented to us under liberal hegemony toward an ingenious futurity. Departing from other political modalities of futurity that take up a nonnegotiable stance toward the "prison house" of the present and juxtapose a liberating *then and there* against the *here and now* (Muñoz 2009, 1), or those that sustain the duality between surviving and living by urging us to reach beyond the need for basic survival toward struggling for a meaningful life (Cacho 2012, 33), ingenious futurity points to a different political route. It suggests that we live in the present and take the present as a given, but continuously work on and recraft the present to reshape and reorient it in different directions. It insists on the concreteness of the present as the foundation of one's politics, asking: What happens when you cannot look to the past or to the future to retrieve and save purity, but can only create purity from within contamination? It also sees surviving and living not as dualistic modes of existence but as inextricable ways of being as we strive to both survive *and* to live, being both romantic (having hope for the purity of justice) and pragmatic (negotiating limits and complicities). It further signals that, sometimes, we might need to use survival (i.e., bread) to leverage and earn more spaces of meaningful life (i.e., roses).

In this ingenious futurity, democracy should no longer be seen as a transcendent ideal to be set on a pedestal and realized purely and chastely in practice. Rather, it is an always already tainted cultural script that implicates all human beings living through its hegemonic replication, where any hope and aspiration for the purity of justice and equality must be sought and achieved inside this inescapable contamination. This material state of democratic politics need not be taken negatively or pessimistically. To the contrary, in their clever, inventive, and resourceful ways, abject improvisations of nonexistent citizenship have offered us lessons that, as a lived cultural script, democracy is *meant for ingenious appropriation*. The key to crafting the most potent improvisation of social change will precisely lie in human creativity and inventiveness in negotiating the elements of the romantic and pragmatic, practicality and hopefulness, limits and aspiration, to persistently disrupt the democratic script in generating more cultural and material spaces of rights, justice, and equality for all citizen-subjects to appropriate and live in. This entails an ingenious reconfiguration of the system at a collective level, as we, with whatever means are available, come up with ever more innovative and unordinary methods in politics without politics to fluidly remold the given liberal citizenship script in manifold and heterogeneous ways, helping to bring about powerful and unexpected transformation in actually existing liberal life.

Still, my foregoing discussion does not suggest a disregard for the need to be pure, just, and democratic. Despite the issues I raise with democratic agency, I believe it is crucial to continue expanding and cultivating democratic values, principles, and rights wherever possible and appropriate. In fact, in spite of his gestures toward tactics and cunning, what Lee represented as a martial artist and a filmic character is, indeed, justice, an inextinguishable purifying force against contaminating bullies, belligerents, and even imperialists. As he cautions at one point: "It is all right to change one's style to adapt to various circumstances, but remember not to change your basic form" (Lee, 15).

While by "basic form" Lee is referring to the matter of technique, I argue that we may extend the phrase to mean one's original purpose of employing politics without politics: to create and regenerate democratic purity. Any political contestation cannot happen without a vision of purity, and if this aspiration is overtaken by contamination—that is, if one uses politics without politics simply to remain contaminated—then the combat stance loses its purpose and dynamic balance, turning into a linear and unitary form that itself undermines social change. It then needs to be disrupted and reappropriated to be brought back to a balanced, rejuvenating state that mixes contamination and purity. Here, we might say, ingenious agency needs the interiorization of democratic agency to continue directing and rejuvenating its aspiration and purpose, as much as democratic agency needs the crafting of ingenious agency to fulfill its latent strength.

At the same time, just as Lee uses JKD to expand the potency and reach of justice, and just as abject subjects take the limits and complicities of their modes of operating as a given basis in improvising disruption and claiming a more dignified state of being, I argue that to move things forward and advance a vision of democratic purity, critical scholars and social activists need to boldly and designingly stage their resistance and contestation via the contaminated field of liberal citizenship for the vision's partial, and progressive, realization.

Returning once again to the admonition of politics without politics: social activism needs to *flow like water* in the perpetual combat of social justice struggles. Thus, while there are moments when it would be helpful for democratic agency to be visible and vocal, there are also times when its foregrounding may not prove effective, when it should remain hidden in the background and be packaged or substituted with other forms of logics, discourses, ethics, and intervention strategies. This includes, following James Ferguson, shifting from the normative routine of "critiquing power" to the creative practice of a "left art of government," wherein "empirical experimentation rather than moralistic denunciation takes center place" (2011, 61). As politics without politics teaches us, it is not enough that we be critical of hegemony through a universalizing will to purity. Rather, while being critical, we also need to be ingenious—with purposeful elasticity, necessary modesty, and contextual sensitivity—in unendingly recrafting the sphere of social change.

Notes

Introduction. Ingenious Agency

1. Ad Council, *I Am an American*, 2001, accessed August 9, 2012, http://adcouncil.org /default.aspx?id=141.

2. See also Cynthia Weber, *"I Am an American": Video Portraits of Unsafe U.S. Citizens*, 2007, accessed August 13, 2012, http://www.opendemocracy.net/article/democracy_power /america_power_world/citizen_identity.

3. This critical take on the discourse of national identity resonates with Lauren Berlant's discussion of the 1993 special issue of *Time* magazine on immigration entitled "The New Face of America" (Berlant 1997). See also Banet-Weiser 1999.

4. For other works in radical democratic theory, see, e.g., Mouffe 1993; Honig 1993; Connolly 1995; Trend 1996; Isin and Wood 1999; Rancière 1999; Castronovo and Nelson 2002b; Isin 2002.

5. For an overview of the liberal, civic republican, communitarian, and radical democratic conceptions of citizenship, see the chapters by Peter H. Schuck, Richard Dagger, Gerard Delanty, and Claire Rasmussen and Michael Brown, respectively, in Isin and Turner 2002. For an overview of the deliberative democratic model of citizenship, see Habermas 1996.

6. For instance, while Bayat identifies the presence of "passive networks" in public spaces such as neighborhoods, street corners, mosques, bus stops, detention centers, migrant camps, and public parks as crucial for the formation of nonmovements in the Middle East (2010, 22), the quiet encroachment of the ordinary may advance through different routes and in varying fashions in other sociopolitical, geographic, and cultural contexts.

7. For a critical discussion of how instrumentality operates in progressive ideals such as cosmopolitanism and human rights, see Cheah 2006.

8. Granted, Coles argues—and I agree—that "moving beyond democracy in its dominant forms also entails recognizing and being receptive to the democratic traditions that we inherit from the past" (2005, xii). This double responsibility toward recognizing our intellectual-political debt to "the teleological traditions" and "genealogically interrogat[ing] these traditions and cultivat[ing] a radically ateleological receptivity to what lies beyond" (xvi) is necessary for any responsible and engaged scholarship. Yet questions do emerge when this engagement with, and receptivity to, "democratic traditions" presupposes that all subjects exist within an exclusive paradigm of democratic consciousness and politics, for such a presupposition becomes a universalizing schema that is liberally and willfully deployed without attention to contextual intricacies and differences.

9. Jacques Rancière has previously coined the term "the staging of a nonexistent right" in relation to democratic politics, referring to the ways in which subjects denied status of speaking beings claim rights in advance of sovereign or official recognition (Rancière 1999, 25; see also Honig 2001, 100). While inspired by this idea, here I use "nonexistent citizenship" to refer to the informal spaces of citizenship life that are obtained by the abject through (often nondemocratic) appropriation of the liberal citizenship script.

1. Improvising Citizenship

1. A good example of citizenship as a commodity is the U.S. immigration law that allows foreigners who invest $1 million and create at least ten jobs to obtain a green card (Ong 1996; Miller 2006).

2. Citizenship has been investigated in terms of legal status (Coutin 2003; Bosniak 2006; Varsanyi 2006), democratic institution-building (Benhabib 2004; Somers 2008), identity/difference (Young 1989, 1990; Kymlicka 1995; Rosaldo 1997; Isin and Wood 1999), insurgent political acts (Isin and Nielsen 2008a), and governing technologies (Miller 1993; Cruikshank 1999; Ong 1996, 1999, 2003, 2006), but has not been conceptualized in terms of script.

3. For a helpful source in situating culture within the problematic of "ideology," see works by Stuart Hall and the Birmingham School in the neo-Gramscian, post-Marxist cultural studies approach (Morley and Chen 1996).

4. Judith Butler coined the term "merely cultural." See her articulation of how certain poststructuralist, postcolonial, queer, and cultural studies scholarship is not "merely cultural" but, rather, linked up with the "material" question and constitutes formulations of cultural materialism (Butler 1997).

5. To elaborate on this biopolitical aspect, Michel Foucault has conceptualized the modern form of power as "biopower," wherein the essential measure of liberal governance is to oversee the welfare of the population (wealth, longevity, health, etc.) through mechanisms of calculation, monitoring, regulation, and utilization so that the lives of

citizens are fostered productively in the interests and security of the state (Foucault 1978, 1997). Biopower taps into the bodies and souls of human subjects to ensure the reproduction of the social body in a "proper" mode and "proper" way (Foucault 1980). As a technique of liberal governance, the inscription of subjects into modern citizenship initiates the modern state's systematic surveillance of its population. David Lyon points out that the civil, political, and social rights granted to citizens in the age of modernity imply that "people had to be registered, and their personal details filed, which of course paradoxically facilitated their increased surveillance" (2001, 294). New and minute forms of surveillance and control were established via documentary identification of citizens (i.e., birth certificates, driver's licenses, social security cards, passports, bank books, credit cards) throughout liberal societies by the last quarter of the twentieth century (294). Rather than an autonomous species standing in opposition to corporate bureaucratic power, citizenship is itself entangled in the biopolitical webs of surveillance and subjection, discipline and normalization as a constitutive part of liberal governance in the making of citizen-subjects (Cruikshank 1999).

6. In fact, realignments are underlain by an organic fluidity across these realms, such that a privileged location in particular realms can enable a person to gain a more advantageous position in other realms in times of new political configurations.

7. Even in Latin America, citizenship is structured through the ideology of *mestizaje* (hybrid racial-cultural mixing between indigenous and Spanish) that confers a hegemonic status on whiteness with material investment (Siu 2005).

2. Migrant Domestic Workers

1. Karen D'Souza, "'The Help' Is Poised to Become Chick Flick of the Summer," *San Jose Mercury News*, August 3, 2011, accessed September 5, 2013, http://www.mercurynews .com/movies-dvd/ci_18602288.

2. Tate Taylor, dir., *The Help*, DVD (Walt Disney Studios Motion Pictures, Burbank, CA, 2011).

3. Rinku Sen, "Domestic Workers Use Buzz around 'The Help' to Create Change," *Colorlines.com*, February 24, 2012, accessed September 6, 2013, http://colorlines.com /archives/2012/02/how_domestic_workers_are_using_the_help_and_the_oscars_to _create_change.html.

4. Association of Black Women Historians, "An Open Statement to the Fans of *The Help*," August 14, 2013, accessed September 6, 2013, http://www.abwh.org/index.php ?option=com_content&view=article&id=2%3Aopen-statement-the-help.

5. Sen, "Domestic Workers Use Buzz around 'The Help' to Create Change."

6. National Domestic Workers Alliance, "#BeTheHelp Oscar Party," 2012, DemocracyInAction, accessed Septmber 5, 2013, http://org2.democracyinaction.org/o/6748/p /salsa/web/common/public/signup?signup_page_KEY=6605; Sen, "Domestic Workers Use Buzz around 'The Help' to Create Change."

7. Sen, "Domestic Workers Use Buzz around 'The Help' to Create Change."

8. For a discussion of Disney's sweatshop practices, see "Disney's Sad Sweatshop His-

tory," *Truthout*, September 11, 2006, accessed September 8, 2013, http://www.truth-out
.org/buzzflash/commentary/item/429-disneys-sad-sweatshop-history. For further related readings, see Wasko 2001; Giroux 2010.

9. In arguing this, I am not disregarding the distinctions between the liberal and
the civic republican visions of citizenship in Western political thought, especially the
republican critique of the liberal conception of atomistic and privatistic citizens (Arendt
1958; Wolin 1960; Barber 1984; Sandel 1998). However, my point here is that, whether
in liberal or civic republican thoughts, they inherit the same linear conception of the
"political" in the essential qualities laid out herein: public, visible, audible, legible, and
honorable.

10. While there are important distinctions between (political) refugees and (economic) migrant workers, they are not my primary concern here. I refer to the two
populations broadly to exemplify the diverse range of migrating subjects in the global
political economic system whose life conditions seemingly correspond to Agamben's
conception of "bare life." See also Rajaram and Grundy-Warr 2004, 60n2.

11. A few scholarly works have unveiled alternative forms of social resistance that
sidestep political acts of citizenship and adopt other strategies and appeals on behalf
of migrant subjects. For example, William Walters discusses critical architect activists
in Berlin who map out routes of autonomous escape for refugees and migrants (Walters 2008). While these works also help collapse the binary frame of political life versus
bare life, they do not address the interstitial, ingenious agency of the nonstatus subjects
themselves.

12. National Domestic Workers Alliance, "Employment Protections for Domestic
Workers: An Overview of Federal Law," n.d., accessed September 16, 2013, http://www
.domesticworkers.org/sites/default/files/Domestic_Worker_Employment_Protections
_Federal.pdf.

13. Such tactical display of emotions, however, may be used only occasionally, "since
it loses its punch when utilized frequently" (Parreñas 2001, 190–91). Reluctant compliance with or deviation from the script needs to be exercised precisely to the point that
stops short of a direct insult or overt defiance, lest it jeopardize the worker's employment
(Scott 1985, 26).

14. Linda Burnham and Nik Theodore, "Home Economics: The Invisible and Unreg-
ulated World of Domestic Work," 2012, 9, National Domestic Workers Alliance, accessed
November 6, 2014, http://www.domesticworkers.org/sites/default/files/HomeEconomics
English.pdf.

15. Domestic Workers Bill of Rights Campaign, "State Domestic Workers Bill of
Rights," n.d., accessed November 6, 2014, http://www.knowyourrightsny.org.

16. Domestic Workers Bill of Rights Campaign, "State Domestic Workers Bill of
Rights."

17. International Domestic Workers Federation, "C189: Domestic Workers Are Workers," n.d., accessed November 7, 2014, http://www.idwn.info/c189.php?id=30.

18. International Domestic Workers Federation, "C189."

19. International Labor Organization, "C189—Domestic Workers Convention, 2011

(No. 189)," 2011, accessed November 7, 2014, http://www.ilo.org/dyn/normlex/en/f?p
=NORMLEXPUB:12100:0::NO:12100:P12100_INSTRUMENT_ID:2551460:NO.

20. Laura Flanders, "California Governor Signs Domestic Worker Bill of Rights,"
The Nation, September 26, 2013, accessed November 5, 2014, http://www.thenation.com
/blog/176377/california-governor-signs-domestic-worker-bill-rights#.

21. See the Caring Across Generations website at http://www.caringacrossgenerations
.org.

22. Marisa Lagos, "Jerry Brown Will Launch 'Full-On' Campaign Tuesday, Defends
Domestic Workers, S-Comm Vetoes," *SFGate*, October 13, 2012, accessed January 5,
2013, http://blog.sfgate.com/novo5election/2012/10/13/jerry-brown-will-launch-full-on
-campaign-tuesday-defends-domestic-worker-s-comm-vetoes.

23. Hannah Dreier, "Domestic Workers Bill of Rights in California, AB889, Vetoed by
Gov. Jerry Brown," *Huffington Post*, October 1, 2012, accessed January 5, 2013, http://www
.huffingtonpost.com/2012/10/01/domestic-workers-bill-of-rights-veto_n_1928001.html.

24. Domestic Workers United, "Programs," 2012, accessed November 8, 2014, http://
www.domesticworkersunited.org/index.php/en/our-work/programs. These measures
are adopted by the Domestic Workers United in the United States, which offers job-
skills training courses and programs such as "Nanny Training Program," "Household
Management Course," and "Unemployed Workers Support" to its members alongside
its legal advocacy and social activism initiatives.

3. Global Sex Workers

1. Ken Loach, dir., *Bread and Roses*, DVD (Lions Gate, Santa Monica, CA, 2000).

2. "In Bed with a Los Angeles Prostitute," *The Skyy John Show*, June 8, 2010, accessed
February 20, 2013, http://www.youtube.com/watch?v=6nGD7M5j89g.

3. "In Bed with a Los Angeles Prostitute."

4. "In Bed with a Los Angeles Prostitute."

5. "In Bed with a Los Angeles Prostitute."

6. "In Bed with a Los Angeles Prostitute."

7. For instance, in the United States, strip clubs now often feature "private rooms"
where de facto practices of prostitution take place (Bernstein 2007, 73); in Japan, while
hostesses at nightclubs are far from the classic understanding of prostitutes, some do
engage in direct sexual services outside the clubs to earn extra income (Parreñas 2010,
137). Other issues also exist with terminology: for instance, while pro-prostitution literature considers "sex worker" to be a more progressive and de-stigmatized term than
"prostitute" (Delacoste and Alexander 1987; Leigh 1997), both terms are fraught with
limits. Many migrant women engaging in commercial sex acts do not refer to themselves
as either prostitutes or sex workers, but rather describe the work they do as "that," "the
street," "work," or "business for the time being" (Spanger 2002, 123; Penttinen 2008, 75;
Andrijasevic 2010, 22). This suggests the continuing stigma and taboo associated with
commercial sex irrespective of terminology, and neither "prostitution" nor "sex work"
can aptly capture the complex self-identities understood and claimed by the diverse sub-

jects in global sex commerce. While recognizing these limits, I am using both terms as a common point of reference to undertake my current investigation of these subjects' ingenious agency and the larger lessons about social change that such agency engenders.

8. As Bernstein notes, "In a 2005 analysis of clients arrested for prostitution in Chicago during a four-month period, John Conroy evaluated arrest photos to conclude that of 524 images, more than 80 percent appeared to be African American or Hispanic" (228n41). John Conroy further indicates, "Suburbanites and tourists accounted for less than one mug shot in five, and even in this group nearly three johns in five were black or Hispanic. The wealthy suburbs north of Evanston had not a single representative." John Conroy, "The Electronic Pillory," *Chicago Reader*, April 7, 2006, sec. 1, 20.

9. Sex Workers Project, "Taking the Pledge," n.d., accessed February 20, 2013, http://www.sexworkersproject.org/downloads/TakingThePledgeCurriculum.pdf.

10. This is not to suggest that actual trafficking conditions where women and children are coerced, threatened, or manipulated into prostitution do not exist and need not be combated. Rather, what is critical is to look into the ways in which antitrafficking campaigns reproduce the liberal conditions that abjectify and commodify women's bodies in late capitalism. As an alternative approach, I consider transnational feminist studies on global sex work that call for the removal of the *subjugating conditions* in migration and sexual labor rather than the repression of mobility and elimination of prostitution as a more critically informed remedy to end trafficking (e.g., Kempadoo and Doezema 1998; Thorbek and Pattanaik 2002; Parreñas 2008; Andrijasevic 2010).

11. International Committee on the Rights of Sex Workers in Europe, "Declaration of the Rights of Sex Workers in Europe," 2005, accessed March 1, 2013, http://www.sexworkeurope.org; International Committee on the Rights of Sex Workers in Europe, "Sex Workers in Europe Manifesto," 2005, accessed March 1, 2013, http://www.sexworkeurope.org.

12. Red Umbrella Project, "I Am a Sex Worker," 2009, accessed February 22, 2013, http://www.redumbrellaproject.org/advocate/i-am-a-sex-worker; First Advocates, "Sex Workers Rights—A Public Service Announcement from First," 2010, accessed February 24, 2013, https://www.youtube.com/watch?v=cm9n-WnVDxs.

13. Joanna Walters, "Campaigners Protest against United Nations Stance on Prostitution," *The Guardian*, September 21, 2013, accessed November 30, 2014, http://www.theguardian.com/society/2013/sep/21/united-nations-prostitution-sex-trafficking.

14. For example, the International Covenant on Civil and Political Rights protects all people against discrimination as well as guarantees the right to life, liberty, and personal security, which is relevant to sex workers who suffer from societal stigma in general and sexual violence and police abuse in particular (Mellon 1999, 314). The International Covenant on Economic, Social and Cultural Rights attends to development issues in the Third World, requiring states to provide free and mandatory education at the primary level, thus lessening the burden on migrant women who enter sex work to cover children's education costs (313). Where prostitution is legitimized as work, the minimum labor standards covered in the International Labor Organization apply: "freedom of association, the right to organize, abolition of forced labor, equality of opportunity and treatment, and other

standards regulating work conditions" such as social insurance, sick leave, retirement benefits, vacation pay, and workplace safety and hygiene (Kempadoo and Ghuma 1999, 294). Some also suggest that, while the main thrust of the Convention on the Elimination of All Forms of Discrimination Against Women aims to suppress trafficking, it, along with the Universal Declaration of Human Rights, "contain articles on the inalienable right of all human beings to work and to freely choose their job or profession. Discrimination against sex workers is clearly in violation of this right" (Mellon, 313–14).

15. As Kamala Kempadoo observes, "The international character of the movement has been more wishful thinking than political reality. . . . Much of what was laid out in the Charter and discussed at the congresses was defined by (white) western sex workers and advocates. . . . Many writings in the 1990s have continued to reproduce a skewed representation of the prostitutes rights movement and to ignore sex workers' rights groups in developing countries" (1998a, 20).

16. Although the scope of the World Charter for Prostitutes' Rights in 1985 is international, I use the referent "First World" here to designate that the delegates who drafted the charter were predominantly sex workers from or located in the West. As Gail Pheterson concedes in *A Vindication of the Rights of Whores*: "Only a few Asian countries were represented, and then not by prostitutes themselves; Africa and South America were as yet totally unrepresented" (1989b, 25–26). As such, the voices that went into the drafting of the document reflect those working in the West. This is not to undercut the value of the document, but rather to limit its claims to a specific "location" (which is, after all, a hegemonic one) so that it does not assume certain claims on behalf of others before it transforms into a truly (or relatively more) *international* document. As for the Declaration on the Rights of Sex Workers in Europe in 2005, while "the people involved in the mobilization . . . [include] migrants (regular and irregular), third country nationals (TCNs), and EU [European Union] citizens involved in issues of sex work" (Andrijasevic et al. 2012, 498), the designation of this event as taking place in the "First World" is still pertinent to contextualize its geopolitical configuration.

17. See also International Committee on the Rights of Sex Workers in Europe, "The Declaration of the Rights of Sex Workers in Europe."

4. Trans People

1. Gillian Flaccus, "Man Denied U.S. Citizenship Because Wife Is Transsexual," *Indybay*, November 30, 2004, accessed March 1, 2013, http://www.indybay.org/newsitems /2004/11/30/17078291.php?show_comments=1; "Transsexual Filipino Couple Sues U.S. over Denial of Green Card," *The Filipino Express Online*, December 3, 2004, accessed March 2, 2013, http://www.filipinoexpress.net/18/49_news.html; Yong B. Chavez, "Filipino Man Denied Residency, Marriage to Transgender Challenged," *News America Media*, December 9, 2004, accessed March 1, 2013, http://news.newamericamedia.org/news/view _article.html?article_id=724f1276c8d3521d5542b9a2f50400e4; "Gender Bender," *Metroactive*, March 23–29, 2005, accessed March 2, 2013, http://www.metroactive.com/papers /metro/03.23.05/empaqu-0512.html.

2. "Gender Bender."

3. "Gender Bender."

4. Ronald Pineda, "Couple's Case at the Crosshairs of Debates on Immigration, Marriage and Sexuality," *ColorLines*, April 2005, accessed March 2, 2013, http://arc.org /racewire/050404r_pineda.html.

5. Gayle Rubin's foundational conception of the "sex/gender system," in which she separates sex (a biological category: male or female) from gender (a social construction or an ideological structure: man or woman) is an important distinction (Rubin 1975). However, sex and gender are rarely distinct and detached from one another in their everyday politicized operation. As Shane Phelan observes, "Our sexuality is always partly about gender, though not in any simple sense. Gender, conversely, is partly about sexuality" (2001, 131). In fact, while queer theory is often taken to be the study of sex/sexuality and feminist theory is assigned the interrogation of gender, trans embodiment demonstrates that its ambiguity within and impact on the sex/gender system is expressed dynamically and intertwiningly through both of its "transsexing" and "transgendering" qualities. Without collapsing sex and gender, I wish to indicate that when I speak of the (heteronormative) gender script, I am underlining its signification of the sex/gender system—and that power operates through both the channels of sex and gender rather than one or the other.

6. David Valentine includes the following identity categories under "transgender": "Transsexuals, transvestites, cross-dressers, men or women of transgender or transsexual experience, drag queens, drag kings, female or male impersonators, genderqueers, intersexuals, hermaphrodites, fem queens, girls, boys, trannies, feminine gay men, butch lesbians, male-to-female, female-to-male, female embodied masculine persons, and even, simply, men or women" (2007, 33).

7. For the debate on such terminology issues, see Hale (1998, 341n1) and Cromwell (1999, 24–27).

8. Compare Jay Prosser's characterization of trans-embodiment as following a seemingly linear trajectory "from fragmentation to integration; from alienation to reconciliation; from loss to restoration" (1998, 80). Prosser delineates powerfully and elegantly the felt gender realness and the need of gender location for transsexuals, though his mapping of transgendering through a series of dichotomous constructions such as *departure* and *destination*, *beginning* and *end*, *here* and *there* (116–17) deemphasizes the circuitous and nonlinear routes of "morphing in" that signal critical traces of trans people's ingenious agency.

9. Susan Stryker, "Transgender Activism," *Glbtq.com*, 2004, accessed December 10, 2014, http://www.glbtq.com/social-sciences/transgender_activism.html.

10. Stryker, "Transgender Activism."

11. Stryker, "Transgender Activism."

12. Sandy Stone, "The 'Empire' Strikes Back: A Posttranssexual Manifesto," 1994, accessed December 12, 2014, http://www.actlab.utexas.edu/~sandy/empire-strikes-back.

13. Stone, "The 'Empire' Strikes Back"; emphasis added.

14. International Conference on Transgender Law and Policy, "International Bill of Gender Rights," 1996, accessed March 16, 2013, http://www.transgenderlegal.com.

15. National Gay and Lesbian Task Force, "Employment Non-Discrimination Act (ENDA)," n.d., accessed December 13, 2014, http://www.thetaskforce.org/issues/nondiscrimination /ENDA_main_page.

16. Sylvia Ann Hewlett, "ENDA Vote Is Just the Beginning," *Huffington Post*, July 18, 2013, accessed December 13, 2014, http://www.huffingtonpost.com/sylvia-ann-hewlett /enda-vote-is-just-the—beginning_b_3613199.html.

17. Hewlett, "ENDA Vote Is Just the Beginning."

18. "Pakistan Transgenders Pin Hopes on New Rights," BBC *News*, April 25, 2011, accessed December 14, 2014, http://www.bbc.com/news/world-south-asia-13186958.

19. "Pakistan Transgenders Pin Hopes on New Rights."

5. Suicide Bombers

1. Hilla Medalia, dir., *To Die in Jerusalem*, DVD (Priddy Brothers, Eagle, ID, 2007).

2. Medalia, *To Die in Jerusalem*.

3. Medalia, *To Die in Jerusalem*.

4. Medalia, *To Die in Jerusalem*.

5. George W. Bush, "Bush Roadmap for Peace: First Speech," *About.com*, April 4, 2002, accessed March 18, 2013, http://middleeast.about.com/od/israelandpalestine/a /meo70906.htm.

6. Raja Khalidi, "After the Arab Spring in Palestine: Contesting the Neoliberal Narrative of Palestinian National Liberation," *Jidaliyya*, March 23, 2012, accessed March 20, 2013, http://www.jadaliyya.com/pages/index/4789/after-the-arab-spring-in-palestine _contesting-the—.

7. See also Nasra Hassan, "An Arsenal of Believers: Talking to the 'Human Bombs,'" *New Yorker*, November 19, 2001, 36–41.

8. Michael Ignatieff, "It's War—But It Doesn't Have to Be Dirty," *The Guardian*, October 1, 2001, accessed May 23, 2004, www.theguardian.com/world/2001/oct/01/afghanistan .terrorism; Michael Walzer, "Excusing Terror: The Politics of Ideological Apology," *American Prospect*, October 22, 2001, accessed June 2, 2008, http://www.prospect.org/print/V12 /18/walzer-m.html.

9. Rational strategic choice, for example, has been conceived by many as the central theme in motivating suicide attacks, whether as a political means to end foreign occupation (Pape 2005); an organizational tactic to outbid domestic competitors and mobilize popular support (Bloom 2005); a "weapon of the weak" by a military-technological underdog (Sprinzak 2000; Gambetta 2005a); a Poliheuristic decision-making tool (Mintz et al. 2006); or superior effectiveness through the use of women as the bombing subjects (O'Rourke 2009). Others have further cited religious radicalization and indoctrination (Juergensmeyer 2003; Moghadam 2006b; Sageman 2006); participant altruism (Pedahzur et al. 2003; Gambetta 2005a; Pape 2005); relative economic deprivation (Gurr 2006); personal crisis (Pedahzur 2005); pneumopathology or spiritual disorder (Cooper 2005); desire for vengeance (Rosenberger 2003); and social alienation (Alonso and Reinares 2006; Moghadam 2006b; Sageman 2006) as potential risk factors of suicide missions.

10. Furthermore, the disease narrative that approaches terrorism as if it were a purely biomedical issue does not address the ways in which such discourse itself (such as the AIDS epidemic) is already political and ideological—racialized, sexualized, and colonial (see Cohen 1999; Patton 2002).

11. Hassan, "An Arsenal of Believers," 38.

12. As Mohammed Hafez observes, "Suicide bombers do not lend themselves to easy generalizations. Other than being Muslim, usually unmarried, and in their late teens or early twenties, not much more is common among the bombers. Some bombers come from modest or impoverished backgrounds, whereas many others come from middle class or even affluent families. Some bombers lack secondary education although others are university students and graduates with degrees ranging from engineering, computer programming, journalism, and Islamic law. Some have been engaged in militancy since the first Palestinian uprising, whereas others are recent recruits who joined the movement explicitly for the purpose of carrying out a suicide mission" (2006b, 172).

13. Jacqueline Rose, "Deadly Embrace," *London Review of Books*, November 4, 2004, accessed February 10, 2006, http://www.lrb.co.uk/v26/n21/rose01_.html.

14. U.S. Campaign for the Academic and Cultural Boycott of Israel, n.d., accessed June 18, 2014, http://www.usacbi.org.

15. Elizabeth Redden, "A First for the Israel Boycott?" *Inside Higher Ed*, April 24, 2013, accessed June 18, 2014, http://www.insidehighered.com/news/2013/04/24/asian-american-studies-association-endorses-boycott-israeli-universities#sthash.Zerns4oA.dpbs.

16. American Studies Association, "Council Resolution on Boycott of Israeli Academic Institutions," December 4, 2013, accessed June 18, 2014, http://www.theasa.net/american_studies_association_resolution_on_academic_boycott_of_israel.

17. U.S. Campaign for the Academic and Cultural Boycott of Israel.

18. Michael Roth, "Boycott of Israeli Universities: A Repugnant Attack on Academic Freedom," *Los Angeles Times*, December 19, 2013, accessed June 19, 2014, http://articles.latimes.com/2013/dec/19/opinion/la-oe-roth-academic-boycott-israel-20131219; Cary Nelson, "The Problem with Judith Butler: The Political Philosophy of the Movement to Boycott Israel," *Los Angeles Review of Books*, March 16, 2014, accessed June 19, 2014, https://lareviewofbooks.org/essay/problem-judith-butler-political-philosophy-movement-boycott-israel.

19. Khalidi, "After the Arab Spring in Palestine."

20. Edith M. Lederer, "Palestinian Statehood Vote: Palestinians Certain to Win UN Recognition as a State," *Huffington Post*, November 29, 2012, accessed March 21, 2013, http://www.huffingtonpost.com/2012/11/29/palestinian-statehood-vote-certain-to-win_n_2210431.html?utm_hp_ref=email_share.

21. Max Ajl, "Israeli Tent Protests Ignore Link between Neoliberalism, Occupation," *Truthout*, August 13, 2011, accessed March 19, 2013, http://www.truth-out.org/news/item/2589:israeli-tent-protests-ignore-link-between-neoliberalism-occupation.

22. Ajl, "Israeli Tent Protests Ignore Link between Neoliberalism, Occupation."

23. Ajl, "Israeli Tent Protests Ignore Link between Neoliberalism, Occupation."

24. Khalidi, "After the Arab Spring in Palestine."

25. Khalidi, "After the Arab Spring in Palestine."

26. Khalidi, "After the Arab Spring in Palestine."

27. Khalidi, "After the Arab Spring in Palestine."

28. Khalidi, "After the Arab Spring in Palestine."

Conclusion. Politics without Politics

1. The broader implications of Bruce Lee's thought for contemporary social philosophy and critical cultural studies have surfaced in recent academic discussions. See, e.g., Bowman 2009, 2013. For the present analysis, here I focus specifically on the political implications of Bruce Lee's thought for social activism.

2. John Little, dir., *Bruce Lee: A Warrior's Journey*, DVD (Warner Home Video, Burbank, CA, 2000).

3. Bruce Lee, quoted at http://www.goodreads.com/author/quotes/32579.Bruce_Lee.

Works Cited

Aarens, Blake, Hima B., Gina Gold, Jade Irie, Madeleine Lawson, and Gloria Lockett. 1997. "Showing Up Fully: Women of Color Discuss Sex Work." In *Whores and Other Feminists*, ed. Jill Nagle. New York: Routledge.

Abad, Angelita, Marena Briones, Tatiana Cordero, Rosa Manzo, and Marta Marchán. 1998. "The Association of Autonomous Women Workers, Ecuador, '22nd June.'" In *Global Sex Workers: Rights, Resistance, and Redefinition*, ed. Kamala Kempadoo and Jo Doezema. New York: Routledge.

Agamben, Georgio. 1998. *Homo Sacer: Sovereign Power and Bare Life*, trans. Daniel Heller-Roazen. Stanford, CA: Stanford University Press.

———. 2000. *Means without End: Notes on Politics*, trans. Vincenzo Binetti and Cesare Casarino. Minneapolis: University of Minnesota Press.

Allen, Lori. 2008. "Getting by the Occupation: How Violence Became Normal during the Second Palestinian Intifada." *Cultural Anthropology* 23, no. 3: 453–87.

Alonso, Rogelio, and Fernando Reinares. 2006. "Maghreb Immigrants Becoming Suicide Terrorists: A Case Study on Religious Radicalization Processes in Spain." In *Root Causes of Suicide Terrorism: The Globalization of Martyrdom*, ed. Ami Pedahzur. New York: Routledge.

Andoni, Lamis. 1997. "Searching for Answers: Gaza's Suicide Bombers." *Journal of Palestine Studies* 26, no. 4: 33–45.

Andrijasevic, Rutvica. 2010. *Migration, Agency and Citizenship in Sex Trafficking*. New York: Palgrave Macmillan.

Andrijasevic, Rutvica, Claudia Aradau, Jef Huysmans, and Vicki Squire. 2012. "European Citizenship Unbound: Sex Work, Mobility, Mobilization." *Environment and Planning D: Society and Space* 30: 497–514.

Ang, Ien. 1995. "'I'm a Feminist but . . .': 'Other' Women and Postnational Feminism." In *Transitions: New Australian Feminisms*, ed. Barbara Caine and Rosemary Pringle. New York: Palgrave Macmillan.

Apostolidis, Paul. 2010. *Breaks in the Chain: What Immigrant Workers Can Teach America about Democracy*. Minneapolis: University of Minnesota Press.

Araj, Bader. 2008. "Harsh State Repression as a Cause of Suicide Bombing: The Case of the Palestinian-Israeli Conflict." *Studies in Conflict and Terrorism* 31: 284–303.

Arendt, Hannah. 1958. *The Human Condition*. Chicago: University of Chicago Press.

Arjomand, Said Amir. 2002. "Can Rational Analysis Break a Taboo? A Middle Eastern Perspective." In *Critical Views of September 11: Analyses from around the World*, ed. Eric Hershberg and Kevin W. Moore. New York: New Press.

Banet-Weiser, Sarah. 1999. *The Most Beautiful Girl in the World: Beauty Pageants and National Identity*. Berkeley: University of California Press.

Banet-Weiser, Sarah, and Roopali Mukherjee, eds. 2012a. *Commodity Activism: Cultural Resistance in Neoliberal Times*. New York: New York University Press.

———. 2012b. "Introduction: Commodity Activism in Neoliberal Times." In *Commodity Activism: Cultural Resistance in Neoliberal Times*, ed. Sarah Banet-Weiser and Roopali Mukherjee. New York: New York University Press.

Banner, Francine. 2006. "Uncivil Wars: 'Suicide Bomber Identity' as a Product of Russo-Chechen Conflict." *Religion, State and Society* 34, no. 3: 215–53.

Bapat, Sheila. 2014. *Part of the Family? Nannies, Housekeepers, Caregivers and the Battle for Domestic Workers' Rights*. Brooklyn, NY: Ig.

Barber, Benjamin. 1984. *Strong Democracy: Participatory Politics for a New Age*. Berkeley: University of California Press.

Bayat, Asef. 2010. *Life as Politics: How Ordinary People Change the Middle East*. Stanford, CA: Stanford University Press.

Beauchamp, Toby. 2013. "Artful Concealment and Strategic Visibility: Transgender Bodies and U.S. State Surveillance after 9/11." In *The Transgender Studies Reader 2*, ed. Susan Stryker and Aren Z. Aizura. New York: Routledge.

Bell, Derrick. 1995. "Racial Realism." In *Critical Race Theory: The Key Writings That Formed The Movement*, ed. Kimberlé Crenshaw, Neil Gotanda, Gary Peller, and Kendall Thomas. New York: New Press.

Bell, Shannon. 1994. *Reading, Writing, and Rewriting the Prostitute Body*. Bloomington: Indiana University Press.

Benhabib, Seyla. 2004. *The Rights of Others: Aliens, Residents, and Citizens*. New York: Cambridge University Press.

Berlant, Lauren. 1997. *The Queen of America Goes to Washington City: Essays on Sex and Citizenship*. Durham, NC: Duke University Press.

Bernstein, Elizabeth. 2007. *Temporarily Yours: Intimacy, Authenticity, and the Commerce of Sex*. Chicago: University of Chicago Press.

Bhabha, Homi. 2004. "Foreword: Framing Fanon." In *The Wretched of the Earth*, trans. Richard Philcox. New York: Grove.

Bhargava, Rajeev. 2002. "Ordinary Feelings, Extraordinary Events: Moral Complexity in

9/11." In *Understanding September 11*, ed. Craig Calhoun, Paul Price, and Ashley Timmer. New York: New Press.

Bishop, Ryan, and Lillian S. Robinson. 1998. *Night Market: Sexual Cultures and the Thai Economic Miracle*. New York: Routledge.

Bloom, Mia. 2005. *Dying to Kill: The Allure of Suicide Terror*. New York: Columbia University Press.

Bordo, Susan. 1992. "Postmodern Subjects, Postmodern Bodies (Review Essay)." *Feminist Studies* 18, no. 1: 159–75.

Bornstein, Kate. 1995. *Gender Outlaw: On Men, Women, and the Rest of Us*. New York: Vintage.

Bosniak, Linda. 2006. *The Citizen and the Alien: Dilemmas of Contemporary Membership*. Princeton, NJ: Princeton University Press.

Bower, Lisa. 1997. "Queer Problems/Straight Solutions: The Limits of a Politics of 'Official Recognition.'" In *Playing with Fire: Queer Politics, Queer Theories*, ed. Shane Phelan. New York: Routledge.

Bowman, Paul. 2009. *Theorizing Bruce Lee: Film-Fantasy-Fighting-Philosophy*. Amsterdam: Rodopi.

———. 2013. *Beyond Bruce Lee: Chasing the Dragon through Film, Philosophy, and Popular Culture*. New York: Columbia University Press.

Brass, Tom. 2012. "Scott's 'Zomia,' or a Populist Post-modern History of Nowhere." *Journal of Contemporary Asia* 42, no. 1: 123–33.

Brennan, Denise. 1999. "Women at Work: Sex Tourism in Sosúa, the Dominican Republic." *Critical Matrix* 11, no. 2: 17–41.

———. 2002. "Selling Sex for Visas: Sex Tourism as a Stepping-Stone to International Migration." In *Global Woman: Nannies, Maids, and Sex Workers in the New Economy*, ed. Barbara Ehrenreich and Arlie Russell Hochschild. New York: Metropolitan.

Brown, Wendy. 1995. *States of Injury: Power and Freedom in Late Modernity*. Princeton, NJ: Princeton University Press.

———. 2005. "Neoliberalism and the End of Liberal Democracy." In *Edgework: Critical Essays on Knowledge and Politics*. Princeton, NJ: Princeton University Press.

Bukatman, Scott. 2000. "Taking Shape: Morphing and the Performance of Self." In *Meta-Morphing: Visual Transformation and the Culture of Quick-Change*, ed. Vivian Sobchack. Minneapolis: University of Minnesota Press.

Butler, Judith. 1988. "Performative Acts and Gender Constitution: An Essay in Phenomenology and Feminist Theory." *Theatre Journal* 40, no. 4: 519–31.

———. 1990. *Gender Trouble: Feminism and the Subversion of Identity*. New York: Routledge.

———. 1993. *Bodies that Matter: On the Discursive Limits of "Sex."* New York: Routledge.

———. 1997. "Merely Cultural." *Social Text* 15, nos. 3–4: 265–77.

———. 1999. "Preface." In *Gender Trouble: Feminism and the Subversion of Identity*. New York: Routledge.

———. 2004a. *Precarious Life: The Powers of Mourning and Violence*. New York: Verso.

———. 2004b. *Undoing Gender*. New York: Routledge.

———. 2006. "Undiagnosing Gender." In *Transgender Rights*, ed. Paisley Currah, Richard M. Juang, and Shannon Price Minter. Minneapolis: University of Minnesota Press.

Cabral, Mauro (A. I. Grinspan), and Paula Viturro. 2006. "(Trans)Sexual Citizenship in Contemporary Argentina." In *Transgender Rights*, ed. Paisley Currah, Richard M. Juang, and Shannon Price Minter. Minneapolis: University of Minnesota Press.

Cacho, Lisa Marie. 2012. *Social Death: Racialized Rightlessness and the Criminalization of the Unprotected*. New York: New York University Press.

Califia, Pat. 1997. *Sex Changes: The Politics of Transgenderism*. San Francisco: Cleis.

Castronovo, Russ, and Dana D. Nelson. 2002a. "Introduction: Materializing Democracy and Other Political Fantasies." In *Materializing Democracy: Toward a Revitalized Cultural Politics*, ed. Russ Castronovo and Dana D. Nelson. Durham, NC: Duke University Press.

————, eds. 2002b. *Materializing Democracy: Toward a Revitalized Cultural Politics*. Durham, NC: Duke University Press.

Chambers, Samuel. 2004. "Giving Up (on) Rights? The Future of Rights and the Project of Radical Democracy." *American Journal of Political Science* 48, no. 2: 185–200.

Chang, Grace. 2000. *Disposable Domestics: Immigrant Women Workers in the Global Economy*. Cambridge: South End.

Chapkis, Wendy. 1997. *Live Sex Acts: Women Performing Erotic Labor*. New York: Routledge.

Cheah, Pheng. 2006. *Inhuman Conditions: On Cosmopolitanism and Human Rights*. Cambridge, MA: Harvard University Press.

Chen Kuan-Hsing. 1998. "Introduction: The Decolonization Question." In *Trajectories: Inter-Asia Cultural Studies*, ed. Kuan-Hsing Chen, Hsiu-Ling Kuo, Hans Hang, and Hsu Ming-Chu. New York: Routledge.

Childress, Alice. 1986. *Like One of the Family: Conversations from a Domestic's Life*. Boston: Beacon.

Chin, Christine B. N. 1998. *In Service and Servitude: Foreign Female Domestic Workers and the Malaysian "Modernity" Project*. New York: Columbia University Press.

Cho, Sumi, Kimberlé Williams Crenshaw, and Leslie McCall. 2013. "Toward a Field of Intersectionality Studies: Theory, Applications, and Praxis." *Signs* 38, no. 4: 785–810.

Chuang, Janie A. 2010. "Achieving Accountability for Migrant Domestic Worker Abuse." *North Carolina Law Review* 88, no. 5: 1627–56.

Churchill, Ward. 2003. *On the Justice of Roosting Chickens: Reflections on the Consequences of U.S. Imperial Arrogance and Criminality*. Oakland, CA: AK Press.

Clark-Lewis, Elizabeth. 1996. *Living In, Living Out: African American Domestics and the Great Migration*. New York: Kodansha International.

Cohen, Cathy. 1999. *The Boundaries of Blackness: AIDS and the Breakdown of Black Politics*. Chicago: University of Chicago Press.

Cohen, Erik. 1986. "Lovelorn Farangs: The Correspondence between Foreign Men and Thai Girls." *Anthropological Quarterly* 59, no. 3: 115–27.

Coles, Romand. 2005. *Beyond Gated Politics: Reflections for the Possibility of Democracy*. Minneapolis: University of Minnesota Press.

Colimoro, Claudia. 1998. "A World of People: Sex Workers in Mexico." In *Global Sex Workers: Rights, Resistance, and Redefinition*, ed. Kamala Kempadoo and Jo Doezema. New York: Routledge.

Comella, Lynn, 2012. "Changing the World One Orgasm at a Time: Sex Positive Retail Activism." In *Commodity Activism: Cultural Resistance in Neoliberal Times*, ed. Sarah Banet-Weiser and Roopali Mukherjee. New York: New York University Press.

Constable, Nicole. 2007. *Maid to Order in Hong Kong: Stories of Migrant Workers*, 2nd ed. Ithaca, NY: Cornell University Press.

Cooper, Barry. 2005. "Terrorism and Globalization." *Perspectives on Global Development and Technology* 4, nos. 3–4: 543–75.

Connolly, William E. 1995. *The Ethos of Pluralization*. Minneapolis: University of Minnesota Press.

Coutin, Susan Bibler. 2003. "Illegality, Borderlands, and the Space of Nonexistence." In *Globalization under Construction: Governmentality, Law, and Identity*, ed. Richard Warren Perry and Bill Maurer. Minneapolis: University of Minnesota Press.

Crenshaw, Kimberlé Williams. 1991. "Mapping the Margins: Intersectionality, Identity Politics, and Violence against Women of Color." *Stanford Law Review* 43, no. 6: 1241–99.

Crenshaw, Martha. 1981. "The Causes of Terrorism." *Comparative Politics* 13, no. 4: 379–91.

Cromwell, Jason. 1999. *Transmen and FTMs: Identities, Bodies, Genders, and Sexualities*. Urbana: University of Illinois Press.

Cruikshank, Barbara. 1999. *The Will to Empower: Democratic Citizens and Other Subjects*. Ithaca, NY: Cornell University Press.

Currah, Paisley. 2001. "Queer Theory, Lesbian and Gay Rights, and Transsexual Marriages." In *Sexual Identities, Queer Politics*, ed. Mark Blasius. Princeton, NJ: Princeton University Press.

———. 2006. "Gender Pluralisms under the Transgender Umbrella." In *Transgender Rights*, ed. Paisley Currah, Richard M. Juang, and Shannon Price Minter. Minneapolis: University of Minnesota Press.

Currah, Paisley, Richard M. Juang, and Shannon Price Minter, eds. 2006. "Introduction." In *Transgender Rights*, ed. Paisley Currah, Richard M. Juang, and Shannon Price Minter. Minneapolis: University of Minnesota Press.

Das Gupta, Monisha. 2006. *Unruly Immigrants: Rights, Activism, and Transnational South Asian Politics in the United States*. Durham, NC: Duke University Press.

Davis, Joyce M. 2003. *Martyrs: Innocence, Vengeance, and Despair in the Middle East*. New York: Palgrave Macmillan.

Davis, Mike. 2006. *Planet of Slums*. New York: Verso.

de Certeau, Michel. 1984. *The Practice of Everyday Life*, trans. Steven Rendall. Berkeley: University of California Press.

Delacoste, Fédérique, and Priscilla Alexander, eds. 1987. *Sex Work: Writings by Women in the Sex Industry*. Pittsburgh: Cleiss.

Delgado, Richard, and Jean Stefancic. 2001. *Critical Race Theory: An Introduction*. New York: New York University Press.

Delpit, Lisa. 2003. "Language Diversity and Learning." In *The Critical Pedagogy Reader*, ed. Antonia Darder, Marta P. Baltodano, and Rodolfo D. Torres. New York: Routledge.

Derrida, Jacques. 2002. *Negotiations: Interventions and Interviews, 1971–2001*, ed. and trans. Elizabeth Rottenberg. Stanford, CA: Stanford University Press.

Doezema, Jo. 1998. "Forced to Choose: Beyond the Voluntary v. Forced Prostitution Dichotomy." In *Global Sex Workers: Rights, Resistance, and Redefinition*, ed. Kamala Kempadoo and Jo Doezema. New York: Routledge.

Duggan, Lisa. 2002. "The New Homonormativity: The Sexual Politics of Neoliberalism." In *Materializing Democracy: Toward a Revitalized Cultural Politics*, ed. Russ Castronovo and Dana D. Nelson. Durham, NC: Duke University Press.

Dworkin, Andrea. 1997. *Life and Death: Unapologetic Writings on the Continuing War against Women*. New York: Free Press.

Edelman, Lee. 2004. *No Future: Queer Theory and the Death Drive*. Durham, NC: Duke University Press.

Edwards, Susan. 1993. "Selling the Body, Keeping the Soul: Sexuality, Power, and the Theories and Realities of Prostitution." In *Body Matters: Essays on the Sociology of the Body*, ed. Sue Scott and David Morgan. London: Falmer.

Evans, David T. 1993. *Sexual Citizenship: The Material Construction of Sexualities*. New York: Routledge.

Fanon, Frantz. 1994. *Black Skin, White Masks*. New York: Grove.

———. 2004. *The Wretched of the Earth*. New York: Grove.

Fausto-Sterling, Anne. 2000. *Sexing the Body: Gender Politics and the Construction of Sexuality*. New York: Basic.

Feinberg, Leslie. 1996. *Transgender Warriors: Making History from Joan of Arc to Rupaul*. Boston: Beacon.

Ferguson, James. 2006. *Global Shadows: Africa in the Neoliberal World Order*. Durham, NC: Duke University Press.

———. 2009. "The Uses of Neoliberalism." *Antipode* 41, supp. 1: 166–84.

———. 2011. "Toward a Left Art of Government: from 'Foucauldian Critique' to Foucauldian Politics." *History of the Human Sciences* 24, no. 4: 61–68.

Foster, Morris W., and Jesse W. Butler. 2008. "Cancer, HIV, and Terrorism: Translating Public Health Models for Prevention and Control to Counter-Terrorism." *Critical Studies on Terrorism* 1, no. 1: 81–94.

Foucault, Michel. 1978. *The History of Sexuality, Volume I: An Introduction*, trans. Robert Hurley. New York: Vintage.

———. 1980. "Truth and Power." In *Power/Knowledge: Selected Interviews and Other Writings, 1972–1977*, ed. Colin Gordon. New York: Pantheon.

———. 1997. "Governmentality." In *Power: Essential Works of Foucault, 1954–1984, Volume 3*, ed. James D. Faubion. New York: New Press.

Gagné, Patricia, and Richard Tewksbury. 1998. "Conformity Pressures and Gender Resistance among Transgendered Individuals." *Social Problems* 45, no. 1: 81–101.

Gagné, Patricia, Richard Tewksbury, and Deanna McGaughey. 1997. "Coming Out and Crossing Over: Identity Formation and Proclamation in a Transgender Community." *Gender and Society* 11, no. 4: 478–508.

Gall, Gregor. 2006. *Sex Worker Union Organizing: An International Study*. New York: Palgrave Macmillan.

Gambetta, Diego. 2005a. "Can We Make Sense of Suicide Missions?" In *Making Sense of Suicide Missions*, ed. Diego Gambetta. New York: Oxford University Press.

———. 2005b. "Foreword." In *Making Sense of Suicide Missions*, ed. Diego Gambetta. New York: Oxford University Press.

Gamson, Joshua. 1998. *Freaks Talk Back: Tabloid Talk Shows and Sexual Nonconformity*. Chicago: University of Chicago Press.

Ganzon, Donita. 2008. *Overnight Woman*. Los Angeles: Donita Ganzon.

García Canclini, Néstor. 2001. *Consumers and Citizens: Globalization and Multicultural Conflicts*, trans. George Yúdice. Minneapolis: University of Minnesota Press.

Giroux, Henry A. 2010. *The Mouse that Roared: Disney and the End of Innocence*. Lanham, MD: Rowman and Littlefield.

Glenn, Evelyn Nakano. 2007. "Caring and Inequality." In *Women's Labor in the Global Economy*, ed. Sharon Harley. New Brunswick, NJ: Rutgers University Press.

———. 2008. "Yearning for Lightness: Transnational Circuits in the Marketing and Consumption of Skin Lighteners." *Gender and Society* 22, no. 3: 281–302.

Goldhammer, Jesse. 2005. *The Headless Republic: Sacrificial Violence in Modern French Thought*. Ithaca, NY: Cornell University Press.

Gonzales, Katrina C. 2008. "Undocumented Immigrants and Workers' Compensation: Rejecting Federal Preemption of the California Workers' Compensation Act." *U.C. Davis Law Review* 41, no. 5: 2001–33.

Gordon, Jennifer. 2005. *Suburban Sweatshops: The Fight for Immigrant Rights*. Cambridge, MA: Harvard University Press.

Grewal, Inderpal. 2005. *Transnational America: Feminisms, Diasporas, Neoliberalisms*. Durham, NC: Duke University Press.

Grewal, Inderpal, and Caren Kaplan. 1994. "Introduction: Transnational Feminist Practices and Questions of Postmodernity." In *Scattered Hegemonies: Postmodernity and Transnational Feminist Practices*, ed. Inderpal Grewal and Caren Kaplan. Minneapolis: University of Minnesota Press.

Gurr, Ted Robert. 2006. "Economic Factors." In *The Roots of Terrorism*, ed. Louise Richardson. New York: Routledge.

Habermas, Jürgen. 1996. "Three Normative Models of Democracy." In *Democracy and Difference: Contesting the Boundaries of the Political*, ed. Seyla Benhabib. Princeton, NJ: Princeton University Press.

Hafez, Mohammed M. 2006a. "Dying to be Martyrs: The Symbolic Dimension of Suicide Terrorism." In *Root Causes of Suicide Terrorism: The Globalization of Martyrdom*, ed. Ami Pedahzur. New York: Routledge.

———. 2006b. "Rationality, Culture, and Structure in the Making of Suicide Bombers: A Preliminary Theoretical Synthesis and Illustrative Case Study." *Studies in Conflict and Terrorism* 29: 165–85.

Halberstam, Judith. 1998. *Female Masculinity*. Durham, NC: Duke University Press.

———. 2005. *In a Queer Time and Place: Transgender Bodies, Subcultural Lives*. New York: New York University Press.

————. 2011. *The Queer Art of Failure*. Durham, NC: Duke University Press.

Hale, C. Jacob. 1998. "Consuming the Living, Dis(re)membering the Dead in the Butch/ FTM Borderlands." *GLQ* 4, no. 2: 311–48.

Hall, Stuart. 1980. "Encoding/Decoding." In *Culture, Media, Language: Working Papers in Cultural Studies, 1972–1979*, ed. Stuart Hall, Dorothy Hobson, Andrew Lowe and Paul Willis. New York: Routledge.

————. 1996a. "Gramsci's Relevance for the Study of Race and Ethnicity." In *Stuart Hall: Critical Dialogues in Cultural Studies*, ed. David Morley and Kuan-Hsing Chen. New York: Routledge.

————. 1996b. "The Problem of Ideology: Marxism without Guarantees." In *Stuart Hall: Critical Dialogues in Cultural Studies*, ed. David Morley and Kuan-Hsing Chen. New York: Routledge.

Hannah, Matthew. 2008. "Spaces of Exception and Unexceptionability." In *War, Citizenship, Territory*, ed. Deborah Cowen and Emily Gilbert. New York: Routledge.

Hassan, Nasra. 2006. "Suicide Terrorism." In *The Roots of Terrorism*, ed. Louise Richardson. New York: Routledge.

Hayward, Eva. 2008. "More Lessons from a Starfish: Prefixial Flesh and Transpeciated Selves." *Women's Studies Quarterly* 36, nos. 3–4: 64–85.

Hebdige, Dick. 1979. *Subculture: The Meaning of Style*. New York: Routledge.

Hindess, Barry. 2005. "Citizenship and Empire." In *Sovereign Bodies: Citizens, Migrants, and States in the Postcolonial World*, ed. Thomas Blom Hansen and Finn Stepputat. Princeton, NJ: Princeton University Press.

Hines, Sally. 2009. "(Trans)Forming Gender: Social Change and Transgender Citizenship." In *Intimate Citizenship: Gender, Sexualities, Politics*, ed. Elżbieta H. Olesky. New York: Routledge.

Hoang, Kimberly Kay. 2010. "Economies of Emotion, Familiarity, Fantasy, and Desire: Emotional Labor in Ho Chi Ming City's Sex Industry." In *Intimate Labors: Cultures, Technologies, and the Politics of Care*, ed. Eileen Boris and Rhacel Salazar Parreñas. Stanford, CA: Stanford University Press.

Hondagneu-Sotelo, Pierrette. 2001. *Doméstica: Immigrant Workers Cleaning and Caring in the Shadows of Affluence*. Berkeley: University of California Press.

Honig, Bonnie. 1993. *Political Theory and the Displacement of Politics*. Ithaca, NY: Cornell University Press.

————. 2001. *Democracy and the Foreigner*. Princeton, NJ: Princeton University Press.

Howe, Cymene, Susanna Zaraysky, and Lois Lorentzen. 2008. "Transgender Sex Workers and Sexual Transmigration between Guadalajara and San Francisco." *Latin American Perspectives* 35, no. 1: 31–50.

Human Rights Watch. 2002. *Erased in a Moment: Suicide Bombing Attacks against Israeli Civilians*. New York: Human Rights Watch.

International Committee for Prostitutes' Rights. 1989. "World Charter for Prostitutes' Rights." In *A Vindication of the Rights of Whores*, ed. Gail Pheterson. Seattle: Seal.

Irving, Dan. 2013. "Normalized Transgressions: Legitimizing the Transsexual Body as

Productive." In *The Transgender Studies Reader 2*, ed. Susan Stryker and Aren Z. Aizura. New York: Routledge.

Isin, Engin F. 2002. *Being Political: Genealogies of Citizenship*. Minneapolis: University of Minnesota Press.

———. 2008. "Theorizing Acts of Citizenship." In *Acts of Citizenship*, ed. Engin F. Isin and Greg M. Nielsen. New York: Zed.

———. 2009. "Citizenship in Flux: The Figure of the Activist Citizen." *Subjectivity* 29: 367–88.

Isin, Engin F., and Melissa L. Finn. 2008. "Bombs, Bodies, Acts: The Banalization of Suicide." In *War, Citizenship, Territory*, ed. Deborah Cowen and Emily Gilbert. New York: Routledge.

Isin, Engin F., and Greg M. Nielsen, eds. 2008a. *Acts of Citizenship*. New York: Zed.

———. 2008b. "Introduction." In *Acts of Citizenship*, ed. Engin F. Isin and Greg M. Nielsen. New York: Zed.

Isin, Engin F., and Kim Rygiel. 2007. "Abject Spaces: Frontiers, Zones, Camps." In *The Logics of Biopower and the War on Terror: Living, Dying, Surviving*, ed. Elizabeth Dauphinee and Cristina Masters. New York: Palgrave Macmillan.

Isin, Engin F., and Bryan S. Turner, eds. 2002. *Handbook of Citizenship Studies*. Thousand Oaks, CA: Sage.

Isin, Engin F., and Patricia K. Wood. 1999. *Citizenship and Identity*. Thousand Oaks, CA: Sage.

Jean-Klein, Iris. 2000. "Mothercraft, Statecraft, and Subjectivity in the Palestinian Intifada." *American Ethnologist* 27, no. 1: 100–27.

Johnson, Chalmers. 2004. *The Sorrows of Empire: Militarism, Secrecy, and the End of the Republic*. New York: Metropolitan.

Johnson, Mark. 1997. *Beauty and Power: Transgendering and Cultural Transformation in the Southern Philippines*. New York: Berg.

Juang, Richard M. 2006. "Transgendering the Politics of Recognition." In *Transgender Rights*, ed. Paisley Currah, Richard M. Juang, and Shannon Price Minter. Minneapolis: University of Minnesota Press.

Juergensmeyer, Mark. 2003. *Terror in the Mind of God: The Global Rise of Religious Violence*. Berkeley: University of California Press.

Jung, Moon-Kie, João H. Costa Vargas, and Eduardo Bonilla-Silva, eds. 2011. *State of White Supremacy: Racism, Governance, and the United States*. Stanford, CA: Stanford University Press.

Katsulis, Yasmina. 2008. *Sex Work and the City: The Social Geography of Health and Society in Tijuana, Mexico*. Austin: University of Texas Press.

Kelley, Robin D. G. 1994. *Race Rebels: Culture, Politics, and the Black Working Class*. New York: Free Press.

Kempadoo, Kamala. 1998a. "Introduction: Globalizing Sex Workers' Rights." In *Global Sex Workers: Rights, Resistance, and Redefinition*, ed. Kamala Kempadoo and Jo Doezema. New York: Routledge.

———. 1998b. "The Migrant Tightrope: Experiences from the Caribbean." In *Global Sex Workers: Rights, Resistance, and Redefinition*, ed. Kamala Kempadoo and Jo Doezema. New York: Routledge.

———. 1999. "Continuities and Change: Five Centuries of Prostitution in the Caribbean." In *Sun, Sex, and Gold: Tourism and Sex Work in the Caribbean*, ed. Kamala Kempadoo. Boulder, CO: Rowman and Littlefield.

Kempadoo, Kamala, and Jo Doezema, eds. 1998. *Global Sex Workers: Rights, Resistance, and Redefinition*. New York: Routledge.

Kempadoo, Kamala, and Ranya Ghuma. 1999. "For the Children: Trends in International Policies and Law on Sex Tourism." In *Sun, Sex, and Gold: Tourism and Sex Work in the Caribbean*, ed. Kamala Kempadoo. Boulder, CO: Rowman and Littlefield.

Khosrokhavar, Farhad. 2005. *Suicide Bombers: Allah's New Martyrs*. Ann Arbor: Pluto.

Kinder, Marsha. 2000. "From Mutation to Morphing: Cultural Transformation from Greek Myths to Children's Media Culture." In *Meta-Morphing: Visual Transformation and the Culture of Quick-Change*, ed. Vivian Sobchack. Minneapolis: University of Minnesota Press.

Kirkpatrick, R. George, George N. Katsiaficas, and Mary Lou Emery. 1980. "Critical Theory and the Limits of Sociological Positivism." *Quarterly Journal of Ideology* (Winter): 7–17.

Kristeva, Julia. 1982. *Powers of Horror: An Essay on Abjection*, trans. Leon S. Roudiez. New York: Columbia University Press.

Kulick, Don. 1998. *Travesti: Sex, Gender, and Culture among Brazilian Transgendered Prostitutes*. Chicago: University of Chicago Press.

Kymlicka, Will. 1995. *Multicultural Citizenship: A Liberal Theory of Minority Rights*. New York: Oxford University Press.

Laclau, Ernesto, and Chantal Mouffe. 1985. *Hegemony and Socialist Strategy: Towards a Radical Democratic Politics*. New York: Verso.

Lan, Pei-Chia. 2006. *Global Cinderellas: Migrant Domestics and Newly Rich Employers in Taiwan*. Durham, NC: Duke University Press.

Lavie, Smadar, and Ted Swedenburg. 1996. "Between and among the Boundaries of Culture: Bridging Text and Lived Experience in the Third Timespace." *Cultural Studies* 10, no. 1: 154–79.

Law, Lisa. 2000. *Prostitution in Southeast Asia: The Place of Desire in a Time of* AIDS. New York: Routledge.

Lears, T. J. Jackson. 1985. "The Concept of Cultural Hegemony: Problems and Possibilities." *American Historical Review* 90: 567–93.

Lee, Bruce. 2011. *Tao of Jeet Kune Do*. Valencia, CA: Black Belt.

Leigh, Carol. 1997. "Inventing Sex Work." In *Whores and Other Feminists*, ed. Jill Nagle. New York: Routledge.

Levine, Philippa. 2003. *Prostitution, Race, and Politics: Policing Venereal Disease in the British Empire*. New York: Routledge.

Ling, L. H. M. 2010. "Who Is an American?" *International Political Sociology* 4, no. 1: 99–103.

Lipsitz, George. 1998. *The Possessive Investment in Whiteness: How White People Profit from Identity Politics*. Philadelphia: Tempe University Press.

Lorenz-Meyer, Dagmar. 2004. "Addressing the Politics of Location: Strategies in Feminist Epistemology and Their Relevance to Research Undertaken from a Feminist Perspective." In *Women Scholars and Institutions: Proceedings of the International Conference, Volume 13B*, ed. Sona Štrbánová, Ida H. Stamhuis, and Kateřina Mojsejová. Prague: Research Center for History of Sciences and Humanities.

Lyon, David. 2001. "Under My Skin: From Identification Papers to Body Surveillance." In *Documenting Individual Identity: The Development of State Practices in the Modern World*, ed. Jane Caplan and John Torpey. Princeton, NJ: Princeton University Press.

MacKinnon, Catharine A. 1989. *Toward a Feminist Theory of the State*. Cambridge, MA: Harvard University Press.

Mahmood, Saba. 2001. "Feminist Theory, Embodiment, and the Docile Agent: Some Reflections on Egyptian Islamic Revival." *Cultural Anthropology* 16, no. 2: 202–36.

———. 2005. *Politics of Piety: The Islamic Revival and the Feminist Subject*. Princeton, NJ: Princeton University Press.

Mamdani, Mahmood. 2002. "Good Muslim, Bad Muslim: A Political Perspective on Culture and Terrorism." In *Critical Views of September 11: Analyses from around the World*, ed. Eric Hershberg and Kevin W. Moore. New York: New Press.

Manalansan, Martin F., IV. 2003. *Global Divas: Filipina Gay Men in the Diaspora*. Durham, NC: Duke University Press.

———. 2006. "Queer Intersections: Sexuality and Gender in Migration Studies." *International Migration Review* 40, no. 1: 224–49.

Martinez, Teresa. 1997. "Popular Culture as Oppositional Culture: Rap as Resistance." *Sociological Perspectives* 40, no. 2: 265–86.

Mbembe, Achille. 2003. "Necropolitics," trans. Libby Meintjes. *Public Culture* 15, no. 1: 11–40.

McIntosh Peggy. 1990. "White Privilege: Unpacking the Invisible Knapsack." *Independent School* 49, no. 2: 31–35.

McNevin, Anne. 2006. "Political Belonging in a Neoliberal Era: The Struggle of the Sans-Papiers." *Citizenship Studies* 10, no. 2: 135–51.

Mellon, Cynthia. 1999. "A Human Rights Perspective on the Sex Trade in the Caribbean and Beyond." In *Sun, Sex, and Gold: Tourism and Sex Work in the Caribbean*, ed. Kamala Kempadoo. Boulder, CO: Rowman and Littlefield.

Mercer, Kobena. 1997. "Just Looking for Trouble: Robert Mapplethorpe and Fantasies of Race." In *Dangerous Liaisons: Gender, Nation, and Postcolonial Perspectives*, ed. Anne McClintock, Aamir Mufti, and Ella Shohat. Minneapolis: University of Minnesota Press.

Miller, Toby. 1993. *The Well-Tempered Self: Citizenship, Culture, and the Postmodern Subject*. Baltimore: Johns Hopkins University Press.

———. 2006. *Cultural Citizenship: Cosmopolitanism, Consumerism, and Television in a Neoliberal Age*. Philadelphia: Temple University Press.

Mintz, Alex, J. Tyson Chatagnier, and David J. Brulé. 2006. "Being Bin Laden: An Applied

Decision Analysis Procedure for Analyzing and Predicting Terrorist Decisions." In *Root Causes of Suicide Terrorism: The Globalization of Martyrdom*, ed. Ami Pedahzur. New York: Routledge.

Moallem, Minoo. 2005. *Between Warrior Brother and Veiled Sister: Islamic Fundamentalism and the Politics of Patriarchy in Iran*. Berkeley: University of California Press.

———. 2006. "Feminist Scholarship and the Internationalization of Women's Studies." *Feminist Studies* 32, no. 2: 332–51.

Moghadam, Assaf. 2006a. "The Roots of Suicide Terrorism: A Multi-Causal Approach." In *Root Causes of Suicide Terrorism: The Globalization of Martyrdom*, ed. Ami Pedahzur. New York: Routledge.

———. 2006b. "Suicide Terrorism, Occupation, and the Globalization of Martyrdom: A Critique of Dying to Win." *Studies in Conflict and Terrorism* 29, no. 8: 707–29.

Morley, David, and Kuan-Hsing Chen, eds. 1996. *Stuart Hall: Critical Dialogues in Cultural Studies*. New York: Routledge.

Mouffe, Chantal. 1993. *The Return of the Political*. New York: Verso.

Mulvey, Laura. 1975. "Visual Pleasure and Narrative Cinema." *Screen* 16, no. 3: 6–18.

Muñoz, Jose Esteban. 2009. *Cruising Utopia: The Then and There of Queer Futurity*. New York: New York University Press.

Naaman, Dorit. 2007. "Brides of Palestine/Angels of Death: Media, Gender, and Performance in the Case of the Palestinian Female Suicide Bombers." *Signs* 32, no. 4: 933–55.

Najmabadi, Afsaneh. 2008. "Transing and Transpassing across Sex-Gender Walls in Iran." *Women's Studies Quarterly* 36, nos. 3–4: 23–42.

———. 2013. "Reading Transsexuality in 'Gay' Tehran (around 1979)." In *The Transgender Studies Reader 2*, ed. Susan Stryker and Aren Z. Aizura. New York: Routledge.

Neeley, Barbara. 1993. *Blanche on the Lam*. New York: Penguin.

Nelson, James L. 1998. "The Silence of the Bioethicists: Ethical and Political Aspects of Managing Gender Dysphoria." *GLQ* 4, no. 2: 213–30.

Nyers, Peter. 2003. "Abject Cosmopolitanism: The Politics of Protection in the Anti-Deportation Movement." *Third World Quarterly* 24, no. 6: 1069–93.

O'Brien, Michelle. 2013. "Tracing This Body: Transsexuality, Pharmaceuticals, and Capitalism." In *The Transgender Studies Reader 2*, ed. Susan Stryker and Aren Z. Aizura. New York: Routledge.

Ong, Aihwa. 1996. "Cultural Citizenship as Subject-Making." *Current Anthropology* 37, no. 5: 737–62.

———. 1999. *Flexible Citizenship: The Cultural Logics of Transnationality*. Durham, NC: Duke University Press.

———. 2003. *Buddha Is Hiding: Refugees, Citizenship, the New America*. Berkeley: University of California Press.

———. 2005. "Splintering Cosmopolitanism: Asian Immigrants and Zones of Autonomy in the American West." In *Sovereign Bodies: Citizens, Migrants, and States in the Postcolonial World*, ed. Thomas Blom Hansen and Finn Stepputat. Princeton, NJ: Princeton University Press.

———. 2006. *Neoliberalism as Exception: Mutations in Citizenship and Sovereignty*. Durham, NC: Duke University Press.

O'Rourke, Lindsey A. 2009. "What's Special about Female Suicide Terrorism?" *Security Studies* 18: 681–718.

Pape, Robert. 2005. *Dying to Win: The Strategic Logic of Suicide Terrorism*. New York: Random House.

Parreñas, Rhacel Salazar. 2001. *Servants of Globalization: Women, Migration, and Domestic Work*. Stanford, CA: Stanford University Press.

———. 2008. *The Force of Domesticity: Filipina Migrants and Globalization*. New York: New York University.

———. 2010. "Cultures of Flirtation: Sex and the Moral Boundaries of Filipina Migrant Hostesses in Tokyo." In *Intimate Labors: Cultures, Technologies, and the Politics of Care*, ed. Eileen Boris and Rhacel Salazar Parreñas. Stanford, CA: Stanford University Press.

———. 2012. "The Reproductive Labour of Migrant Workers." *Global Networks* 12, no. 2: 269–75.

Pateman, Carole. 1988. *The Sexual Contract*. Stanford, CA: Stanford University Press.

Patton, Cindy. 2002. *Globalizing AIDS*. Minneapolis: University of Minnesota Press.

Pedahzur, Ami, 2005. *Suicide Terrorism*. Cambridge: Polity.

Pedahzur, Ami, Arie Perliger, and Leonard Weinberg. 2003. "Altruism and Fatalism: the Characteristics of Palestinian Suicide Terrorists." *Deviant Behavior* 24: 405–23.

Penttinen, Elina. 2008. *Globalization, Prostitution, and Sex-Trafficking: Corporeal Politics*. New York: Routledge.

Perez, Nancy. 2011. "Corporeal Citizenship: Embodying Domestic Workers' Bill of Rights." Unpublished ms., Arizona State University, Tempe, AZ.

———. 2014. "Immigrant Domestic Worker Activism." Unpublished ms., Arizona State University, Tempe, AZ.

Petzer, Shane A., and Gordon M. Issacs. 1998. "SWEAT: The Development and Implementation of a Sex Worker Advocacy and Intervention Program in Post-Apartheid South Africa." In *Global Sex Workers: Rights, Resistance, and Redefinition*, ed. Kamala Kempadoo and Jo Doezema. New York: Routledge.

Phelan, Shane. 2001. *Sexual Strangers: Gays, Lesbians, and Dilemmas of Citizenship*. Philadelphia: Temple University Press.

Pheterson, Gail, ed. 1989a. *A Vindication of the Rights of Whores*. Seattle: Seal.

———. 1989b. "Not Repeating History." In *A Vindication of the Rights of Whores*, ed. Gail Pheterson. Seattle: Seal.

———. 1993. "The Whore Stigma: Female Dishonor and Male Unworthiness." *Social Text*, no. 37: 39–64.

Polan, Dana. 1993. "The Public's Fear; or, Media as Monster in Habermas, Negt, and Kluge." In *The Phantom Public Sphere*, ed. Bruce Robbins. Minneapolis: University of Minnesota Press.

Prosser, Jay. 1998. *Second Skins: The Body Narratives of Transsexuality*. New York: Columbia University Press.

Puar, Jasbir K. 2007. *Terrorist Assemblages: Homonationalism in Queer Times*. Durham, NC: Duke University Press.

Rajan, V. G. Julie. 2011. *Women Suicide Bombers: Narratives of Violence*. New York: Routledge.

Rajaram, Prem Kumar, and Carl Grundy-Warr. 2004. "The Irregular Migrant as Homo Sacer: Migration and Detention in Australia, Malaysia, and Thailand." *International Migration* 42, no. 1: 33–63.

Rancière, Jacques. 1999. *Dis-agreement: Politics and Philosophy*. Minneapolis: University of Minnesota Press.

———. 2004. "Who Is the Subject of the Rights of Man?" *South Atlantic Quarterly* 103, nos. 2–3: 297–310.

Reddy, Chandan. 2011. *Freedom with Violence: Race, Sexuality, and the U.S. State*. Durham, NC: Duke University Press.

Reuter, Christoph. 2004. *My Life is a Weapon: A Modern History of Suicide Bombing*. Princeton, NJ: Princeton University Press.

Richardson, Louise. 2006. "The Roots of Terrorism: An Overview." In *The Roots of Terrorism*, ed. Louise Richardson. New York: Routledge.

Rofel, Lisa. 2007. *Desiring China: Experiments in Neoliberalism, Sexuality, and Public Culture*. Durham, NC: Duke University Press.

Romero, Mary. 1992. *Maid in the U.S.A.* New York: Routledge.

———. 2012. "The Real Help." *Contexts* 11, no. 2: 54–56.

Rosaldo, Renato. 1997. "Cultural Citizenship, Inequality, and Multiculturalism." In *Latino Cultural Citizenship: Claiming Identity, Space, and Rights*, ed. William V. Flores and Rina Benmayor. Boston: Beacon.

Rose, Nikolas. 1999. *Powers of Freedom: Reframing Political Thought*. New York: Cambridge University Press.

Rosen, David M. 2005. *Armies of the Young: Child Soldiers in War and Terrorism*. New Brunswick, NJ: Rutgers University Press.

Rosenberger, John. 2003. "Discerning the Behavior of the Suicide Bomber: The Role of Vengeance." *Journal of Religion and Health* 42, no. 1: 13–20.

Ross, Becki. 2010. "Sex and (Evacuation from) the City: The Moral and Legal Regulation of Sex Workers in Vancouver's West End, 1975–1985." In *Intimate Labors: Cultures, Technologies, and the Politics of Care*, ed. Eileen Boris and Rhacel Salazar Parreñas. Stanford, CA: Stanford University Press.

Rubin, Gayle. 1975. "The Traffic in Women: Notes on the 'Political Economy' of Sex." In *Toward an Anthropology of Women*, ed. Rayna R. Reiter. New York: Monthly Review Press.

Rubin, Henry. 2003. *Self-Made Men: Identity and Embodiment among Transsexual Men*. Nashville, TN: Vanderbilt University Press.

Rushbrook, Dereka. 2002. "Cities, Queer Space, and the Cosmopolitan Tourist." GLQ 8, nos. 1–2: 183–206.

Sageman, Marc. 2006. "Islam and al Qaeda." In *Root Causes of Suicide Terrorism: The Globalization of Martyrdom*, ed. Ami Pedahzur. New York: Routledge.

Said, Edward. 1979. *Orientalism*. New York: Vintage.

Salter, Mark B. 2008. "When the Exception Becomes the Rule: Borders, Sovereignty, and Citizenship." *Citizenship Studies* 12, no. 4: 365–80.

Sandel, Michael. 1998. *Democracy's Discontent: America's Search of a Public Philosophy*. Cambridge, MA: Harvard University Press.

Sandoval, Chela. 2000. *Methodology of the Oppressed*. Minneapolis: University of Minnesota Press.

Sanger, Tam. 2008. "Trans Governmentality: The Production and Regulation of Gendered Subjectivities." *Journal of Gender Studies* 17, no. 1: 41–53.

Schilt, Kristen. 2006. "Just One of the Guys: How Transmen Make Gender Visible at Work." *Gender and Society* 20, no. 4: 465–90.

Schrock, Douglas, Lori Reid, and Emily M. Boyd. 2005. "Transsexuals' Embodiment of Womanhood." *Gender and Society* 19, no. 3: 317–35.

Schweitzer, Yoram. 2006. "Al-Qaeda and the Global Epidemic of Suicide Attacks." In *Root Causes of Suicide Terrorism: The Globalization of Martyrdom*, ed. Ami Pedahzur. New York: Routledge.

Scott, James C. 1985. *Weapons of the Weak: Everyday Forms of Peasant Resistance*. New Haven, CT: Yale University Press.

———. 1990. *Domination and the Arts of Resistance: Hidden Transcripts*. New Haven, CT: Yale University Press.

———. 1998. *Seeing like a State: How Certain Schemes to Improve the Human Condition Have Failed*. New Haven, CT: Yale University Press.

———. 2009. *The Art of Not Being Governed: An Anarchist History of Upland Southeast Asia*. New Haven, CT: Yale University Press.

———. 2012. *Two Cheers for Anarchism: Six Easy Pieces on Autonomy, Dignity, and Meaningful Work and Play*. Princeton, NJ: Princeton University Press.

Sedgwick, Eve Kosofsky. 1997. "A Response to C. Jacob Hale." *Social Text* 15, nos. 3–4: 237–39.

Sereewat, Sudarat. 1985. *Prostitution, Thai-European Connection: An Action-Oriented Study*. Geneva: World Council of Churches.

Shah, Hina, and Marci Seville. 2012. "Domestic Worker Organizing: Building a Contemporary Movement for Dignity and Power." *Albany Law Review* 75, no. 1: 413–47.

Shimizu, Celine Parreñas. 2007. *The Hypersexuality of Race: Performing Asian/American Women on Screen and Scene*. Durham, NC: Duke University Press.

Siu, Lok C. D. 2005. *Memories of a Future Home: Diasporic Citizenship of Chinese in Panama*. Stanford, CA: Stanford University Press.

Sjoberg, Laura, Grace D. Cooke, and Stacy Reiter Neal. 2011. "Introduction: Women, Gender, and Terrorism." In *Women, Gender, and Terrorism*, ed. Laura Sjoberg and Caron E. Gentry. Athens: University of Georgia Press.

Snorton, C. Riley, and Jin Haritaworn. 2013. "Trans Necropolitics: A Transnational Reflection on Violence, Death, and the Trans of Color Afterlife." In *The Transgender Studies Reader 2*, ed. Susan Stryker and Aren Z. Aizura. New York: Routledge.

Sobchack, Vivian. 2000a. "'At the Still Point of the Turning World': Meta-Morphing and Meta-Stasis." In *Meta-Morphing: Visual Transformation and the Culture of Quick-Change*, ed. Vivian Sobchack. Minneapolis: University of Minnesota Press.

————, ed. 2000b. *Meta-Morphing: Visual Transformation and the Culture of Quick-Change.* Minneapolis: University of Minnesota Press.

Somers, Margaret R. 2008. *Genealogies of Citizenship: Markets, Statelessness, and the Right to Have Rights.* New York: Cambridge University Press.

Spade, Dean. 2011. *Normal Life: Administrative Violence, Critical Trans Politics, and the Limits of Law.* Brooklyn: South End.

Spanger, Marlene. 2002. "Black Prostitutes in Denmark." In *Transnational Prostitution: Changing Global Patterns,* ed. Susanne Thorbek and Bandana Pattanaik. New York: Zed.

Sprinzak, Ehud. 2000. "Rational Fanatics." *Foreign Policy* 120 (September–October): 66–73.

Stasiulus, Daiva K., and Abigail B. Bakan. 2003. *Negotiating Citizenship: Migrant Women in Canada and the Global System.* New York: Palgrave Macmillan.

Stockett, Kathryn. 2009. *The Help.* New York: Penguin.

Stoddart, Mark C. J. 2007. "Ideology, Hegemony, Discourse: A Critical Review of Theories of Knowledge and Power." *Social Thought and Research* 28: 191–225.

Stoller, Robert. 1975. *Sex and Gender, Volume II: The Transsexual Experiment.* New York: Jason Aronson.

Stone, Jennie, and Katherine Pattillo. 2011. "Al-Qaeda's Use of Female Suicide Bombers in Iraq: A Case Study." In *Women, Gender, and Terrorism,* ed. Laura Sjoberg and Caron E. Gentry. Athens: University of Georgia Press.

Stryker, Susan. 2013. "*Kaming Mga Talyada (We Who Are Sexy)*: The Transsexual Whiteness of Christine Jorgensen in the (Post)colonial Philippines." In *The Transgender Studies Reader 2,* ed. Susan Stryker and Aren Z. Aizura. New York: Routledge.

Stryker, Susan, and Aren Z. Aizura. 2013. "Introduction: Transgender Studies 2.0." In *The Transgender Studies Reader 2,* ed. Susan Stryker and Aren Z. Aizura. New York: Routledge.

Sturken, Marita. 2007. *Tourists of History: Memory, Kitsch, and Consumerism from Oklahoma City to Ground Zero.* Durham, NC: Duke University Press.

————. 2012. "Foreword." In *Commodity Activism: Cultural Resistance in Neoliberal Times,* ed. Sarah Banet-Weiser and Roopali Mukherjee. New York: New York University Press.

Thorbek, Susanne, and Bandana Pattanaik, eds. 2002. *Transnational Prostitution: Changing Patterns in a Global Context.* New York: Zed.

Tilly, Charles. 1984. "Social Movements and National Politics." In *State-Making and Social Movements: Essays in History and Theory,* ed. Charles Bright and Susan Harding. Ann Arbor: University of Michigan Press.

Trend, David, ed. 1996. *Radical Democracy: Identity, Citizenship, and the State.* New York: Routledge.

Valentine, David. 2007. *Imagining Transgender: An Ethnography of a Category.* Durham, NC: Duke University Press.

Varsanyi, Monica. 2006. "Interrogating 'Urban Citizenship' vis-à-vis Undocumented Migration." *Citizenship Studies* 10, no. 2: 229–49.

Victor, Barbara. 2003. *Army of Roses: Inside the World of Palestinian Women Suicide Bombers.* Emmaus, PA: Rodale.

Walters, William. 2008. "Acts of Demonstration: Mapping the Territory of (Non-) Citizenship." In *Acts of Citizenship,* ed. Engin F. Isin and Greg M. Nielsen. New York: Zed.

Ward, Jane. 2010. "Gender Labor: Transmen, Femmes, and Collective Work of Transgression." In *Intimate Labors: Culture, Technologies, and the Politics of Care,* ed. Eileen Boris and Rhacel Salazar Parreñas. Stanford, CA: Stanford University Press.

Wasko, Janet. 2001. *Understanding Disney: The Manufacture of Fantasy.* Cambridge: Polity.

Weber, Cynthia. 2010. "Citizenship, Security, Humanity." *International Political Sociology* 4, no. 1: 80–85.

———. 2011. *"I Am an American": Filming the Fear of Difference.* Chicago: University of Chicago Press.

Weinberg, Leonard. 2006. "Democracy and Terrorism." In *The Roots of Terrorism,* ed. Louise Richardson. New York: Routledge.

Weinberg, Martin, Frances Shaver, and Colin J. Williams. 1999. "Gendered Sex Work in the San Francisco Tenderloin." *Archives of Sexual Behavior* 28, no. 6: 503–21.

White, Melanie. 2008. "Can an Act of Citizenship Be Creative?" In *Acts of Citizenship,* ed. Engin F. Isin and Greg M. Nielsen. New York: Zed.

Wilchins, Riki Anne. 1997. *Read My Lips: Sexual Subversion and the End of Gender.* Ithaca, NY: Firebrand.

Wolf, Mark J. P. 2000. "A Brief History of Morphing." In *Meta-Morphing: Visual Transformation and the Culture of Quick-Change,* ed. Vivian Sobchack. Minneapolis: University of Minnesota Press.

Wolin, Sheldon. 1960. *Politics and Vision: Continuity and Innovation in Western Political Thought.* Boston: Little, Brown.

Young, Iris Marion. 1989. "Polity and Group Difference: A Critique of the Ideal of Universal Citizenship." *Ethics* 99: 250–74.

———. 1990. *Justice and the Politics of Difference.* Princeton, NJ: Princeton University Press.

Young, Robert J. C. 2001. *Postcolonialism: An Historical Introduction.* Malden, MA: Wiley-Blackwell.

Yúdice, George. 2001. "From Hybridity to Policy: For a Purposeful Cultural Studies." In *Consumers and Citizens: Globalization and Multicultural Conflicts,* trans. George Yúdice. Minneapolis: University of Minnesota Press.

Zivi, Karen. 2011. *Making Rights Claims: A Practice of Democratic Citizenship.* New York: Oxford University Press.

Index

abject cosmopolitanism, use of term, 77
abjection: as act of force, 15; agency
  and, 5, 14–20, 26, 57; citizenship and,
  42–43, 49–57; complicity and, 248;
  identity and, 16; improvisation and,
  16; levels of meaning, 14–16; negotiation and, 53–54; neoliberal, 110, 113,
  120–21, 136–39, 143, 144, 147; normality and, 15–17, 18, 38–39, 52, 54–55, 71,
  75–76, 86, 104–11, 120, 128, 130, 136,
  147, 150–51, 155, 189, 196–97, 236–44,
  247; rights and, 29; use of term, 14, 23.
  See also calculated abjection
abject spaces, 64, 76–77, 79
Action Committee of Non-Status Algerians (CASS), 77
activism. See social activism
ACT UP. See AIDS Coalition to Unleash
  Power
Afghanistan, Soviet invasion of, 197–98
Agamben, Giorgio: on bare life, 67–69,
  72–76, 81; critics of, 70, 71, 76–79, 100;
  on political agency, 69, 76, 87, 100

agency: abjection and, 5, 14–20, 26; in
  camp, 68; creative, 27; nonlinear, 152;
  state-evading, 10–11; in suicide
  bombing, 195, 197, 200, 205, 227; un-
  predictable, 16. See also democratic
  agency; ingenious agency; political
  agency
AIDS Coalition to Unleash Power (ACT
  UP), 181
Aizura, Aren, 161, 188
Ajl, Max, 239–40
Akhbar, Al- (journal), 207
Akhras, Ayat, 18, 191–94, 227
Allen, Lori, 228
America, ideal of, 19–20, 47
American Ad Council, 1–4
American exceptionalism, 19
Andoni, Lamis, 222
Andrijasevic, Rutvica, 111–12, 134–35
Ang, Ien, 46–47, 54–55, 130
antideportation campaigns, 77
antitrafficking assemblages, 111–21
Apostolidis, Paul, 23

appropriation: of economic citizenship, 105, 106–7, 110, 113, 116, 119, 121–35, 136, 144–47; of gendered citizenship, 165–78, 186–89; ingenious, 57, 71, 83, 86, 228, 243, 254–56; of liberal citizenship script, 18, 27, 31, 37–39, 41, 42–43, 48, 49–57, 247, 248, 254–55, 258n9; of life itself, 195–98, 200, 227–35, 240, 242; of neoliberalism, 48, 96, 110, 144, 242; of nonexistent rights, 29, 91–100; of political citizenship, 68, 70–71, 76, 79, 81, 84–86, 88, 92, 96–100; of sacrificial violence, 201–10, 238, 243

Araj, Bader, 228

Arendt, Hannah, 69

Association of Autonomous Women Workers, 141

Association of Black Women Historians, 64

Bakan, Abigail, 84–85

Banet-Weiser, Sarah, 143, 237

Bapat, Sheila, 89

bare life, 67–69, 72–76, 78, 81; political, resurrection of, 76–79

Basic Income Grant (BIG), 48

Bayat, Asef, 6–8, 30, 56, 257n6

BDS movement. See boycott, divestment, and sanctions (BDS) movement

Bell, Derrick, 249

Bell, Shannon, 23, 109

belonging. See inclusion and belonging

Bergson, Henri, 219

Berlant, Lauren, 197

Bernstein, Elizabeth, 113–20, 121, 126, 127, 262n8

Beverly LeHaye Institute, 117

Beyond Gated Politics (Coles), 21

Bhabha, Homi, 199–200

Bhargava, Rajeev, 198

BIG. See Basic Income Grant

biopower, 72, 80–81, 258–59n5

bios: capitalist, 93; script of, 70, 72–76, 78–79, 80, 81, 100; sovereign, 74, 84; sphere of, 69, 93–94

biowelfare, 96–97

Black Skin, White Masks (Fanon), 217

Bloom, Mia, 213, 216

Bodies that Matter (Butler), 163–64

Bordo, Susan, 163

Bornstein, Kate, 173–74

Bourdieu, Pierre, 50

Bower, Lisa, 182

boycott, divestment, and sanctions (BDS) movement, 236–38

Brass, Tom, 10–11

Bread and Roses (film), 101–6

Brennan, Denise, 132

Brown, Jerry, 94

Brown, Wendy, 28, 114, 125

Bukatman, Scott, 160

Bush, George W., 118, 193–94

Butler, Jesse, 215

Butler, Judith, 15, 157, 162–64, 216

Cacho, Lisa Marie, 13, 249

calculated abjection, 108, 110, 122–25, 126–27, 130, 131, 136, 138, 141–42, 145, 147, 196

Califa, Pat, 173

California Homemakers Association, 89

Call Off Your Old Tired Ethics (COYOTE), 137

camp space, 67–68, 72–75, 76, 78, 79

Caring Across Generations campaign, 93, 95, 99

CASS. See Action Committee of Non-Status Algerians

Castronovo, Russ, 2–3

Chang, Grace, 90

Cheah, Pheng, 71, 79, 80, 87, 92–93, 97–98

Chen, Kuan-Hsing, 25

Chin, Christine, 49–51, 63, 87

citizenship: acts of, 77–78, 103, 218–20, 225; commodity consumption and,

37; and consumerism, 22, 37–38, 47, 237–38; as cultural script, 26–27, 248; democratic, 22, 103; economic, 43, 104, 105, 106–7, 113, 116, 119, 136, 138, 145; exclusion from, 41–42, 52, 68–69, 72–74, 78–80, 179, 192, 218, 229; gendered, 43, 149, 153, 165–78; global, 47; improvisation of, 23, 27, 31, 42, 56, 96, 174, 235, 254–55; innocent, 197; insurgent, 77; life script, 44, 197, 198, 200, 228, 229, 230, 231, 232, 237, 242; limits of, 41; narcissism and, 15; noncitizen, 70, 77, 103, 218; nonexistent, 27, 42, 56, 68–69, 83, 96, 123, 137, 165, 235, 248, 254–55, 258n9; normality and, 17; otherness and, 15–16; political, 43, 81, 88, 92, 95; practices of, 4; sacrificial violence and, 211, 225–26; unequal access to, 2. *See also* ingenious citizenship; liberal citizenship

Civil Rights movement, 64

Coalition Against Trafficking in Women, 117

Cohen, Erik, 132

Cold War, 197

Coles, Romand, 21–22, 258n8

Comella, Lynn, 147

commercial morphing. *See under* morphing technologies

commodity activism, 111, 139, 143–47

complicity: domestic employers and, 50; gender normativity and, 152–57, 161–62, 168, 172, 174, 178; of ingenious citizenship, 87, 88, 100, 248; morphing and, 180, 186; in objectification, 122, 128; refusal of, 182, 250; reuse of, 162–65; social change and, 8, 12, 13, 18–19, 29, 43, 55–56, 61–71, 94, 100, 159, 248–49; structural inevitability of, 54, 130, 184–85; suicide bombing and, 196, 200, 201, 210, 228, 231–32; use of term, 53; value-free science and, 215

Concerned Residents of the West End (CROWE), 115

Concerned Women for America, 117

Constable, Nicole, 82–83, 85–86, 98–99

consumerism: academic boycott and, 237–38; citizenship and, 22, 37–38, 47; domestic workers and, 50–52, 89, 93, 99–100; Islamic fundamentalism and, 205, 233; neoliberalism and, 42, 110, 125–30; in Palestine, 204–05, 241–42; sex workers and, 107, 110, 111, 125–30, 131, 142, 143–47; transgender people and, 152–53, 160, 167, 186–89

Consumers and Citizens (García Canclini), 37

contamination: defined, 10; ingenious citizenship and, 87, 88, 253; as instrumentality, 189; purity and, 9–14, 253; reuse of, 12; sacrificial violence and, 231; social change and, 29, 43, 55–56, 94; use of term, 53

corporate culture, 22

COYOTE. *See* Call Off Your Old Tired Ethics

Crenshaw, Martha, 211

critical contextualization, 13; ingenious citizenship and, 29, 66–67; as interpretive strategy, 22–27; liberal citizenship and, 41; rights and, 28–29

Cromwell, Jason, 171, 175–76

CROWE. *See* Concerned Residents of the West End

cultural script, 27, 43, 44, 49. *See under* liberal citizenship

Currah, Paisley, 156, 183

Das Gupta, Monisha, 29, 82, 250

Davis, Joyce, 221

decentering, 22–23, 24, 25, 27, 29

de Certeau, Michel, 70

"Declaration of Independence" (Palestine), 207

Declaration on the Rights of Sex Workers in Europe, 138, 140, 263n16 decolonization, 46, 241

democracy: antidemocratic powers in, 21–22; as democratization, 21; exclusion in, 5; for ingenious appropriation, 254–56; liberal, 2–3; radical, 3, 5

democratic agency, 3–9, 22, 152, 255–56; defined, 3; enacting, 90; in domestic workers' movements, 89–94; ingenious agency and, 5, 12, 17, 19–20, 32, 90–91, 95, 255; in Israeli-Palestine conflict, 236–37; oppositional stance, 250; prescription of, 9, 21, 57, 67, 70, 98, 100, 122; purity and, 250; in sex workers' rights movements, 139–43; in suicide bombing, 217–27; in terrorism research, 217; in trans activism, 152, 180–85

democratic citizenship, 4, 5, 22, 47, 67, 69, 77, 103, 193, 199, 217

democratic cosmopolitanism, use of term, 77

Derrida, Jacques, 53

Diagnostic and Statistical Manual of Mental Disorders (DSM-V), 167, 187

differential oppositional consciousness, use of term, 250

Disney movies, 61

disruption: contamination and, 53; of liberal citizenship script, 41, 52–53

diversity: belonging and, 3; ethnic, 115; patriotism and, 2; sexual, 115, 123, 179, 189

Doezema, Jo, 137–38, 139, 140–41

domestic workers, 23; consumerism and, 50–52, 89, 93, 99–100; entrepreneurialism and, 99–100; Filipina, 82–85, 98–99; global capitalism and, 67, 87; hidden tactics, 70–71, 79–86, 88, 99, 196, 235; human rights and, 17, 74, 91–93, 95–98; Indonesian, 82–83; ingenious agency of, 64, 70–71, 88, 91, 95, 100; ingenious citizenship of, 50–52, 95, 99; labor rights, 79–80,

89, 91–100; liberal citizenship script and, 39; Malaysian modernity project, 49–51, 54, 56, 63, 68, 85; professionalization, 98–99; West Indian, 84–85

Domestic Workers' Association (DWA), 90

Domestic Workers Bill of Rights, 91, 92, 99–100

Domestic Workers Convention (C189), 91–92, 95, 139

Don't Ask, Don't Tell campaigns, 77

DreamWorks, 61

DSM-V. See Diagnostic and Statistical Manual of Mental Disorders

DWA. See Domestic Workers' Association

Dying to Win (Pape), 212

economic script, 43

Edelman, Lee, 249

Edwards, Susan, 126–27

Embracing the Movement for Pinays and Queers (EMPAQ), 151

EMPAQ. See Embracing the Movement for Pinays and Queers (EMPAQ)

"The 'Empire' Strikes Back" (Stone), 182

Employment Non-Discrimination Act (2013), 186

ENDA. See Employment Non-Discrimination Act (2013)

entrepreneurialism: domestic workers and, 99–100; neoliberalism and, 43–44, 48, 109–10, 125–30; in Palestine, 240, 241–42, 243; sex workers and, 105, 107, 110, 111, 115, 119, 120, 125–30, 131, 136, 139, 143–47; transgender people and, 188–89

Equality NOW, 117

European Conference on Sex Work, Human Rights, Labor and Migration, 137–38

exclusion: abjection and, 14, 15, 16, 25, 54; from citizenship, 41–42, 52, 68–69, 72–74, 78–80, 179, 192, 218, 229; in democracy, 5; from global economy, 40; from labor protections, 89, 120

failure, virtues of, 249–50
Fair Labor Standards Act (1938; Final Rule, 2015), 80, 89
Family Research Council, 117
Fanon, Frantz, 124, 199–200, 216, 217–18, 224
Fausto-Sterling, Anne, 172
Feinberg, Leslie, 187–88
female-to-males (FTMs). *See under* transgender people
Ferguson, James, 24, 30, 40, 42, 47, 48, 256
Finn, Melissa, 226–27
Foster, Morris, 215
Foucault, Michel, 45, 107, 114, 154–55, 258n5
freedom as normative, 5–6
French Revolution (1789-1799), 205–7

Gagné, Patricia, 155, 157–58
Gall, Gregor, 137
Gambetta, Diego, 210–11, 214
Gamson, Joshua, 9
Ganzon, Donita, 149–52
García Canclini, Néstor, 37
gay index, 115
gender: binary system, 43, 153, 155, 157–58, 163, 165, 166, 168, 171, 172–74, 177–80, 182, 187; citizenship, 149, 153–55, 165–78; dislocation, 153; dysphoria, 167, 187; identity, 151, 157–59, 162, 167–69, 179, 181–82, 184, 186–89; improvisation, 167, 171, 174, 177, 182; normativity, 149–53, 163, 168, 172, 174, 177, 178; performativity, 162, 164; script, 43–44, 153–54, 157–58, 161, 165–66, 168, 170, 172, 173–74, 177, 178, 188, 264n5; self-identification, 174–75, 187–88; sex vs., use of terms, 264n5. *See also* transgender people

Gender Recognition Act (2005), 179
Gender Trouble (Butler), 162–63
gentrification. *See* urban gentrification
"Girlfriend Experience." *See under* sex workers
GLBTQ rights movement, 181
Glenn, Evelyn Nakano, 47–48, 79–80
global capitalism, 11, 13, 22, 29; domestic workers and, 67, 87; human rights and, 92–93; Islamic fundamentalism and, 205; sex workers and, 112–13, 134, 136, 145; transgender people and, 185. *See also* neoliberalism
global economy, 40, 42, 47, 94, 110, 119, 132, 137. *See also* neoliberalism
Global Sex Workers (Kempadoo/Doezema), 137–38, 140–41
glocalization, 115
Goldhammer, Jesse, 202, 206–9
Gordon, Jennifer, 77
Gramsci, Antonio, 45, 258n3
Grewal, Inderpal, 22, 40, 47
Grundy-Warr, Carl, 73, 74

Hafez, Mohammed, 224, 234, 266n12
Halberstam, Judith, 66, 156, 177–78, 249
Hale, C. Jacob, 173
Hall, Stuart, 53, 258n3
Hamas, 203, 204, 208, 224
Hassan, Nasra, 222
Hazza al-Ghoul, Muhammad, 208, 224
Headless Republic, The (Goldhammer), 202
Hebdige, Dick, 55, 126
hegemony, concept of, 45
Help, The (Stockett book/DreamWorks film), 61–67, 70, 99, 100; criticism of, 64, 67; democratic agency and, 67; ingenious agency in, 61–63, 67; NDWA endorsement, 65–66; as popular cultural product, 61–62, 64, 65–67; themes, 62
Hezbollah, 203
hidden tactics, 70–71, 79–86, 88, 99, 196

hidden transcripts, 9, 55
Hindess, Barry, 46
Hines, Sally, 168, 179
HIV/AIDS, 118, 211, 215
Hoang, Kimberly Kay, 133
homoeroticism, 24–25
homonationalism, 13
Homo Sacer (Agamben), 67–68, 72
homo sacer, concept of, 74, 78
Honig, Bonnie, 19
Howe, Cymene, 153
human rights: domestic workers and, 17,
74, 91–93, 95–98; in Israeli-Palestinian
conflict, 220, 236–37, 238, 244; sex
workers and, 110–11, 113, 137–43, 144,
145, 147; transgender people and, 156,
159, 184

"I Am an American" (ad campaign), 1–4
"I Am an American" (video project), 2–4
ICPR. *See* International Committee for
Prostitutes' Rights
identity: disturbance of, 16, 25; gender,
151, 157–59, 162, 167–69, 179, 181–82,
184, 186–89; Islamic, 195; national, 2;
nation-state and, 223–24; resistance
and, 77; transgender categories,
264n6; victim, 131–32, 135
Idris, Wafa, 207
ILO. *See* International Labor
Organization
improvisation: abjection and, 16; of citizenship, 23, 27, 31, 42, 56, 96, 174, 235,
254–55; in complicity, 12; gender, 167,
171, 174, 177, 182; ingenious, 14, 18, 27,
63–64, 71, 137; of resistance, 6, 8, 17,
43; subcultural, 136; in suicide bombing, 196, 199, 210, 228, 231
"In Bed with a Los Angeles Prostitute"
(*Skyy John Show* episode), 105–6
inclusion and belonging, 3, 5, 68; citizenship and, 226, 235; gender script and,
172; script of *bios* on, 75; spaces of, 17,

37–38, 39, 49, 56–57, 127, 141, 150, 174,
195, 200, 242, 247–48
infrapolitics, 9, 10, 11
ingenious agency, 9–14, 16–19, 27, 39,
49, 51, 57, 247; in collective resistance,
90–91, 138; in commodity activism,
147; democratic agency and, 5, 12, 17,
19–20, 90–91, 95, 255; in domestic
worker activism, 64, 88, 91, 95, 100; in
The Help, 61–62, 63, 67; interstitiality
and, 55; of migrant subjects, 67, 68,
69–70, 71, 77–78, 90–91; negotiation
and, 53; neoliberalism and, 237, 242;
nonexistent rights and, 91–100; of
sex workers, 108, 110, 111, 123, 125,
138, 141; suicide bombing and, 197,
200, 201, 227, 228, 235, 238, 243–44; of
transgender people, 161, 165, 166, 168,
184–85. *See also* calculated abjection;
hidden tactics; morphing technologies; sacrificial violence
ingenious citizenship, 39, 41, 48; abjection and, 179–80; complicity and, 87,
88, 100; contamination and, 87, 88,
253; critical contextualization and,
29; of domestic workers, 50–52, 95,
99; dynamics of, 136, 247; improvisations of, 71, 137; interstitiality in, 55,
71; in neoliberal economy, 87; of sex
workers, 136, 142; social activism and,
20–21, 248, 250–54; subcultural script
of, 233–34; suicide bombing as, 197,
230, 235; of transgender people, 178,
179–80; use of term, 12, 27. *See also* calculated abjection; hidden tactics; morphing technologies; sacrificial violence
ingenious futurity, 19, 254–56
International Bill of Gender Rights, 184
International Committee for Prostitutes'
Rights (ICPR), 137
International Convention on the Protection of the Rights of All Migrant Workers and Members of Their Families, 96

martyrdom, 18, 194, 203–4, 207–9, 224, 234

Masri, Izzidene al, 224

Mbembe, Achille, 197, 218, 220–21, 225

McGaughey, Deanna, 166

McNevin, Anne, 74, 77

Mercer, Kobena, 24–26

Meta-Morphing (Sobchack), 160

mētis, 9

migrant subjects, 10, 19; bare life and, 67–69, 74–75, 78, 81; citizenship and, 70, 73, 76, 77; complicity of, 67; consumer citizenship and, 237–38; as disposable labor, 73–74; ingenious agency of, 67, 68, 69–70, 71, 77–78, 90–91; political resurrection of, 76–79; as racialized labor, 94; sex work, 18, 111–12, 121–23, 127, 128–29, 131, 134–35, 136, 145; sovereignty and, 78, 79, 81, 84. *See also* domestic workers; sex workers

Migration, Agency and Citizenship in Sex Trafficking (Andrijasevic), 111–12

Mission district (San Francisco), 117

Moallem, Minoo, 195, 205, 233

Moghadam, Assaf, 212

morphing technologies: commercial, 160; complicity and, 164–65, 180, 186; corporeal, 160–61; morphing in, 165, 166–72; morphing out, 165, 172–78; rights and, 178–89; use of term, 157, 159–60

Mouffe, Chantal, 3

Mujeres Unidas y Activas, 90

Mukherjee, Roopali, 143, 237

multinational corporations, 22

Naaman, Dorit, 212, 216

Nadasen, Premilla, 90

narcissism, 15, 19

Nasser, Jamal, 222–23

National Association of Evangelicals, 117

National Domestic Workers Alliance (NDWA), 65–66, 89, 91, 93–95, 99, 142, 186

National Labor Relations Act (1935), 80, 89, 90

National Organization for Women (NOW), 117

National Task Force on Prostitution (NTFP), 137

NDWA. *See* National Domestic Workers Alliance

necropower, 220

Nelson, Dana, 2–3

Nelson, James, 186–87

neoliberalism, 22, 30; abjection, 110, 113, 120–21, 136–39, 143, 144, 147; appropriation of, 48, 96; competing scripts and, 45–46; consumerism and, 42, 110, 125–30; democratic agency and, 250; entrepreneurialism and, 43–44, 48, 109–10, 125–30; global culture and, 42; ingenious agency and, 237, 242; market logic, 109–10, 120; networks of, 40; sacrificial violence of, 236–44

New Deal, 89

9-11 attacks. *See* September 11, 2001 terrorist attacks

nongovernmental organizations (NGOs), 49, 96–97, 112, 117

normality. *See under* abjection

NTFP. *See* National Task Force on Prostitution

Nyers, Peter, 14, 77

O'Brien, Michelle, 185

Ong, Aihwa, 40, 95, 96–97, 98, 120

Oslo Accords (1993-1995), 203–4

otherness, 2; citizenship and, 15–16

Palestinian Authority (PA), 204, 238, 240–41, 243

Pape, Robert, 203, 212, 214, 226

Paris Is Burning (film), 164

Parreñas, Rhacel Salazar, 71, 82, 83–84, 87

Sprinzak, Ehud, 215
Stasiulus, Daiva, 84–85
state-making, 10–11
Stoddart, Mark, 44–45
Stoller, Robert, 175
Stone, Sandy, 182
Stonewall Riots, 181
Stryker, Susan, 159, 161, 181, 188
Sturken, Marita, 143, 197
subaltern subjects, 7, 10, 11, 12, 23
subcultures, 55–56, 125–30, 233–34
suicide bombing, 23; agency in, 39, 195,
    197, 198–99, 200, 205, 215–17, 226, 227;
    characteristics of bombers, 266n12; by
    children, 216–17; complicity and, 196,
    200, 201, 210, 228, 231–32; by females,
    191–95, 207, 216, 231–33; improvisation
    in, 196, 199, 210, 228, 231; ingenious
    agency and, 197, 200, 201, 227, 228, 235,
    238, 243–44; as ingenious citizenship,
    197, 230, 235; interstitial quality of,
    232–33; as leap of faith, 219–20, 225,
    226; negotiation and, 230–31; origins
    of, 203; purity and, 209; reanimating
    toward life, 217–27; as sacrificial vio-
    lence, 195–96, 205; terrorism research
    on, 210–17; as threat, 215–17; use
    of term, 200–201. See also sacrificial
    violence
Super Doméstica (comic book), 90
survival strategies, 10, 86, 109, 132
SWEAT. See Sex Worker Education and
    Advocacy Taskforce

Taylor, Charles, 183
Tenderloin district (San Francisco),
    114–15, 117
terrorism: as death, 210–17; as life,
    217–27; origins of, 197, 203; relation-
    ship with liberalism, 198–99. See also
    suicide bombing
Terrorist Assemblages (Puar), 13, 113
Tewksbury, Richard, 155, 157–58

"Theorizing Acts of Citizenship" (Isin),
    218–19
To Die in Jerusalem (documentary), 192, 227
Trafficking Victims' Protection Reautho-
    rization Act (2005), 117
Transexual Menace, 181
Transgender Nation, 181
transgender people: abjection of, 149,
    153, 161–62, 178; activism of, 157–58,
    178–89; categories, 264n6; consum-
    erism and, 152–53, 160, 167, 186–89;
    democratic agency of, 152, 180, 183,
    184–85; distress of, 153, 167; entre-
    preneurialism and, 188–89; FTMs,
    158, 171, 172–78; gender identity,
    39, 151, 157–59, 162, 167–69, 179,
    181–82, 184, 186–89; gender identity
    disorder, 167–68; gender normativity
    and, 149–54, 163, 168, 172, 174, 178;
    global capitalism and, 185; human
    rights and, 156, 159, 184; ingenious
    agency of, 161, 165, 166, 168, 184–85;
    ingenious citizenship of, 178, 179–80;
    MTFs, 158, 166–72; performativity,
    162, 164; self-identification, 174–75,
    187–88; sex work, 153–54; sovereignty
    and, 149–50, 188; use of terms, 158,
    159, 264n5. See also gender; morphing
    technologies
Transgender Rights (Currah et al.), 156
transnational sex tourism, 123, 129, 131,
    132, 133, 135, 136, 145
"Transsexuals' Embodiment of Woman-
    hood" (Schrock et al.), 152–53
Transvestia (journal), 181

Únion Unica, La, 141
United Nations, 96; Commission on the
    Status of Women, 117; General Assem-
    bly, 238, 241
unsafe U.S. citizens, use of term, 2–4,
    19–20
urban gentrification, 113, 114, 116, 117, 119

INDEX   297

U.S. Agency for International Development (USAID), 118

Valentine, David, 158–59, 264n6
veiling, 233
Victims of Trafficking and Violence Protection Act (2000), 113, 117, 118
Vindication of the Rights of Whores, A (Pheterson), 137, 263n16
violence: Fanon on, 199–200, 217–18; rights-based politics and, 28; against transgender subjects, 161; transgressive, 206. *See also* terrorism; sacrificial violence; suicide bombing

Walters, William, 73, 76, 260n11
Ward, Jane, 176–77
warring mentality, 250–54
water metaphor, 252–54, 256
weapons of the weak, 9, 10, 11, 63–64, 265n9

Weber, Cynthia, 2–4, 5, 19
Weinberg, Leonard, 213–14
West End neighborhood (Vancouver), 115
Westernness, 46–47, 54
White, Melanie, 219–20
whiteness, 13, 46–47, 54, 65, 113, 116, 124, 159, 259n7
Wilchins, Riki Anne, 181–82
World Charter for Prostitutes' Rights, 137, 140, 141
World Whores' Congress, 137

Young, Robert, 200
Young Women's Christian Association (YWCA), 89

Zaraysky, Susanna, 153
Zivi, Karen, 28
zoē, 69, 72